Itsuwaribito・空・

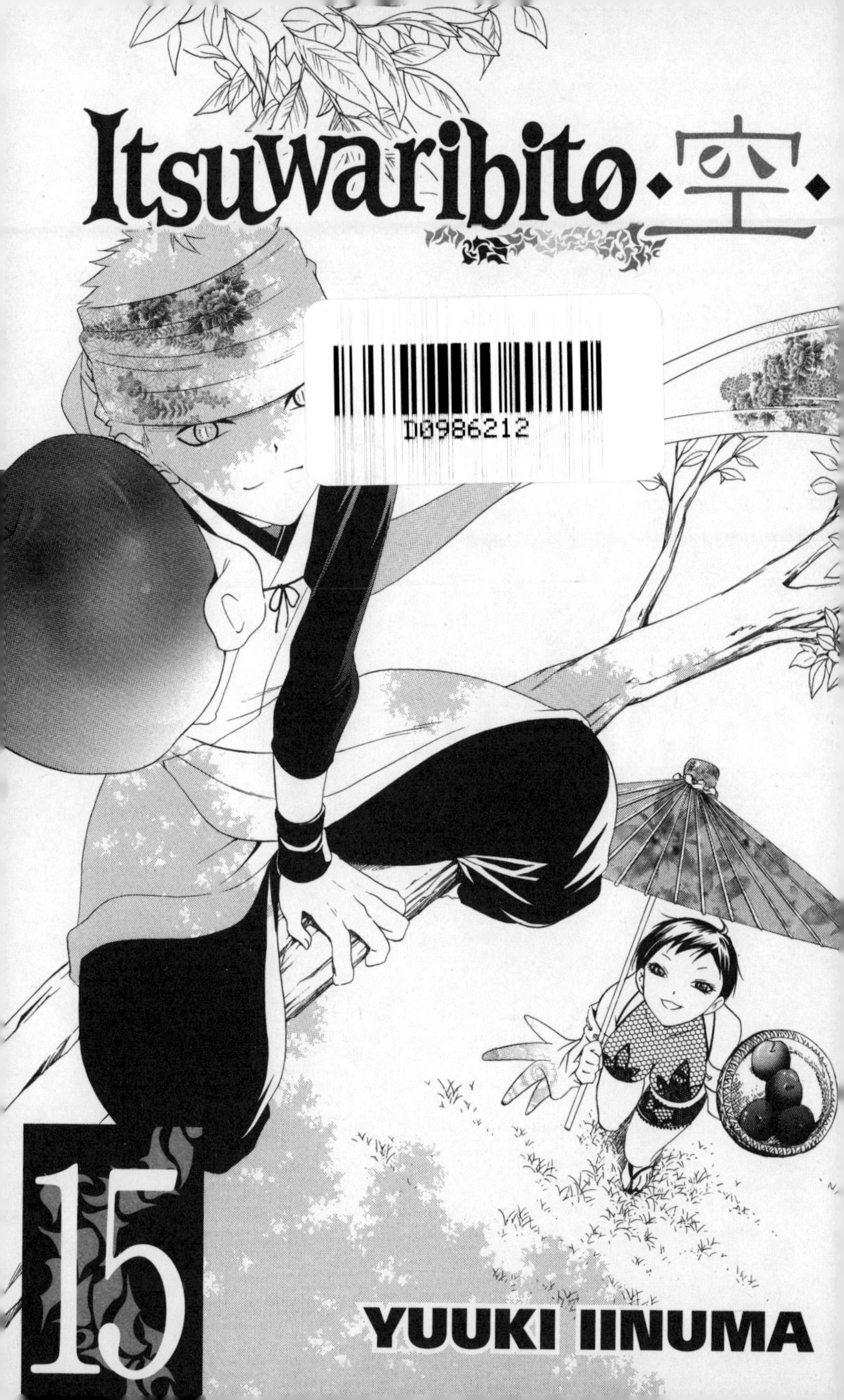

15

YUUKI IINUMA

Contents

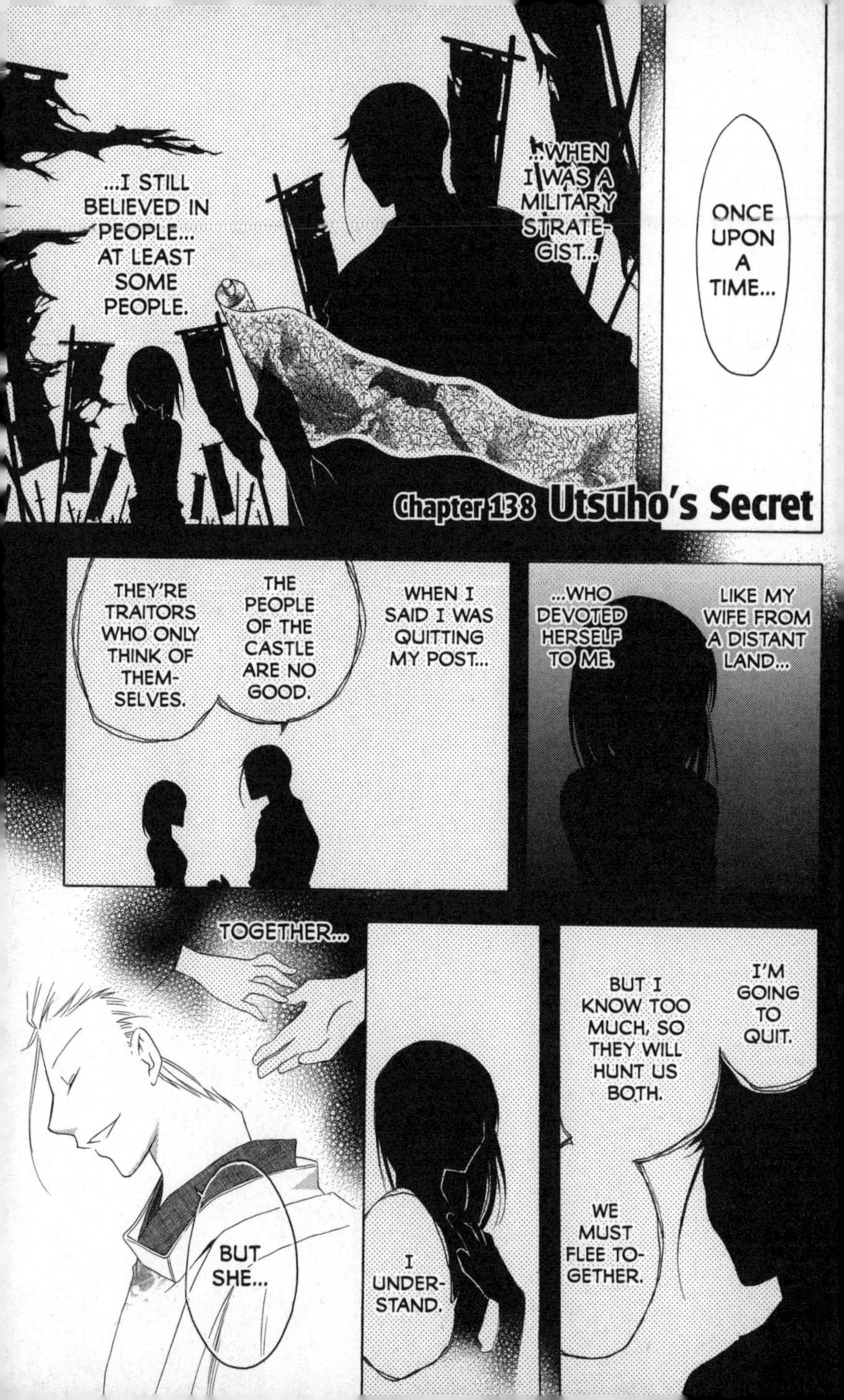
ONCE UPON A TIME...
...WHEN I WAS A MILITARY STRATE-GIST...
...I STILL BELIEVED IN PEOPLE... AT LEAST SOME PEOPLE.
Chapter 138 Utsuho's Secret
LIKE MY WIFE FROM A DISTANT LAND...
...WHO DEVOTED HERSELF TO ME.
WHEN I SAID I WAS QUITTING MY POST...
THE PEOPLE OF THE CASTLE ARE NO GOOD.
THEY'RE TRAITORS WHO ONLY THINK OF THEM-SELVES.
I'M GOING TO QUIT.
BUT I KNOW TOO MUCH, SO THEY WILL HUNT US BOTH.
WE MUST FLEE TO-GETHER.
I UNDER-STAND.
TOGETHER...
BUT SHE...

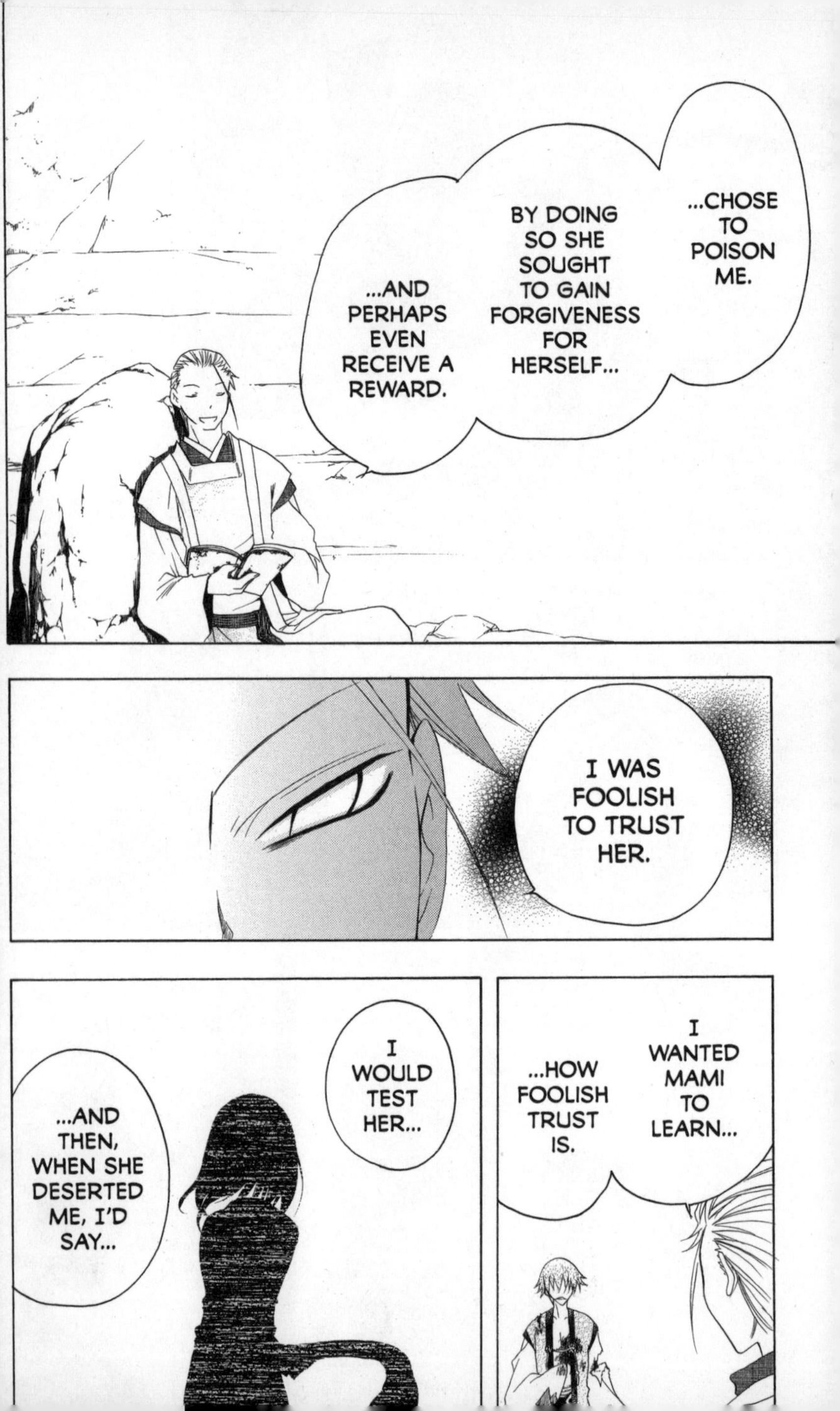
...CHOSE TO POISON ME.
BY DOING SO SHE SOUGHT TO GAIN FORGIVENESS FOR HERSELF...
...AND PERHAPS EVEN RECEIVE A REWARD.
I WAS FOOLISH TO TRUST HER.
I WANTED MAMI TO LEARN...
...HOW FOOLISH TRUST IS.
I WOULD TEST HER...
...AND THEN, WHEN SHE DESERTED ME, I'D SAY...

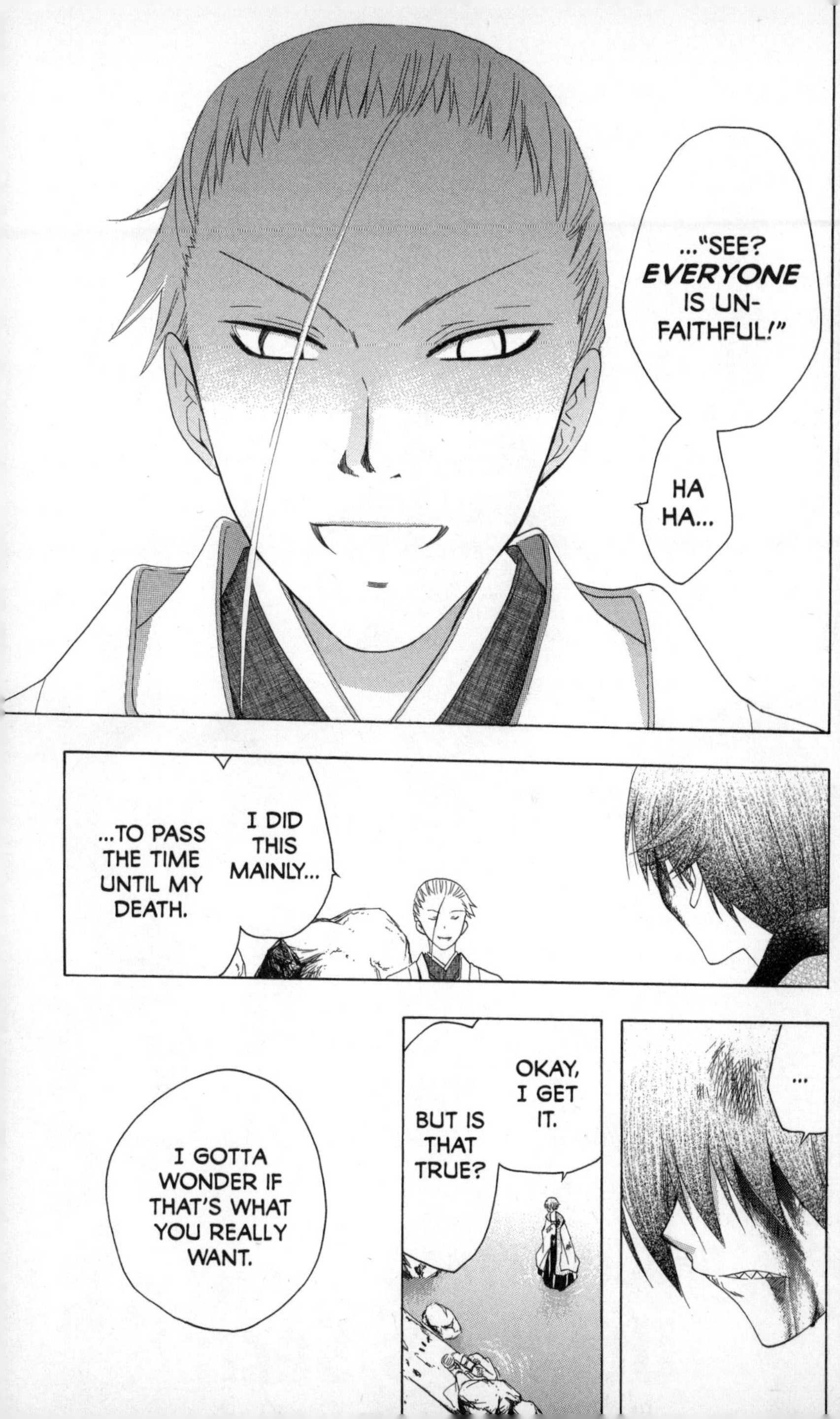
..."SEE? *EVERYONE* IS UN-FAITHFUL!"
HA HA...
I DID THIS MAINLY...
...TO PASS THE TIME UNTIL MY DEATH.
...
OKAY, I GET IT.
BUT IS THAT TRUE?
I GOTTA WONDER IF THAT'S WHAT YOU REALLY WANT.

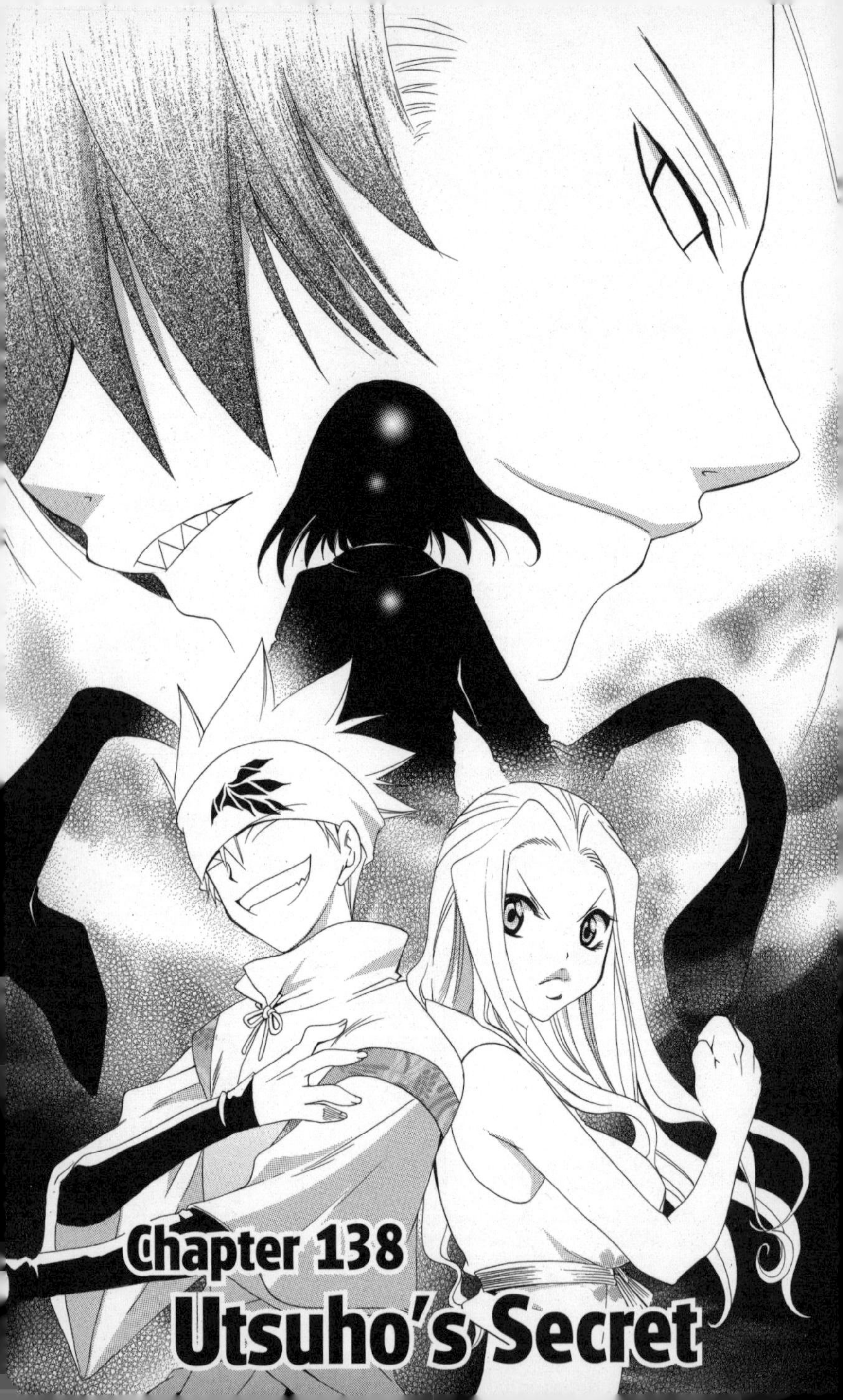
Chapter 138
Utsuho's Secret

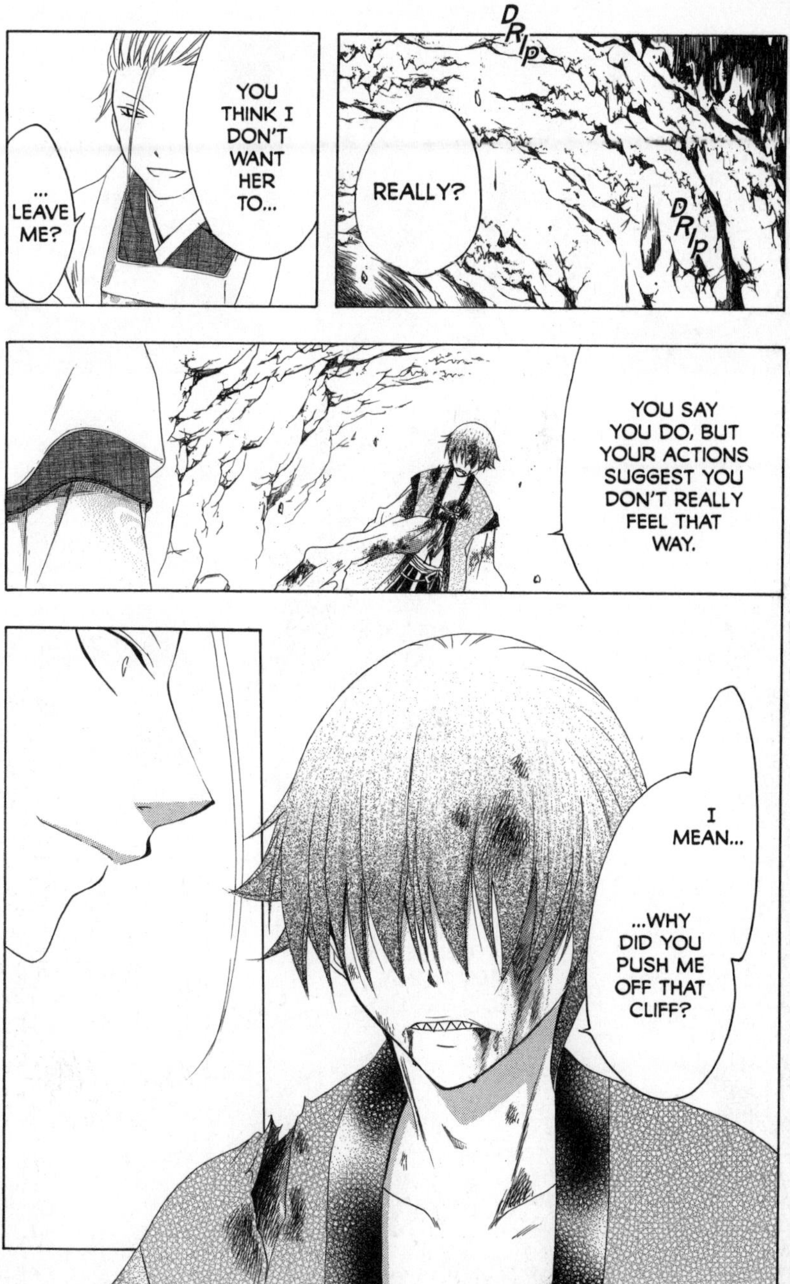
DRIP
REALLY?
DRIP
YOU THINK I DON'T WANT HER TO...
...LEAVE ME?
YOU SAY YOU DO, BUT YOUR ACTIONS SUGGEST YOU DON'T REALLY FEEL THAT WAY.
I MEAN...
...WHY DID YOU PUSH ME OFF THAT CLIFF?

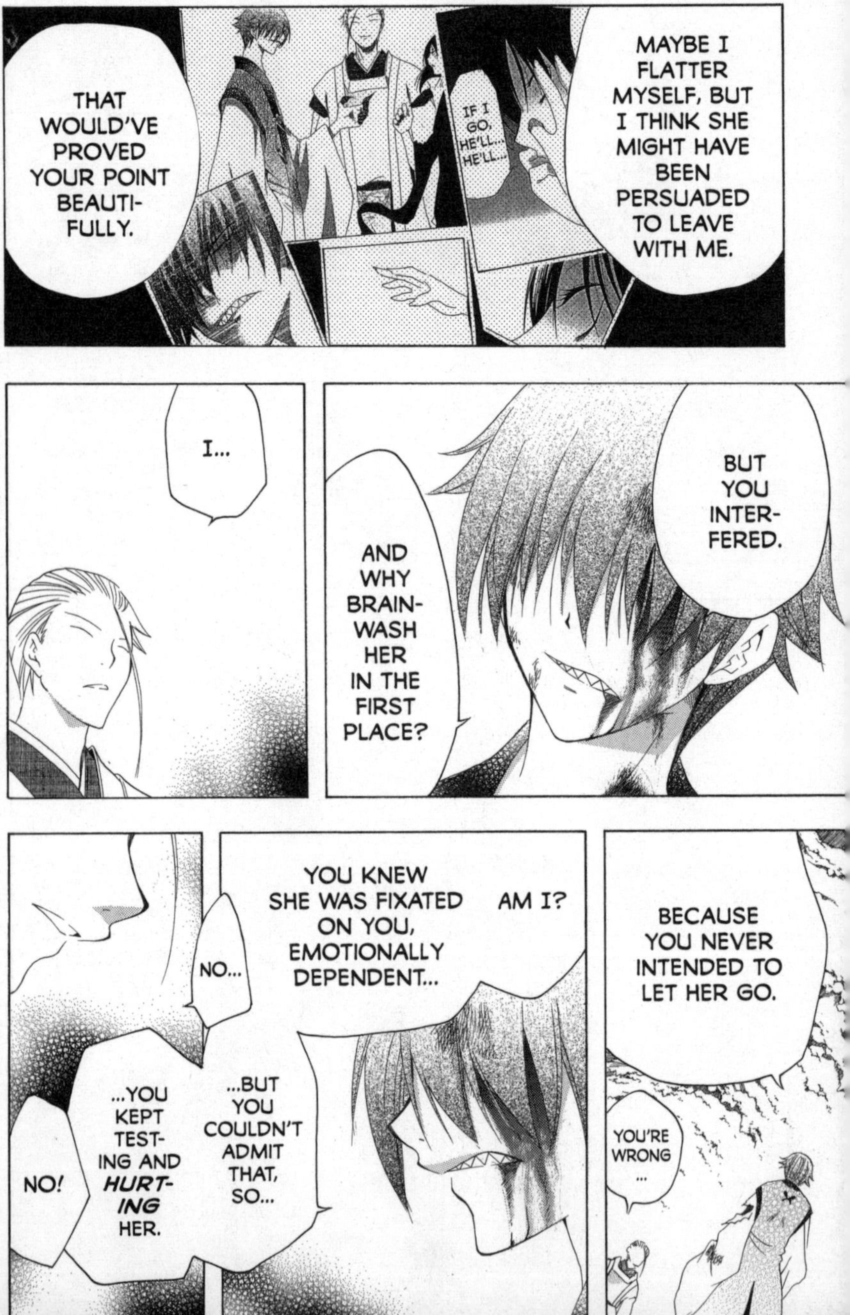
MAYBE I FLATTER MYSELF, BUT I THINK SHE MIGHT HAVE BEEN PERSUADED TO LEAVE WITH ME.
IF I GO, HE'LL... HE'LL...
THAT WOULD'VE PROVED YOUR POINT BEAUTIFULLY.
BUT YOU INTERFERED.
AND WHY BRAINWASH HER IN THE FIRST PLACE?
I...
BECAUSE YOU NEVER INTENDED TO LET HER GO.
YOU'RE WRONG...
AM I?
YOU KNEW SHE WAS FIXATED ON YOU, EMOTIONALLY DEPENDENT...
...BUT YOU COULDN'T ADMIT THAT, SO...
...YOU KEPT TESTING AND *HURTING* HER.
NO...
NO!

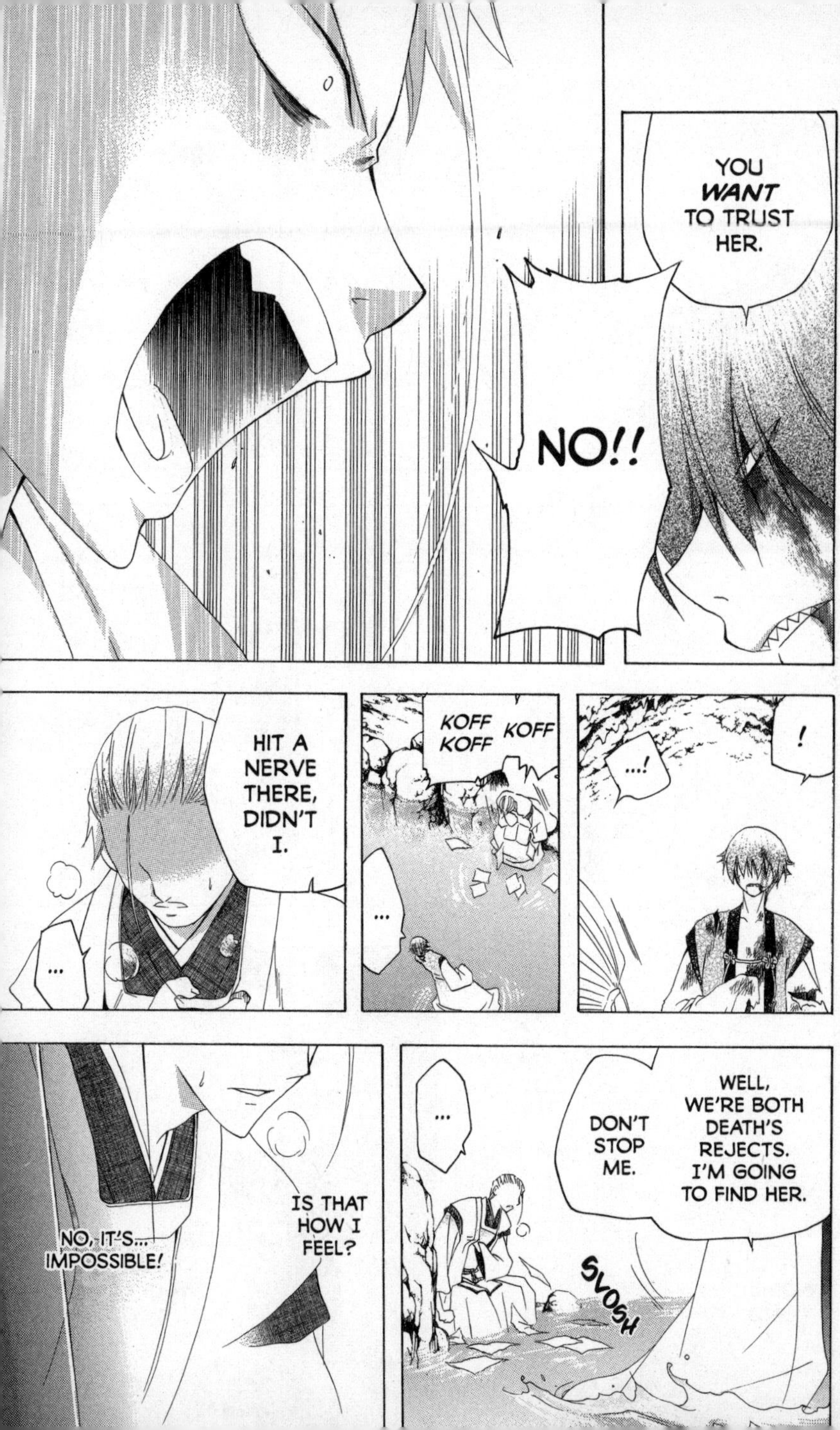
YOU WANT TO TRUST HER.
NO!!
!
...!
KOFF KOFF KOFF
...
HIT A NERVE THERE, DIDN'T I.
...
WELL, WE'RE BOTH DEATH'S REJECTS. I'M GOING TO FIND HER.
DON'T STOP ME.
...
SVOSH
IS THAT HOW I FEEL?
NO, IT'S... IMPOSSIBLE!

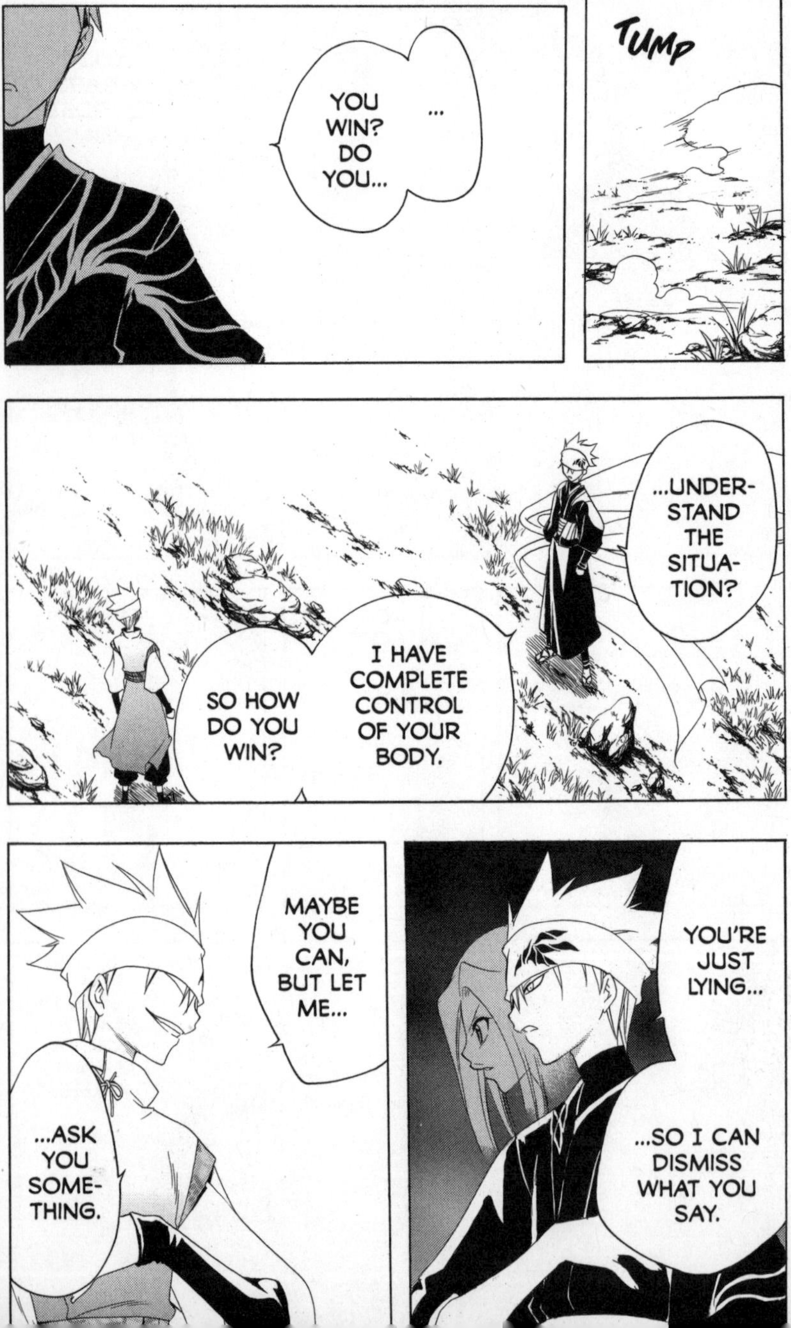
TUMP
... YOU WIN? DO YOU...
...UNDER-STAND THE SITUA-TION?
I HAVE COMPLETE CONTROL OF YOUR BODY.
SO HOW DO YOU WIN?
YOU'RE JUST LYING...
...SO I CAN DISMISS WHAT YOU SAY.
MAYBE YOU CAN, BUT LET ME...
...ASK YOU SOMETHING.

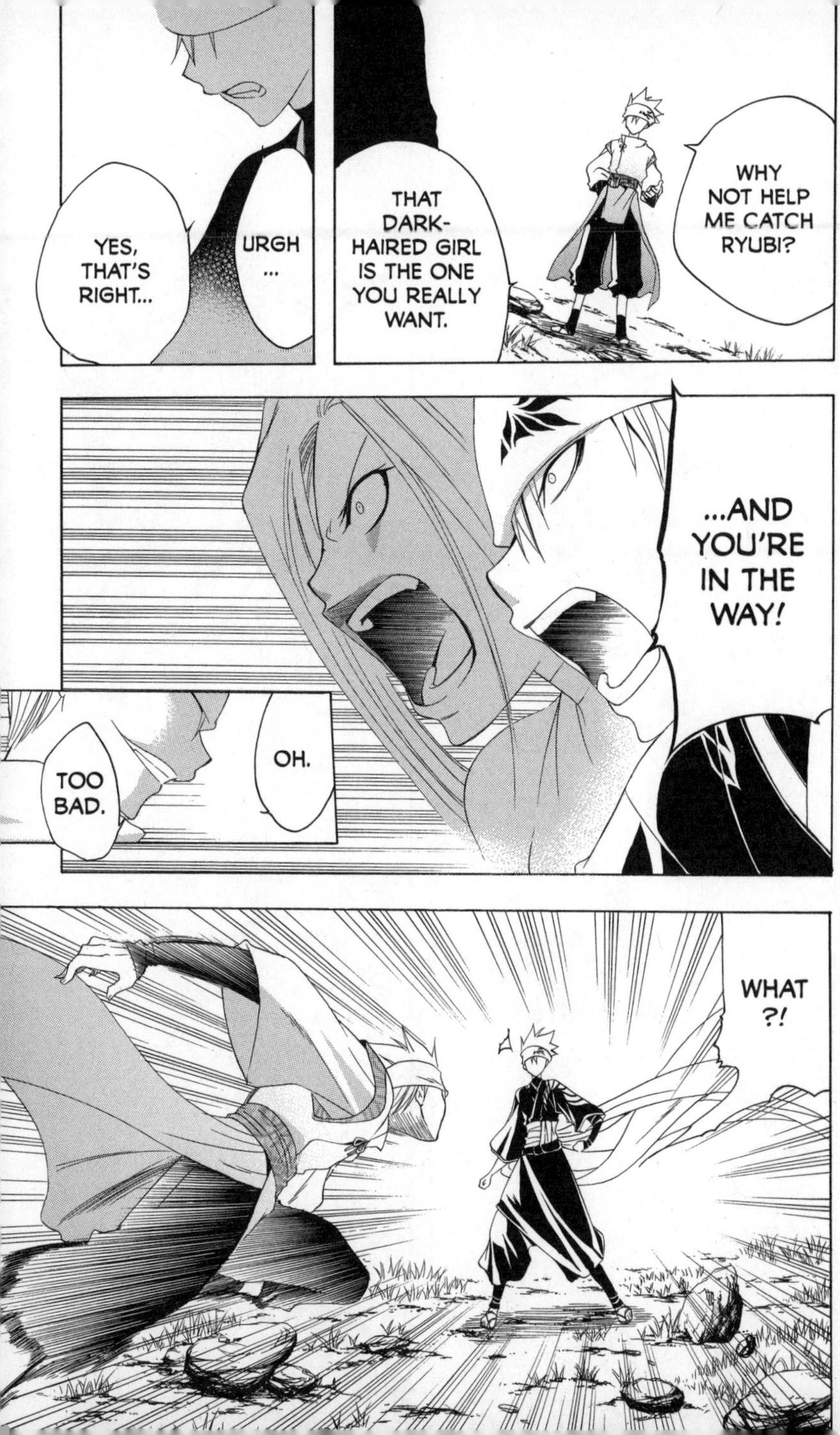
WHY NOT HELP ME CATCH RYUBI?
THAT DARK-HAIRED GIRL IS THE ONE YOU REALLY WANT.
URGH ...
YES, THAT'S RIGHT...
...AND YOU'RE IN THE WAY!
OH.
TOO BAD.
WHAT ?!

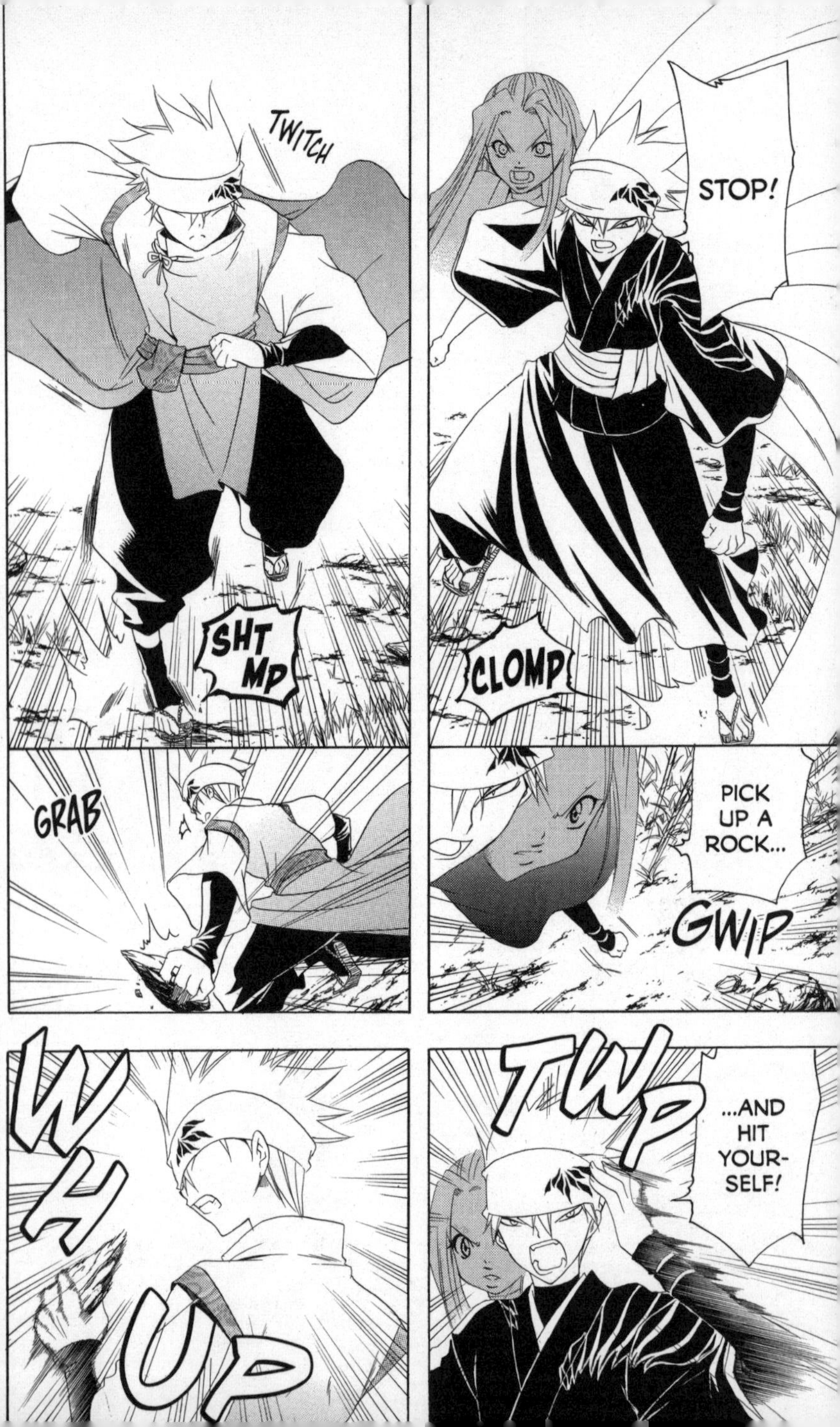
STOP!
CLOMP
TWITCH
SHTMP
PICK UP A ROCK...
GWIP
GRAB
TWP
...AND HIT YOURSELF!
WHUP

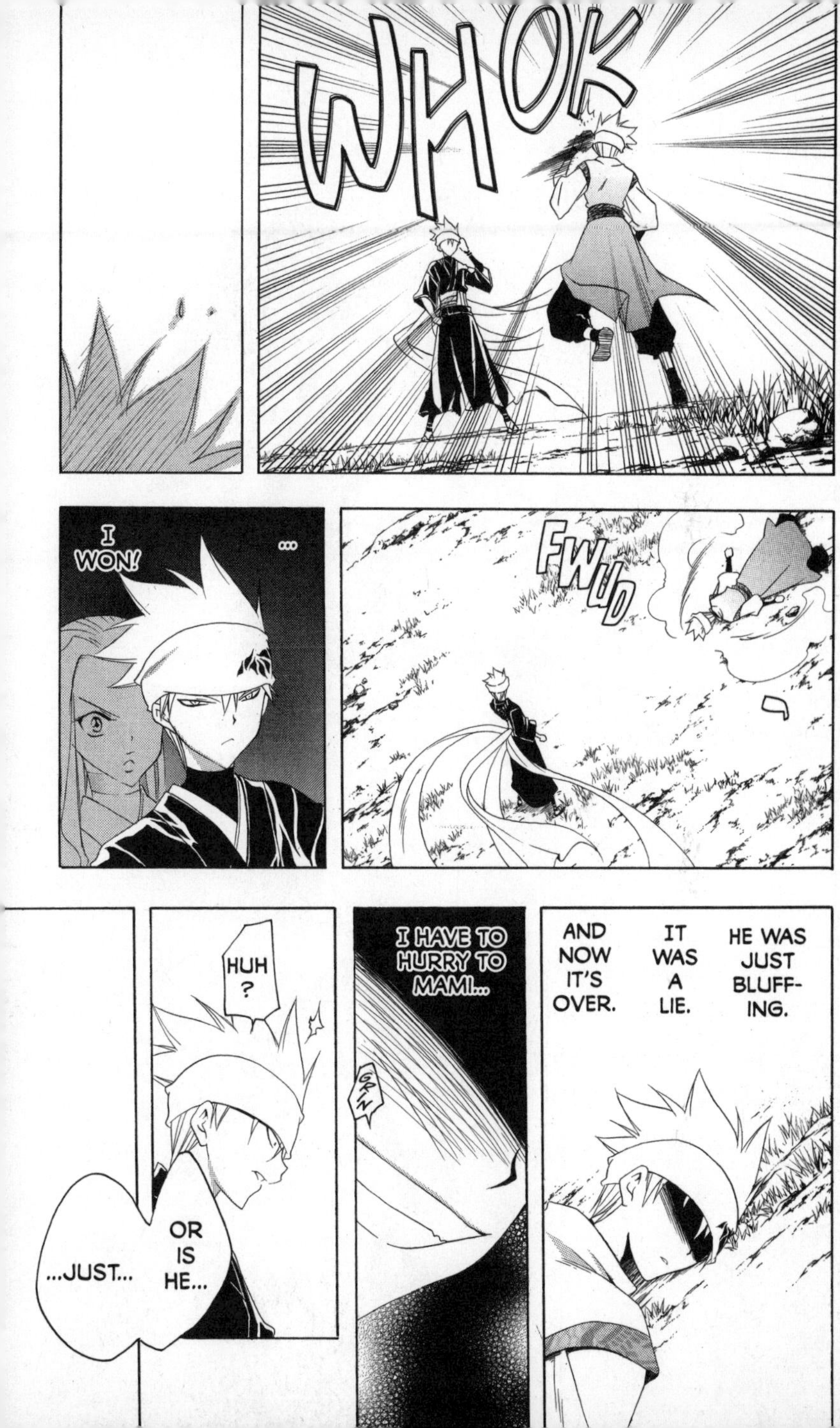
WHOK
FWUD
...
I WON!
HE WAS JUST BLUFF-ING.
IT WAS A LIE.
AND NOW IT'S OVER.
I HAVE TO HURRY TO MAMI...
GRIN
HUH?
OR IS HE...
...JUST...

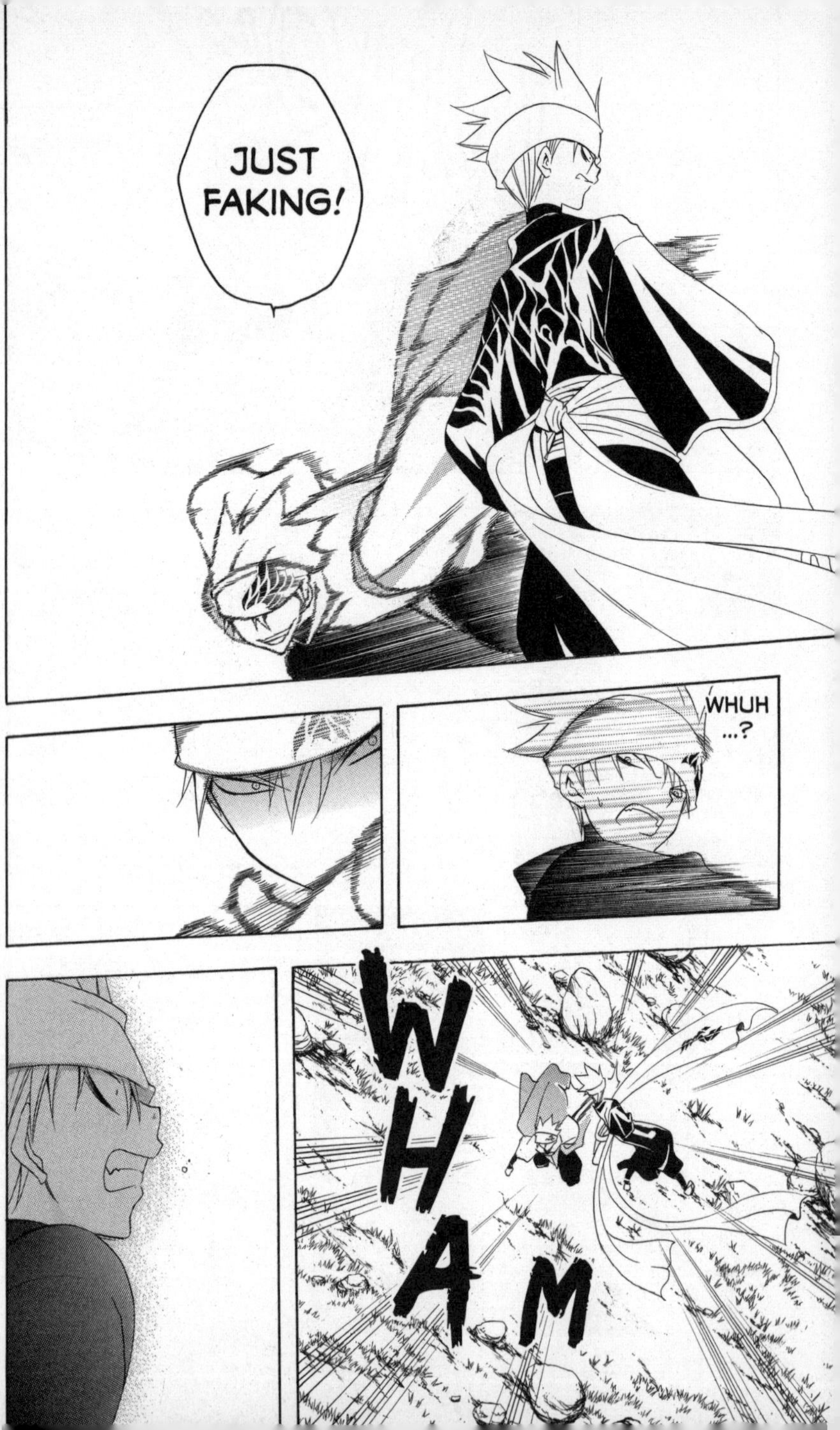
JUST FAKING!
WHUH ...?
WHAM

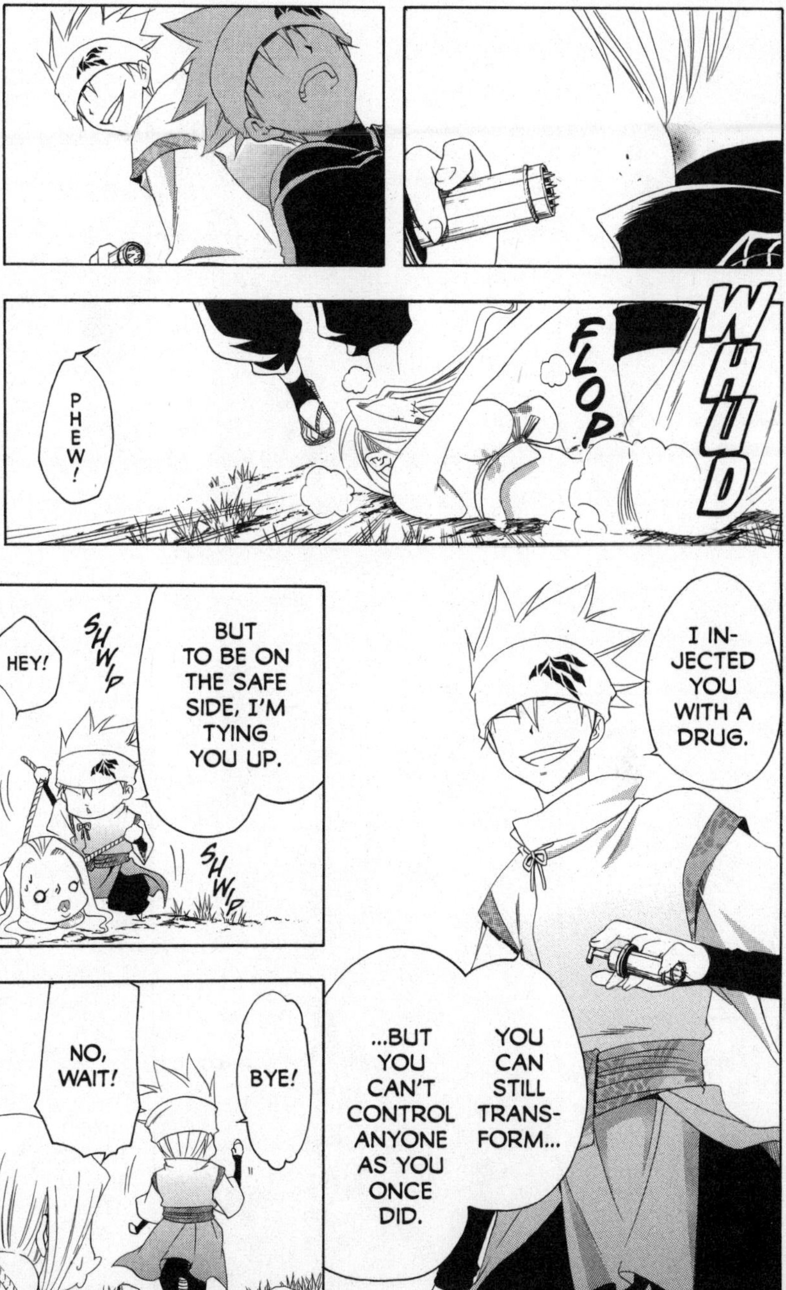
WHUD
FLOP
PHEW!
I INJECTED YOU WITH A DRUG.
YOU CAN STILL TRANSFORM...
...BUT YOU CAN'T CONTROL ANYONE AS YOU ONCE DID.
BUT TO BE ON THE SAFE SIDE, I'M TYING YOU UP.
SHWIP
HEY!
SHWIP
BYE!
NO, WAIT!

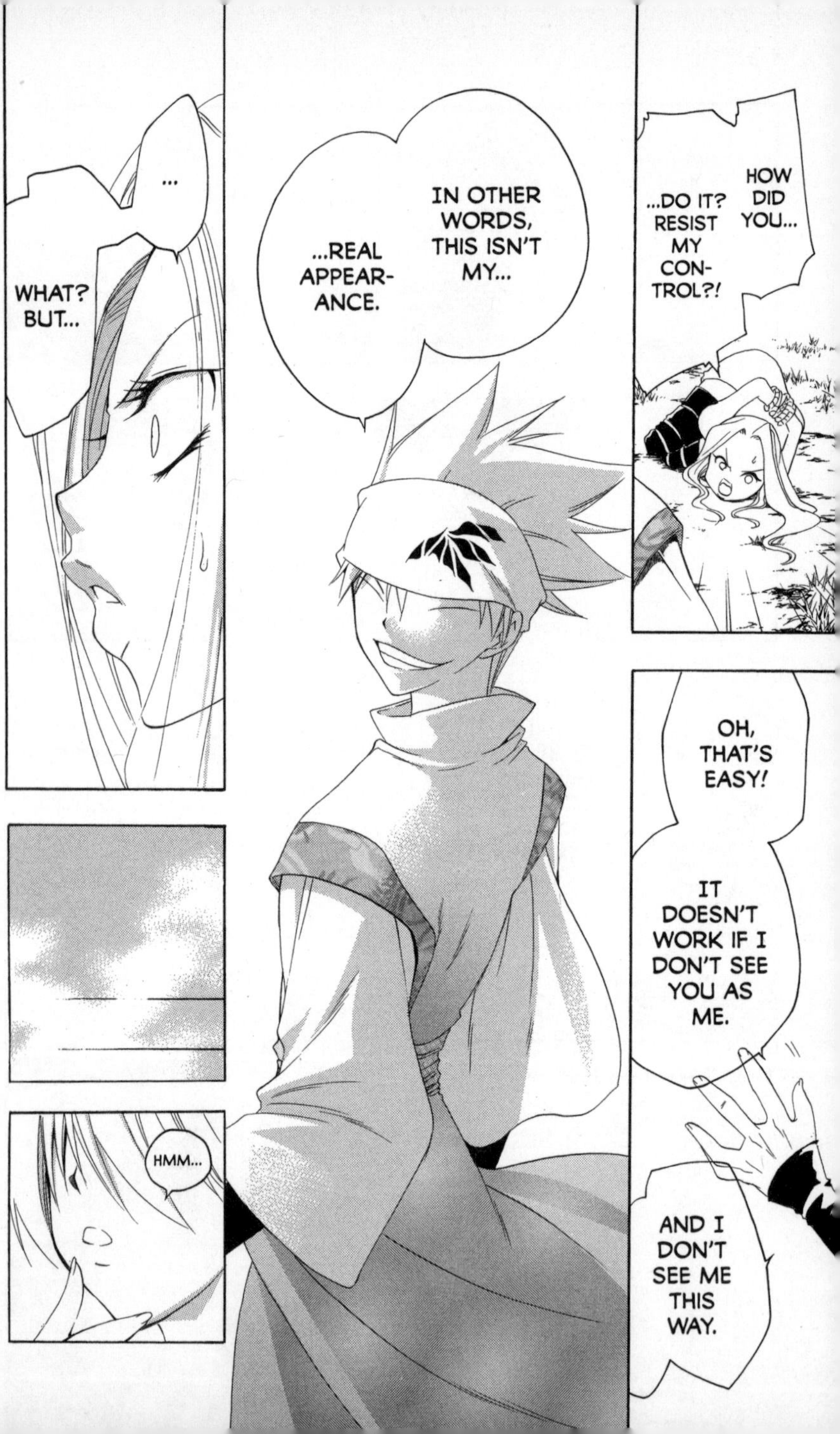
HOW DID YOU...
...DO IT? RESIST MY CONTROL?!
OH, THAT'S EASY!
IT DOESN'T WORK IF I DON'T SEE YOU AS ME.
AND I DON'T SEE ME THIS WAY.
IN OTHER WORDS, THIS ISN'T MY...
...REAL APPEARANCE.
...
WHAT? BUT...
HMM...

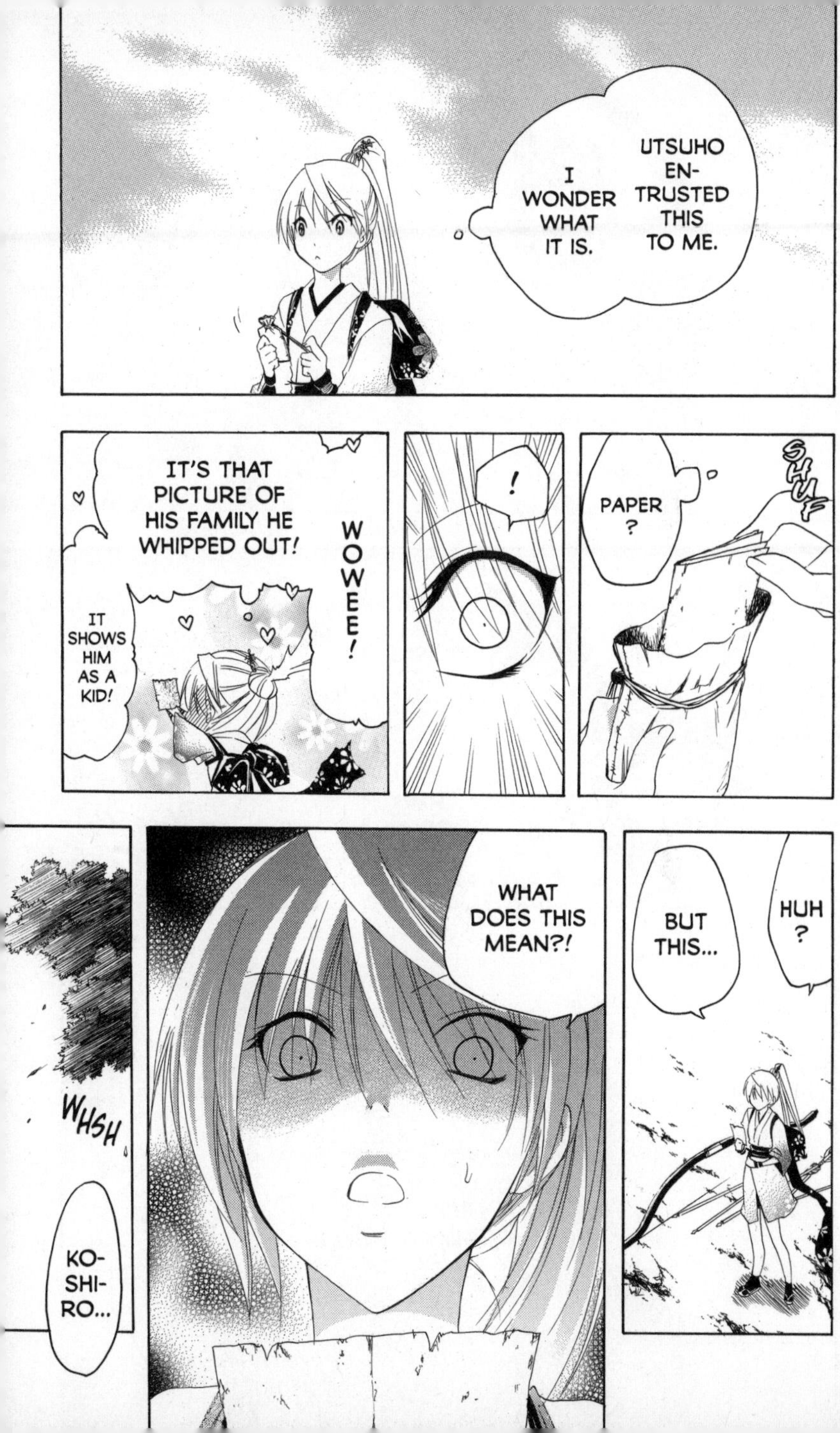
UTSUHO ENTRUSTED THIS TO ME.
I WONDER WHAT IT IS.
SHUF
PAPER?
!
IT'S THAT PICTURE OF HIS FAMILY HE WHIPPED OUT!
WOWEE!
IT SHOWS HIM AS A KID!
HUH?
BUT THIS...
WHAT DOES THIS MEAN?!
WHSH
KOSHIRO...

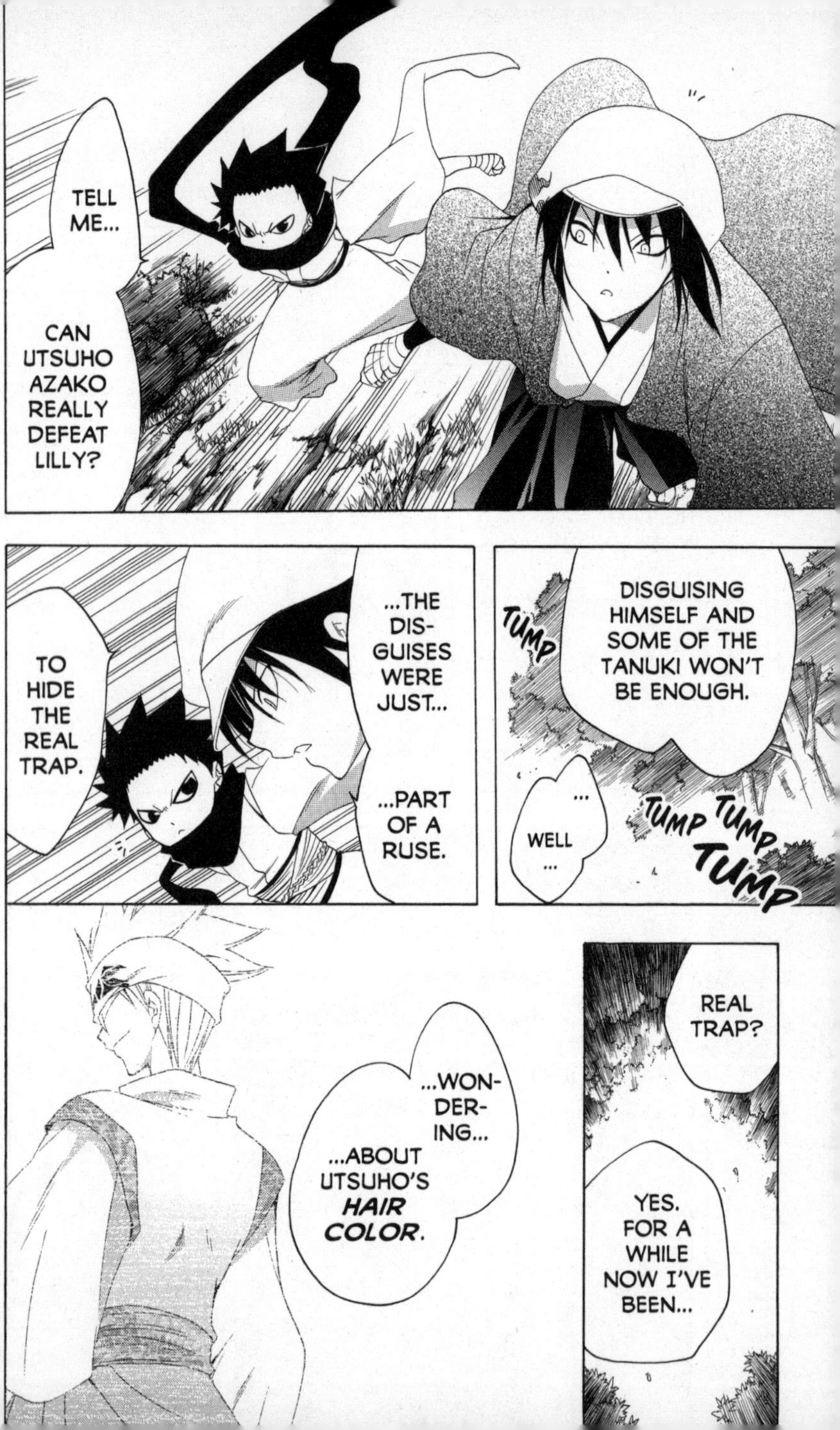
TELL ME...
CAN UTSUHO AZAKO REALLY DEFEAT LILLY?
DISGUISING HIMSELF AND SOME OF THE TANUKI WON'T BE ENOUGH.
TUMP
... WELL ...
TUMP TUMP TUMP
...THE DISGUISES WERE JUST...
...PART OF A RUSE.
TO HIDE THE REAL TRAP.
REAL TRAP?
YES. FOR A WHILE NOW I'VE BEEN...
...WONDERING...
...ABOUT UTSUHO'S *HAIR COLOR*.

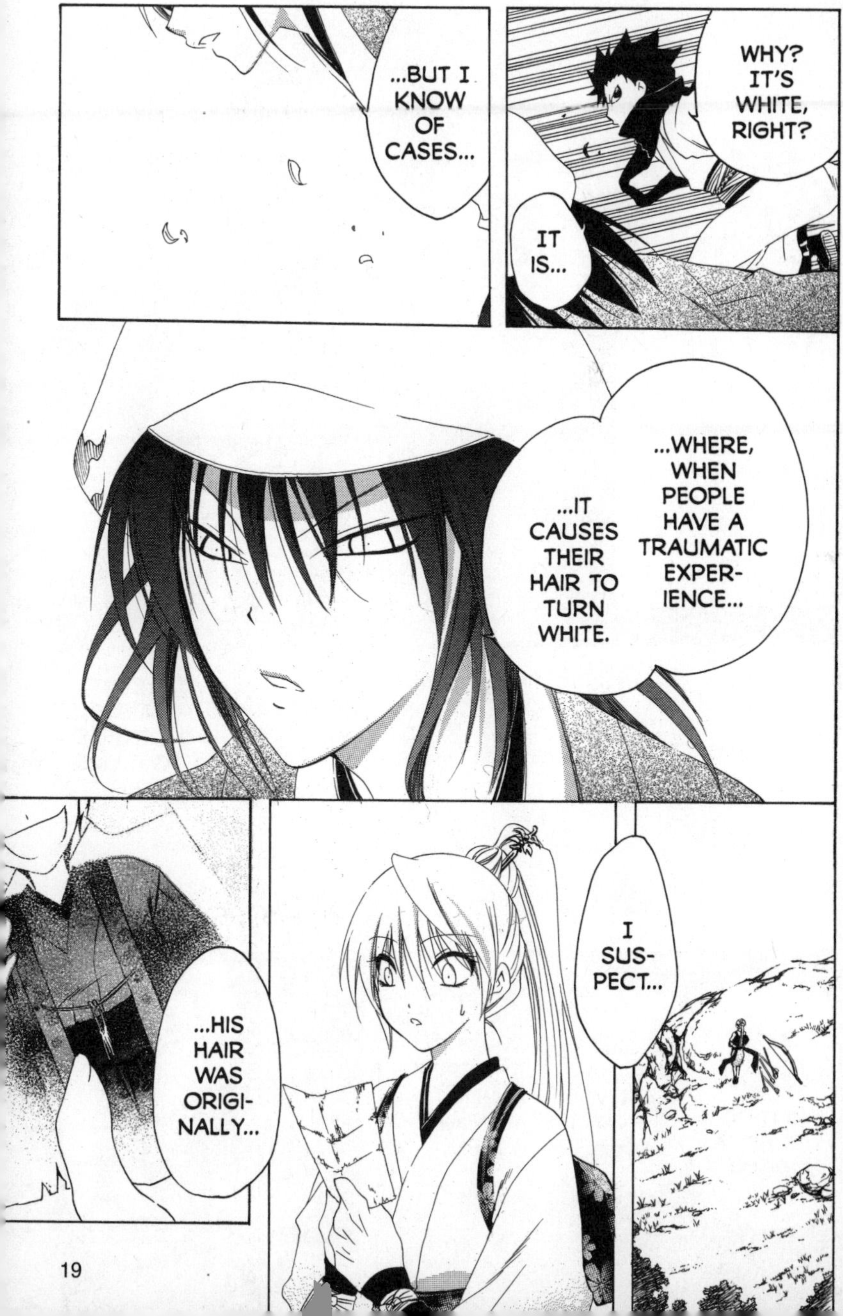
WHY? IT'S WHITE, RIGHT?
IT IS...
...BUT I KNOW OF CASES...
...WHERE, WHEN PEOPLE HAVE A TRAUMATIC EXPER-IENCE...
...IT CAUSES THEIR HAIR TO TURN WHITE.
I SUS-PECT...
...HIS HAIR WAS ORIGI-NALLY...

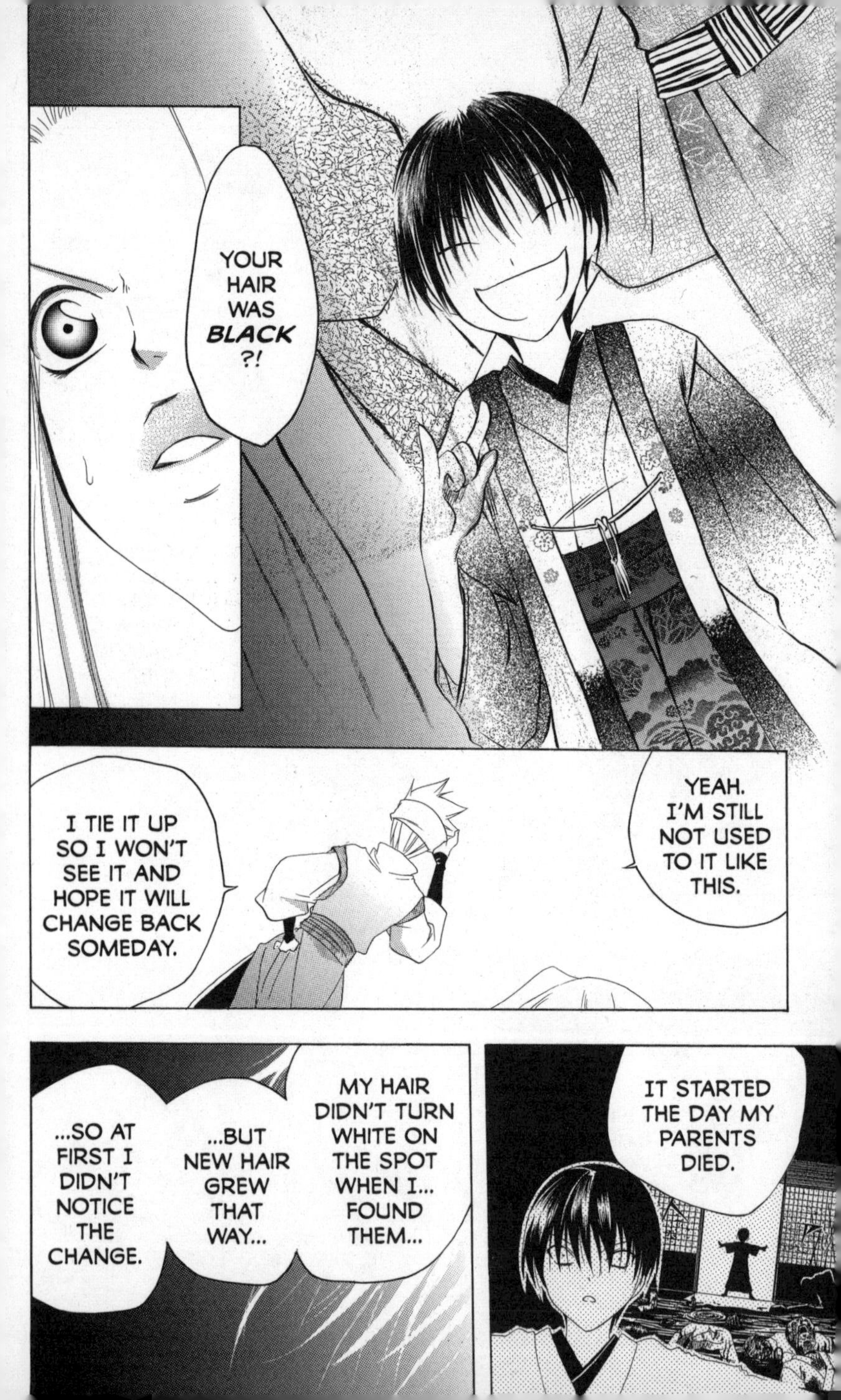
YOUR HAIR WAS BLACK ?!
YEAH. I'M STILL NOT USED TO IT LIKE THIS.
I TIE IT UP SO I WON'T SEE IT AND HOPE IT WILL CHANGE BACK SOMEDAY.
IT STARTED THE DAY MY PARENTS DIED.
MY HAIR DIDN'T TURN WHITE ON THE SPOT WHEN I... FOUND THEM...
...BUT NEW HAIR GREW THAT WAY...
...SO AT FIRST I DIDN'T NOTICE THE CHANGE.

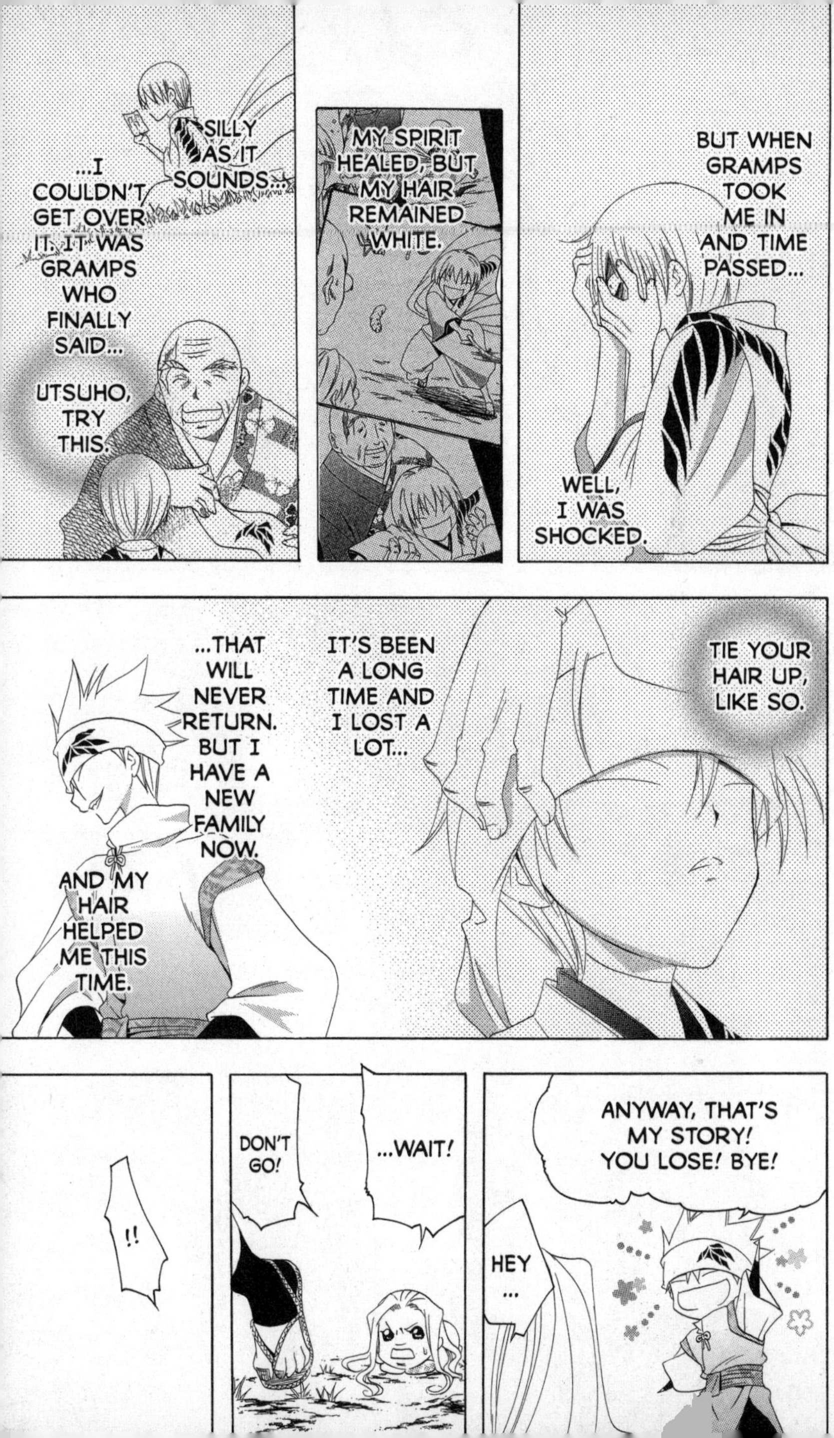
BUT WHEN GRAMPS TOOK ME IN AND TIME PASSED...
WELL, I WAS SHOCKED.
MY SPIRIT HEALED, BUT MY HAIR REMAINED WHITE.
SILLY AS IT SOUNDS...
...I COULDN'T GET OVER IT. IT WAS GRAMPS WHO FINALLY SAID...
UTSUHO, TRY THIS.
TIE YOUR HAIR UP, LIKE SO.
IT'S BEEN A LONG TIME AND I LOST A LOT...
...THAT WILL NEVER RETURN. BUT I HAVE A NEW FAMILY NOW.
AND MY HAIR HELPED ME THIS TIME.
ANYWAY, THAT'S MY STORY! YOU LOSE! BYE!
HEY ...
...WAIT!
DON'T GO!
!!

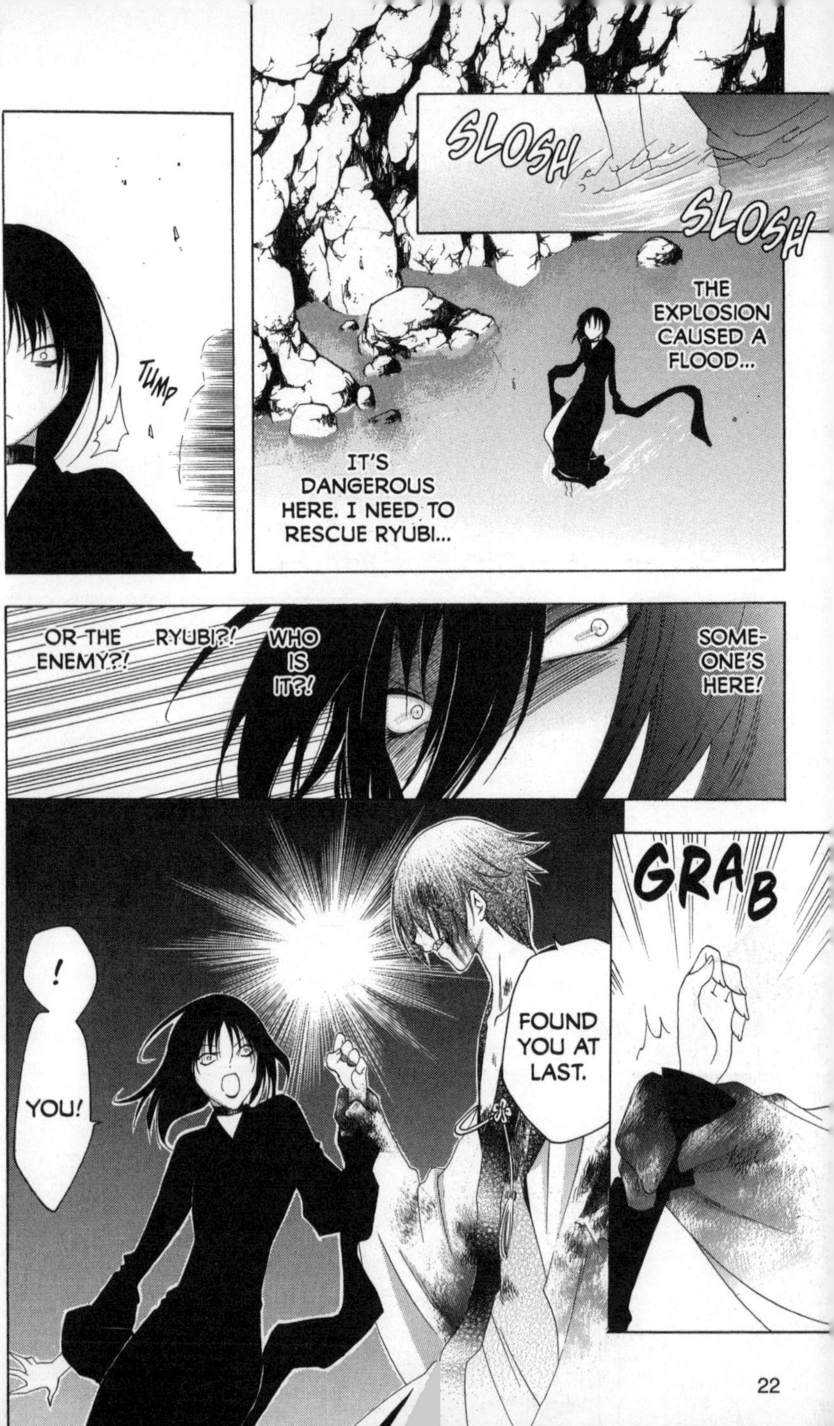
SLOSH
SLOSH
THE EXPLOSION CAUSED A FLOOD...
IT'S DANGEROUS HERE. I NEED TO RESCUE RYUBI...
TUMP
SOME-ONE'S HERE!
WHO IS IT?!
RYUBI?!
OR THE ENEMY?!
GRAB
FOUND YOU AT LAST.
!
YOU!

Chapter 139 Choza and Mami

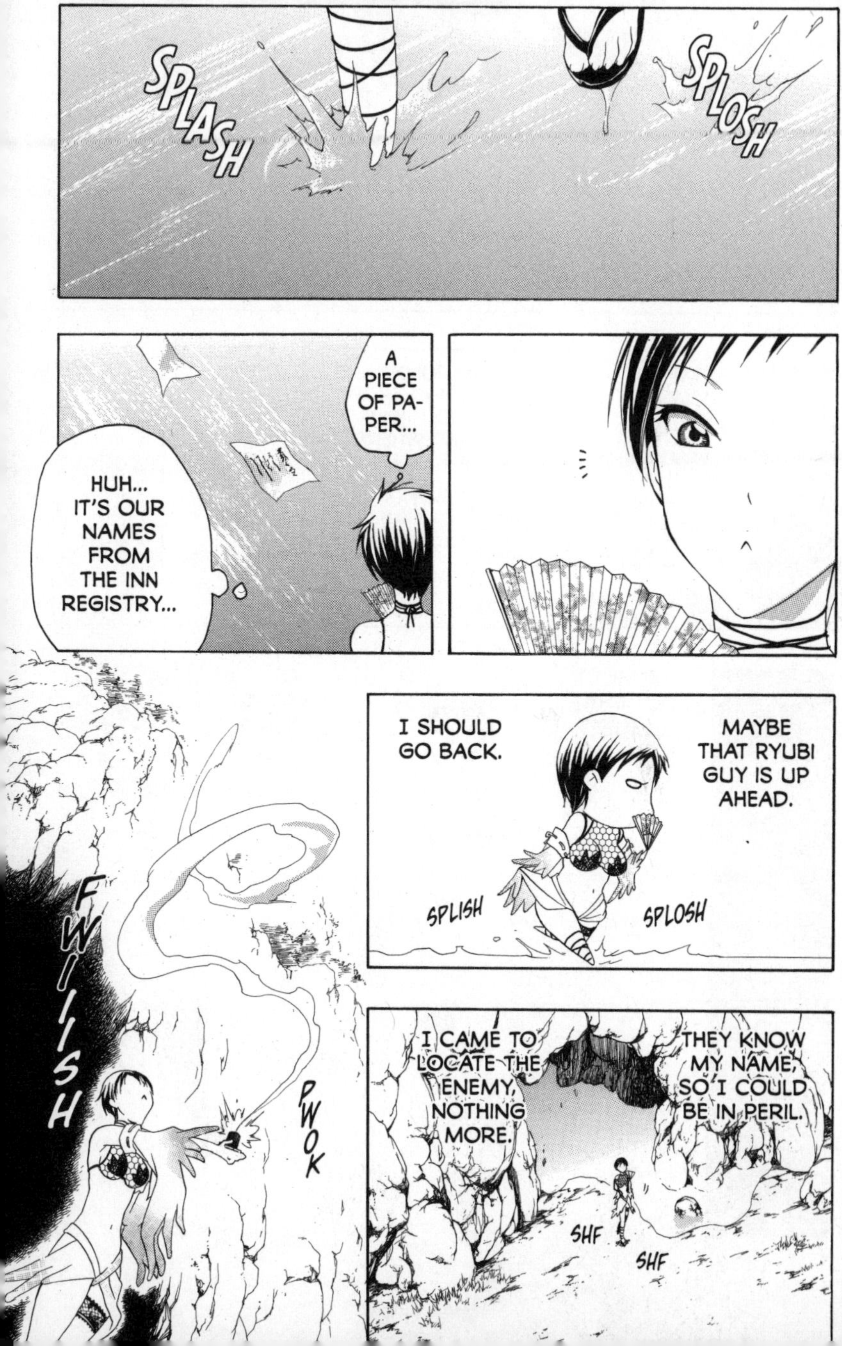
SPLOSH
SPLASH
A PIECE OF PA-PER...
HUH... IT'S OUR NAMES FROM THE INN REGISTRY...
MAYBE THAT RYUBI GUY IS UP AHEAD.
I SHOULD GO BACK.
SPLOSH
SPLISH
THEY KNOW MY NAME, SO I COULD BE IN PERIL.
I CAME TO LOCATE THE ENEMY, NOTHING MORE.
SHF
SHF
PWOK
FWIIISH

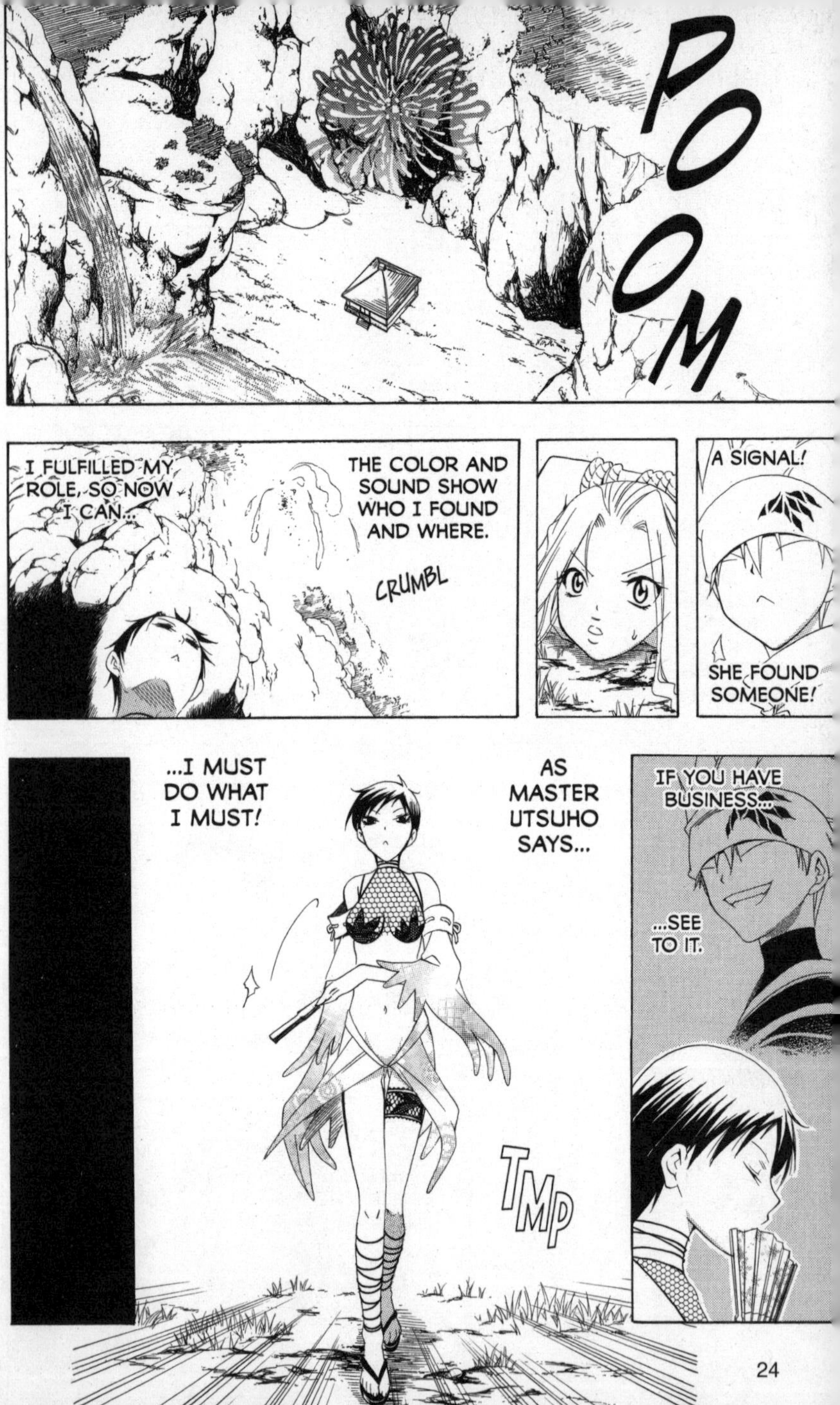
POOM
A SIGNAL!
SHE FOUND SOMEONE!
THE COLOR AND SOUND SHOW WHO I FOUND AND WHERE.
I FULFILLED MY ROLE, SO NOW I CAN...
CRUMBL
IF YOU HAVE BUSINESS...
...SEE TO IT.
AS MASTER UTSUHO SAYS...
...I MUST DO WHAT I MUST!
TMP

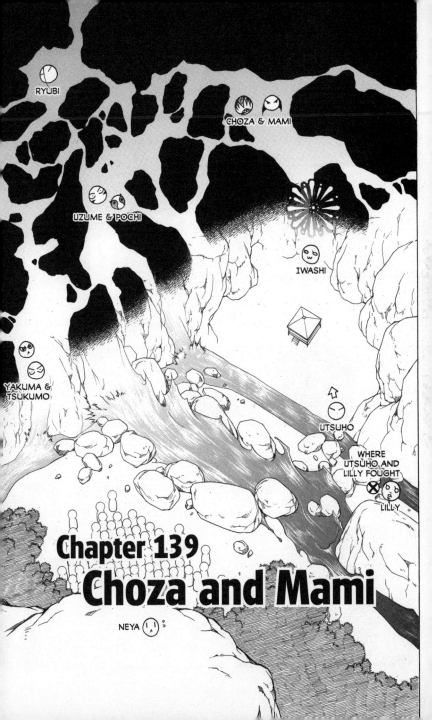

RYUBI

CHOZA & MAMI

UZUME & POCHI

IWASHI

YAKUMA &
TSUKUMO

UTSUHO

WHERE
UTSUHO AND
LILLY FOUGHT

LILLY

Chapter 139
Choza and Mami

NEYA

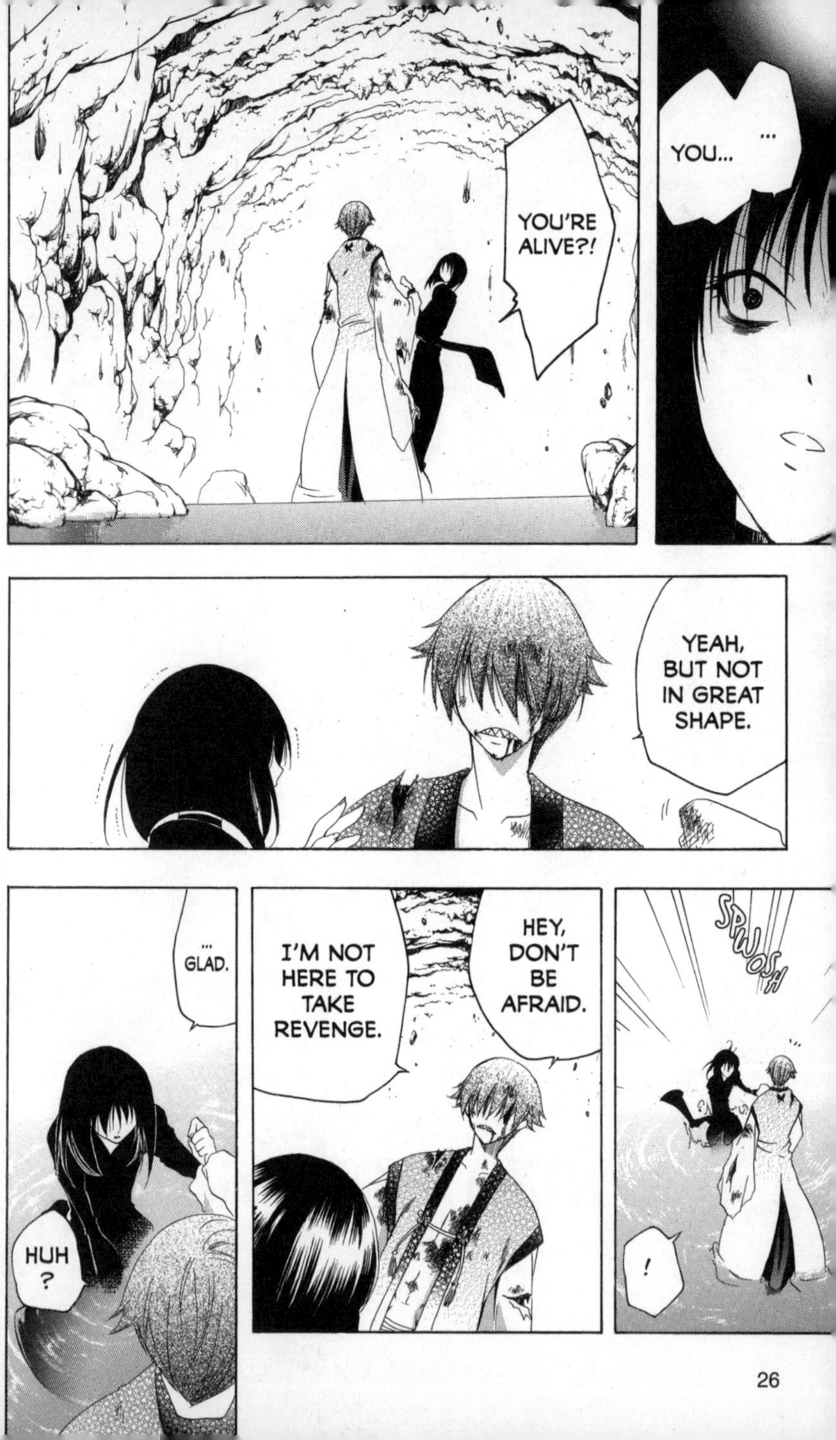
...
YOU...
YOU'RE ALIVE?!
YEAH, BUT NOT IN GREAT SHAPE.
SPWOSH
...
!
HEY, DON'T BE AFRAID.
I'M NOT HERE TO TAKE REVENGE.
... GLAD.
HUH?

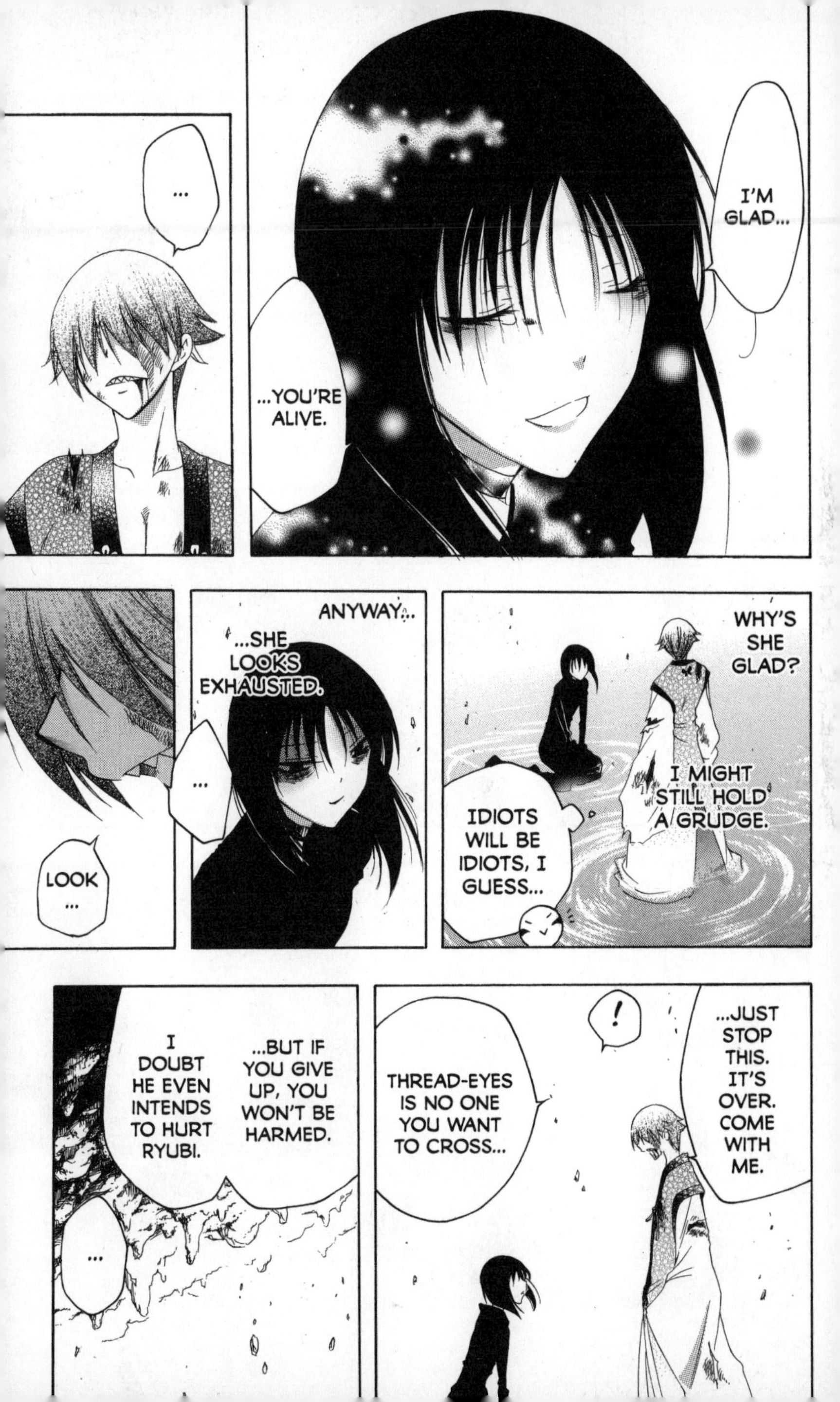

I'M GLAD...
...YOU'RE ALIVE.
...
WHY'S SHE GLAD?
I MIGHT STILL HOLD A GRUDGE.
IDIOTS WILL BE IDIOTS, I GUESS...
ANYWAY...
...SHE LOOKS EXHAUSTED.
...
LOOK ...
!
...JUST STOP THIS. IT'S OVER. COME WITH ME.
THREAD-EYES IS NO ONE YOU WANT TO CROSS...
...BUT IF YOU GIVE UP, YOU WON'T BE HARMED.
I DOUBT HE EVEN INTENDS TO HURT RYUBI.
...

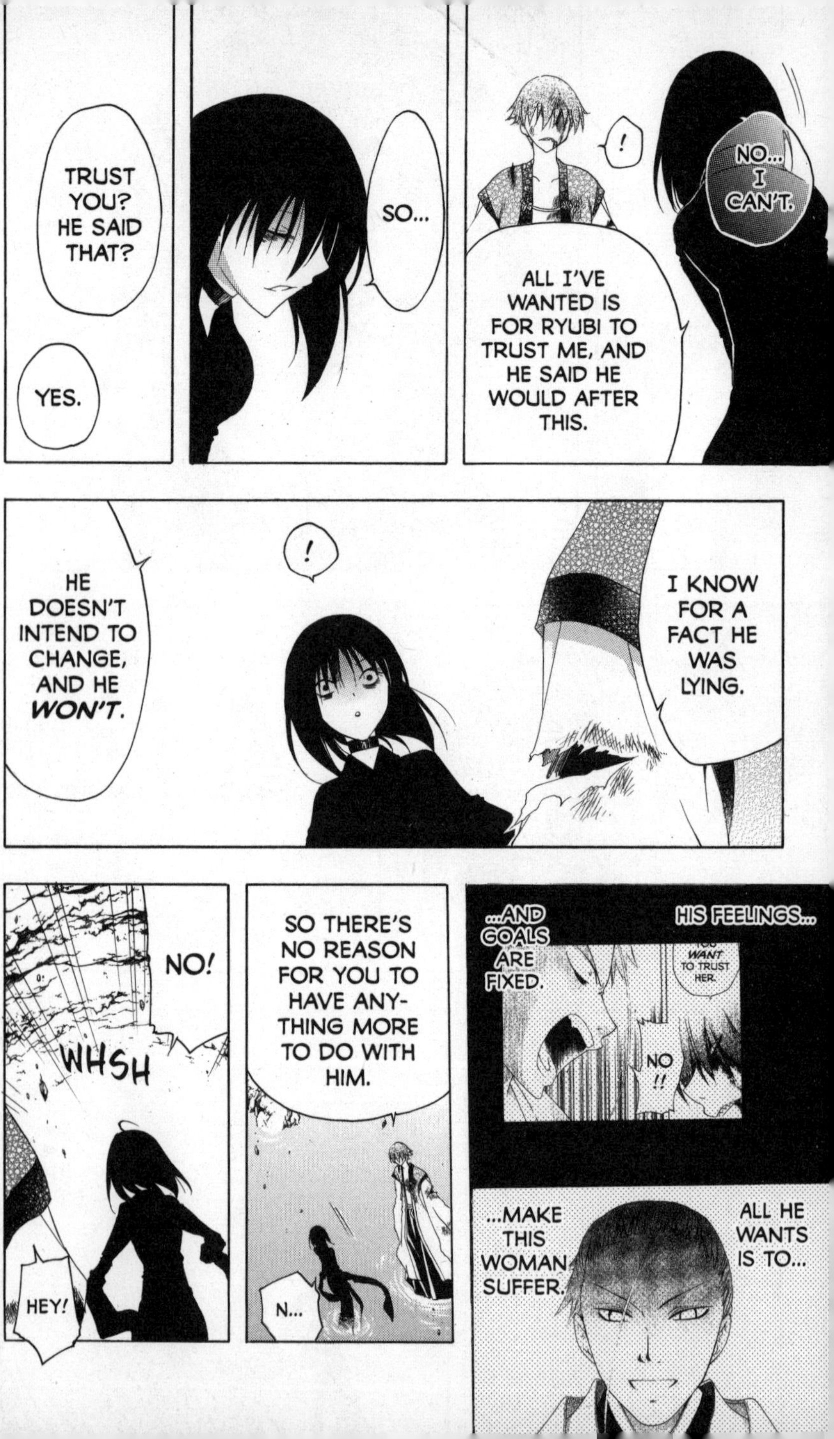
NO... I CAN'T.
!
ALL I'VE WANTED IS FOR RYUBI TO TRUST ME, AND HE SAID HE WOULD AFTER THIS.
SO...
TRUST YOU? HE SAID THAT?
YES.
I KNOW FOR A FACT HE WAS LYING.
!
HE DOESN'T INTEND TO CHANGE, AND HE *WON'T*.
HIS FEELINGS...
...AND GOALS ARE FIXED.
WANT TO TRUST HER.
NO !!
ALL HE WANTS IS TO...
...MAKE THIS WOMAN SUFFER.
SO THERE'S NO REASON FOR YOU TO HAVE ANY-THING MORE TO DO WITH HIM.
N...
NO!
WHSH
HEY!

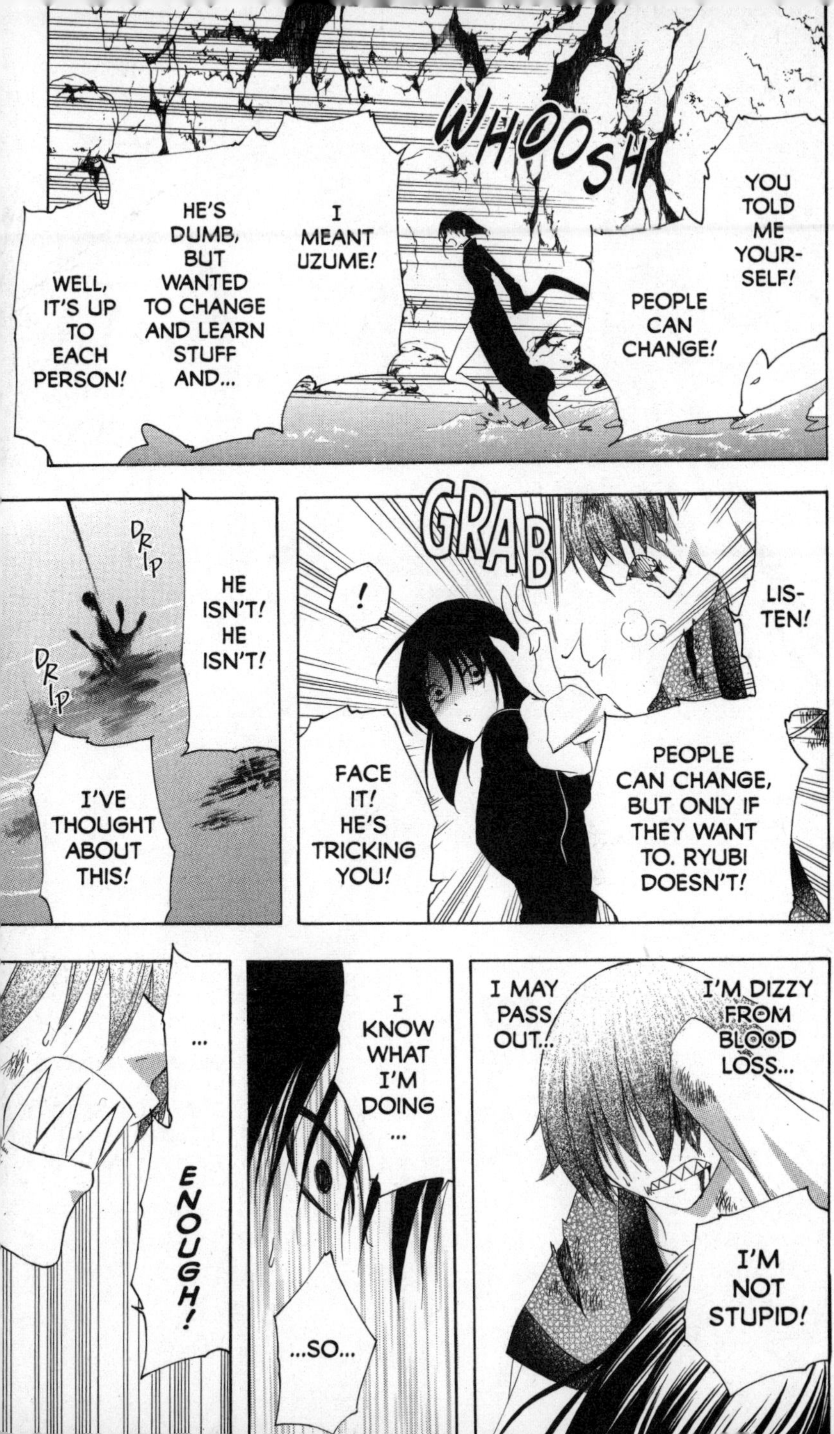
YOU TOLD ME YOUR-SELF!
PEOPLE CAN CHANGE!
WHOOSH
I MEANT UZUME!
HE'S DUMB, BUT WANTED TO CHANGE AND LEARN STUFF AND...
WELL, IT'S UP TO EACH PERSON!
GRAB
LIS-TEN!
!
PEOPLE CAN CHANGE, BUT ONLY IF THEY WANT TO. RYUBI DOESN'T!
FACE IT! HE'S TRICKING YOU!
DRIP
DRIP
HE ISN'T! HE ISN'T!
I'VE THOUGHT ABOUT THIS!
I'M DIZZY FROM BLOOD LOSS...
I MAY PASS OUT...
I'M NOT STUPID!
I KNOW WHAT I'M DOING...
...SO...
...
ENOUGH!

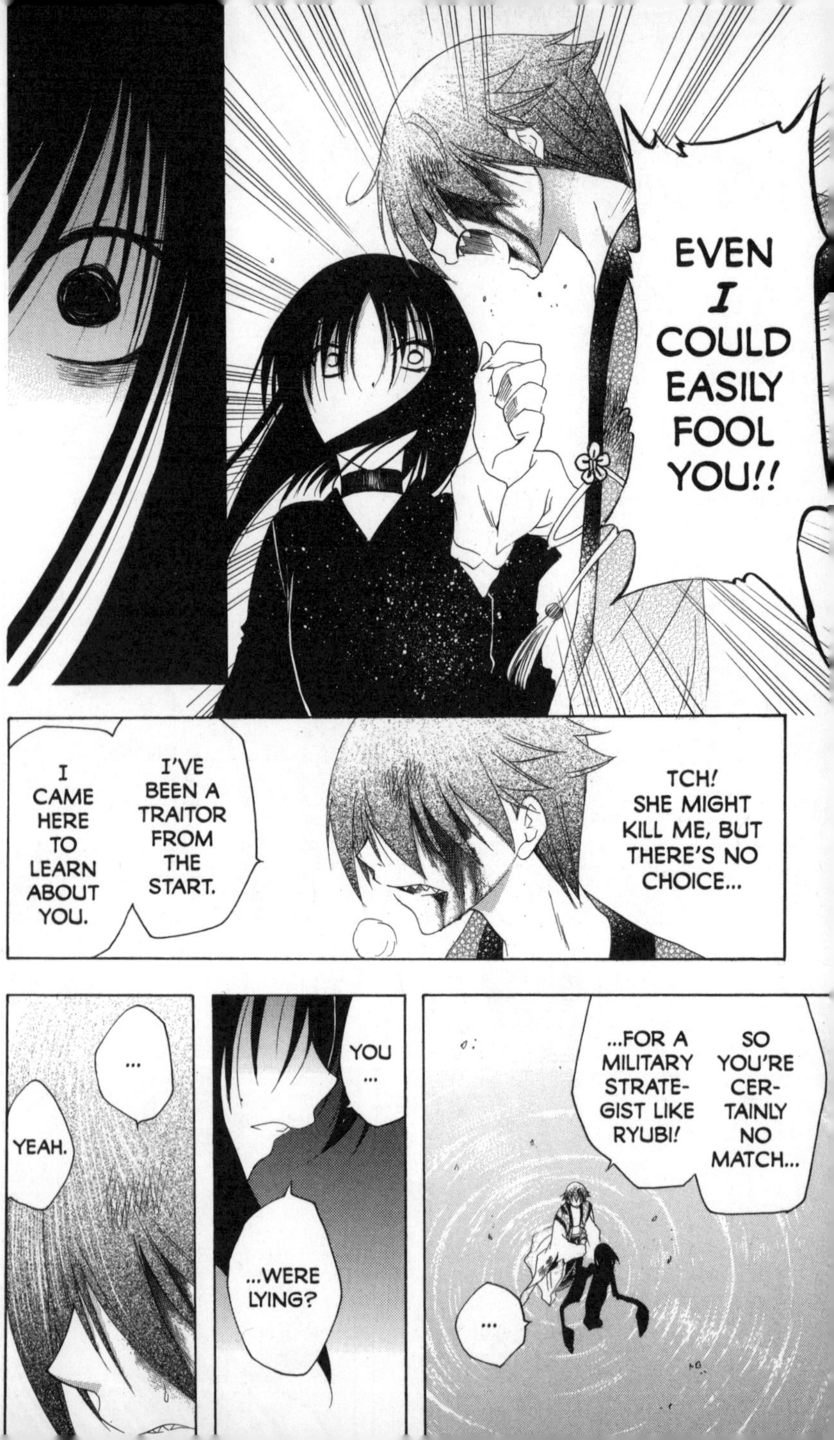
EVEN *I* COULD EASILY FOOL YOU!!
TCH! SHE MIGHT KILL ME, BUT THERE'S NO CHOICE...
I'VE BEEN A TRAITOR FROM THE START.
I CAME HERE TO LEARN ABOUT YOU.
SO YOU'RE CER-TAINLY NO MATCH...
...FOR A MILITARY STRATE-GIST LIKE RYUBI!
...
YOU...
...WERE LYING?
...
YEAH.

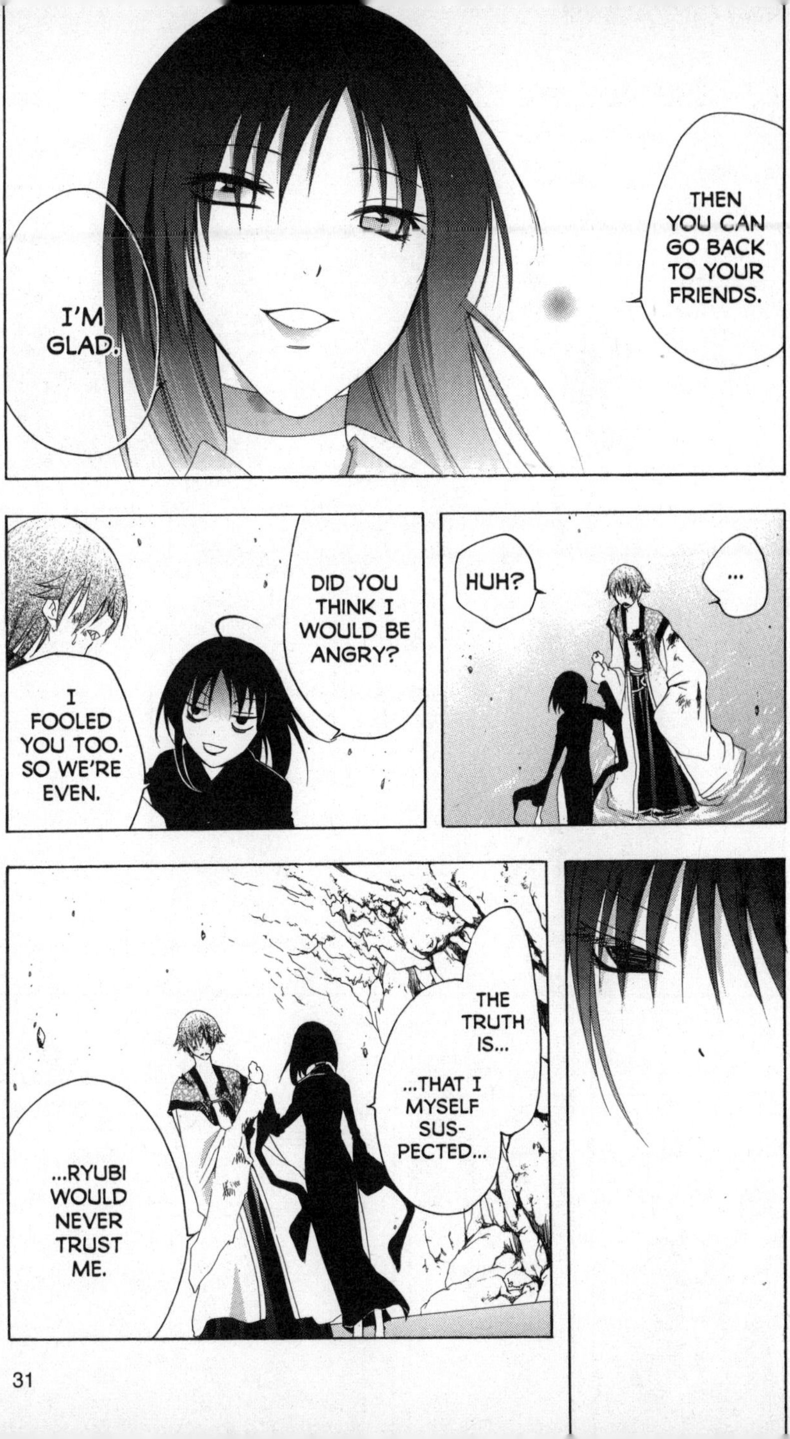
THEN YOU CAN GO BACK TO YOUR FRIENDS.
I'M GLAD.
...
HUH?
DID YOU THINK I WOULD BE ANGRY?
I FOOLED YOU TOO. SO WE'RE EVEN.
THE TRUTH IS...
...THAT I MYSELF SUSPECTED...
...RYUBI WOULD NEVER TRUST ME.

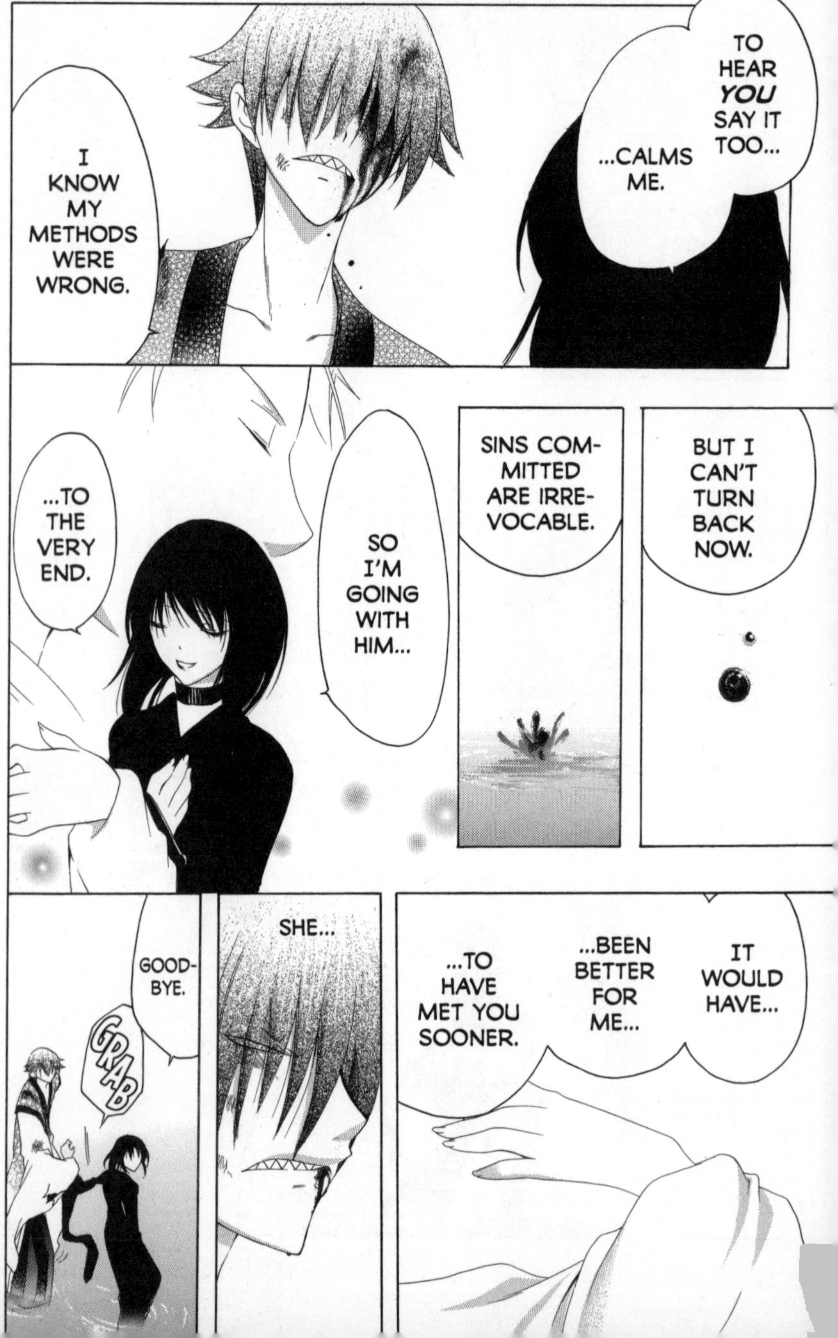
TO HEAR *YOU* SAY IT TOO...
...CALMS ME.
I KNOW MY METHODS WERE WRONG.
BUT I CAN'T TURN BACK NOW.
SINS COM-MITTED ARE IRRE-VOCABLE.
SO I'M GOING WITH HIM...
...TO THE VERY END.
IT WOULD HAVE...
...BEEN BETTER FOR ME...
...TO HAVE MET YOU SOONER.
SHE...
GOOD-BYE.
GRAB

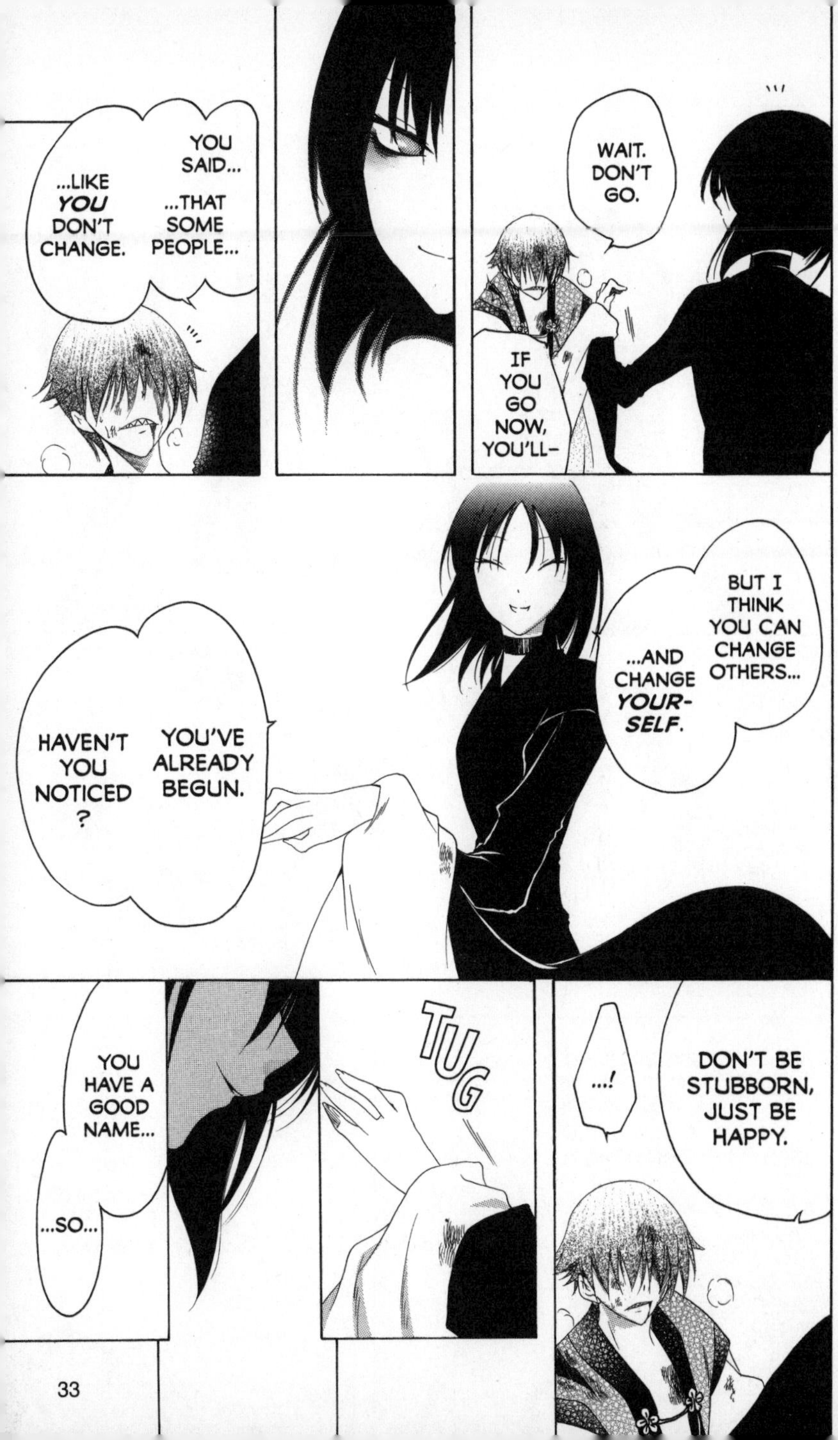
WAIT. DON'T GO.
IF YOU GO NOW, YOU'LL-
YOU SAID...
...THAT SOME PEOPLE...
...LIKE *YOU* DON'T CHANGE.
BUT I THINK YOU CAN CHANGE OTHERS...
...AND CHANGE *YOURSELF*.
YOU'VE ALREADY BEGUN.
HAVEN'T YOU NOTICED?
DON'T BE STUBBORN, JUST BE HAPPY.
...!
TUG
YOU HAVE A GOOD NAME...
...SO...

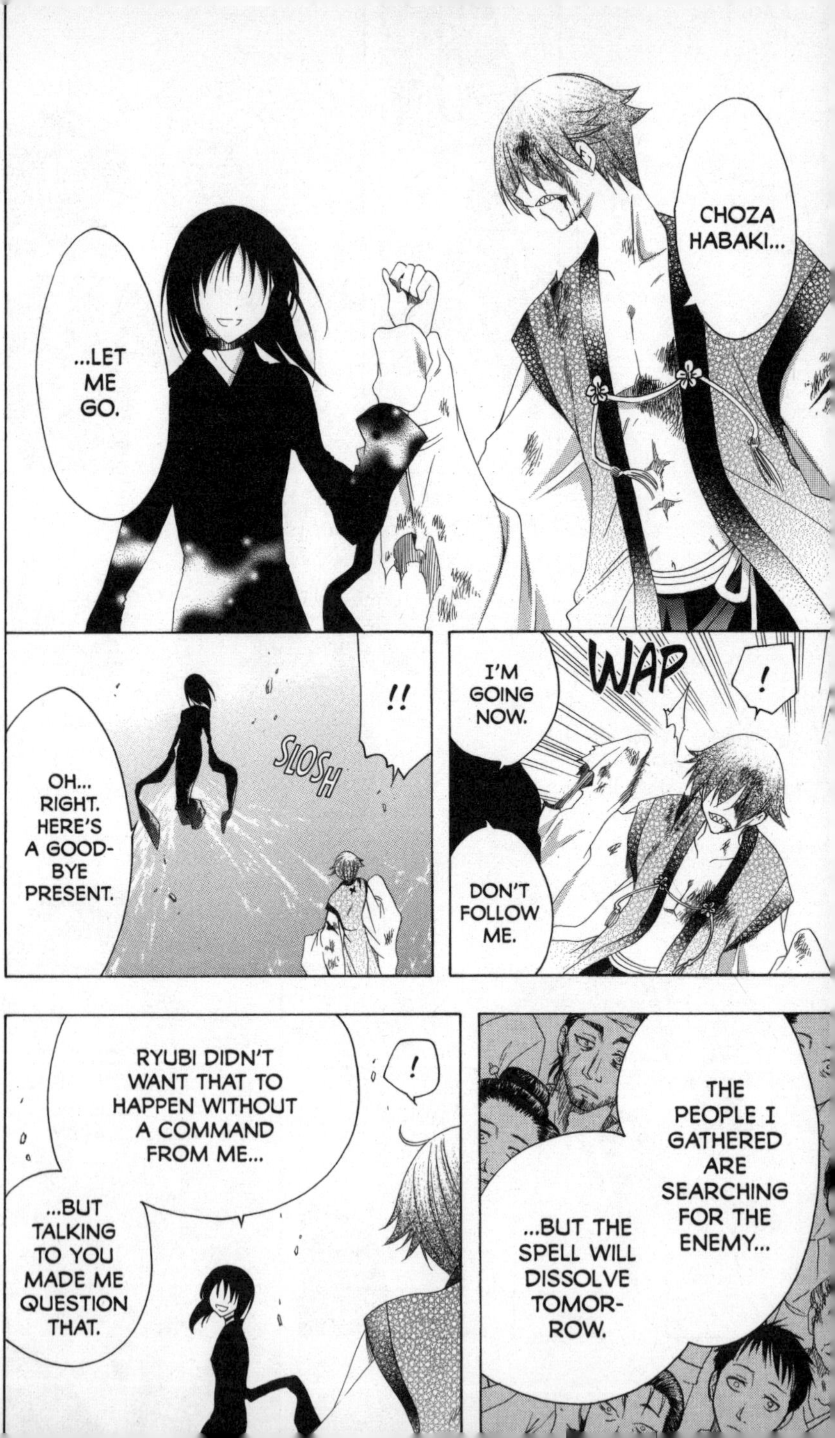
CHOZA HABAKI...
...LET ME GO.
!
WAP
I'M GOING NOW.
DON'T FOLLOW ME.
!!
SLOSH
OH... RIGHT. HERE'S A GOOD-BYE PRESENT.
THE PEOPLE I GATHERED ARE SEARCHING FOR THE ENEMY...
...BUT THE SPELL WILL DISSOLVE TOMOR-ROW.
!
RYUBI DIDN'T WANT THAT TO HAPPEN WITHOUT A COMMAND FROM ME...
...BUT TALKING TO YOU MADE ME QUESTION THAT.

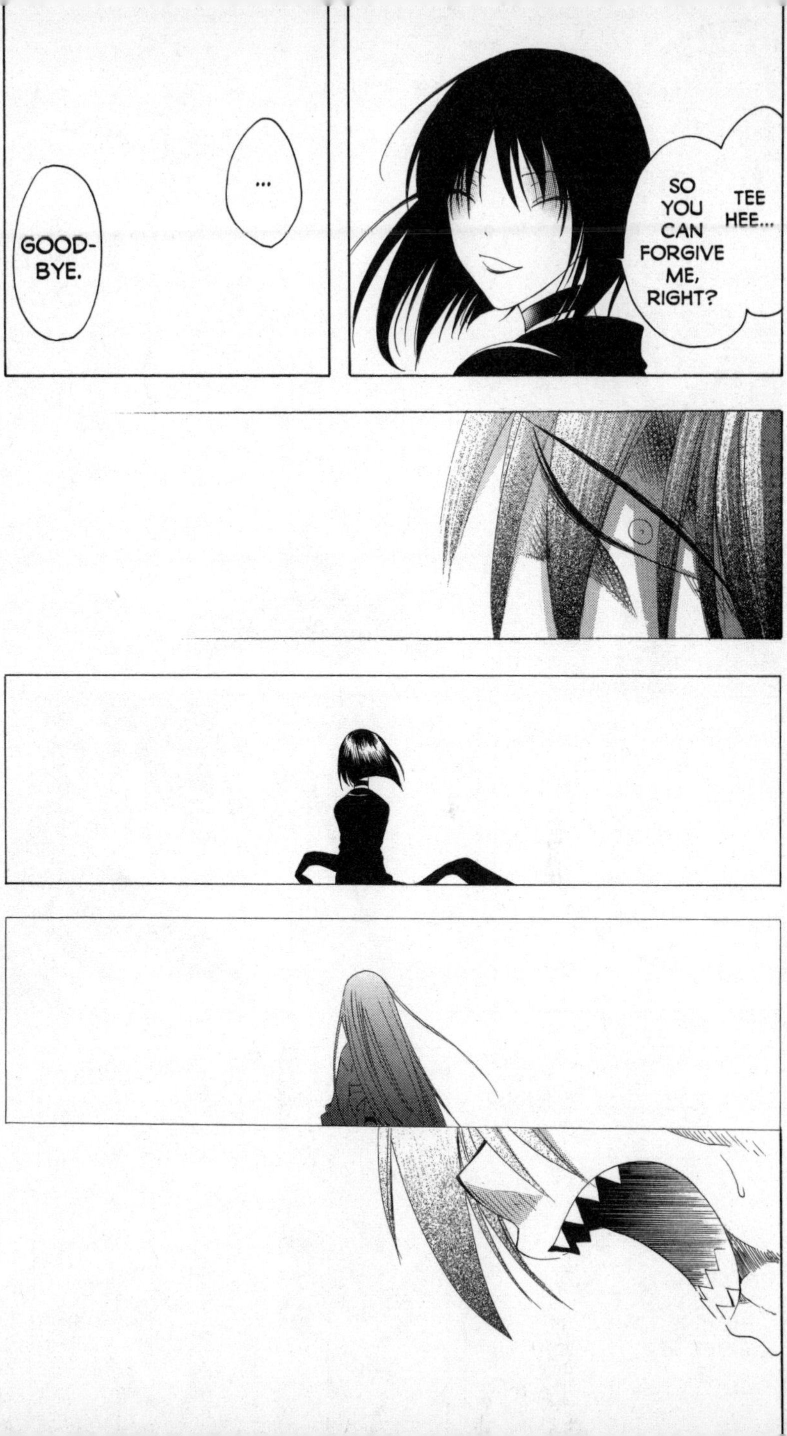
TEE HEE...
SO YOU CAN FORGIVE ME, RIGHT?
...
GOOD-BYE.

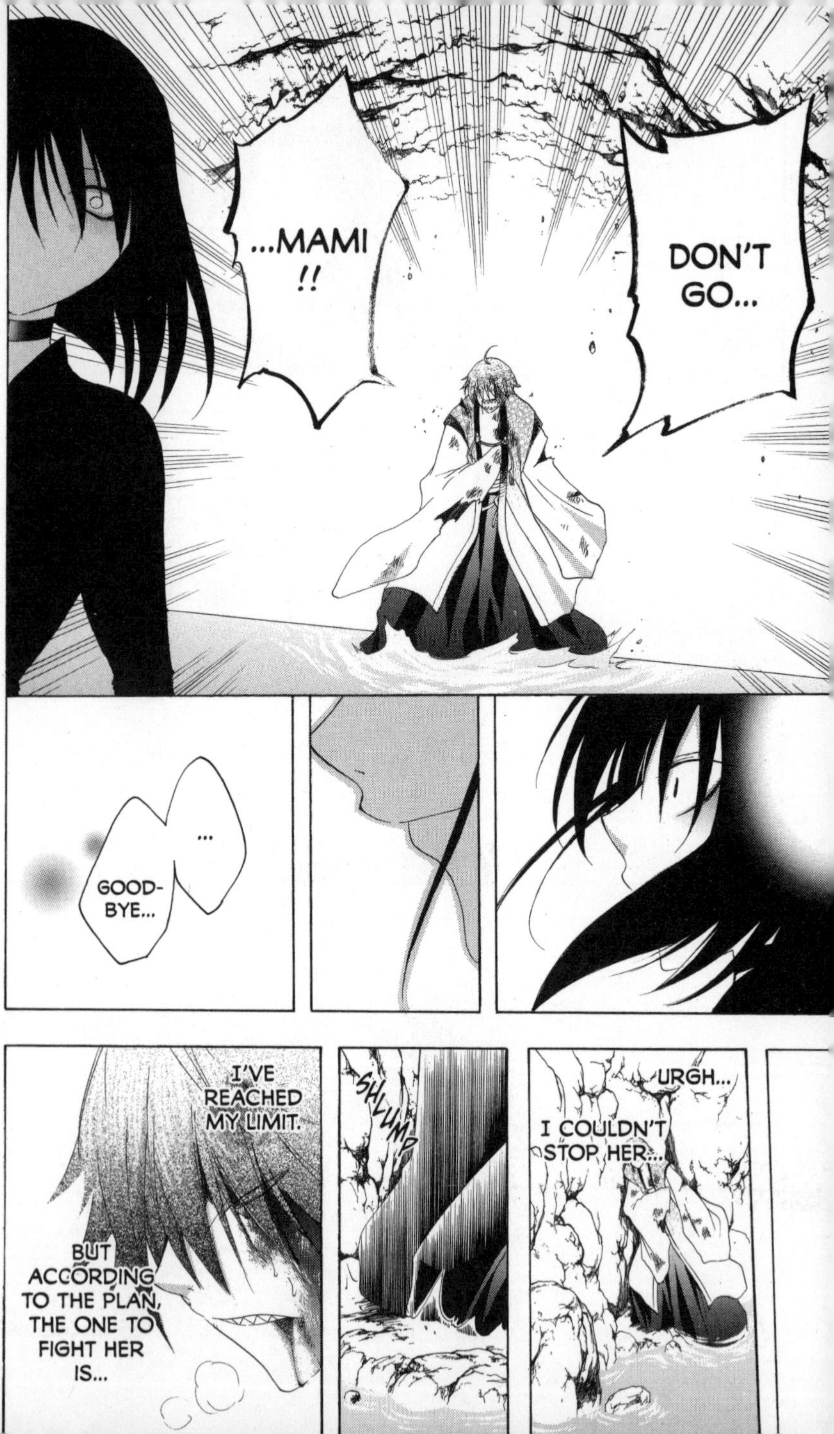
DON'T GO...
...MAMI !!
... GOOD-BYE...
URGH...
I COULDN'T STOP HER...
SHLUMP
I'VE REACHED MY LIMIT.
BUT ACCORDING TO THE PLAN, THE ONE TO FIGHT HER IS...

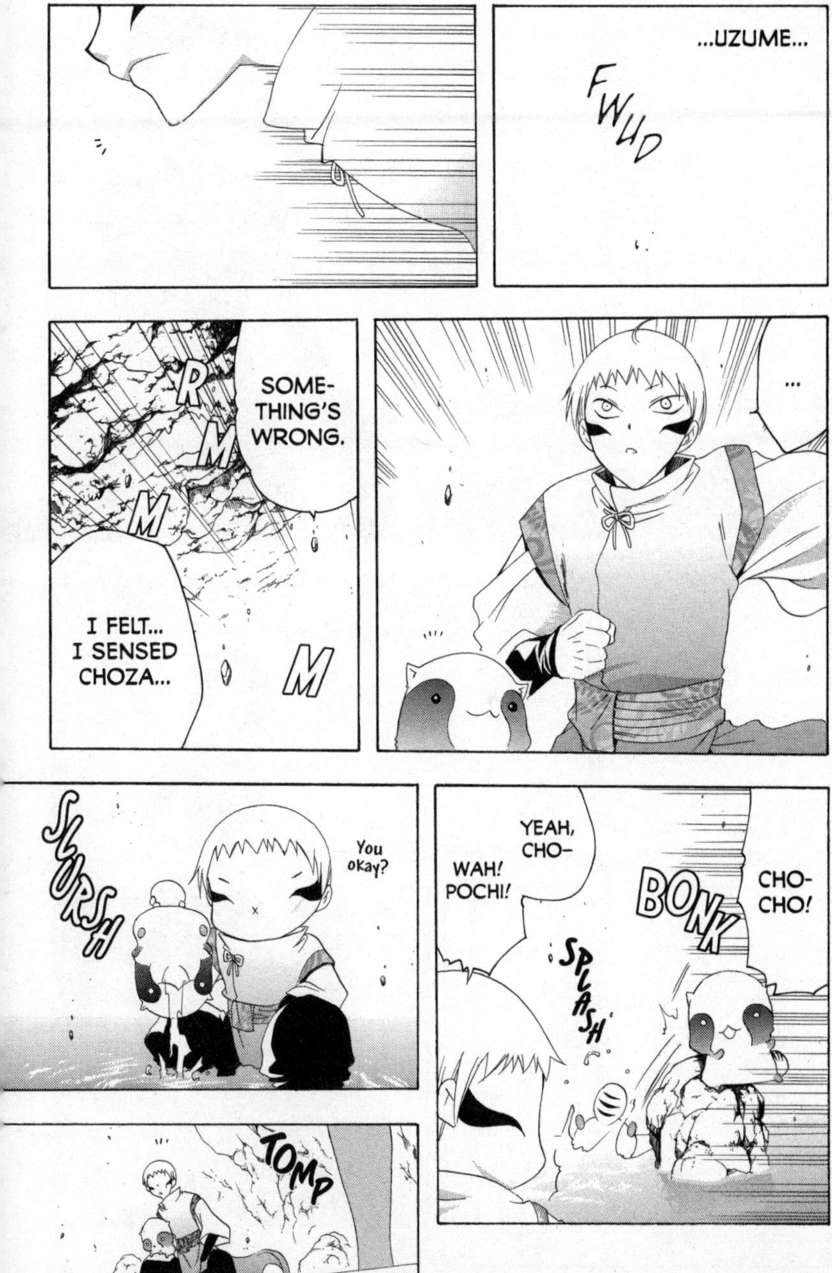
...UZUME...
FWUD
...
SOME-THING'S WRONG.
RMMM
I FELT... I SENSED CHOZA...
M
CHO-CHO!
BONK
YEAH, CHO-
WAH! POCHI!
SPLASH
SLURSH
You okay?
TOMP

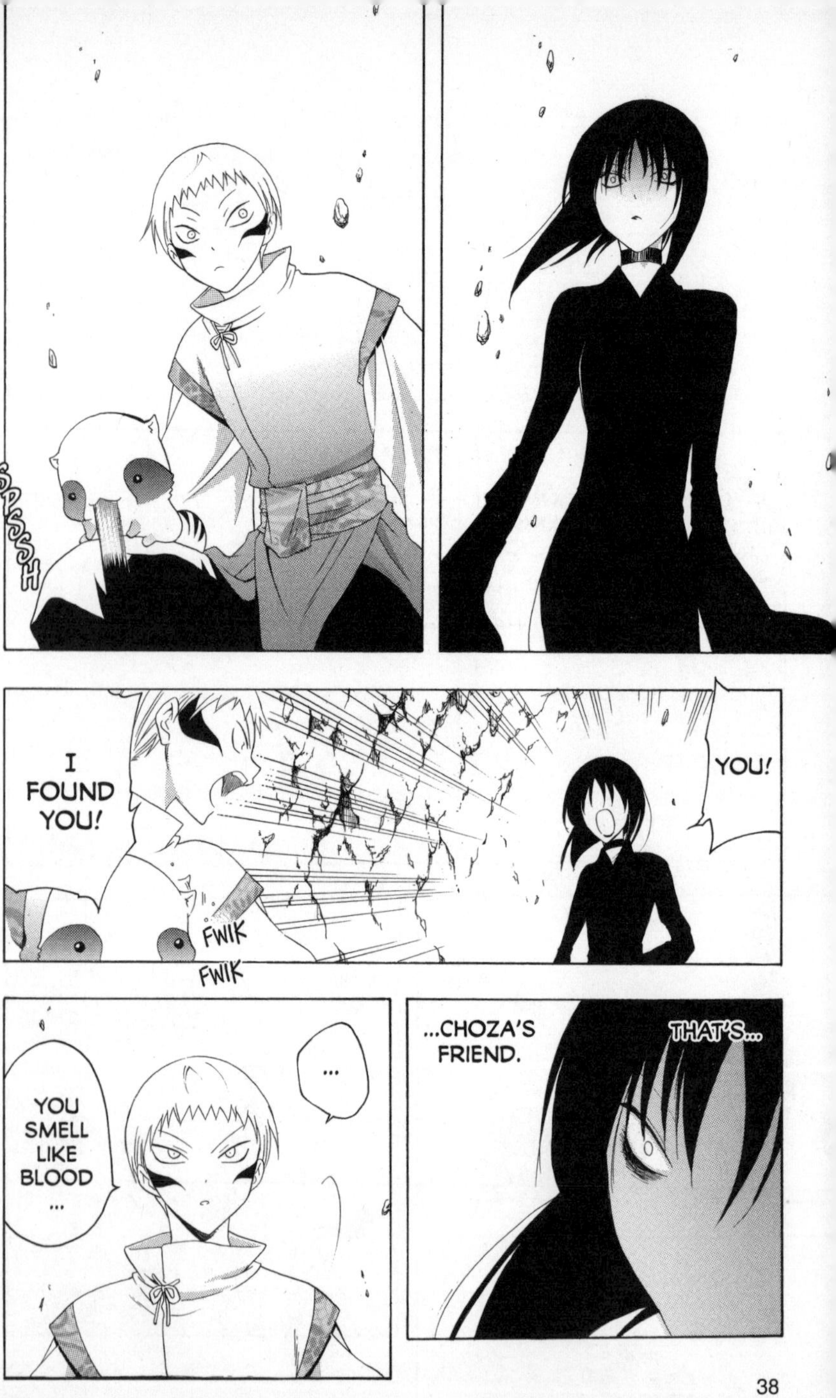
SPSSH
YOU!
I FOUND YOU!
FWIK
FWIK
THAT'S...
...CHOZA'S FRIEND.
...
YOU SMELL LIKE BLOOD ...

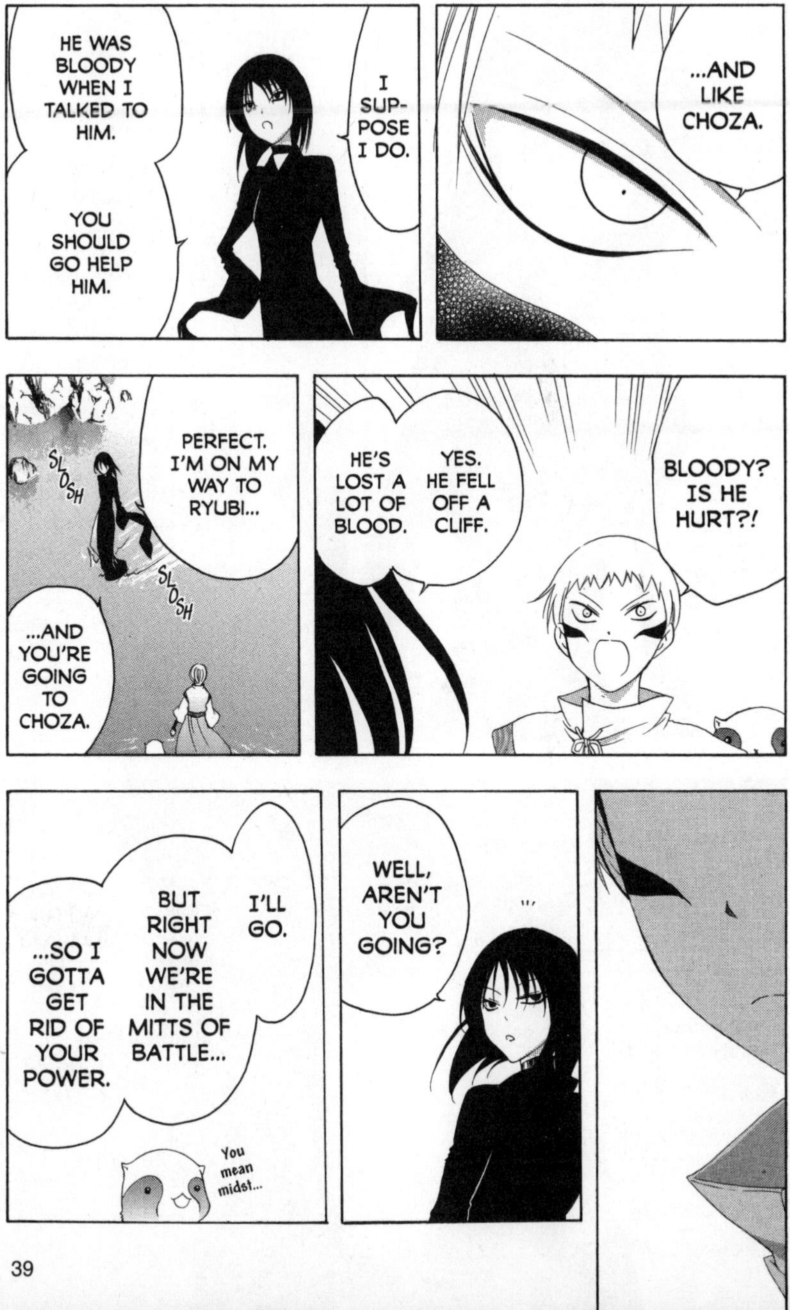
...AND LIKE CHOZA.
I SUPPOSE I DO.
HE WAS BLOODY WHEN I TALKED TO HIM.
YOU SHOULD GO HELP HIM.
BLOODY? IS HE HURT?!
YES. HE FELL OFF A CLIFF.
HE'S LOST A LOT OF BLOOD.
PERFECT. I'M ON MY WAY TO RYUBI...
SLOSH
SLOSH
...AND YOU'RE GOING TO CHOZA.
WELL, AREN'T YOU GOING?
...
I'LL GO.
BUT RIGHT NOW WE'RE IN THE MITTS OF BATTLE...
...SO I GOTTA GET RID OF YOUR POWER.
You mean midst...

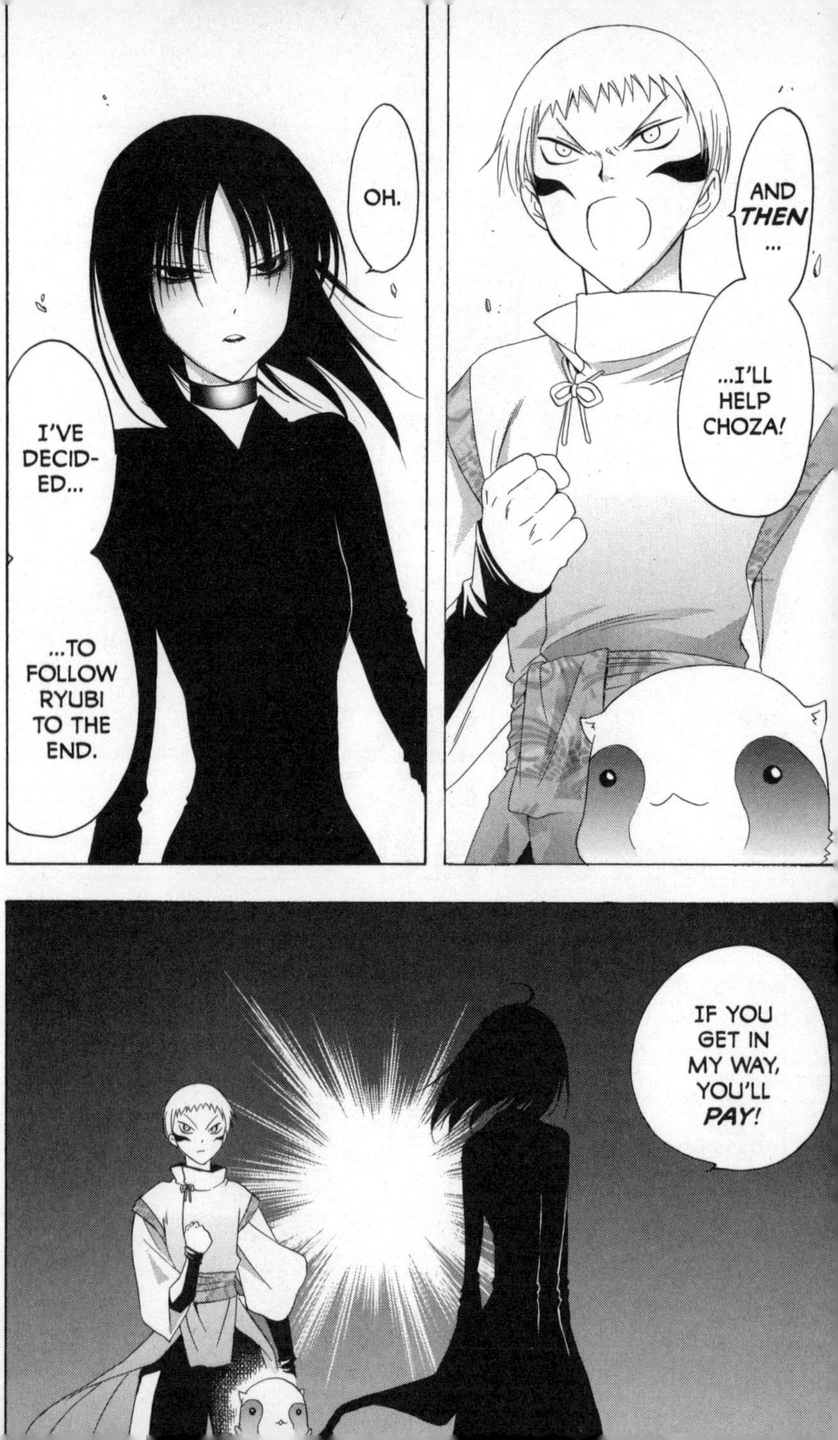
AND *THEN* ...
...I'LL HELP CHOZA!
OH.
I'VE DECID-ED...
...TO FOLLOW RYUBI TO THE END.
IF YOU GET IN MY WAY, YOU'LL *PAY*!

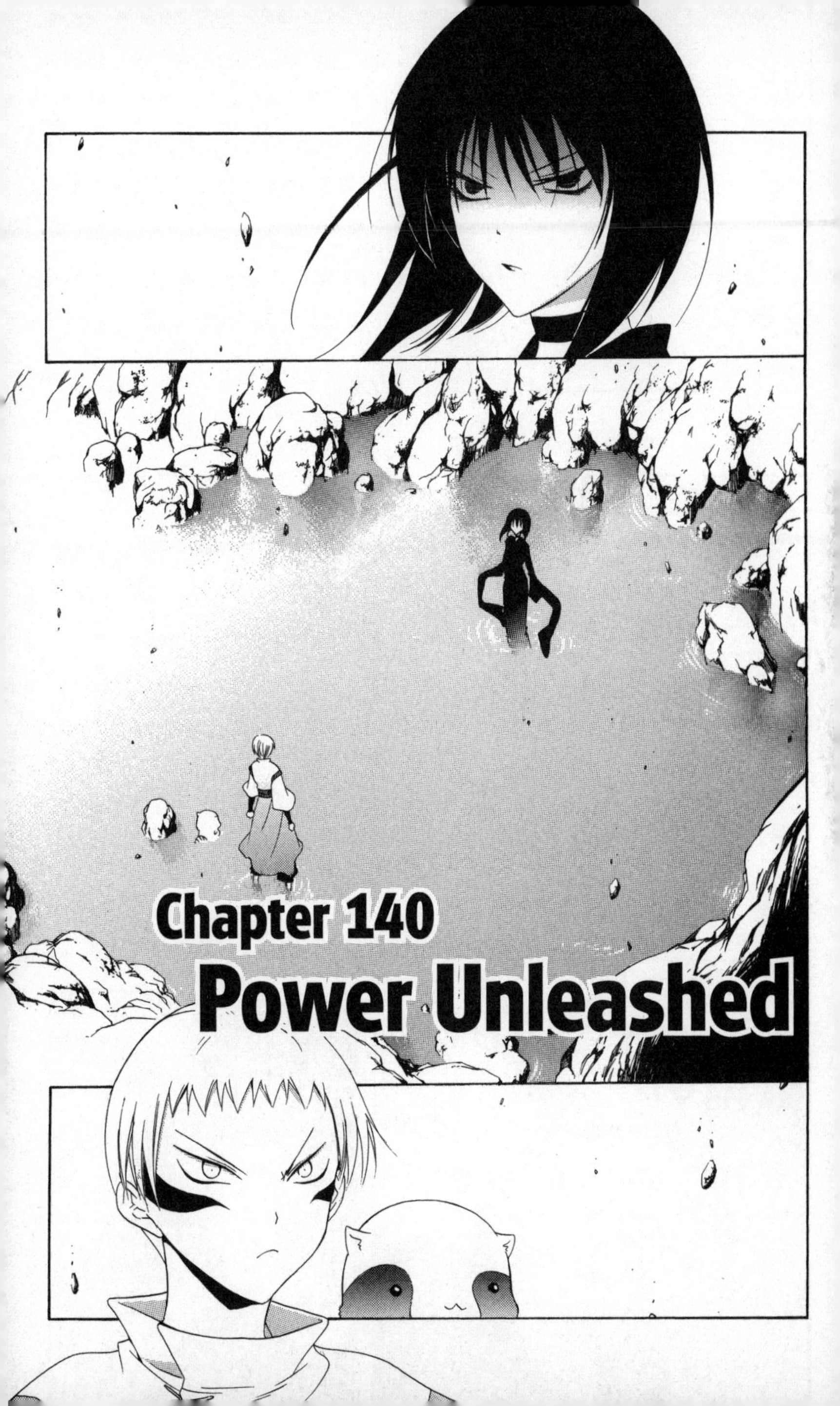

Chapter 140
Power Unleashed

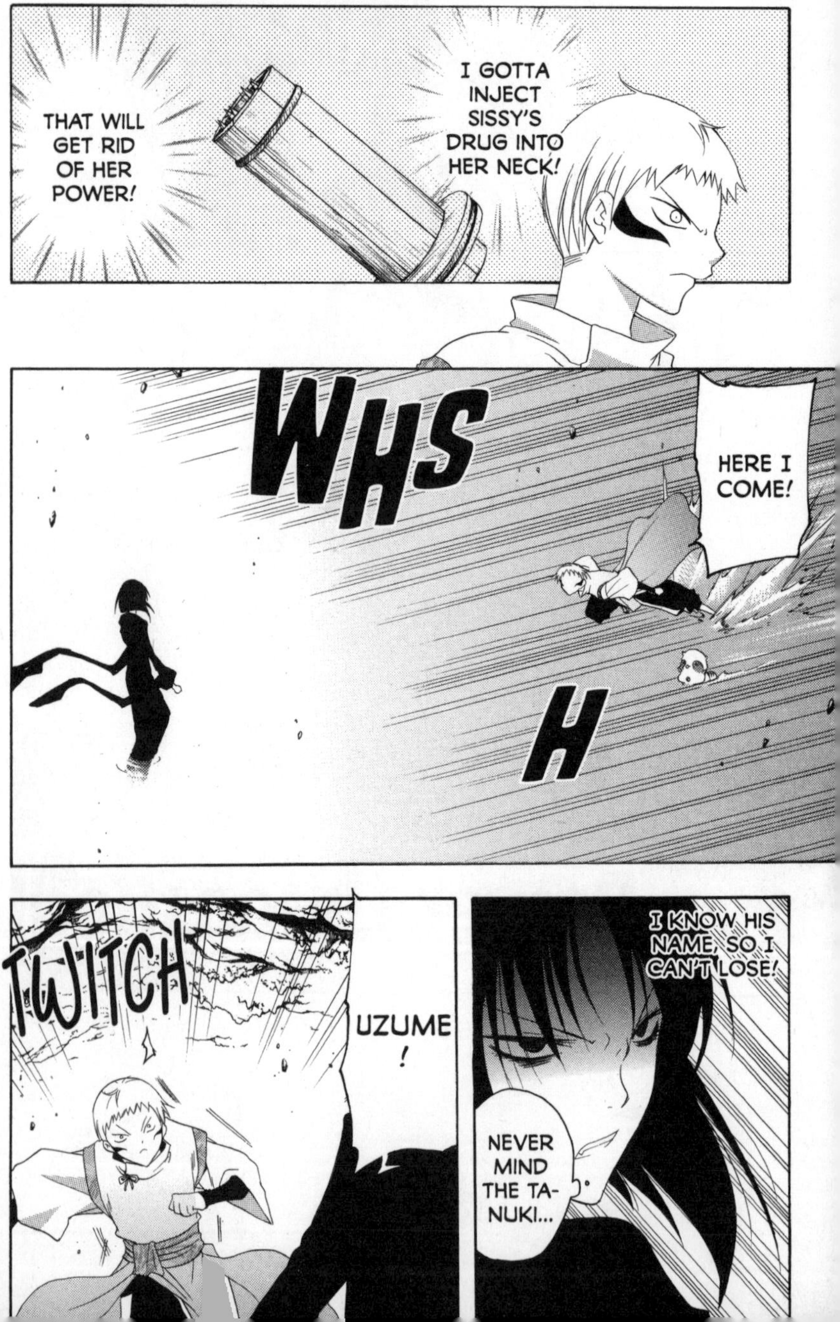
I GOTTA INJECT SISSY'S DRUG INTO HER NECK!
THAT WILL GET RID OF HER POWER!
HERE I COME!
WHSHH
I KNOW HIS NAME, SO I CAN'T LOSE!
NEVER MIND THE TA-NUKI...
UZUME!
TWITCH

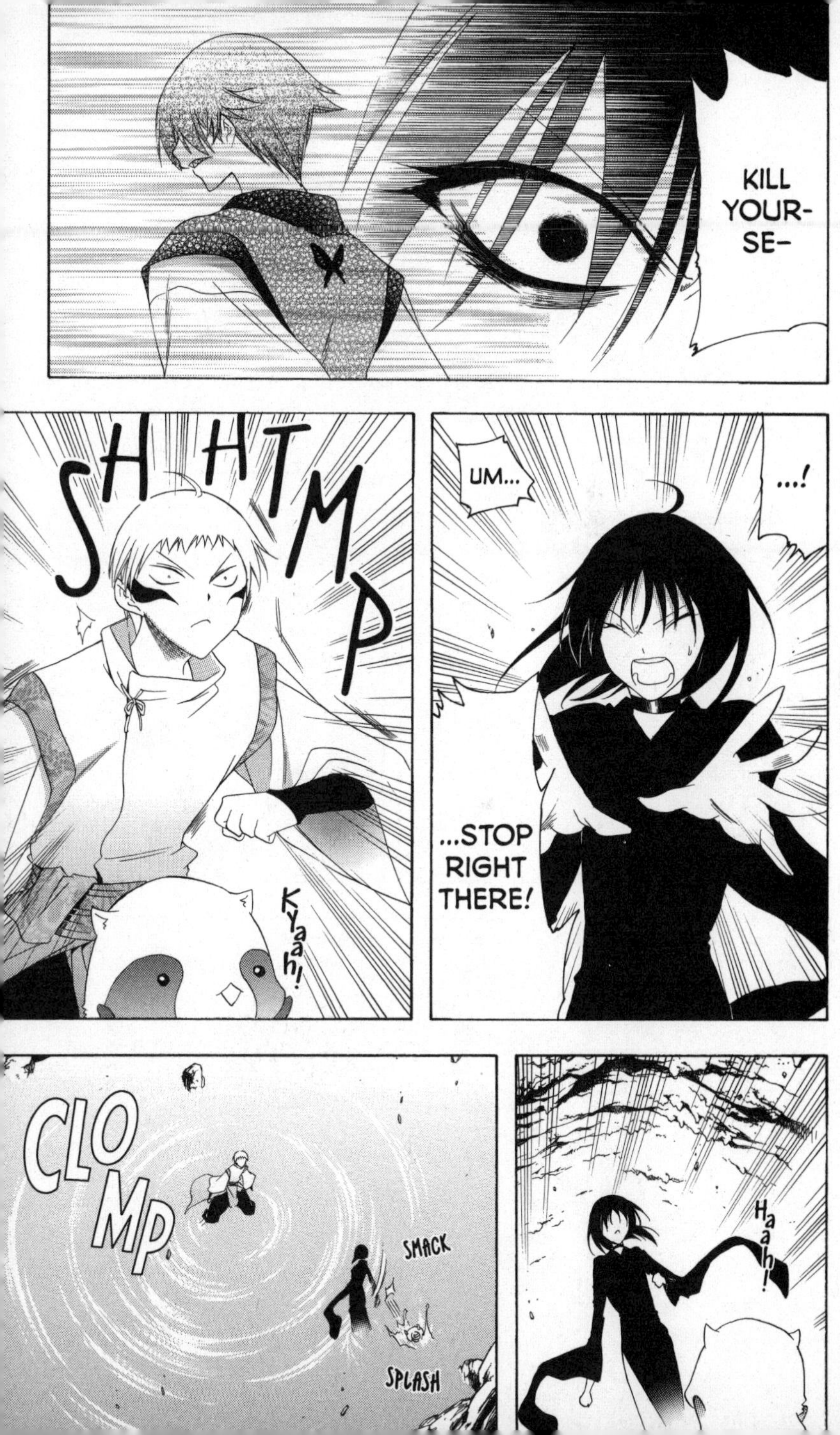
KILL YOURSE–
UM...
...!
...STOP RIGHT THERE!
SHHTMP
Kyaah!
Haaah!
CLOMP
SMACK
SPLASH

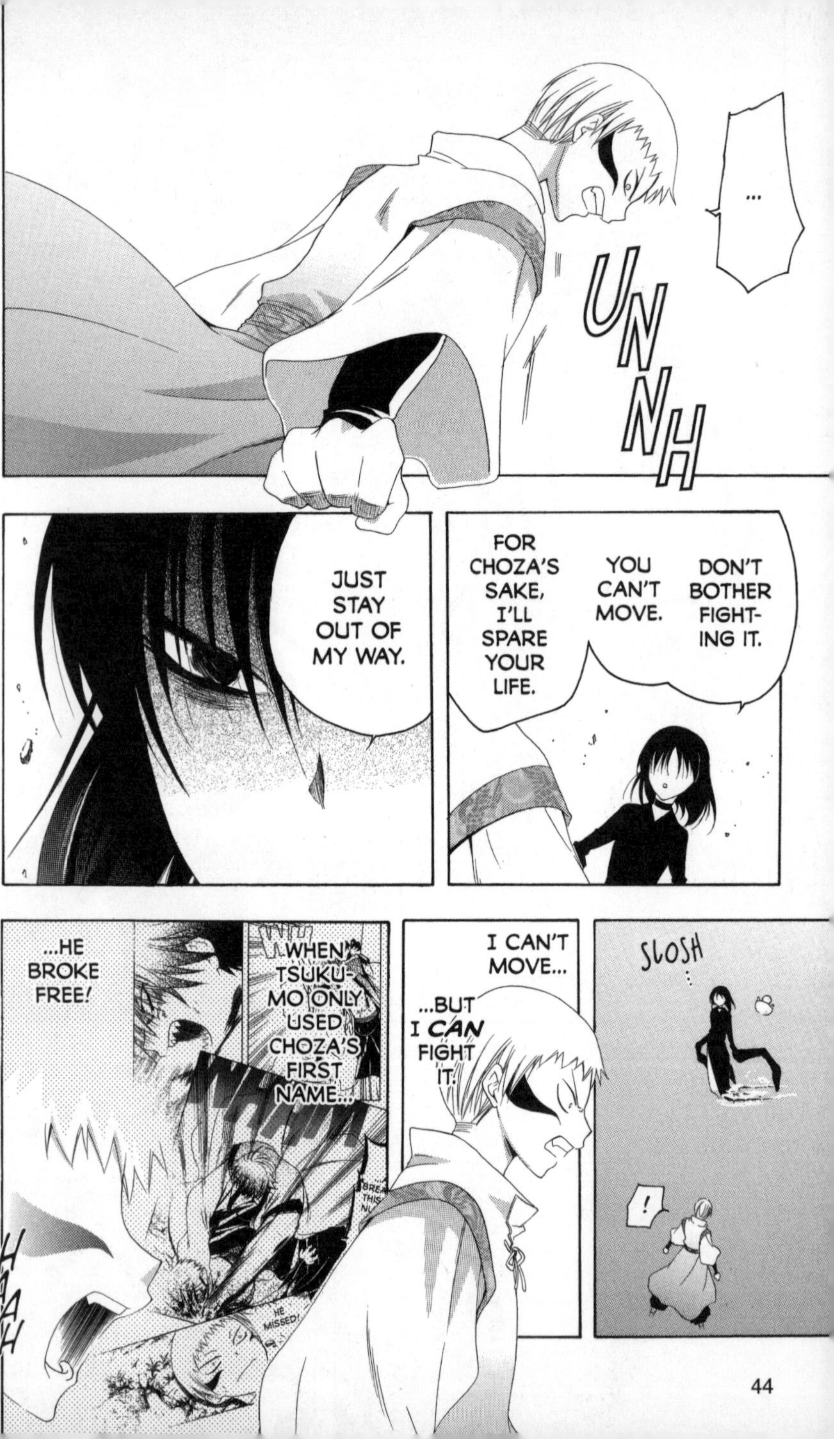
...
UNNH
DON'T BOTHER FIGHTING IT.
YOU CAN'T MOVE.
FOR CHOZA'S SAKE, I'LL SPARE YOUR LIFE.
JUST STAY OUT OF MY WAY.
SLOSH
!
I CAN'T MOVE...
...BUT I *CAN* FIGHT IT.
WHEN TSUKUMO ONLY USED CHOZA'S FIRST NAME...
...HE BROKE FREE!
HE MISSED!
HAAH

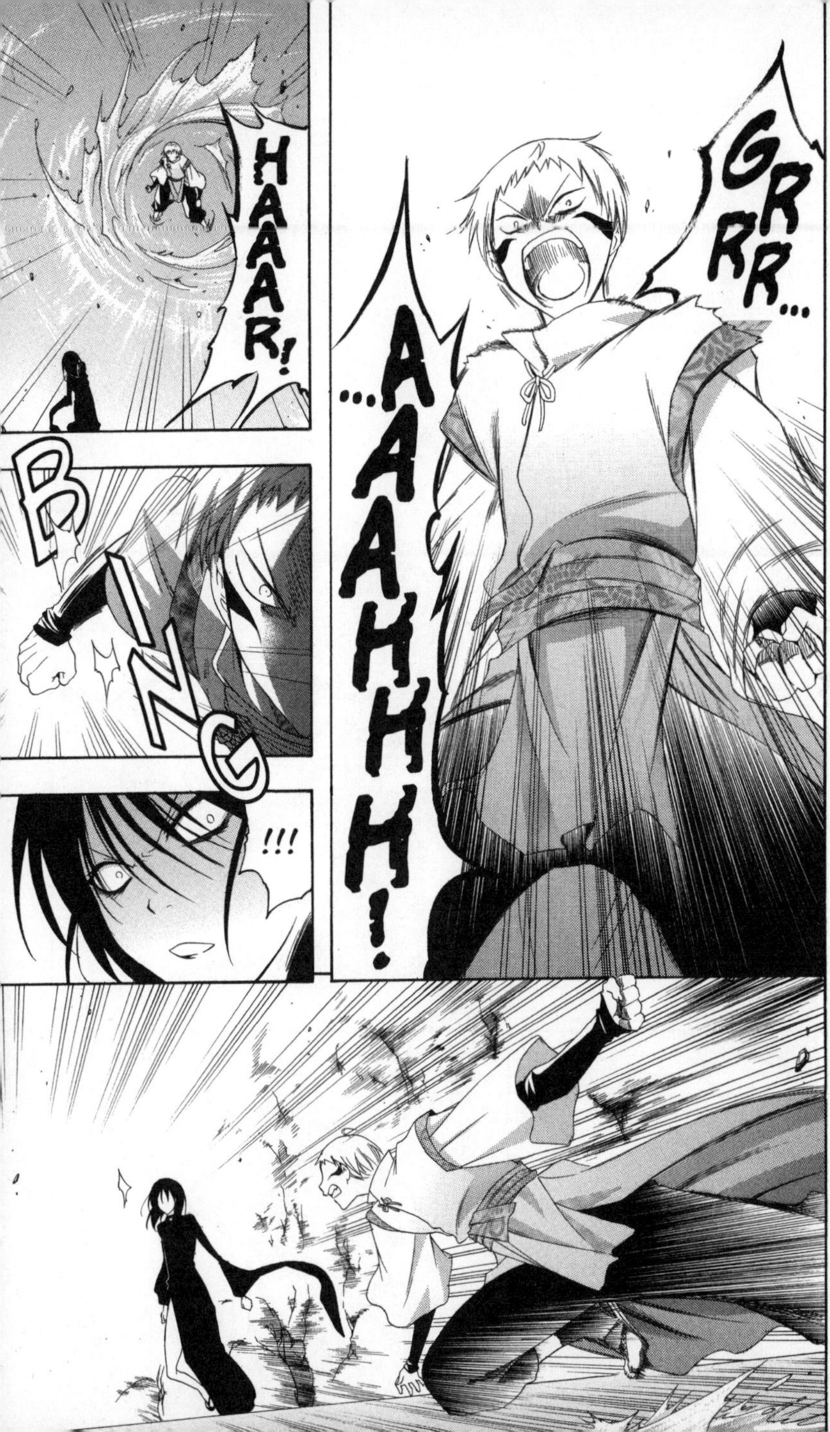
GRRR...
...AAAHHH!
HAAAR!
BING
!!!

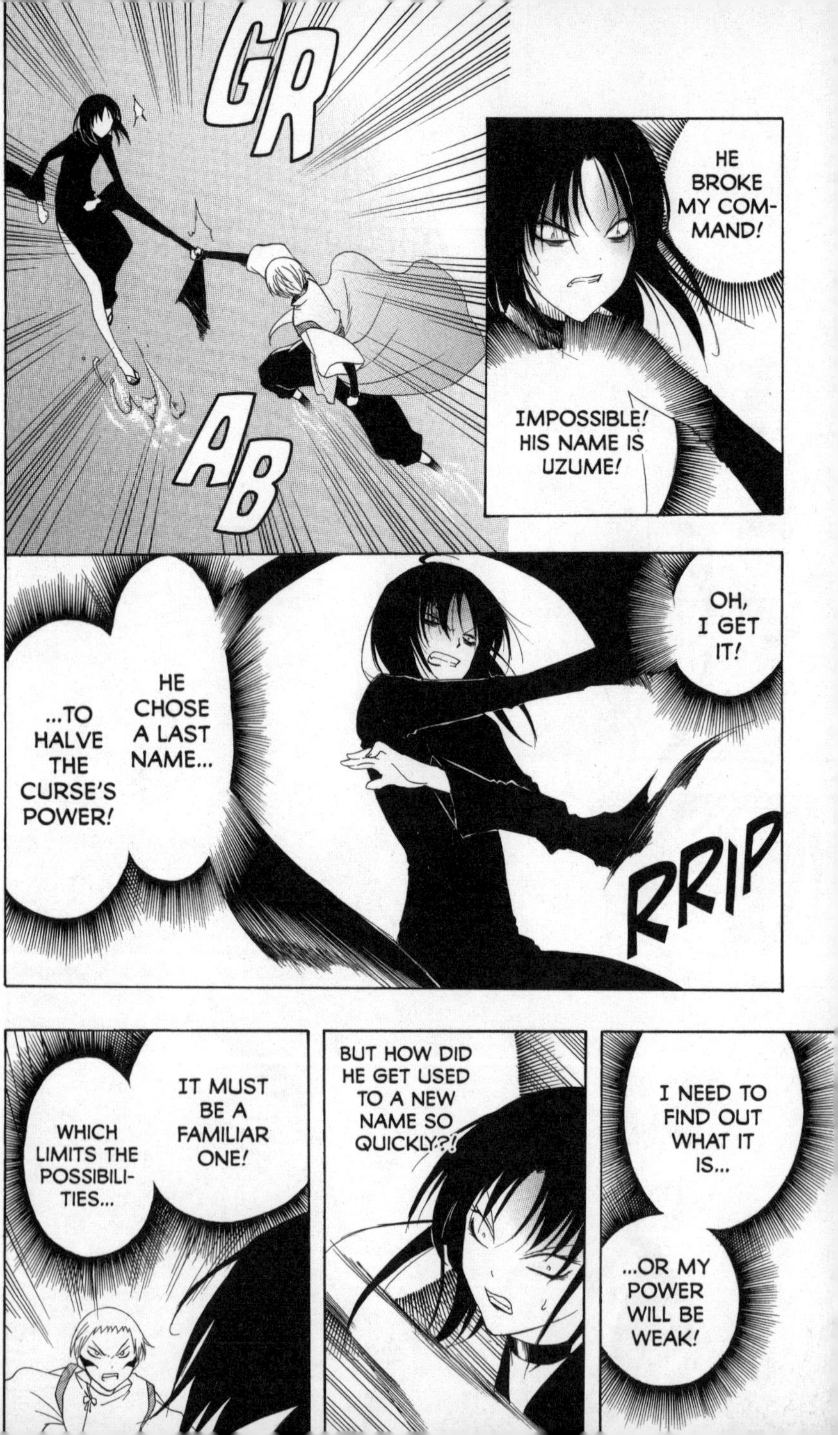
HE BROKE MY COMMAND!
IMPOSSIBLE! HIS NAME IS UZUME!
GRAB
OH, I GET IT!
RRIP
HE CHOSE A LAST NAME...
...TO HALVE THE CURSE'S POWER!
I NEED TO FIND OUT WHAT IT IS...
...OR MY POWER WILL BE WEAK!
BUT HOW DID HE GET USED TO A NEW NAME SO QUICKLY?!
IT MUST BE A FAMILIAR ONE!
WHICH LIMITS THE POSSIBILITIES...

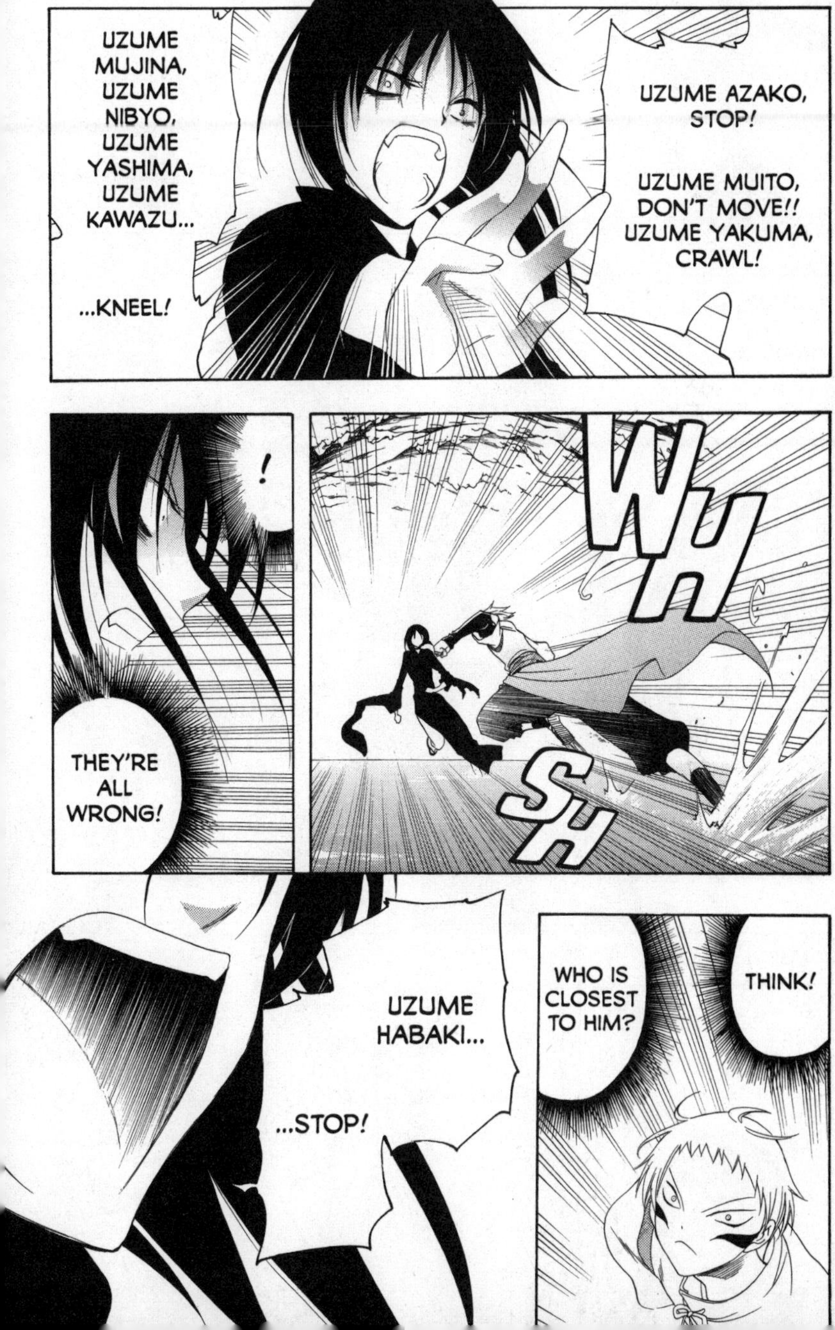
UZUME AZAKO, STOP!
UZUME MUITO, DON'T MOVE!! UZUME YAKUMA, CRAWL!
UZUME MUJINA, UZUME NIBYO, UZUME YASHIMA, UZUME KAWAZU...
...KNEEL!
WHSH
!
THEY'RE ALL WRONG!
THINK!
WHO IS CLOSEST TO HIM?
UZUME HABAKI...
...STOP!

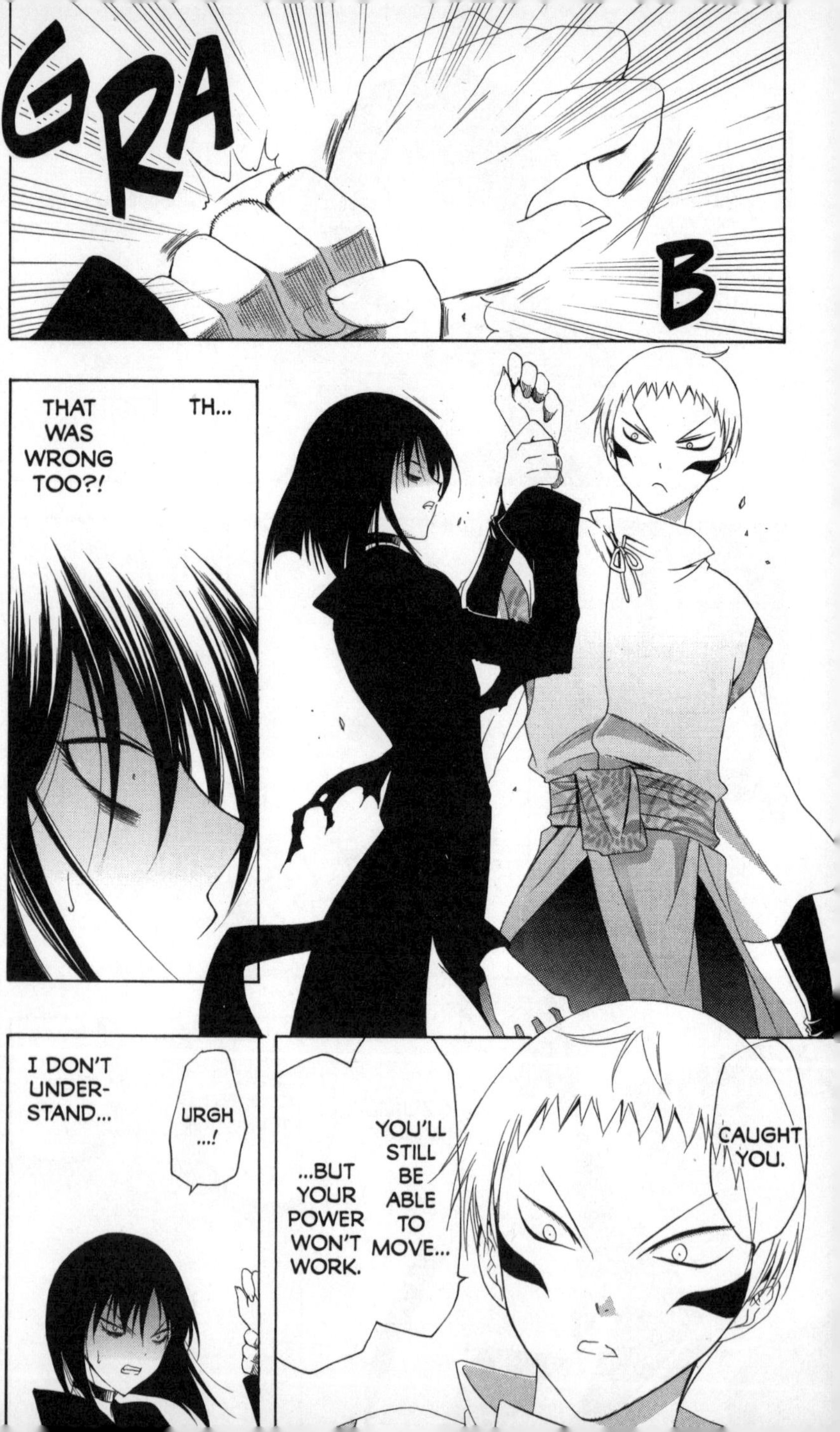
GRAB
TH...
THAT WAS WRONG TOO?!
CAUGHT YOU.
YOU'LL STILL BE ABLE TO MOVE...
...BUT YOUR POWER WON'T WORK.
URGH...!
I DON'T UNDERSTAND...

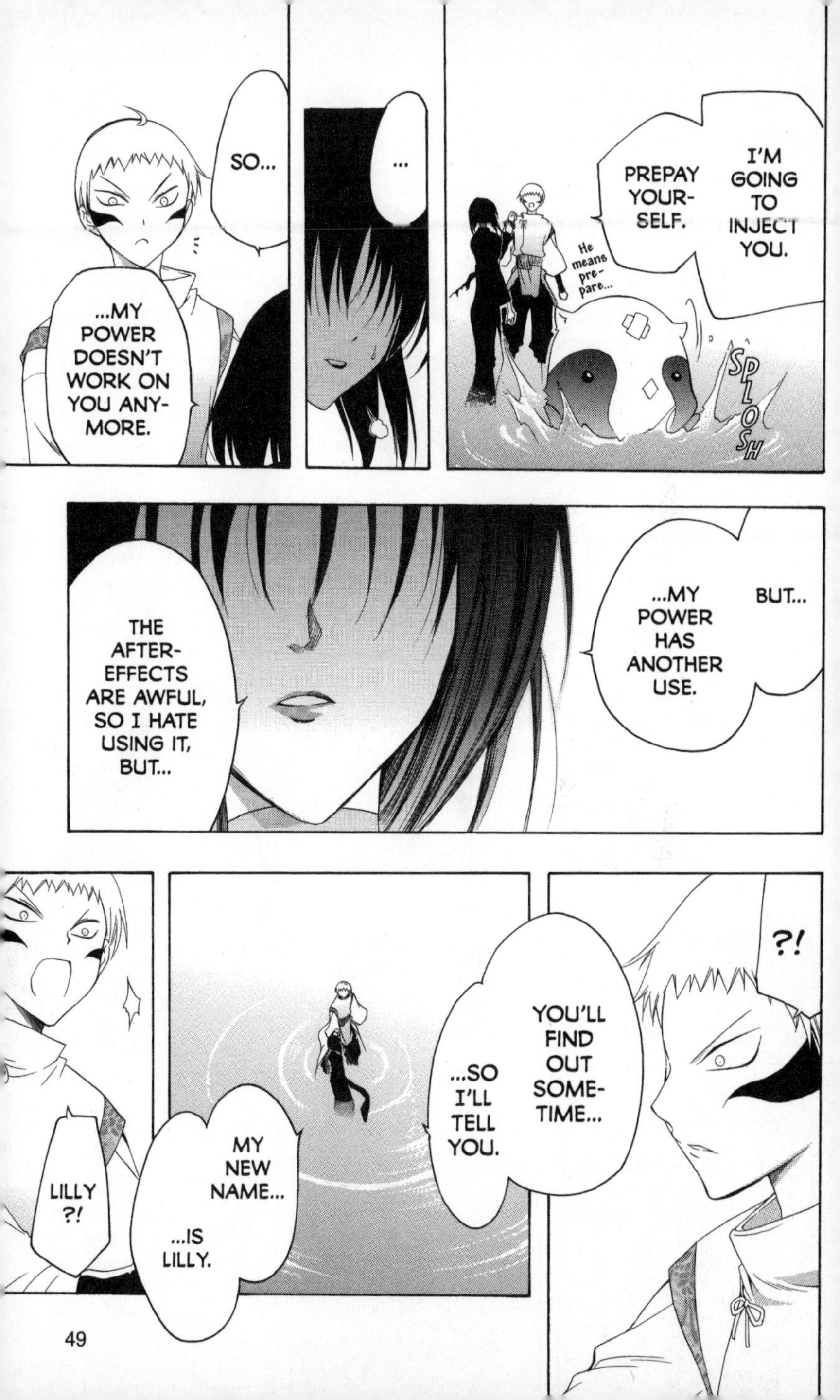
I'M GOING TO INJECT YOU.
PREPAY YOUR-SELF.
He means pre-pare...
SPLOSH
...
SO...
...MY POWER DOESN'T WORK ON YOU ANY-MORE.
BUT...
...MY POWER HAS ANOTHER USE.
THE AFTER-EFFECTS ARE AWFUL, SO I HATE USING IT, BUT...
?!
YOU'LL FIND OUT SOME-TIME...
...SO I'LL TELL YOU.
MY NEW NAME...
...IS LILLY.
LILLY ?!

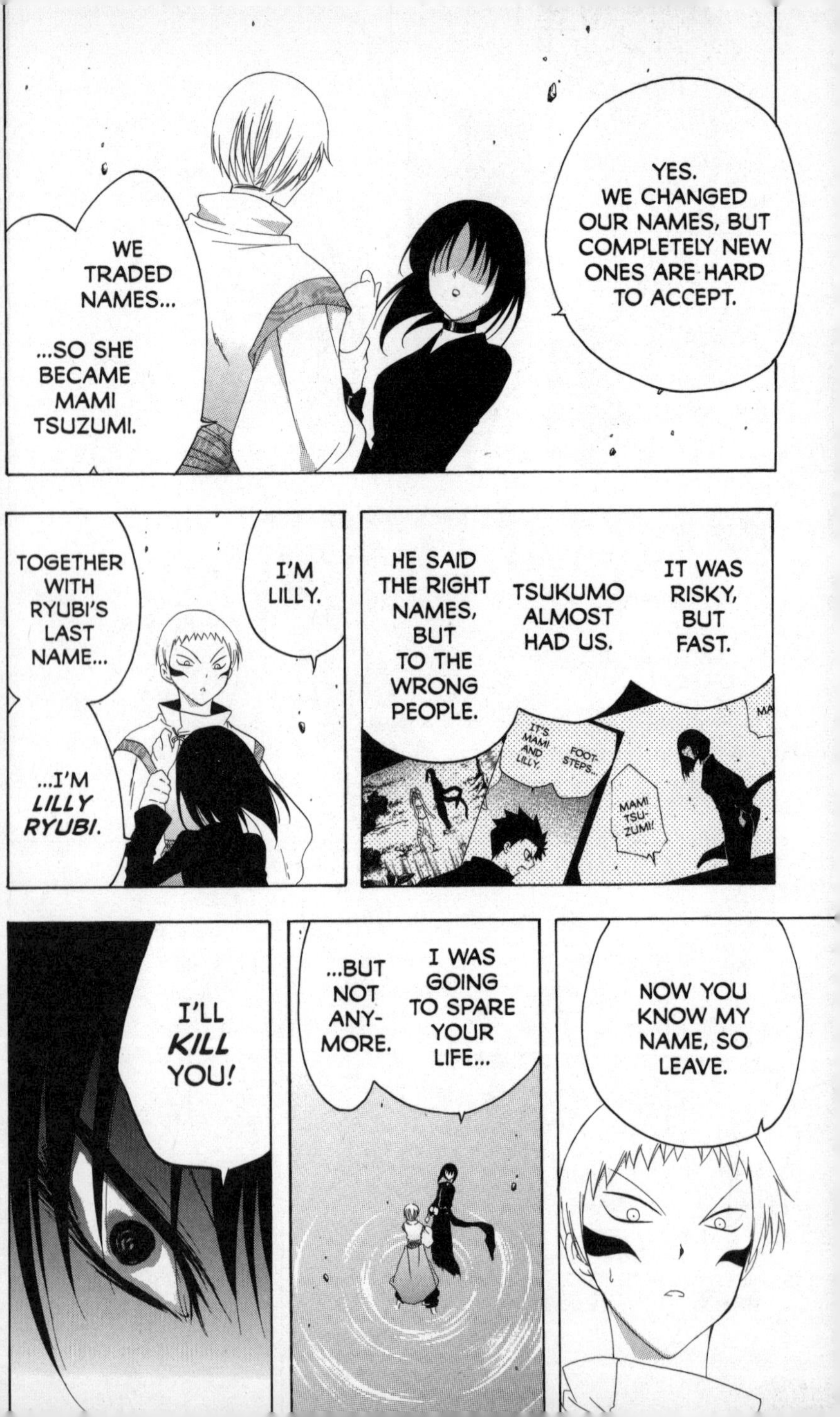
YES. WE CHANGED OUR NAMES, BUT COMPLETELY NEW ONES ARE HARD TO ACCEPT.
WE TRADED NAMES...
...SO SHE BECAME MAMI TSUZUMI.
IT WAS RISKY, BUT FAST.
TSUKUMO ALMOST HAD US.
HE SAID THE RIGHT NAMES, BUT TO THE WRONG PEOPLE.
FOOT-STEPS...
IT'S MAMI AND LILLY.
MAMI TSU-ZUMI!
I'M LILLY.
TOGETHER WITH RYUBI'S LAST NAME...
...I'M *LILLY RYUBI*.
NOW YOU KNOW MY NAME, SO LEAVE.
I WAS GOING TO SPARE YOUR LIFE...
...BUT NOT ANYMORE.
I'LL *KILL* YOU!

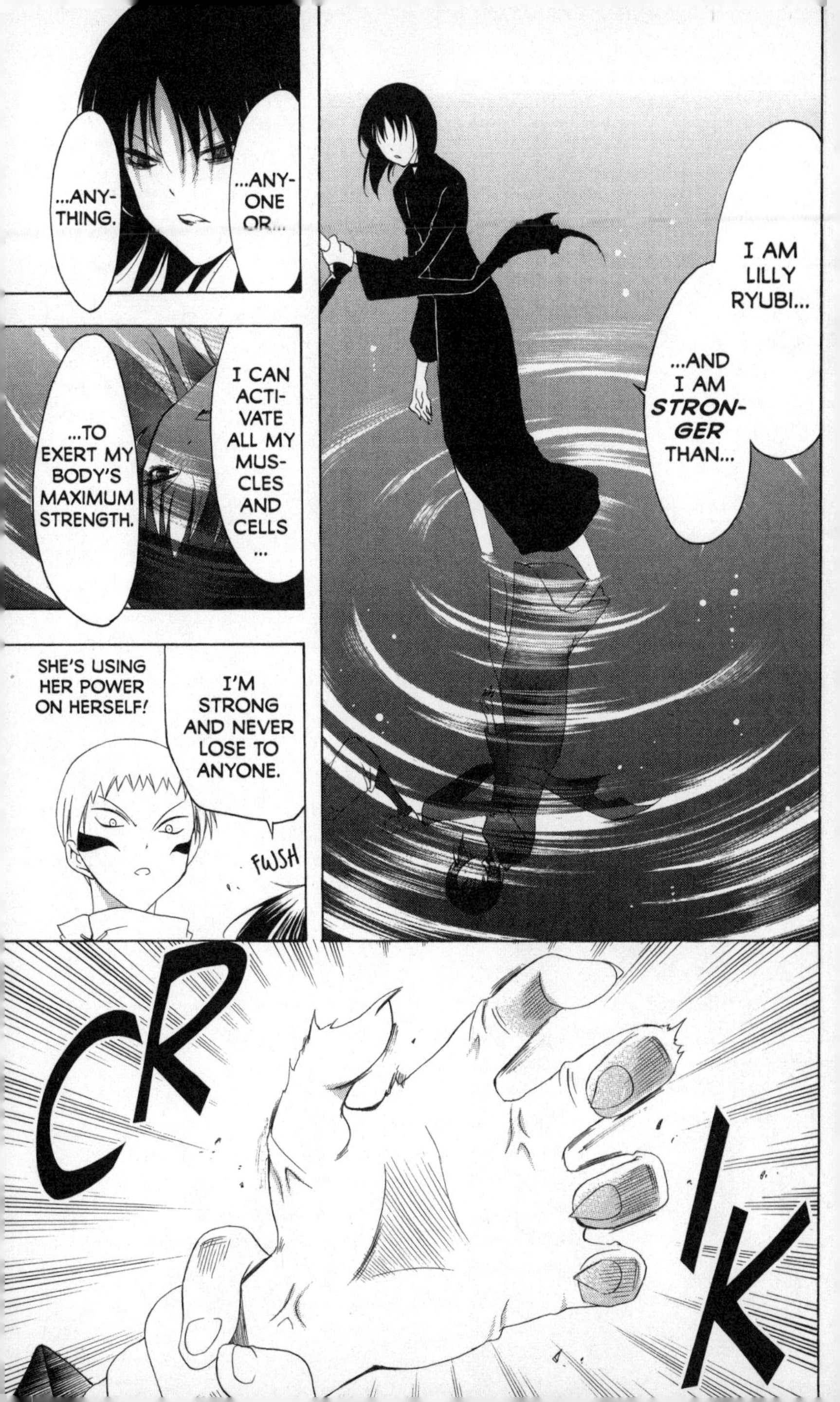

I AM LILLY RYUBI...
...AND I AM STRONGER THAN...
...ANYONE OR...
...ANYTHING.
I CAN ACTIVATE ALL MY MUSCLES AND CELLS...
...TO EXERT MY BODY'S MAXIMUM STRENGTH.
I'M STRONG AND NEVER LOSE TO ANYONE.
SHE'S USING HER POWER ON HERSELF!
FWSH
CRK

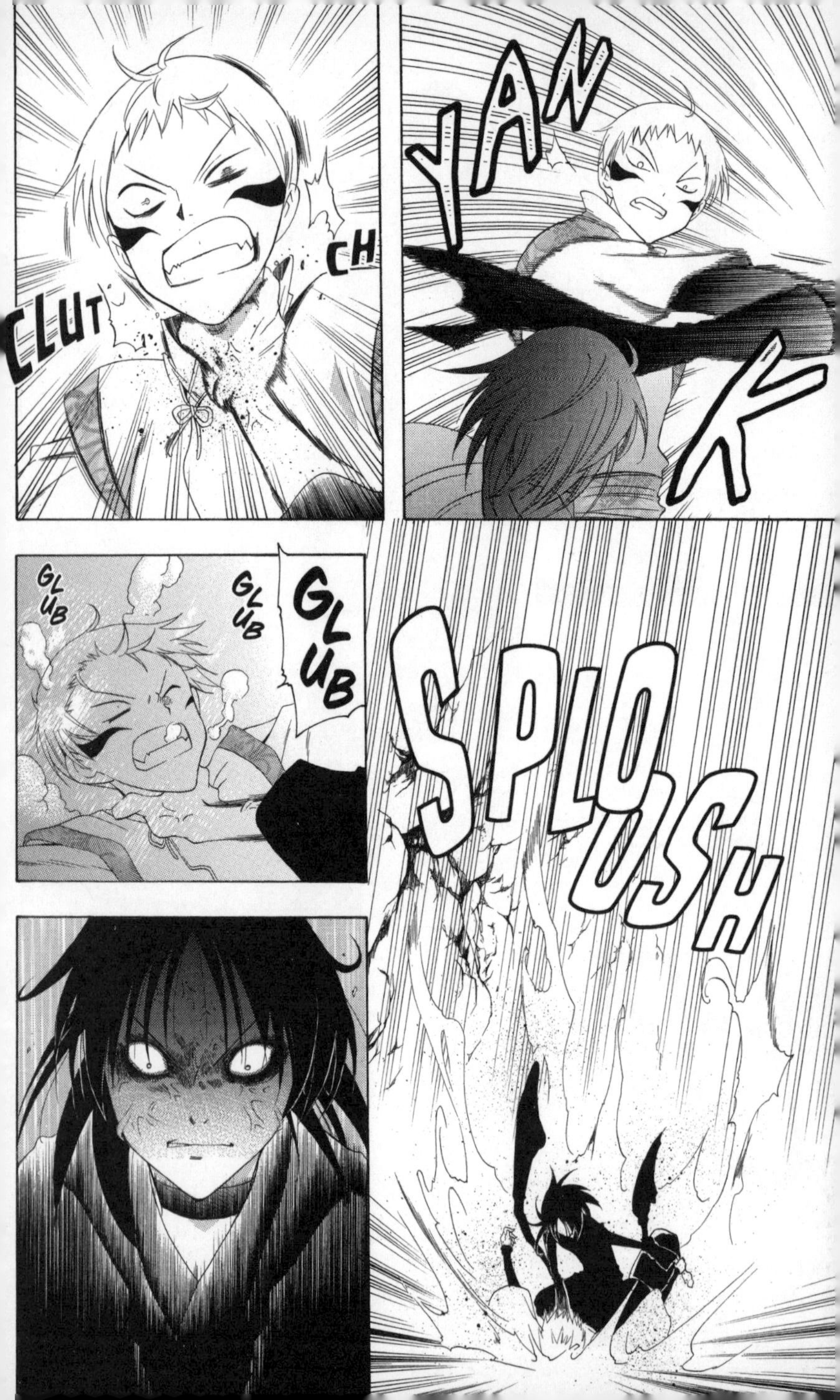
YANK
CLUTCH
SPLOOSH
GLUB
GLUB
GLUB

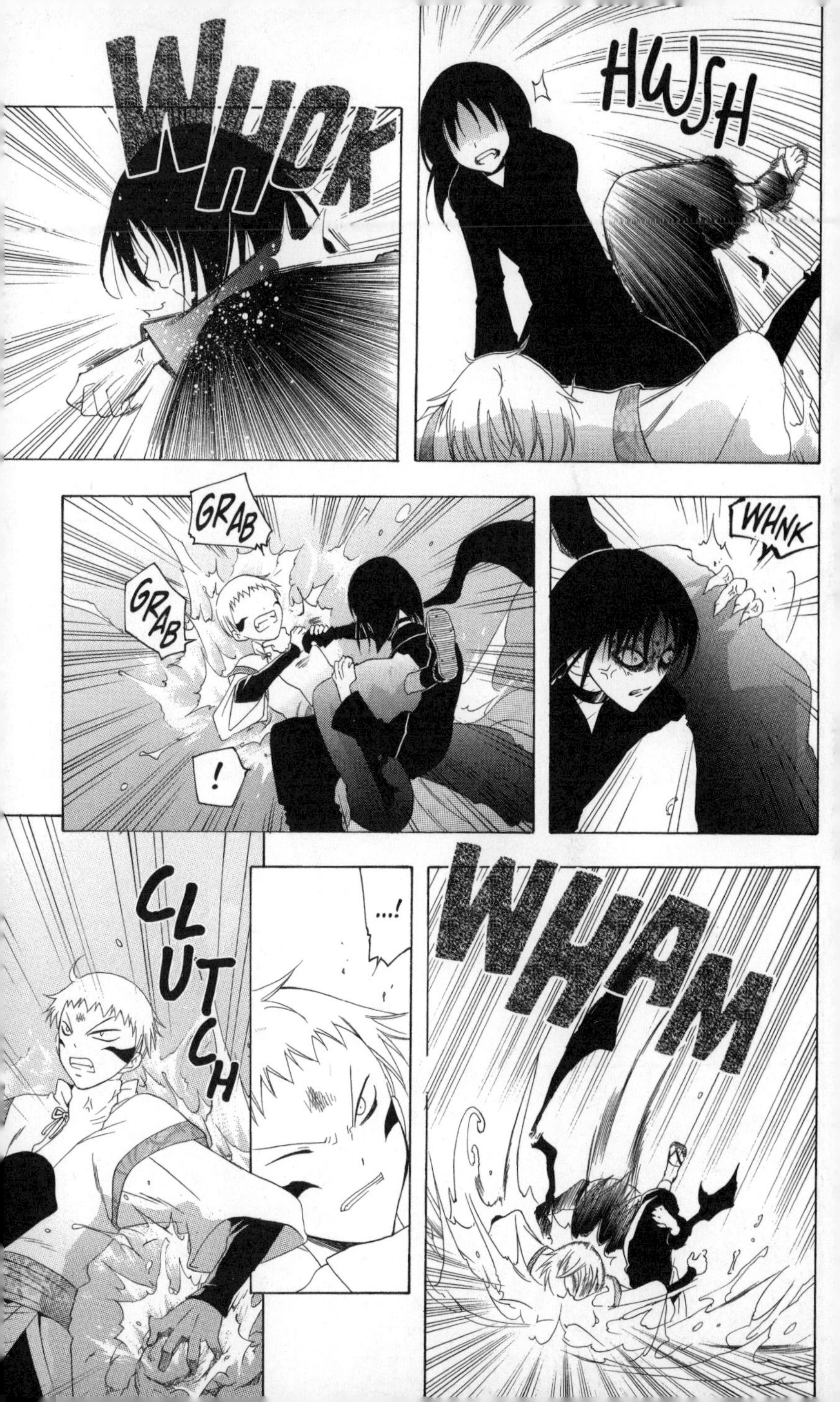
HWSH
WHOK
WHNK
GRAB
GRAB
!
WHAM
...!
CLUTCH

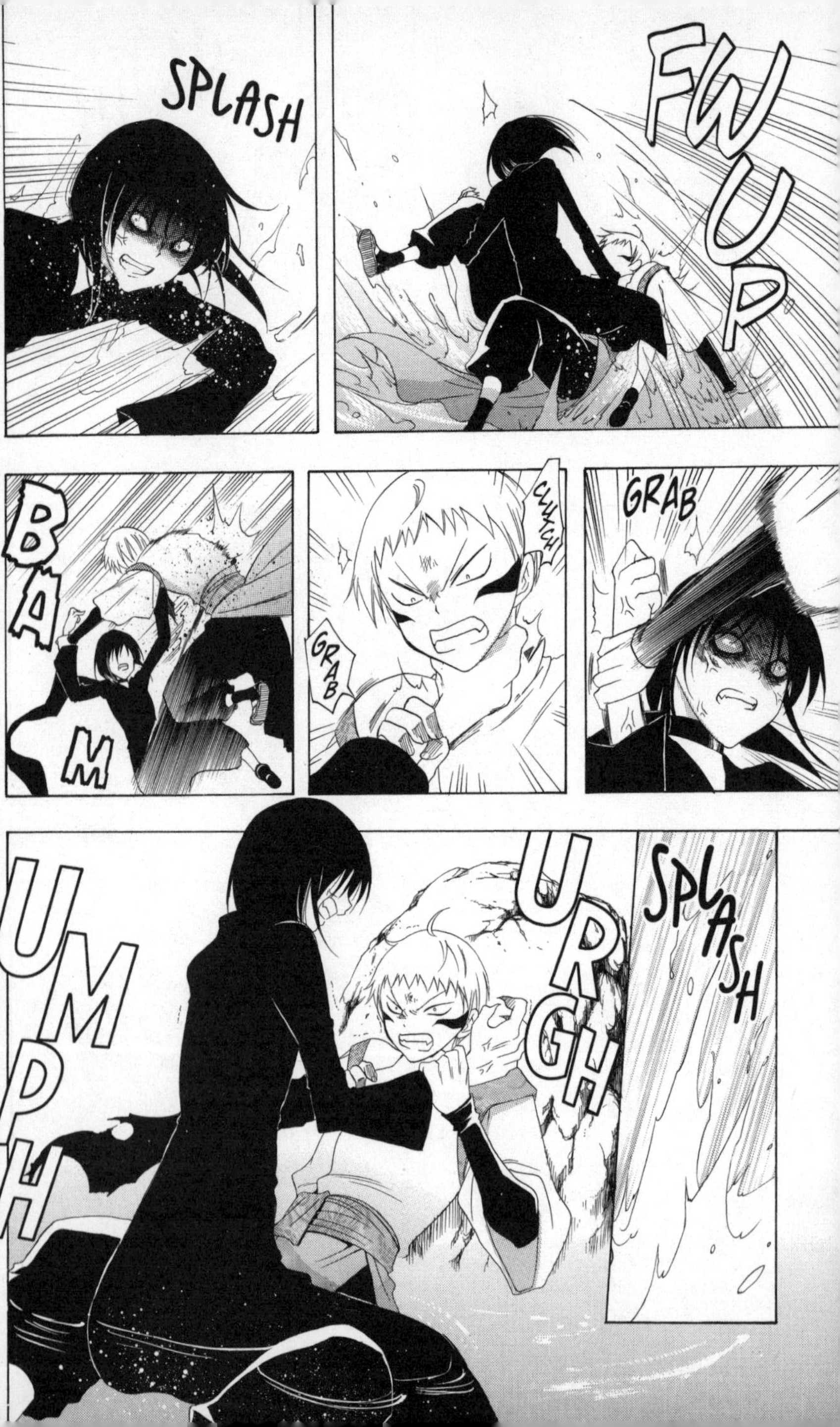
FWUP
SPLASH
GRAB
CLUTCH
GRAB
BAM
SPLASH
URGH
UMPH

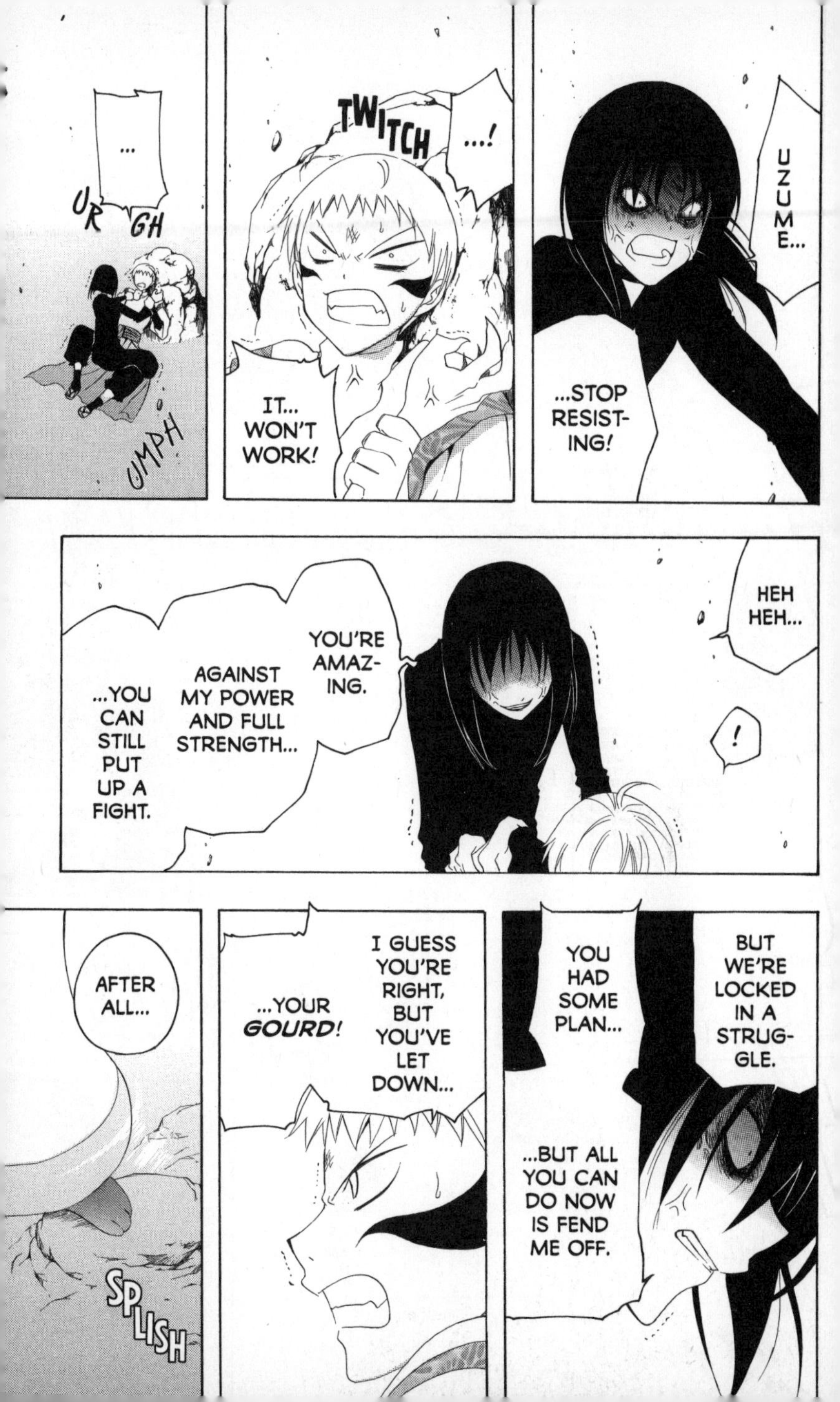
UZUME...
...STOP RESIST-ING!
...!
TWITCH
IT... WON'T WORK!
...
URGH
UMPH
HEH HEH...
!
YOU'RE AMAZ-ING.
AGAINST MY POWER AND FULL STRENGTH...
...YOU CAN STILL PUT UP A FIGHT.
BUT WE'RE LOCKED IN A STRUG-GLE.
YOU HAD SOME PLAN...
...BUT ALL YOU CAN DO NOW IS FEND ME OFF.
I GUESS YOU'RE RIGHT, BUT YOU'VE LET DOWN...
...YOUR *GOURD*!
AFTER ALL...
SPLISH

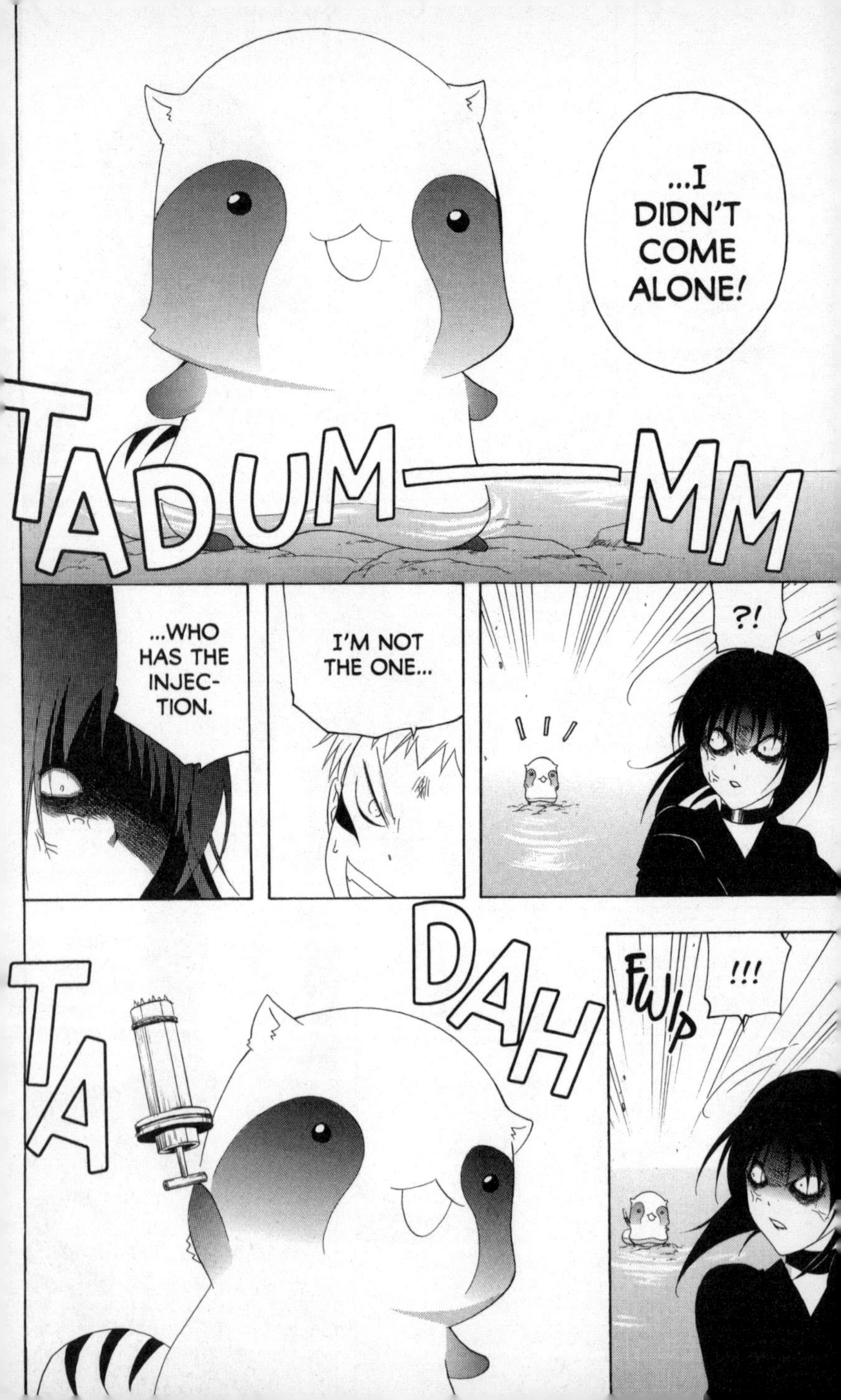
...I DIDN'T COME ALONE!
TADUM—MM
?!
I'M NOT THE ONE...
...WHO HAS THE INJEC-TION.
!!!
FWIP
TA DAH

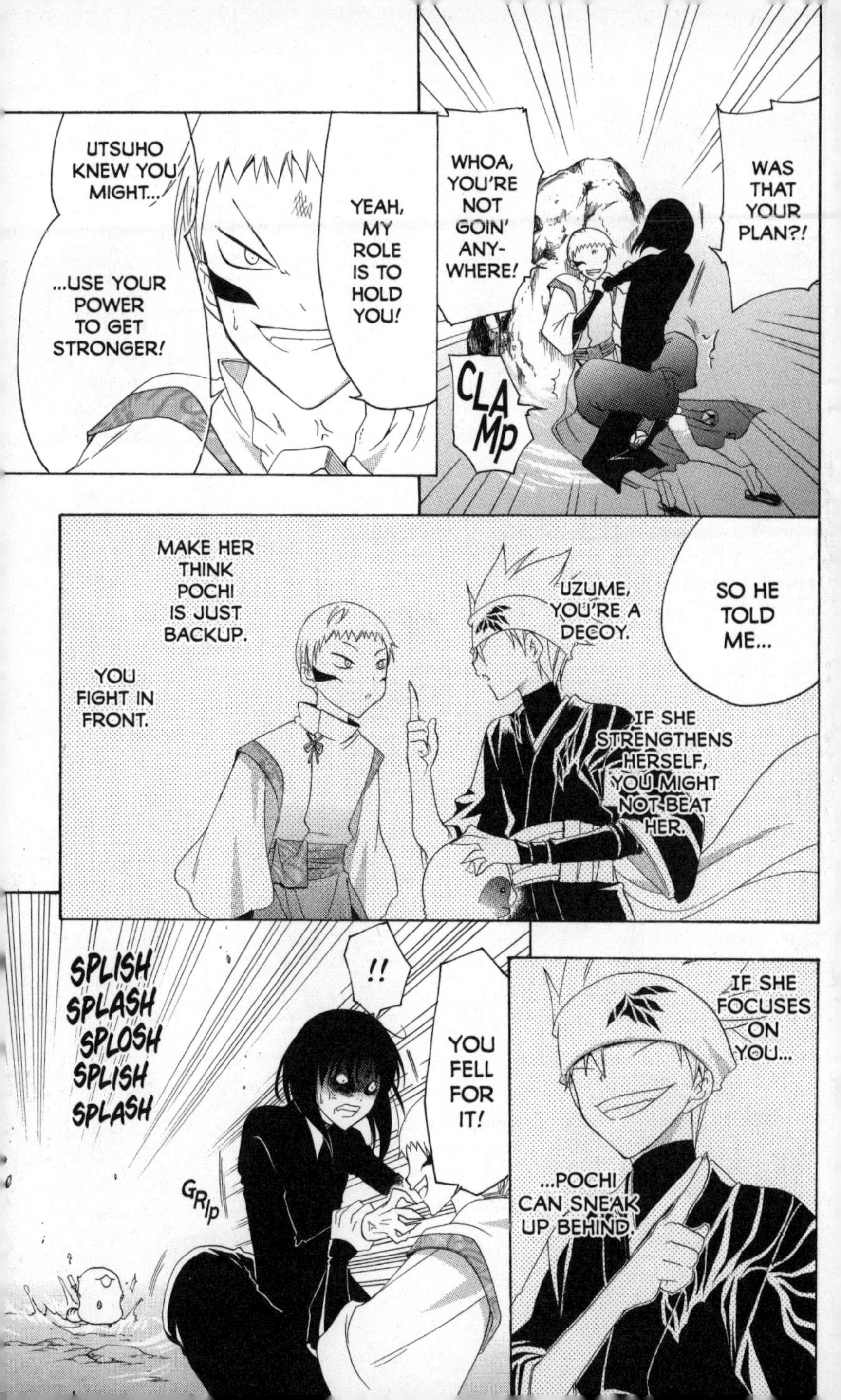
WAS THAT YOUR PLAN?!
WHOA, YOU'RE NOT GOIN' ANY-WHERE!
CLAMP
YEAH, MY ROLE IS TO HOLD YOU!
UTSUHO KNEW YOU MIGHT...
...USE YOUR POWER TO GET STRONGER!
SO HE TOLD ME...
UZUME, YOU'RE A DECOY.
IF SHE STRENGTHENS HERSELF, YOU MIGHT NOT BEAT HER.
MAKE HER THINK POCHI IS JUST BACKUP.
YOU FIGHT IN FRONT.
IF SHE FOCUSES ON YOU...
...POCHI CAN SNEAK UP BEHIND.
!!
YOU FELL FOR IT!
SPLISH SPLASH SPLOSH SPLISH SPLASH
GRIP

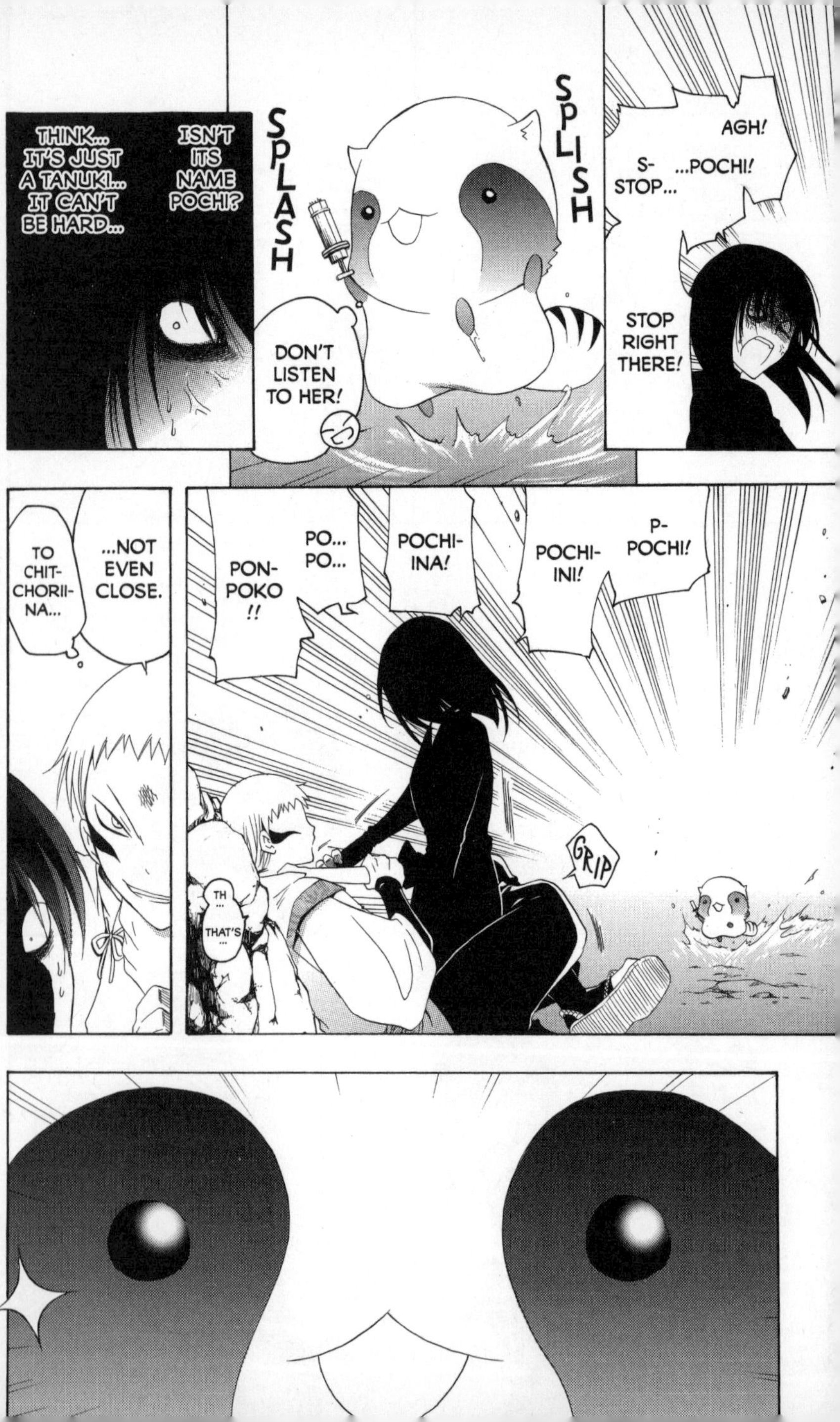
AGH!
S- STOP... ...POCHI!
STOP RIGHT THERE!
SPLISH
SPLASH
DON'T LISTEN TO HER!
ISN'T ITS NAME POCHI?
THINK... IT'S JUST A TANUKI... IT CAN'T BE HARD...
P-POCHI!
POCHI-INI!
POCHI-INA!
PO... PO...
PON-POKO!!
GRIP
TH... THAT'S...
...NOT EVEN CLOSE.
TO CHIT-CHORIINA...

Chapter 141 Uzume's Last Name

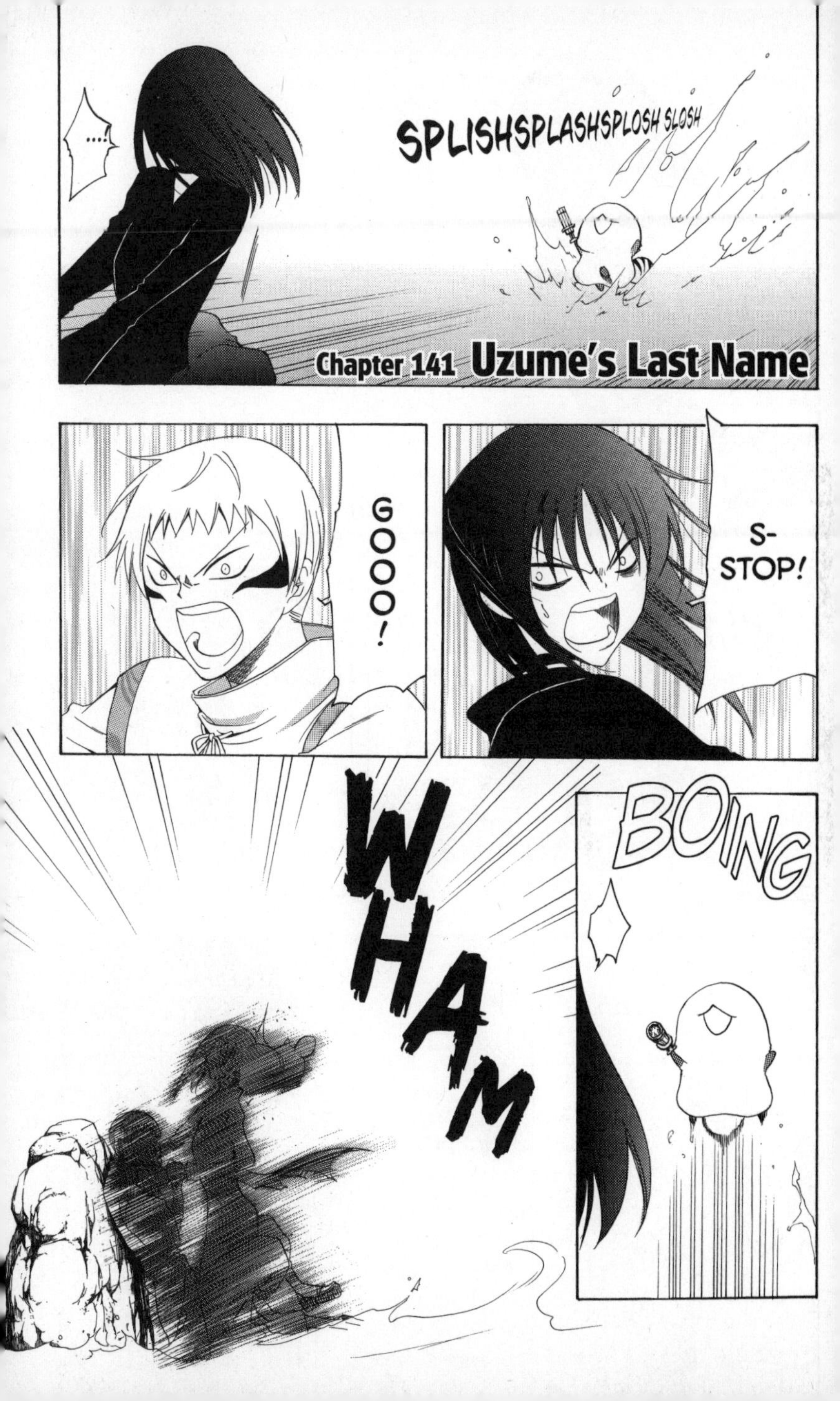
SPLISHSPLASHSPLOSH SLOSH
....!
S-STOP!
GOOO!
BOING
WHAM

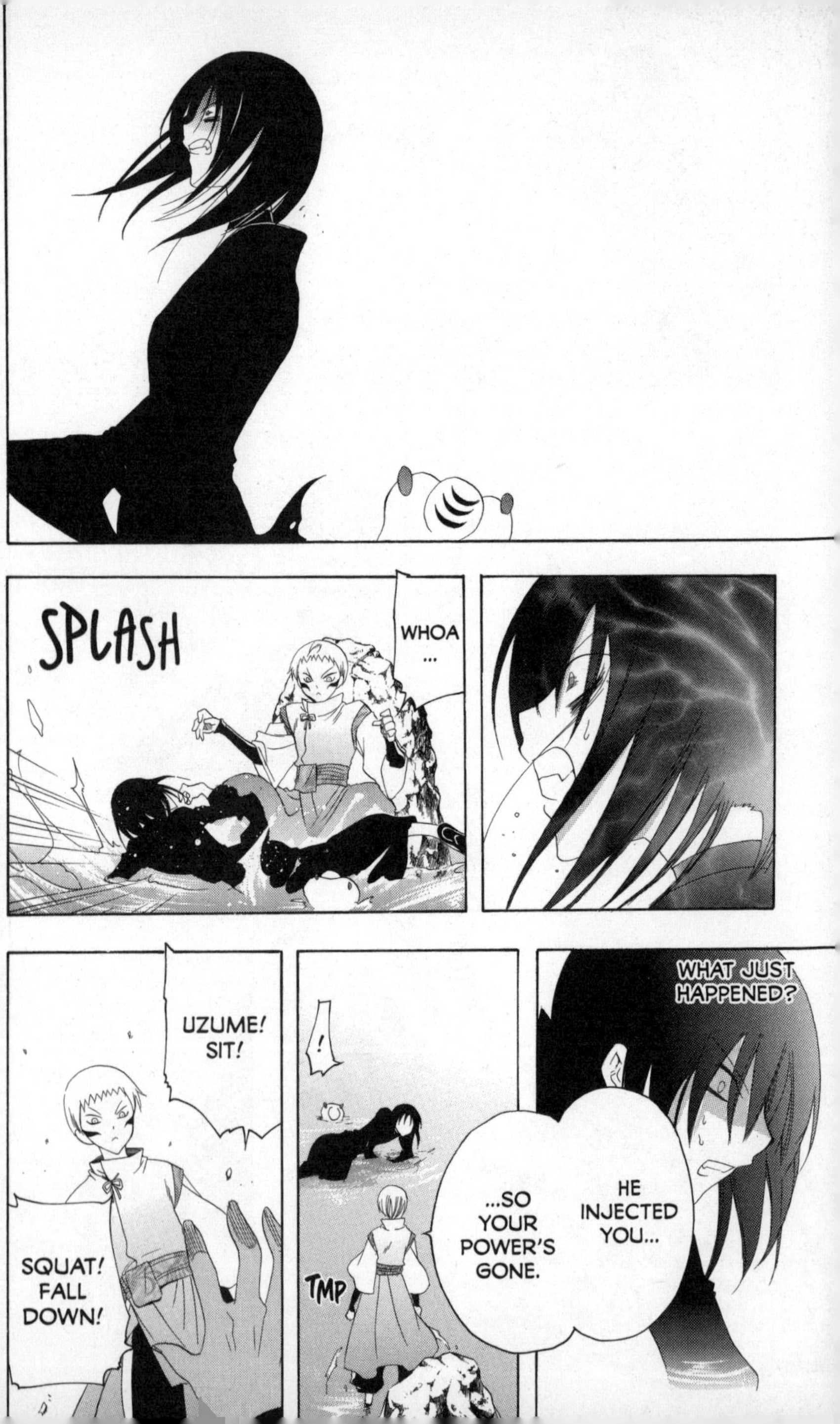
WHOA ...
SPLASH
WHAT JUST HAPPENED?
HE INJECTED YOU...
...SO YOUR POWER'S GONE.
!
TMP
UZUME! SIT!
SQUAT! FALL DOWN!

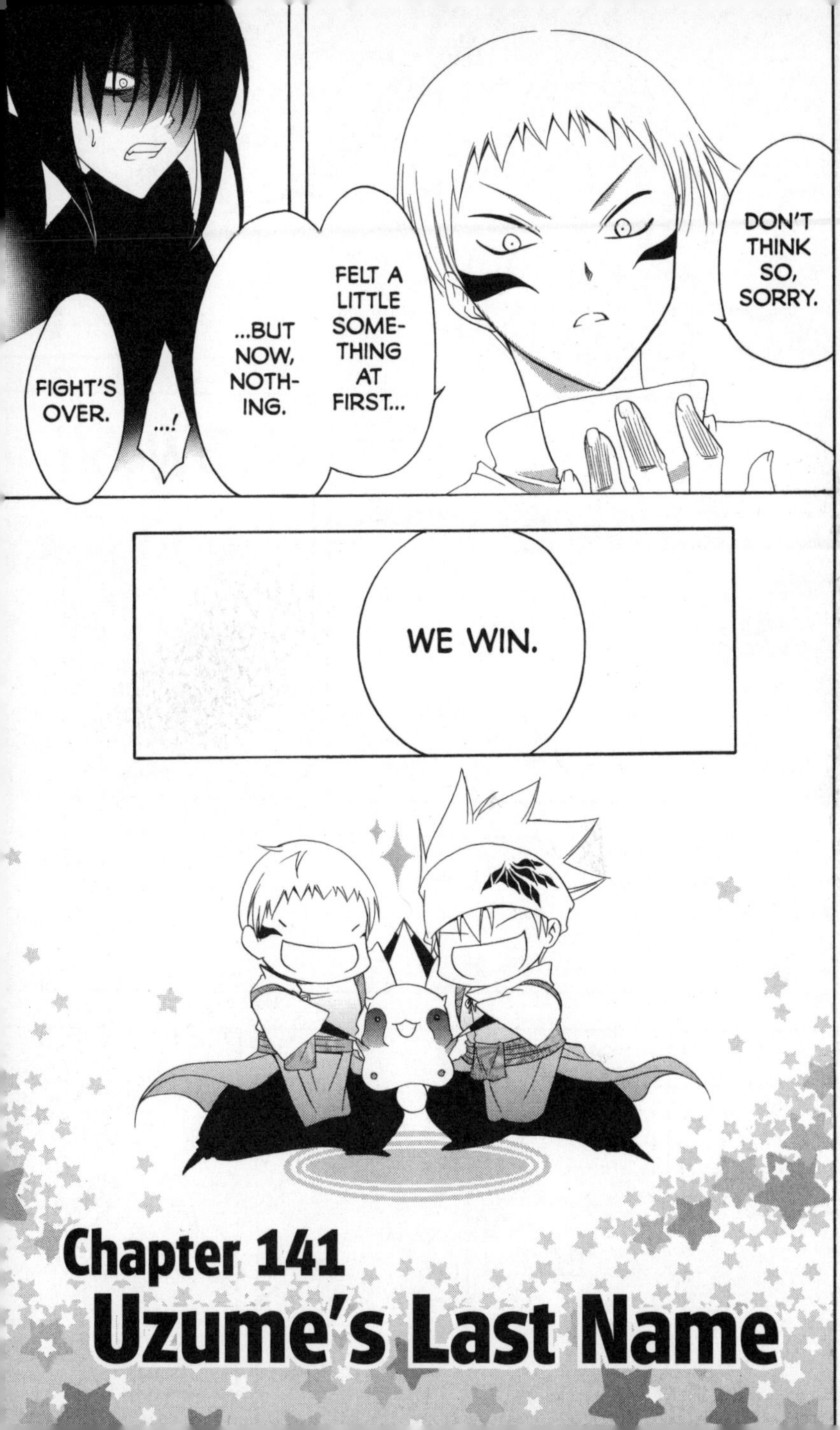
DON'T THINK SO, SORRY.
FELT A LITTLE SOME-THING AT FIRST...
...BUT NOW, NOTH-ING.
...!
FIGHT'S OVER.
WE WIN.

Chapter 141
Uzume's Last Name

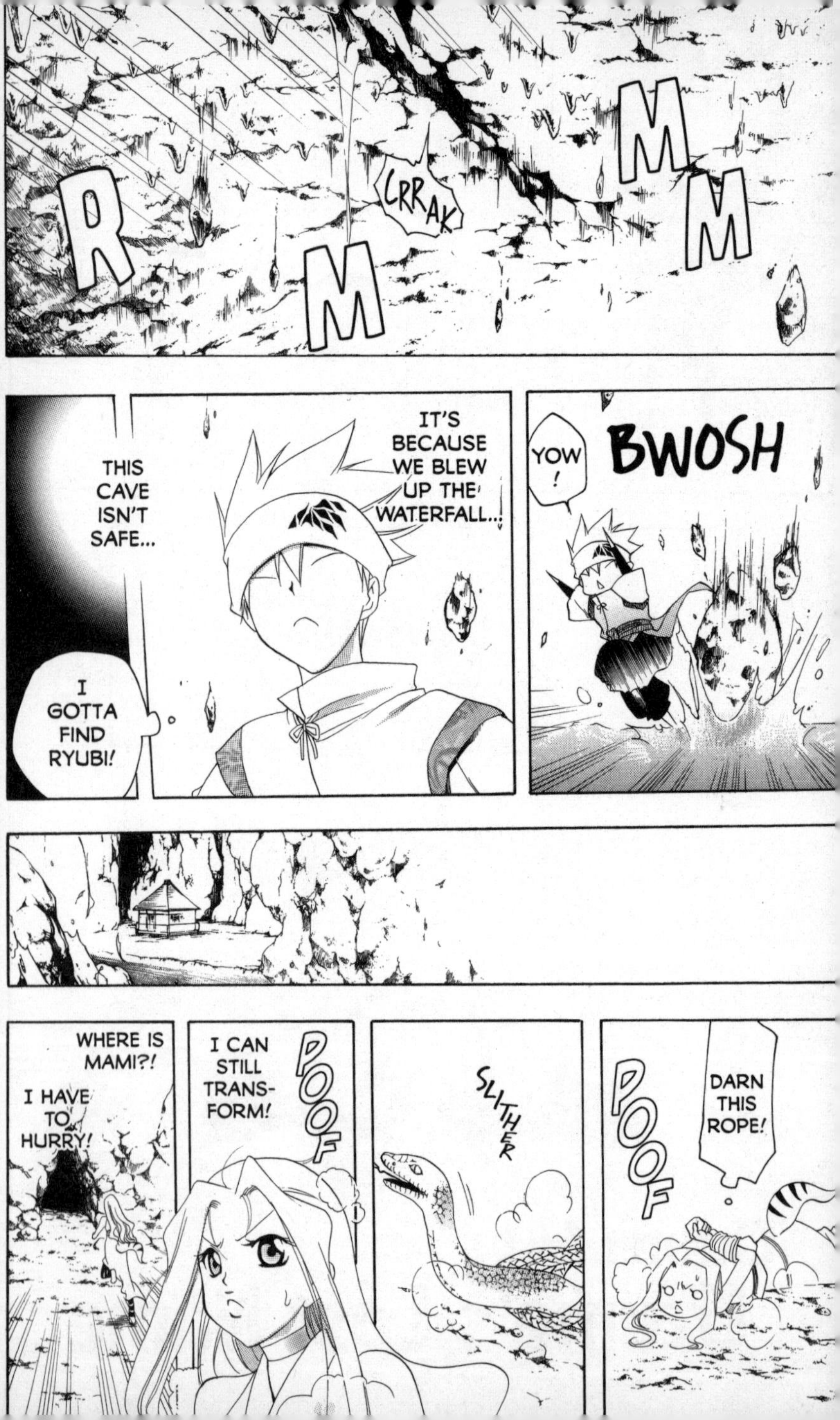
RMMM
CRRAK
BWOSH
YOW!
IT'S BECAUSE WE BLEW UP THE WATERFALL...
THIS CAVE ISN'T SAFE...
I GOTTA FIND RYUBI!
DARN THIS ROPE!
POOF
SLITHER
POOF
I CAN STILL TRANS-FORM!
WHERE IS MAMI?!
I HAVE TO HURRY!

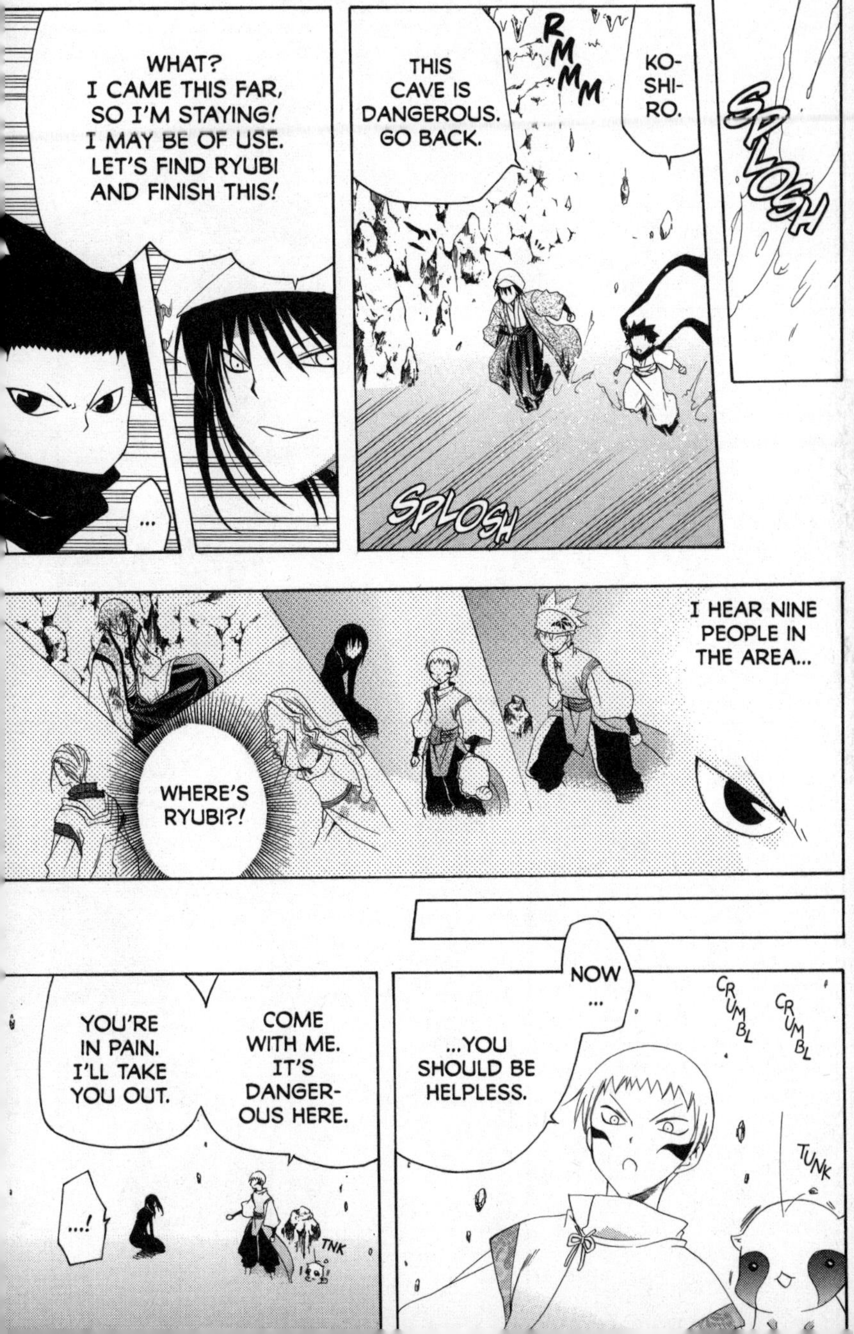
SPLOSH
KO-SHI-RO.
RMMM
THIS CAVE IS DANGEROUS. GO BACK.
SPLOSH
WHAT? I CAME THIS FAR, SO I'M STAYING! I MAY BE OF USE. LET'S FIND RYUBI AND FINISH THIS!
...
I HEAR NINE PEOPLE IN THE AREA...
WHERE'S RYUBI?!
NOW ...
...YOU SHOULD BE HELPLESS.
CRUMBL
CRUMBL
TUNK
COME WITH ME. IT'S DANGER-OUS HERE.
YOU'RE IN PAIN. I'LL TAKE YOU OUT.
...!
TNK

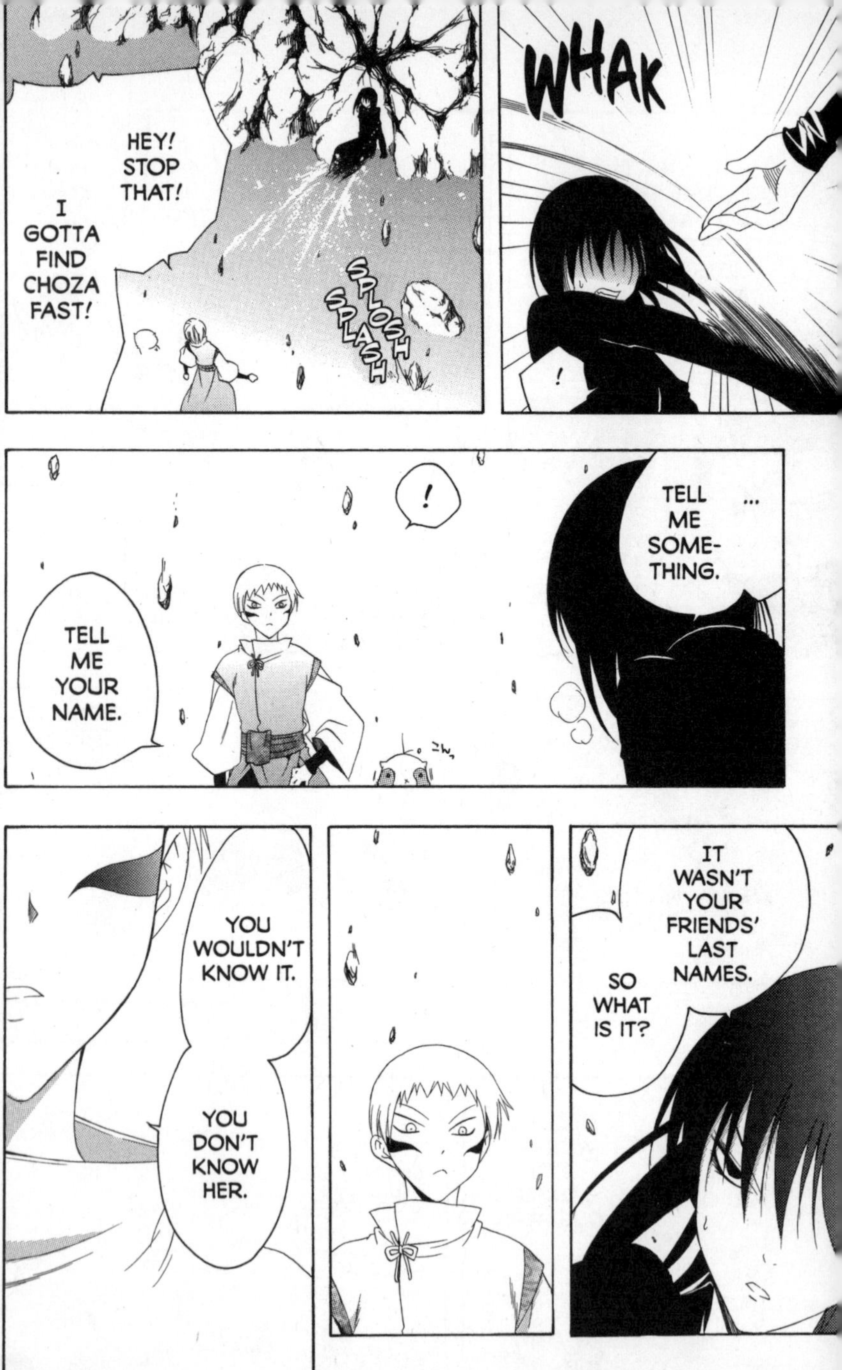
WHAK
!
HEY! STOP THAT!
I GOTTA FIND CHOZA FAST!
SPLOSH
SPLASH
...
TELL ME SOMETHING.
!
TELL ME YOUR NAME.
IT WASN'T YOUR FRIENDS' LAST NAMES.
SO WHAT IS IT?
YOU WOULDN'T KNOW IT.
YOU DON'T KNOW HER.

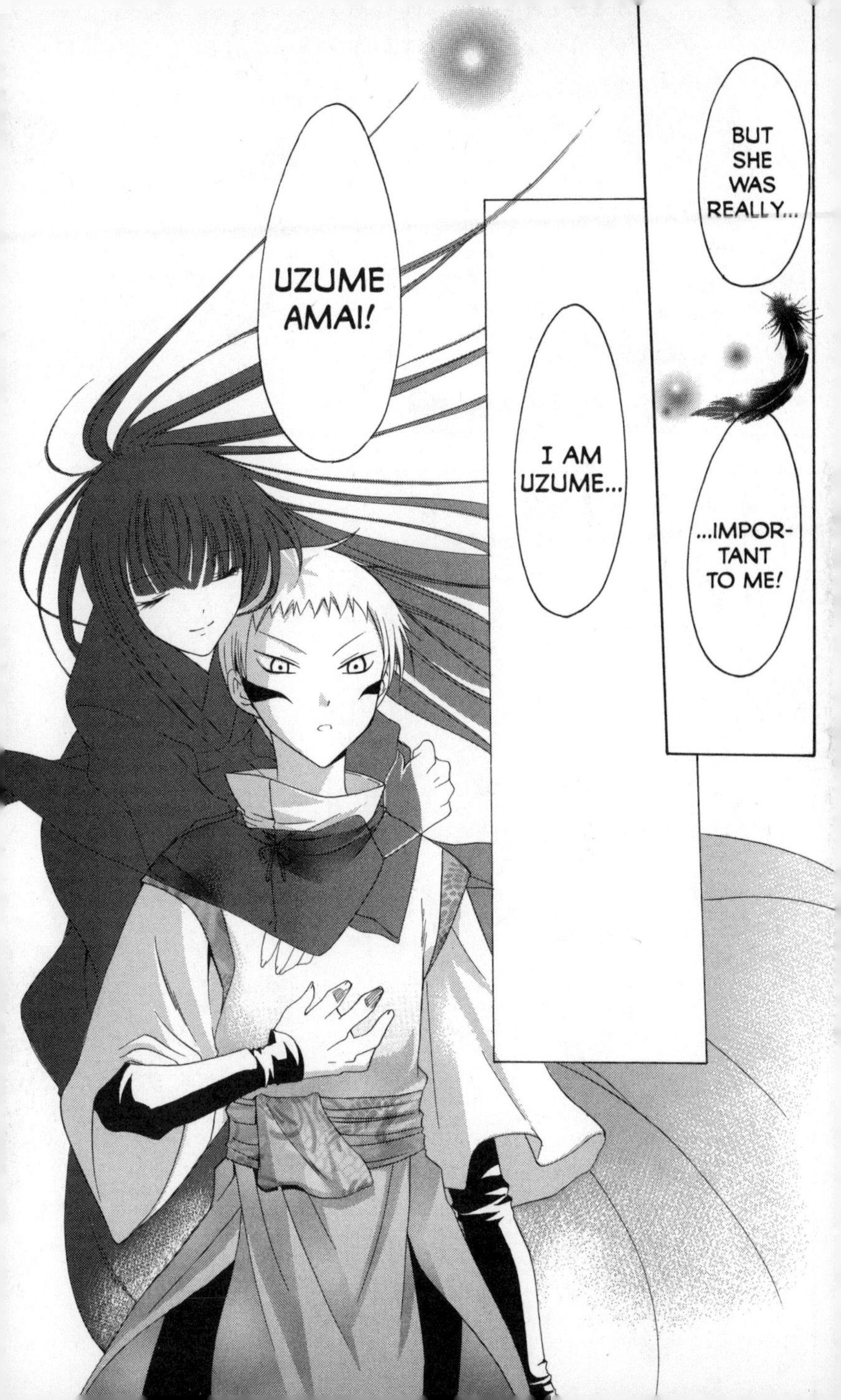
BUT SHE WAS REALLY...
...IMPOR-TANT TO ME!
I AM UZUME...
UZUME AMAI!

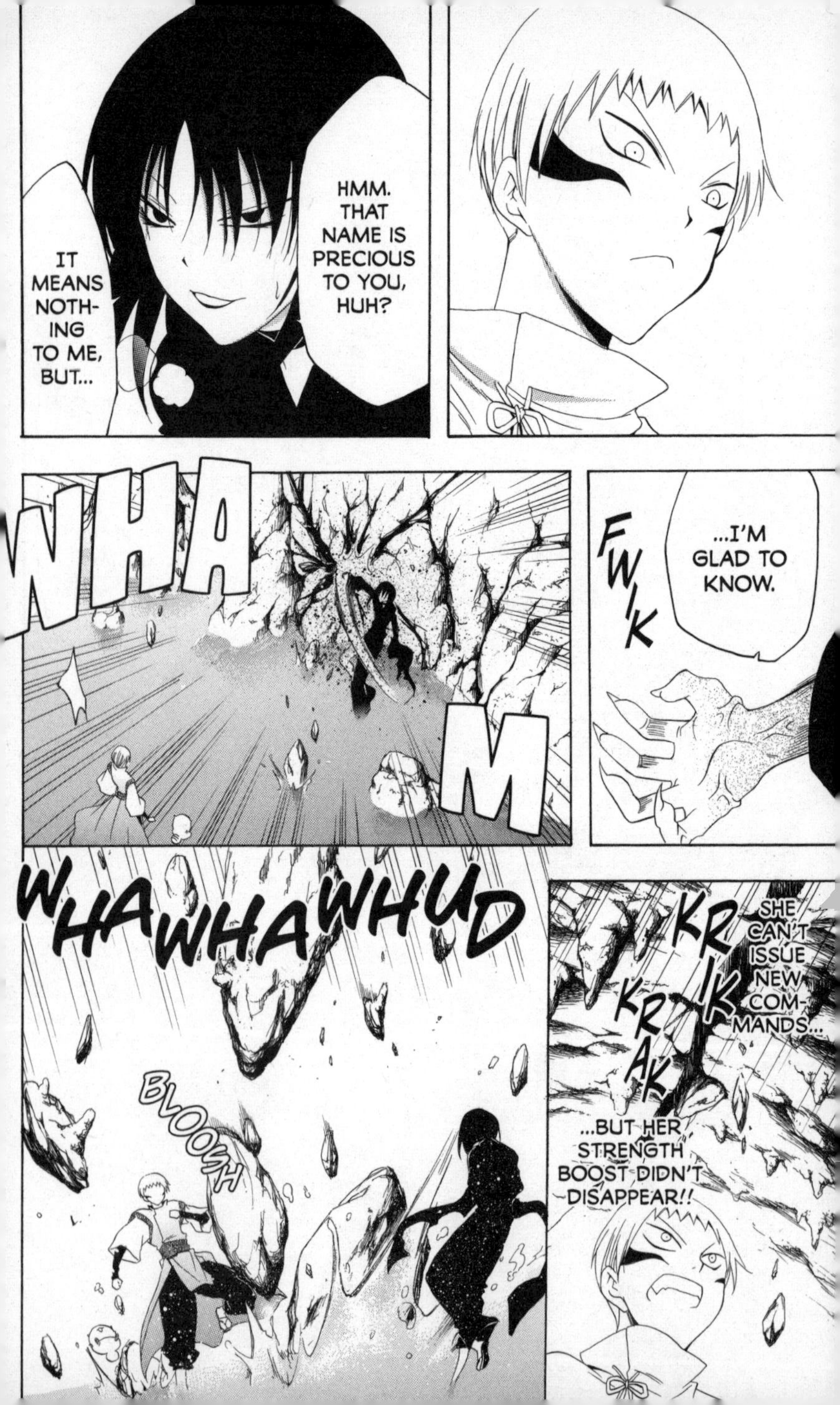
HMM. THAT NAME IS PRECIOUS TO YOU, HUH?
IT MEANS NOTH-ING TO ME, BUT...
FWIK
...I'M GLAD TO KNOW.
WHAM
SHE CAN'T ISSUE NEW COM-MANDS...
KRIK
KRRAK
...BUT HER STRENGTH BOOST DIDN'T DISAPPEAR!!
WHAWHAWHUD
BVOOSH

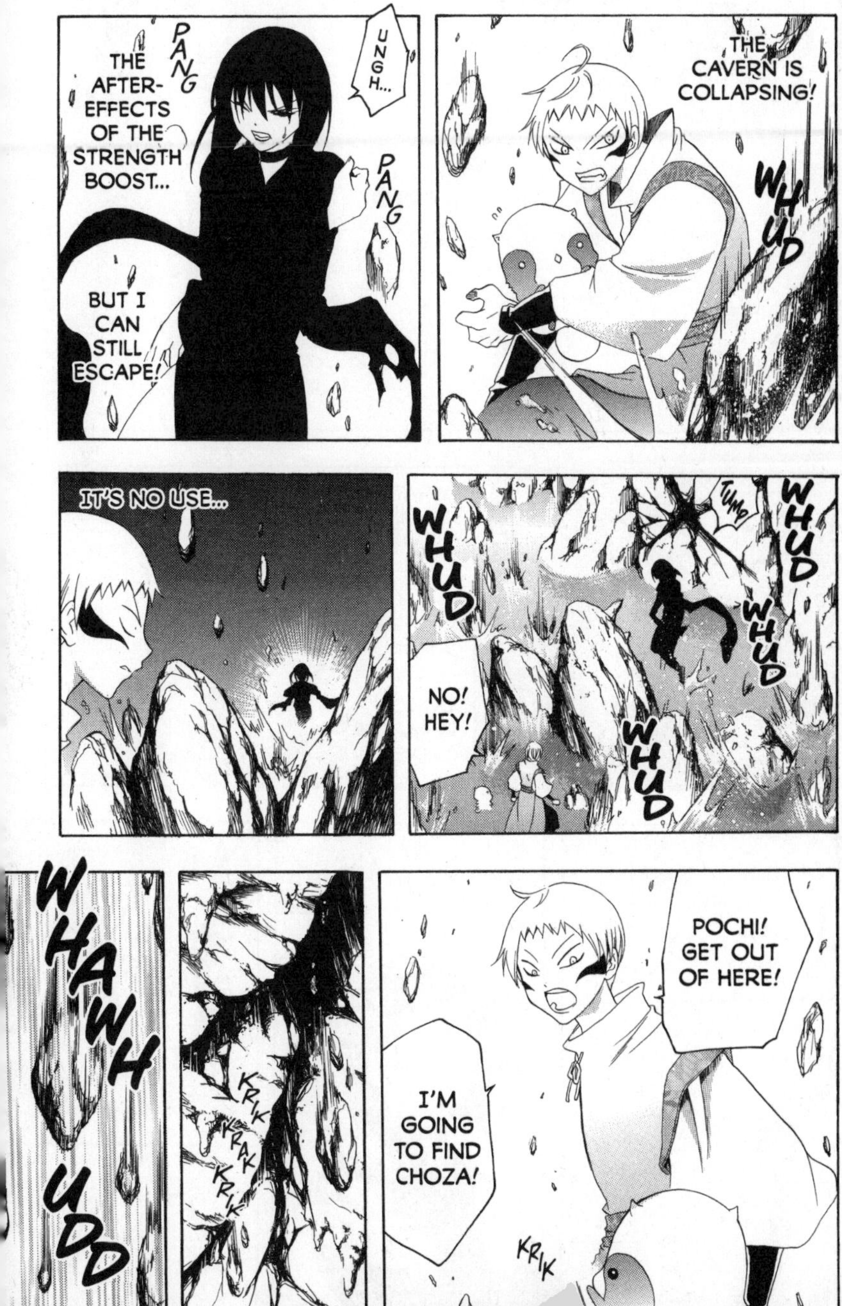
THE CAVERN IS COLLAPSING!
WHUD
UNGH...
PANG
THE AFTER-EFFECTS OF THE STRENGTH BOOST...
PANG
BUT I CAN STILL ESCAPE!
WHUD
TUMP
WHUD
WHUD
WHUD
NO! HEY!
IT'S NO USE...
POCHI! GET OUT OF HERE!
I'M GOING TO FIND CHOZA!
KRIK
KRIK
KRAK
KRIK
WHAWHUDD

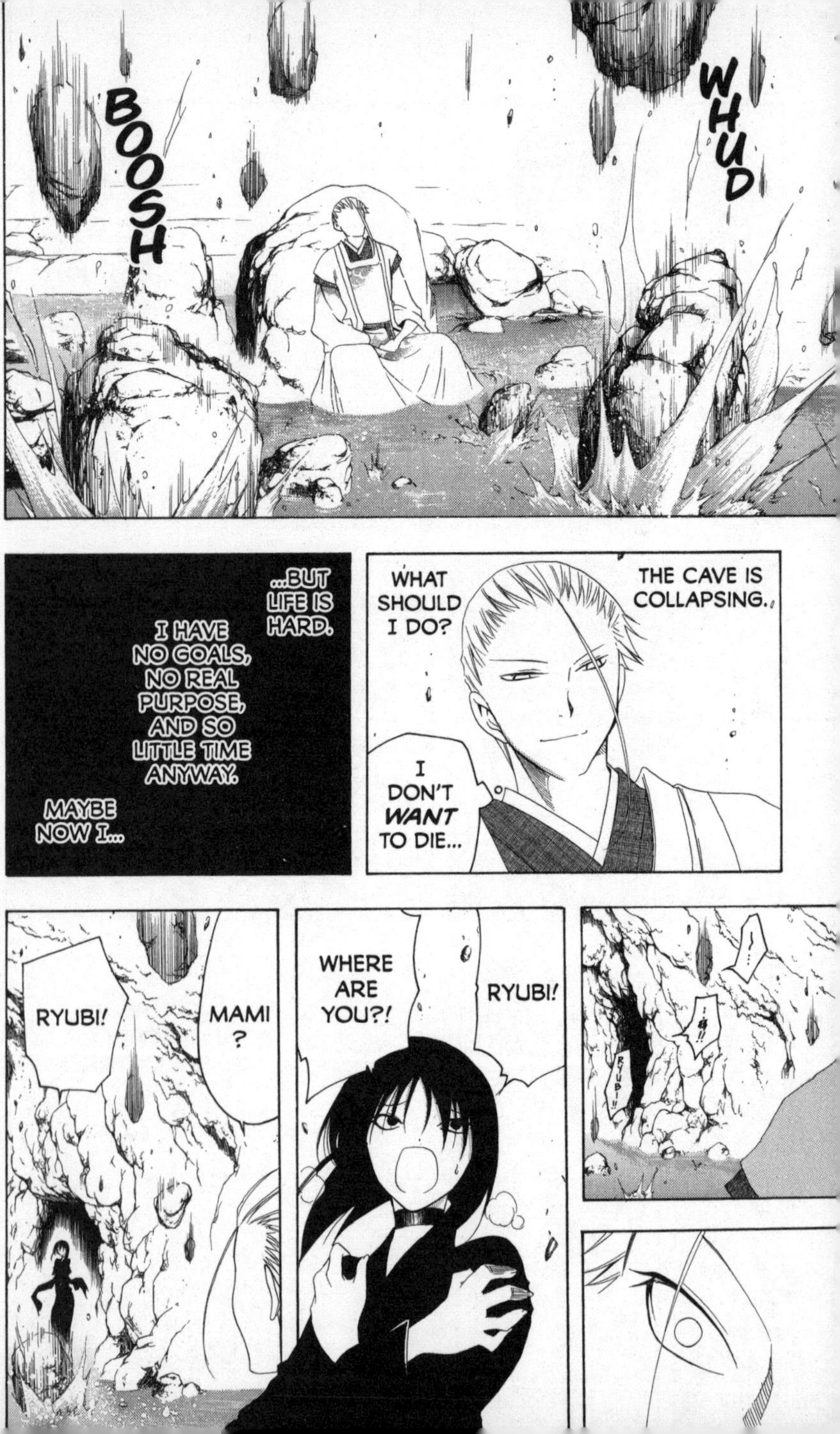
WHUD
BOOSH
THE CAVE IS COLLAPSING.
WHAT SHOULD I DO?
I DON'T *WANT* TO DIE...
...BUT LIFE IS HARD.
I HAVE NO GOALS, NO REAL PURPOSE, AND SO LITTLE TIME ANYWAY.
MAYBE NOW I...
RYUBI!!
RYUBI!
WHERE ARE YOU?!
MAMI?
RYUBI!

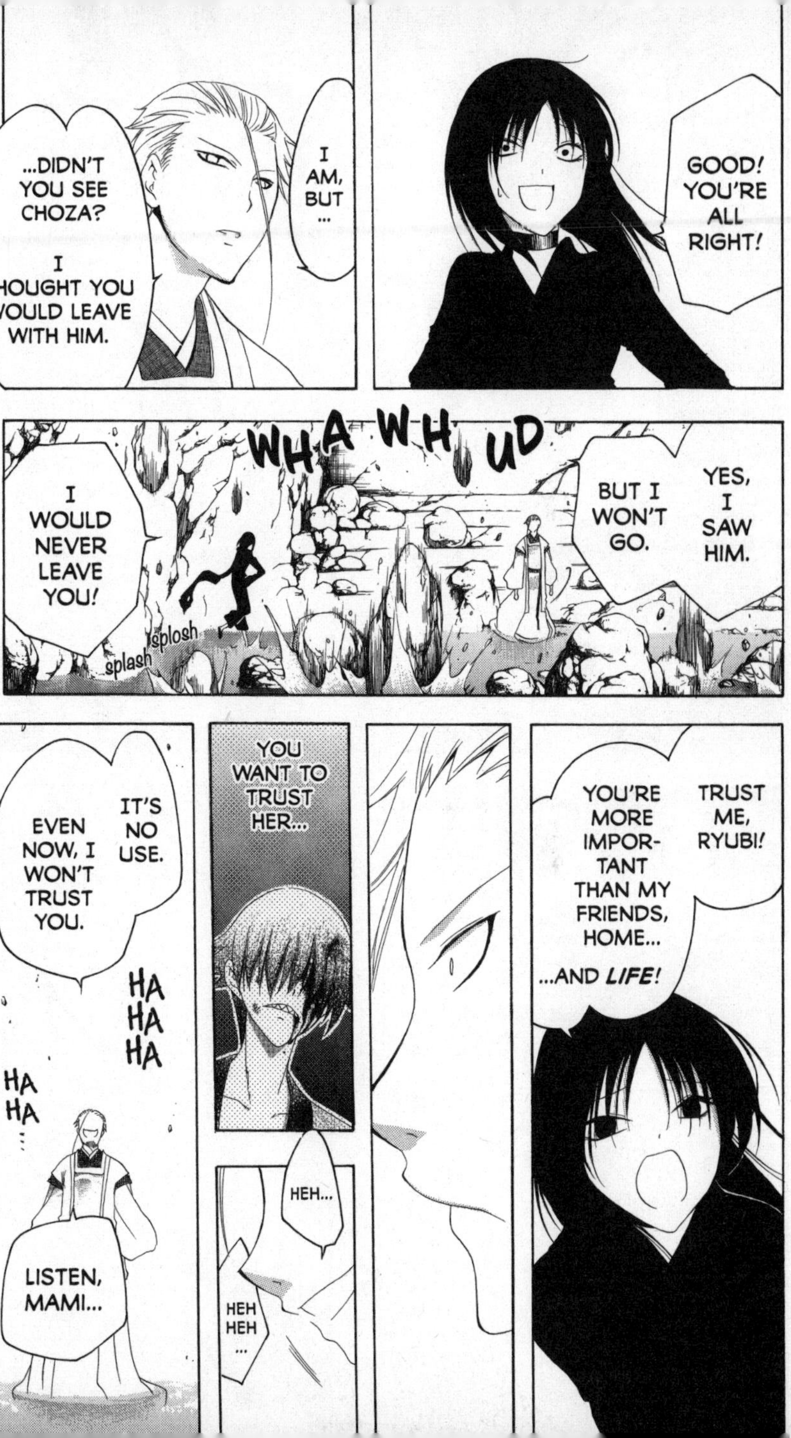
GOOD! YOU'RE ALL RIGHT!
I AM, BUT ...
...DIDN'T YOU SEE CHOZA?
I THOUGHT YOU WOULD LEAVE WITH HIM.
YES, I SAW HIM.
BUT I WON'T GO.
WHA WH UD
I WOULD NEVER LEAVE YOU!
splosh
splash
TRUST ME, RYUBI!
YOU'RE MORE IMPOR-TANT THAN MY FRIENDS, HOME...
...AND *LIFE*!
YOU WANT TO TRUST HER...
HEH...
HEH HEH ...
IT'S NO USE.
EVEN NOW, I WON'T TRUST YOU.
HA HA HA
HA HA ...
LISTEN, MAMI...

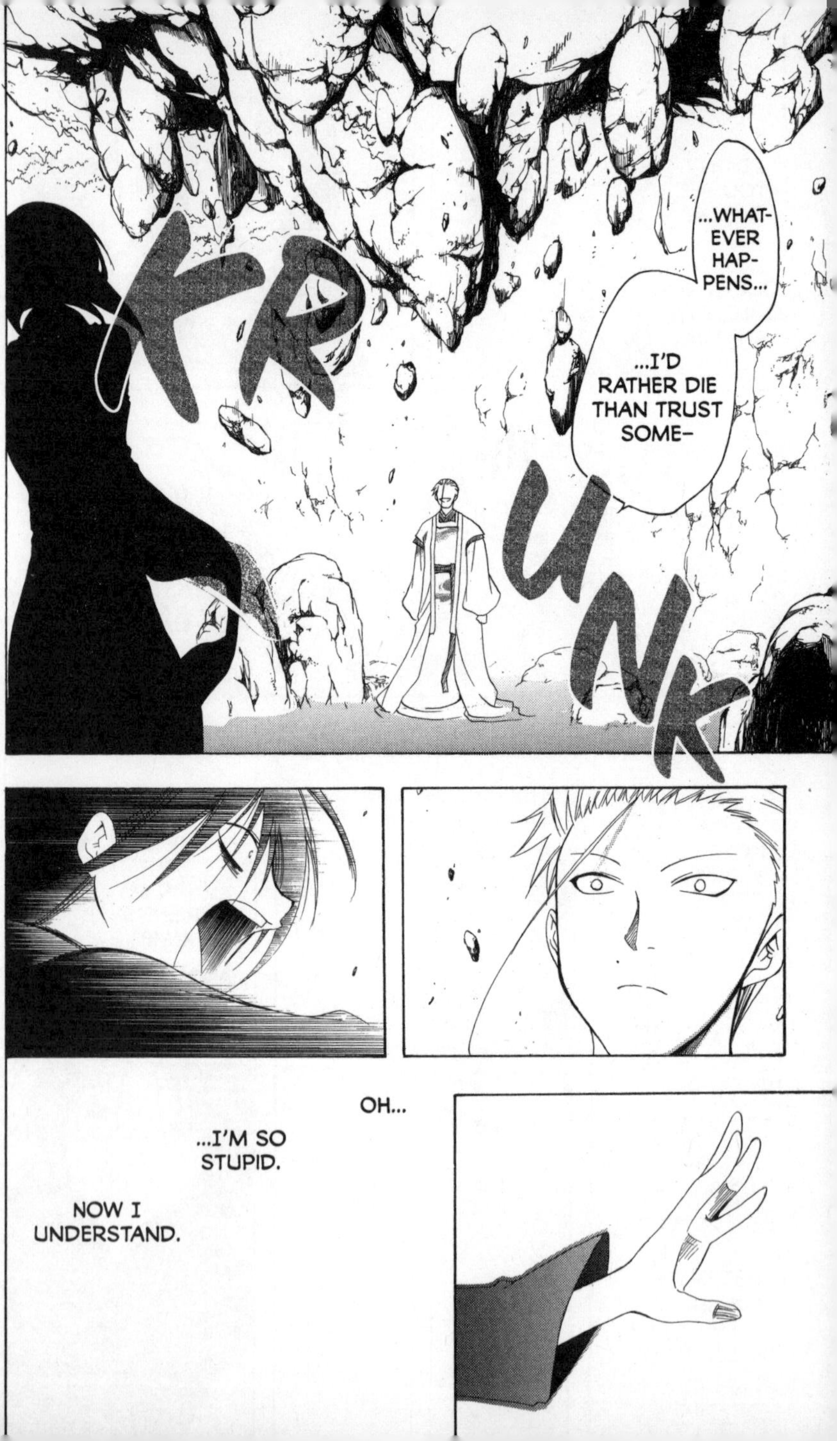
...WHAT-EVER HAP-PENS...
...I'D RATHER DIE THAN TRUST SOME–
KRUNK
OH...
...I'M SO STUPID.
NOW I UNDERSTAND.

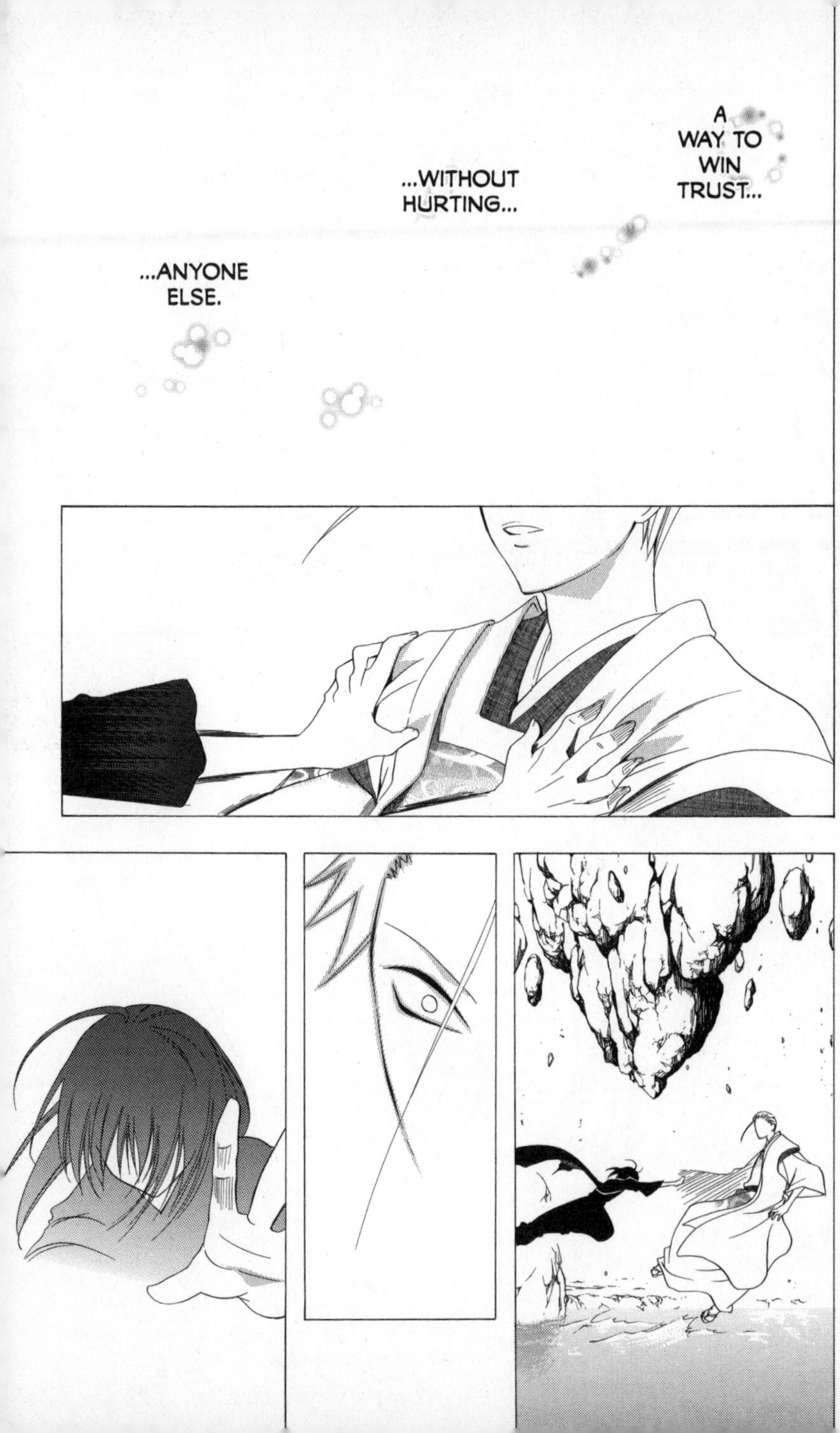
A WAY TO WIN TRUST...
...WITHOUT HURTING...
...ANYONE ELSE.

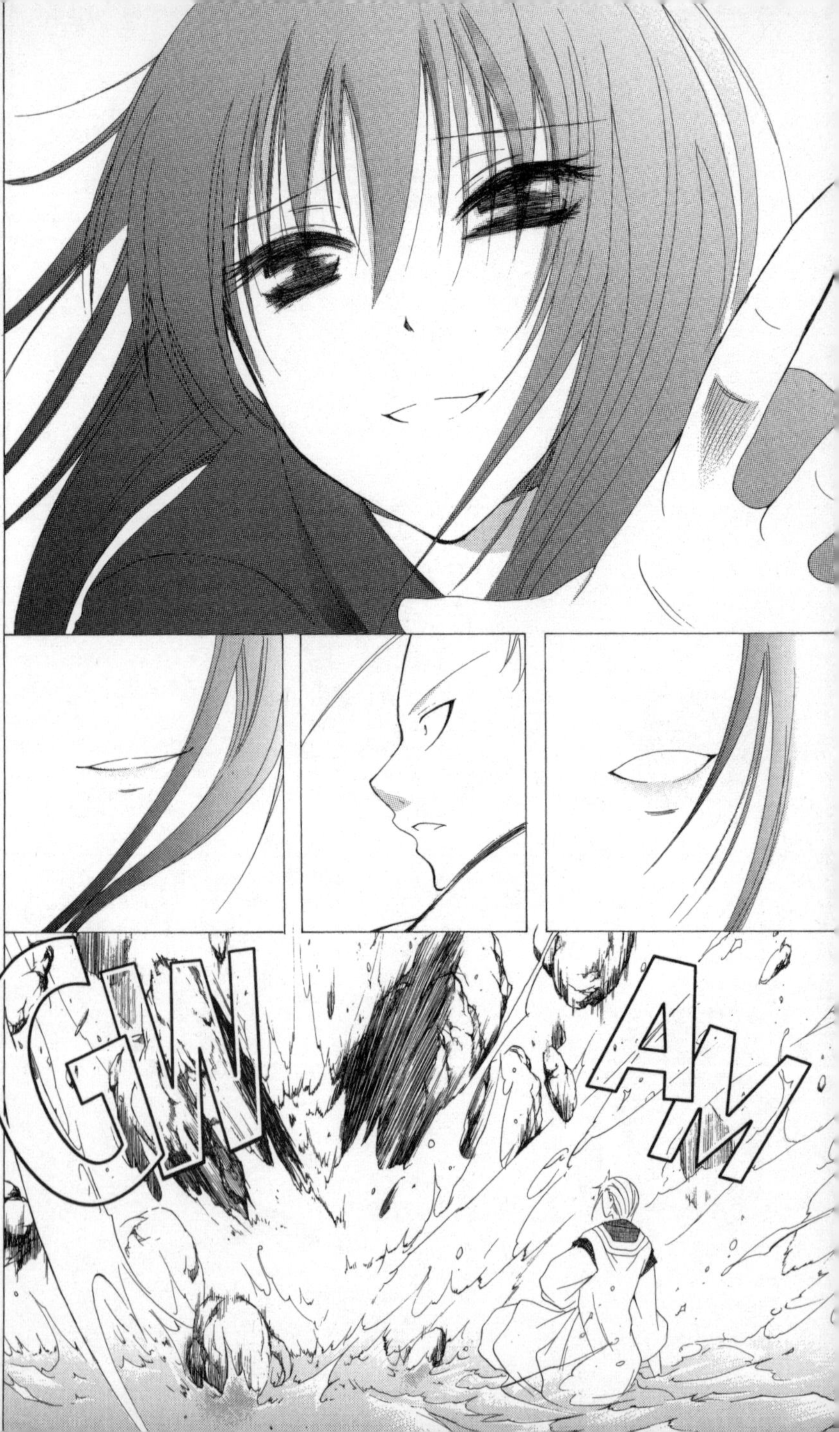
GWAM

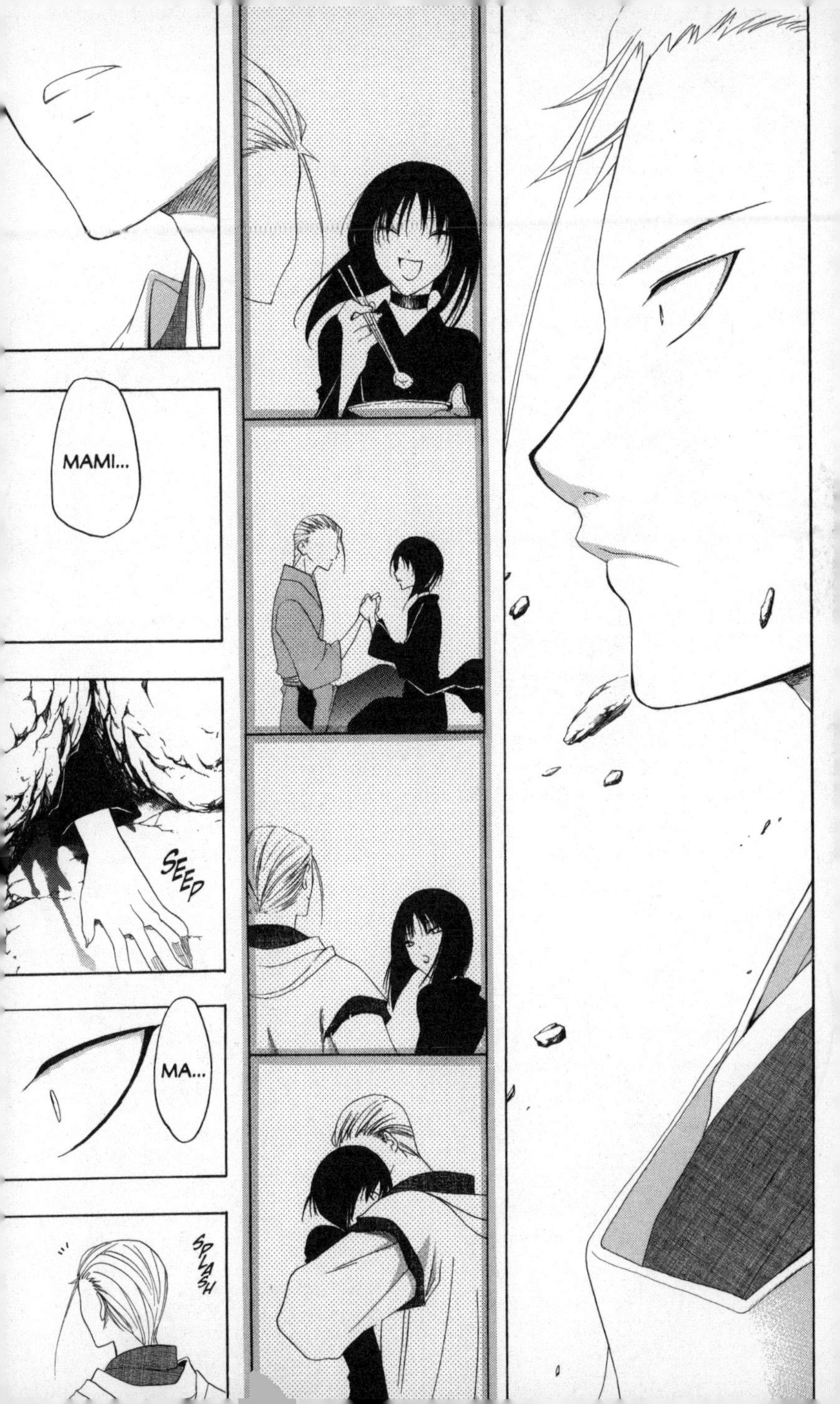
MAMI...
SEEP
MA...
SPLASH

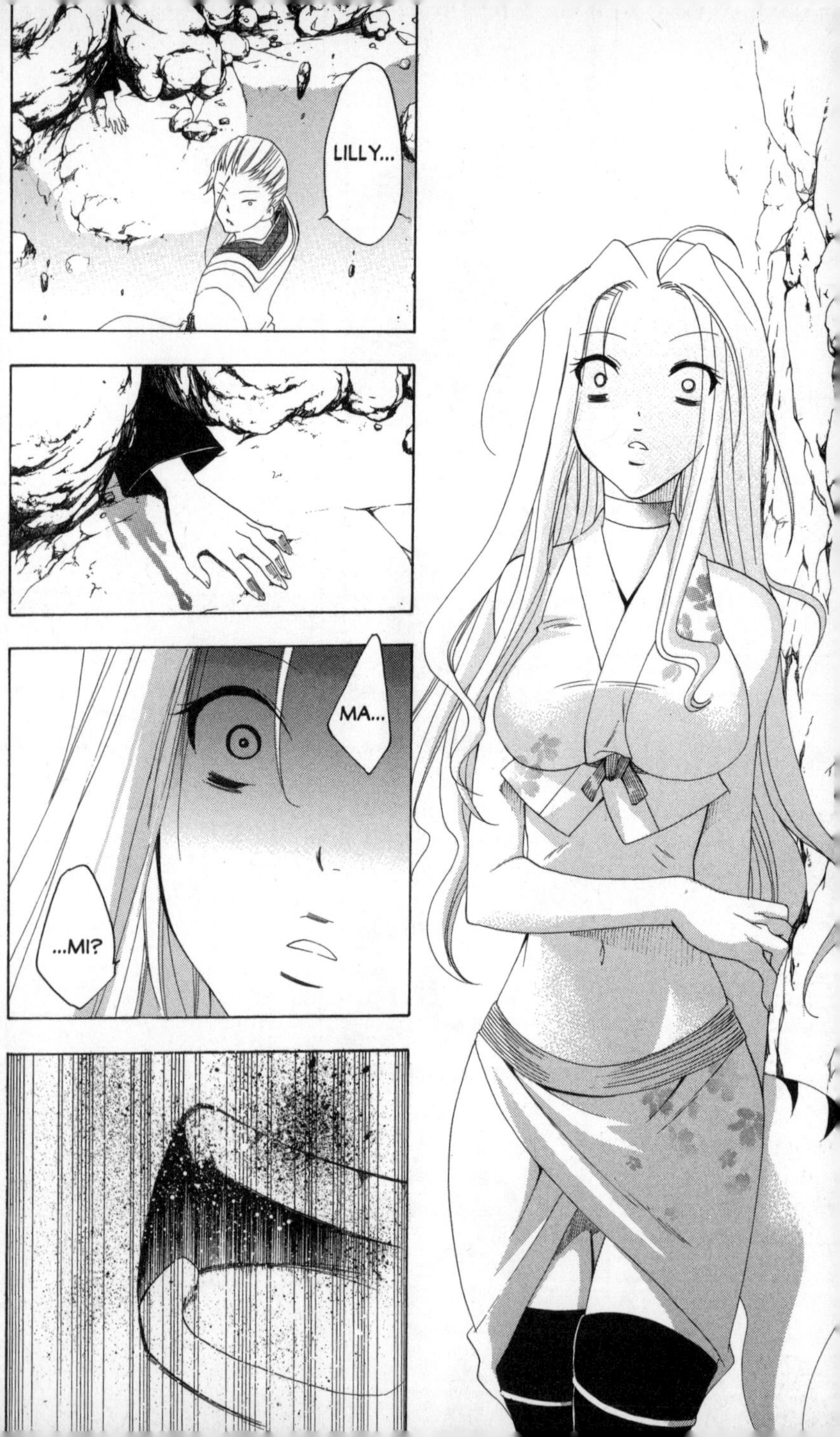
LILLY...
MA...
...MI?

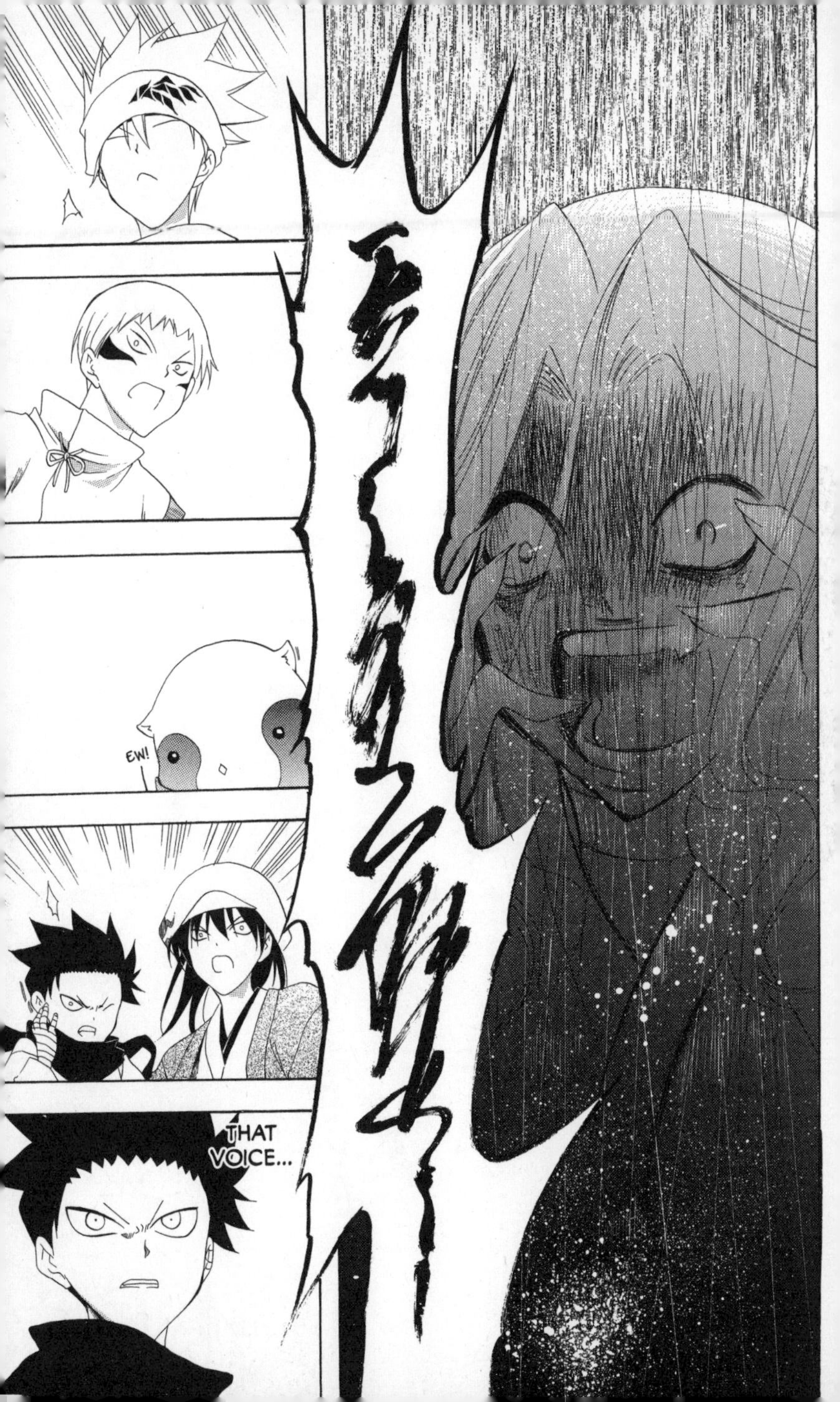
EW!
THAT VOICE...

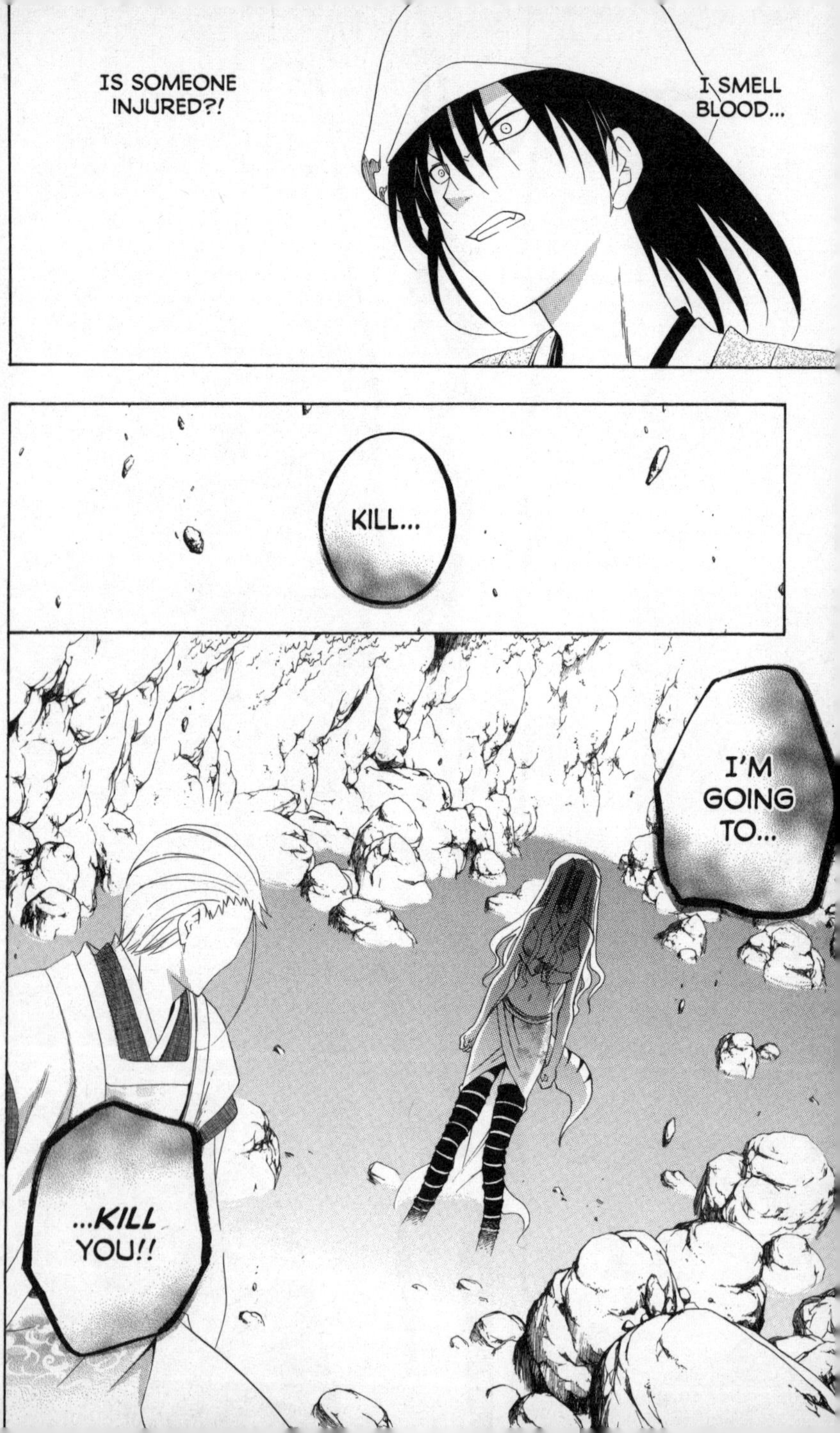
I SMELL BLOOD...
IS SOMEONE INJURED?!
KILL...
I'M GOING TO...
...KILL YOU!!

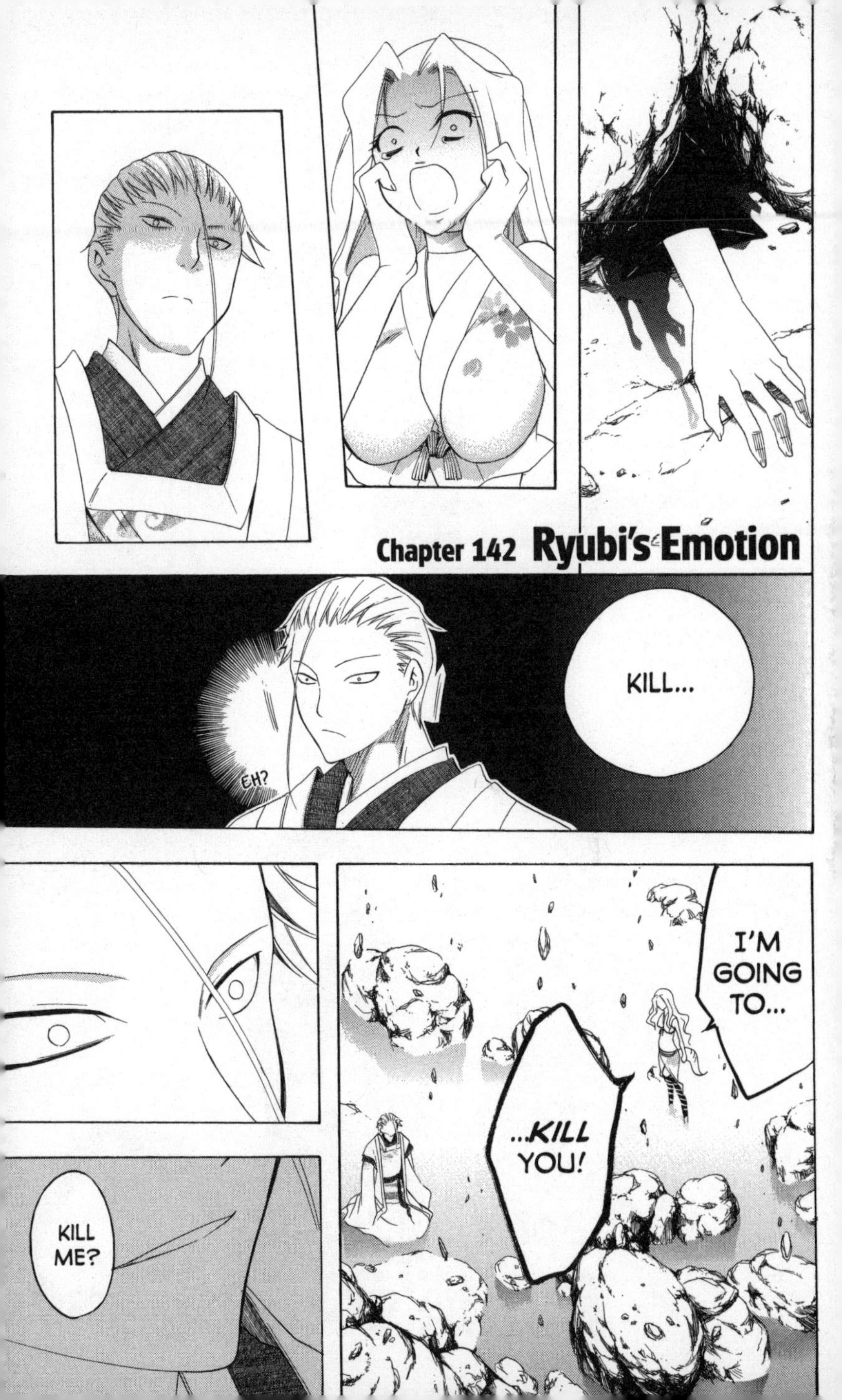
Chapter 142 Ryubi's Emotion
KILL...
EH?
I'M GOING TO...
...KILL YOU!
KILL ME?

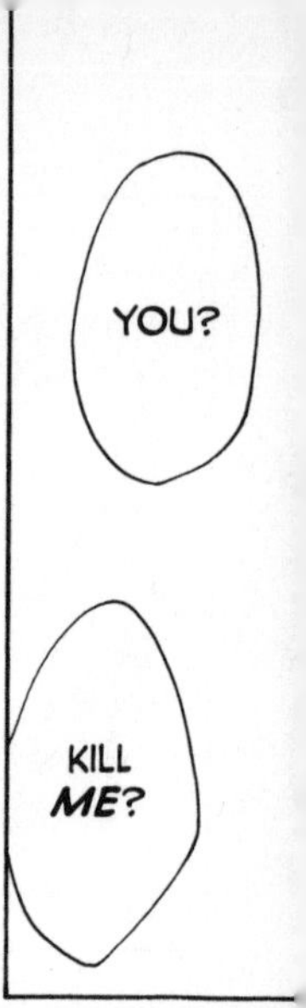
YOU?
KILL *ME*?

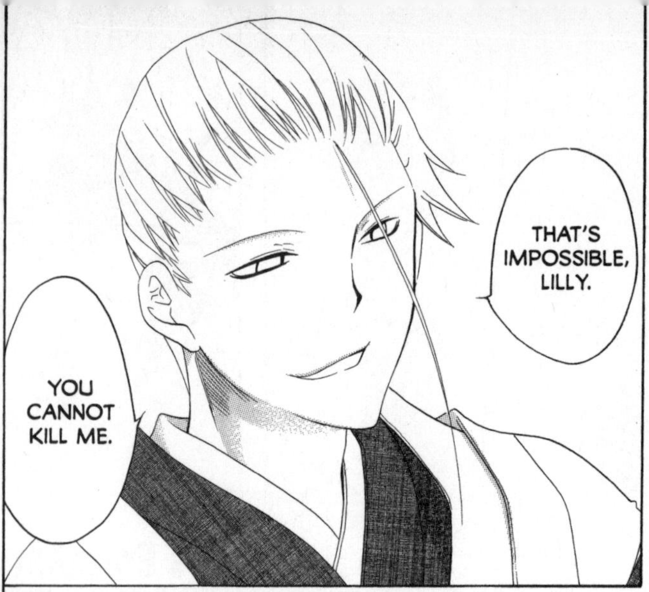
THAT'S IMPOSSIBLE, LILLY.
YOU CANNOT KILL ME.

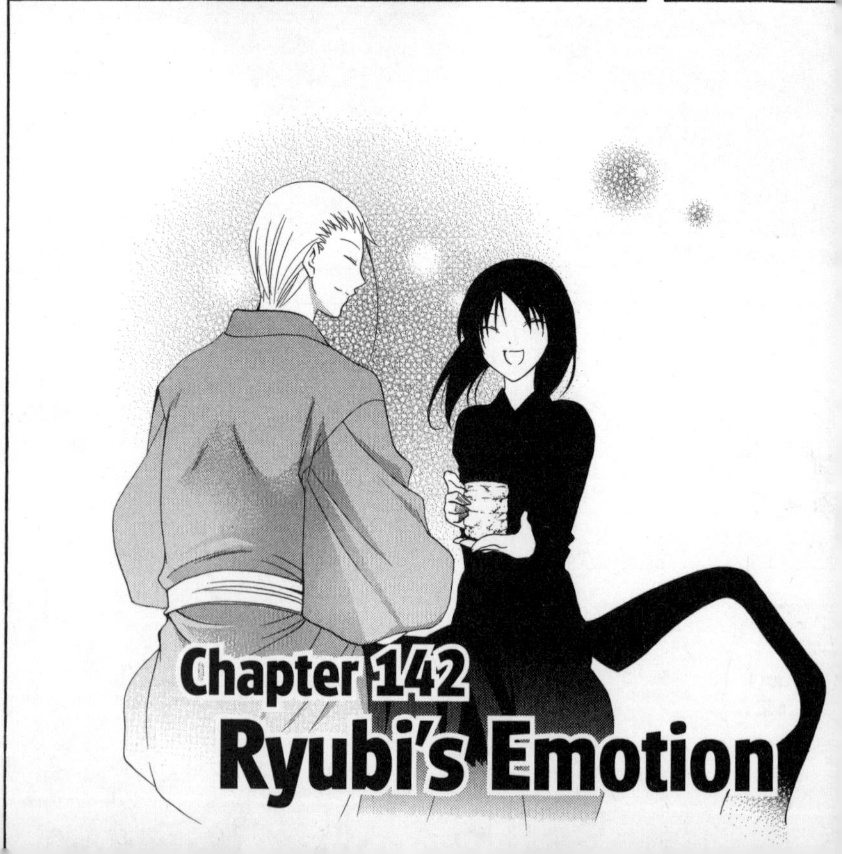
Chapter 142
Ryubi's Emotion

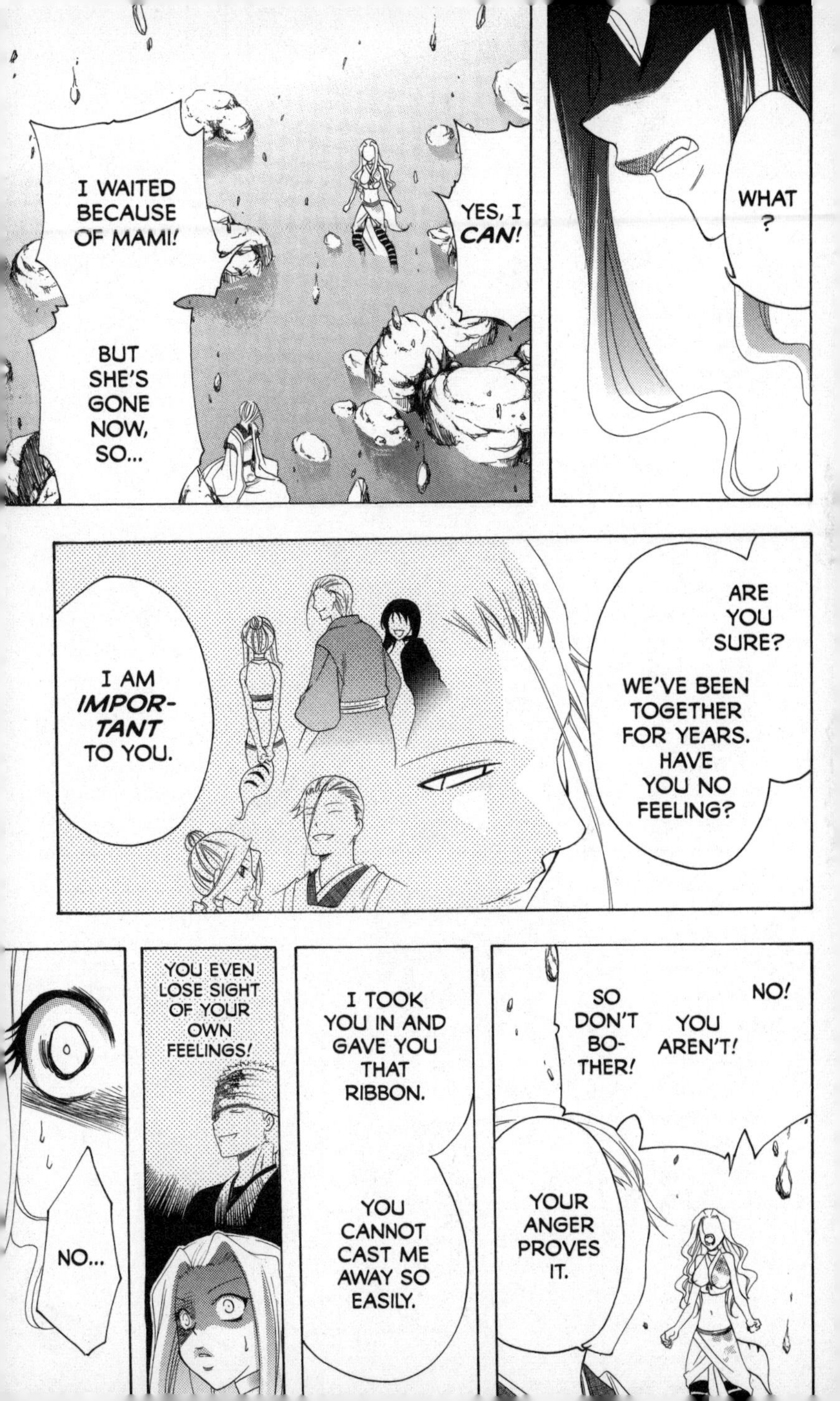
WHAT?
YES, I *CAN*!
I WAITED BECAUSE OF MAMI!
BUT SHE'S GONE NOW, SO...
ARE YOU SURE?
WE'VE BEEN TOGETHER FOR YEARS. HAVE YOU NO FEELING?
I AM *IMPORTANT* TO YOU.
NO!
YOU AREN'T!
SO DON'T BO-THER!
YOUR ANGER PROVES IT.
I TOOK YOU IN AND GAVE YOU THAT RIBBON.
YOU CANNOT CAST ME AWAY SO EASILY.
YOU EVEN LOSE SIGHT OF YOUR OWN FEELINGS!
NO...

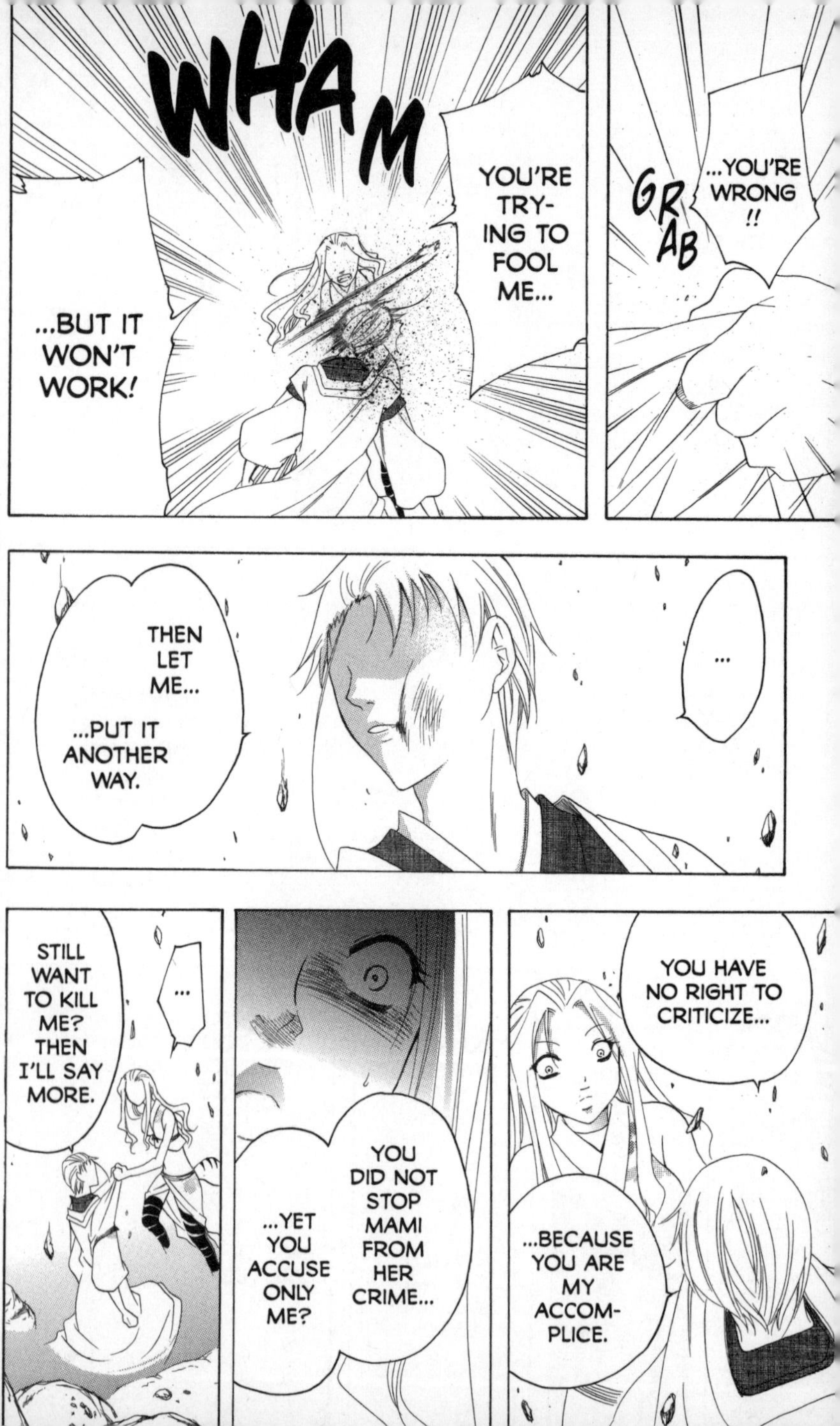
GRAB
...YOU'RE WRONG !!
WHAM
YOU'RE TRY- ING TO FOOL ME...
...BUT IT WON'T WORK!
...
THEN LET ME...
...PUT IT ANOTHER WAY.
YOU HAVE NO RIGHT TO CRITICIZE...
...BECAUSE YOU ARE MY ACCOM- PLICE.
YOU DID NOT STOP MAMI FROM HER CRIME...
...YET YOU ACCUSE ONLY ME?
...
STILL WANT TO KILL ME? THEN I'LL SAY MORE.

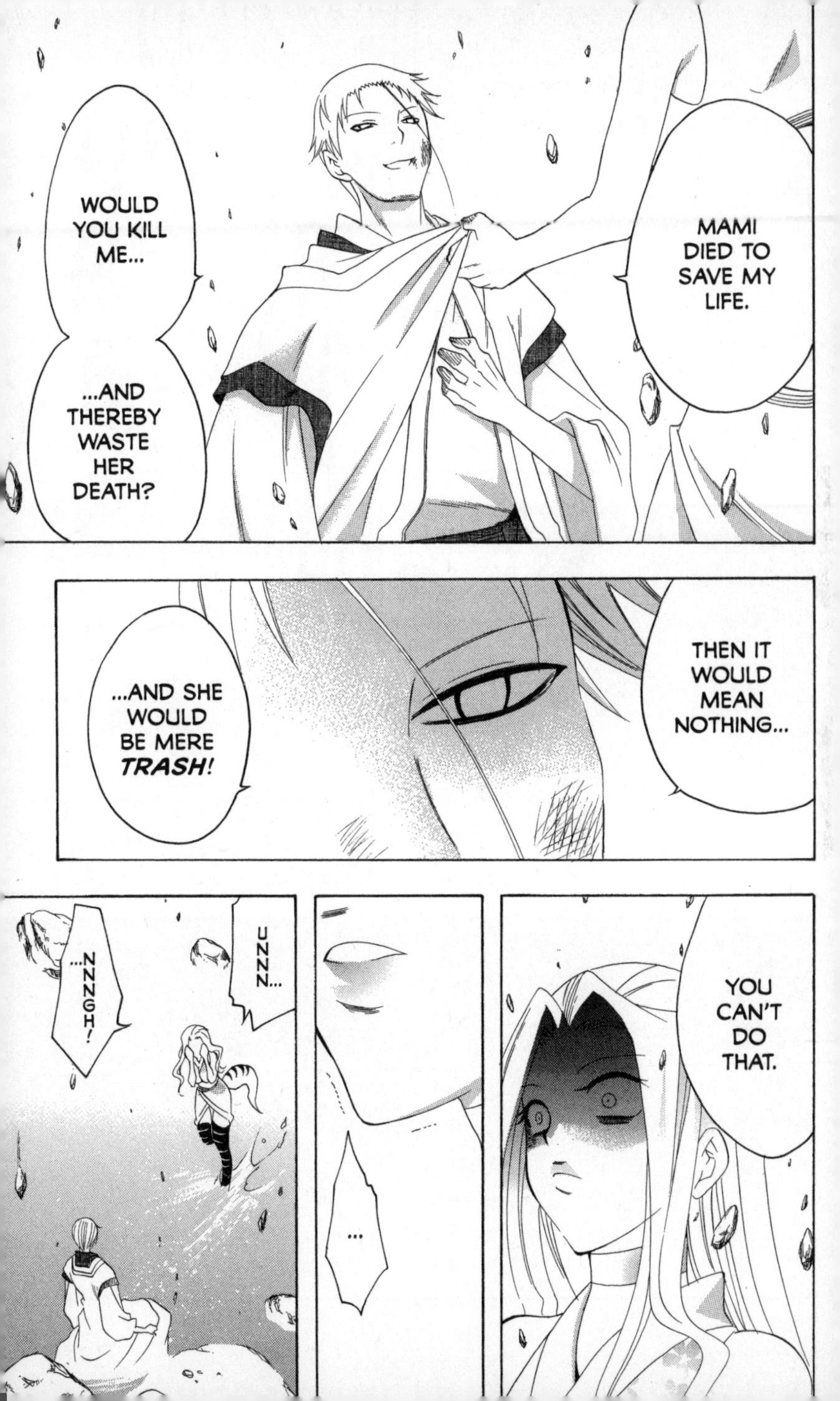
MAMI DIED TO SAVE MY LIFE.
WOULD YOU KILL ME...
...AND THEREBY WASTE HER DEATH?
THEN IT WOULD MEAN NOTHING...
...AND SHE WOULD BE MERE *TRASH*!
YOU CAN'T DO THAT.
...
UNNN...
...NNNGH!

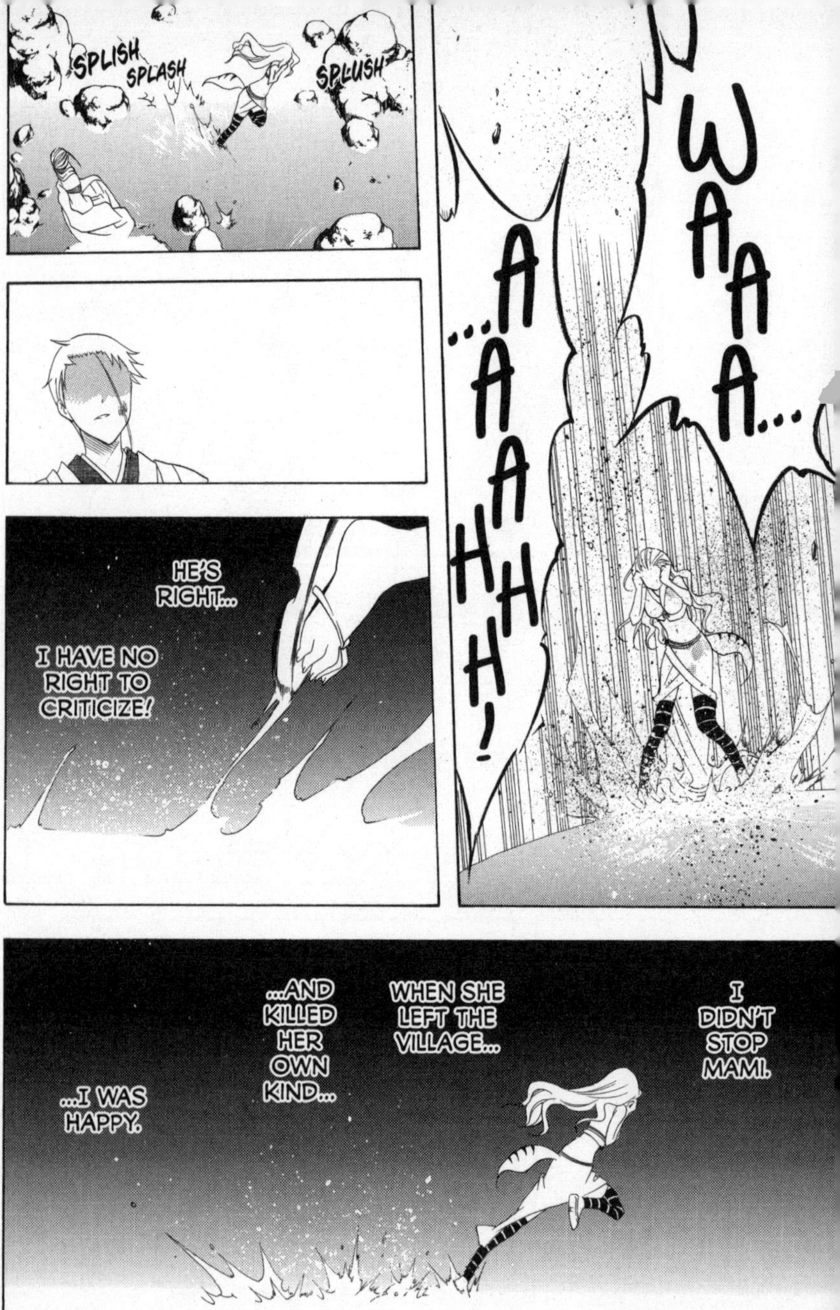
WAAAA...
...AAAHHH!
SPLUSH
SPLISH
SPLASH
HE'S RIGHT...
I HAVE NO RIGHT TO CRITICIZE!
I DIDN'T STOP MAMI.
WHEN SHE LEFT THE VILLAGE...
...AND KILLED HER OWN KIND...
...I WAS HAPPY.

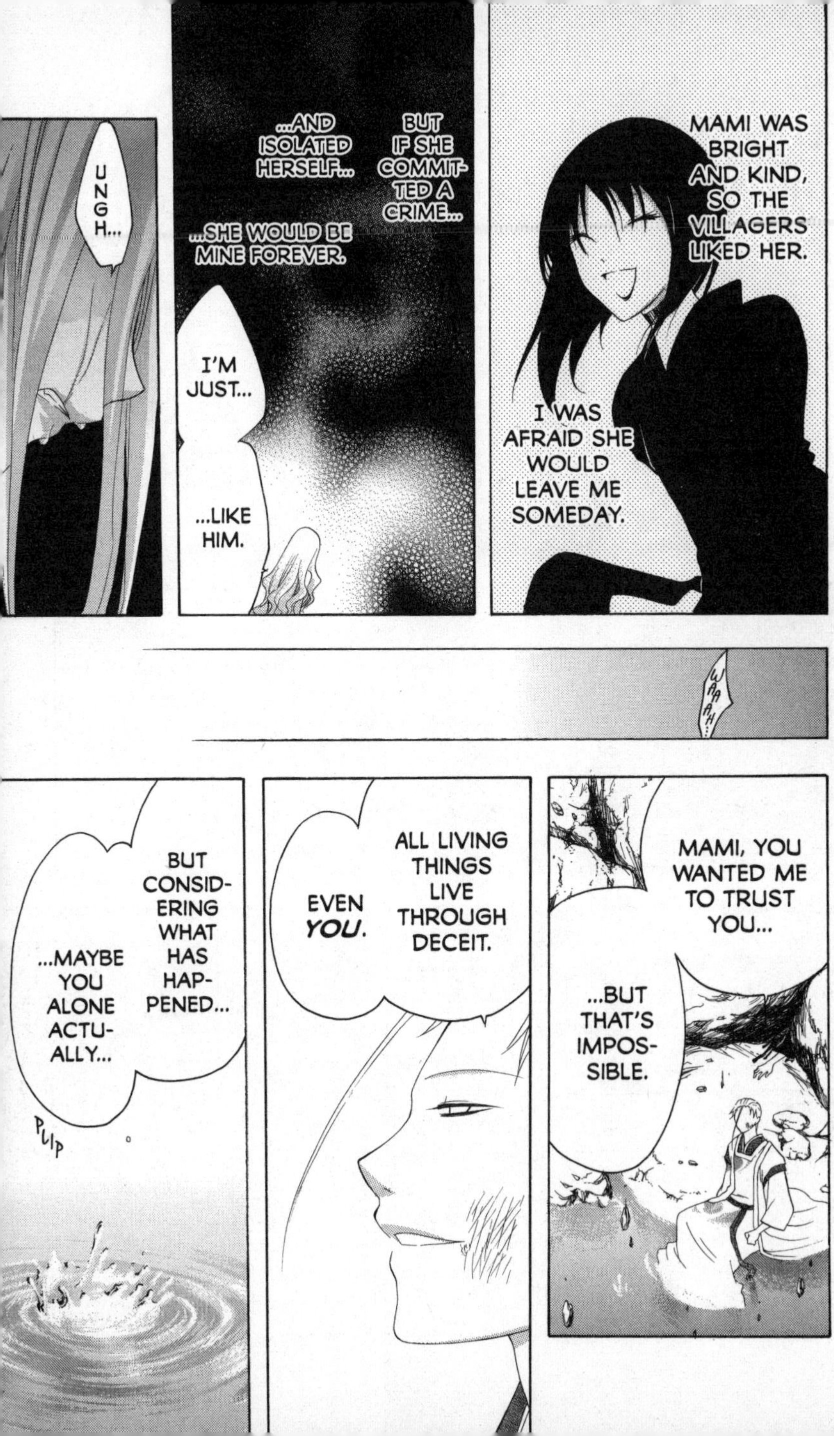
MAMI WAS BRIGHT AND KIND, SO THE VILLAGERS LIKED HER.
I WAS AFRAID SHE WOULD LEAVE ME SOMEDAY.
BUT IF SHE COMMITTED A CRIME...
...AND ISOLATED HERSELF...
...SHE WOULD BE MINE FOREVER.
I'M JUST...
...LIKE HIM.
UNGH...
WAAAH...
MAMI, YOU WANTED ME TO TRUST YOU...
...BUT THAT'S IMPOSSIBLE.
ALL LIVING THINGS LIVE THROUGH DECEIT.
EVEN *YOU*.
BUT CONSIDERING WHAT HAS HAPPENED...
...MAYBE YOU ALONE ACTUALLY...
PLIP

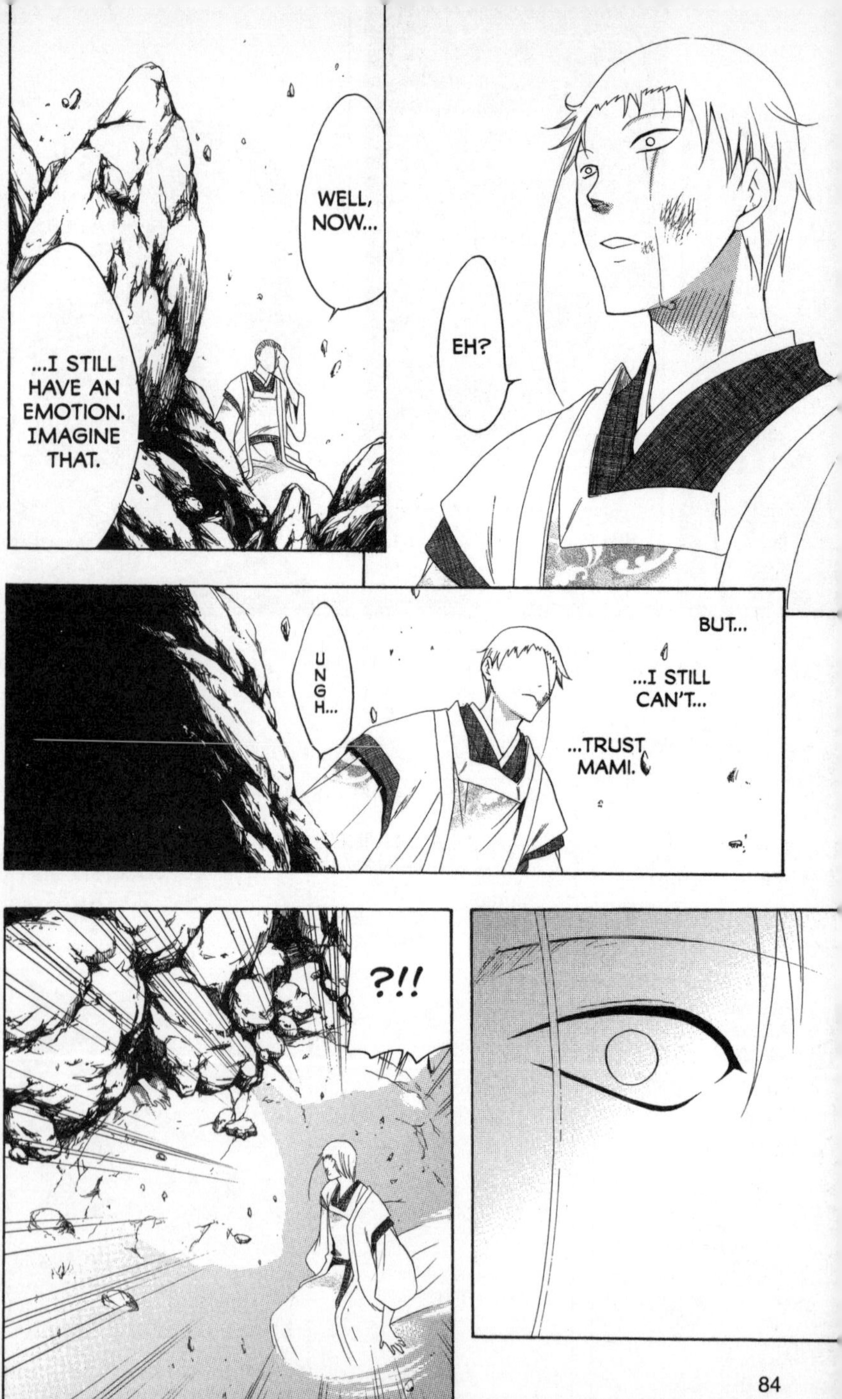
EH?
WELL, NOW...
...I STILL HAVE AN EMOTION. IMAGINE THAT.
BUT...
...I STILL CAN'T...
...TRUST MAMI.
UNGH...
?!!

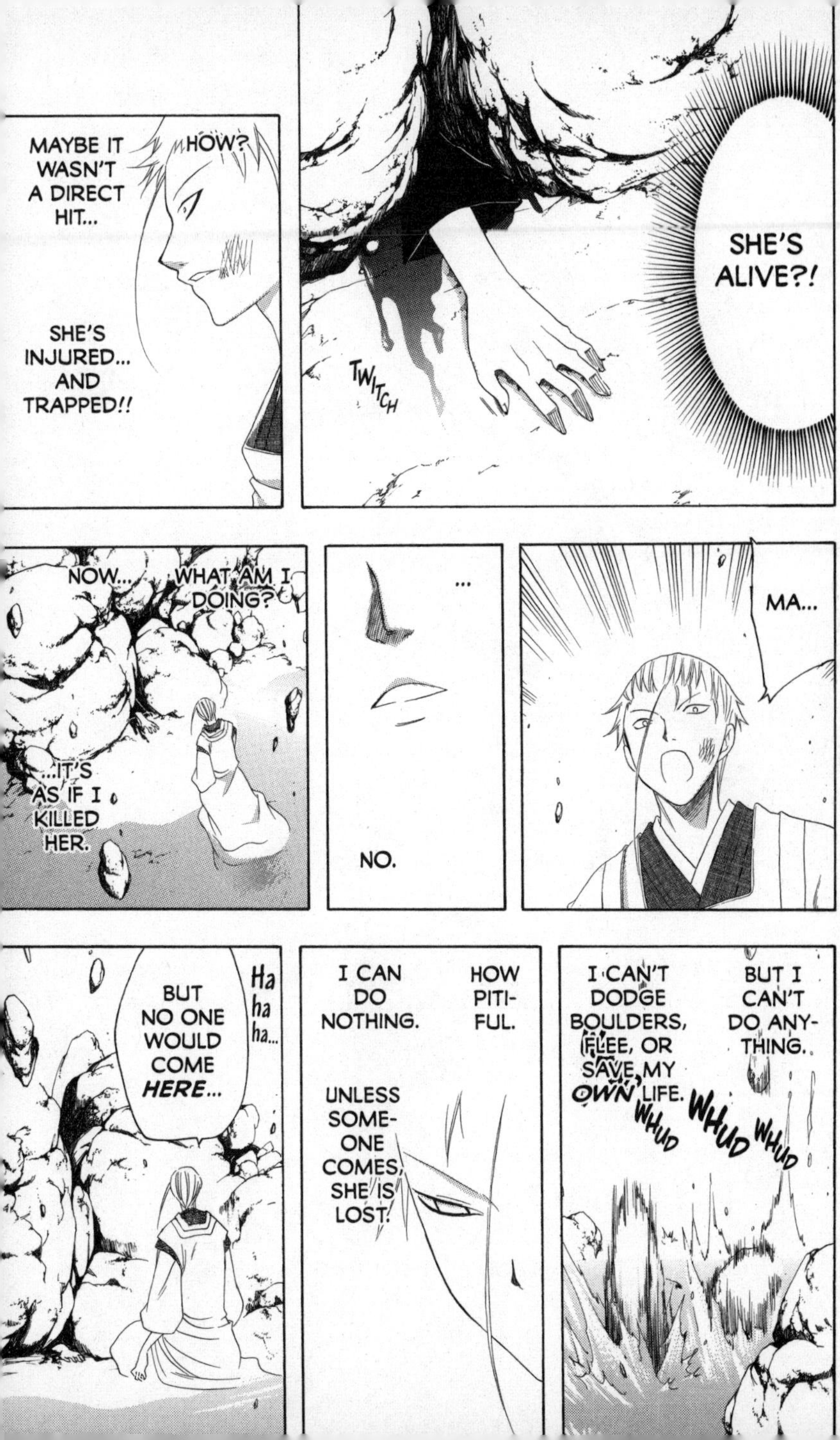
SHE'S ALIVE?!
TWITCH
HOW?
MAYBE IT WASN'T A DIRECT HIT...
SHE'S INJURED... AND TRAPPED!!
MA...
...
NO.
WHAT AM I DOING?
NOW...
...IT'S AS IF I KILLED HER.
BUT I CAN'T DO ANYTHING.
I CAN'T DODGE BOULDERS, FLEE, OR SAVE MY *OWN* LIFE.
WHUD
WHUD
WHUD
HOW PITIFUL.
I CAN DO NOTHING.
UNLESS SOMEONE COMES, SHE IS LOST.
Ha ha ha...
BUT NO ONE WOULD COME *HERE*...

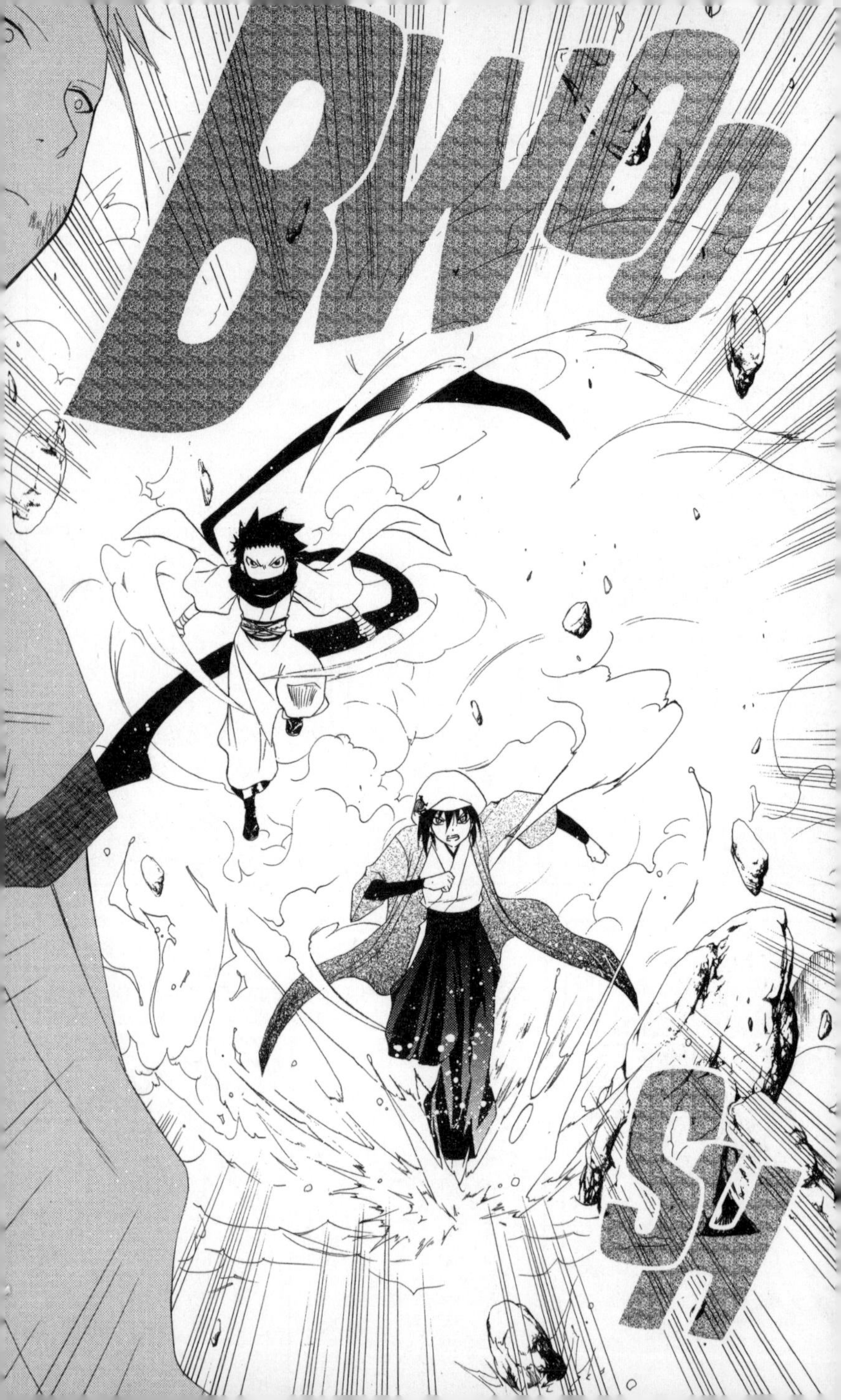
BWOO
S!

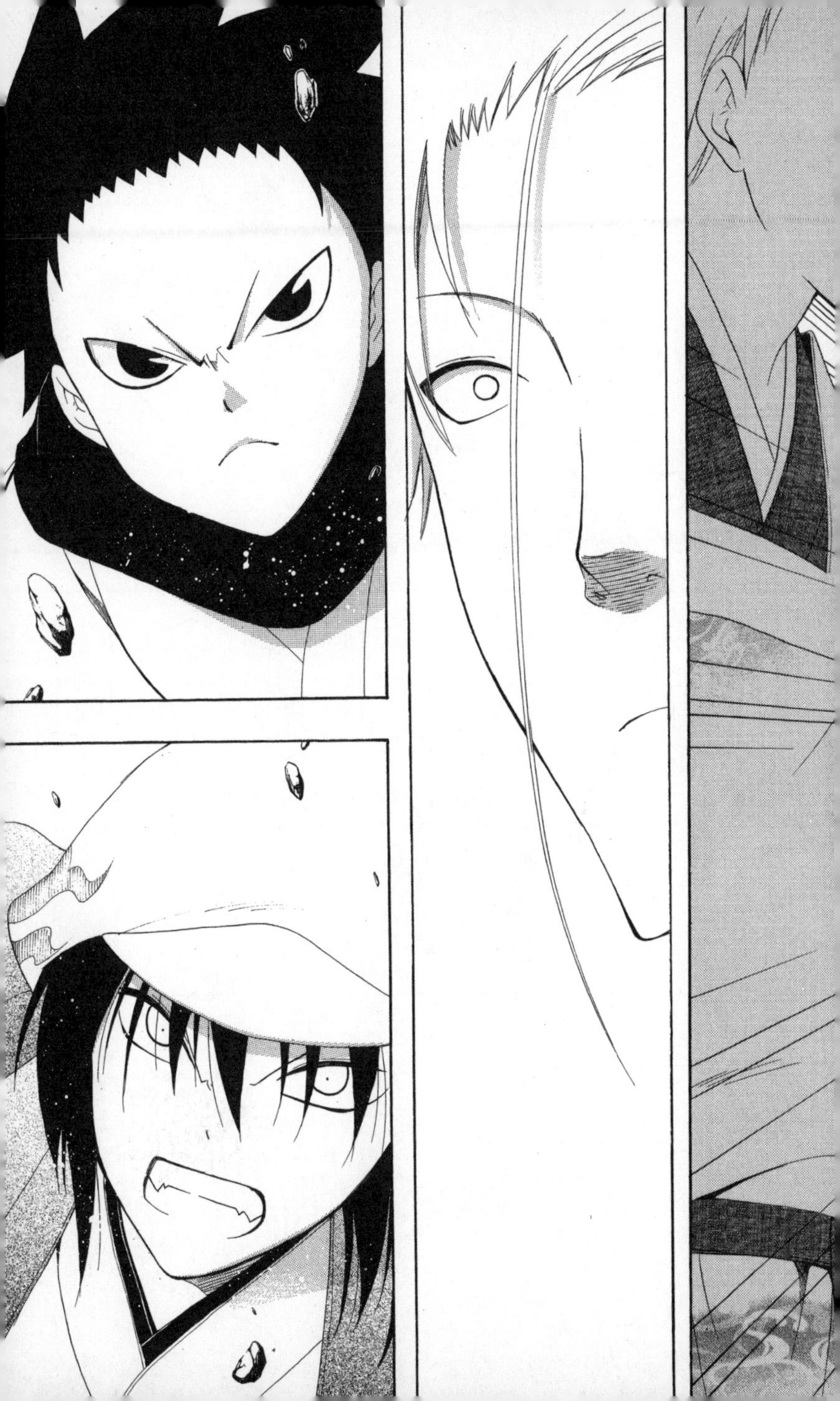

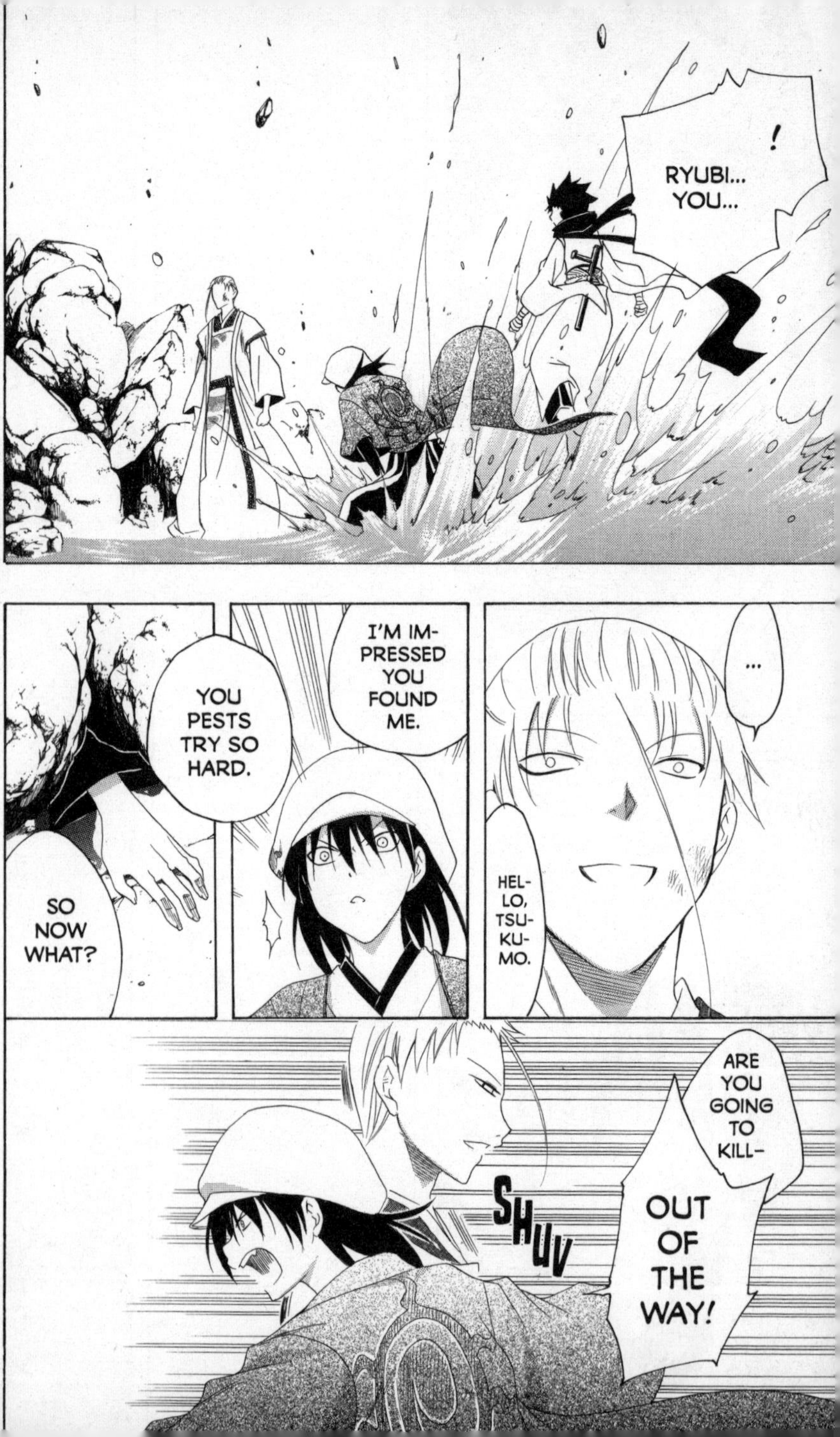
!
RYUBI... YOU...
...
HELLO, TSUKUMO.
I'M IMPRESSED YOU FOUND ME.
YOU PESTS TRY SO HARD.
SO NOW WHAT?
ARE YOU GOING TO KILL-
OUT OF THE WAY!
SHUV

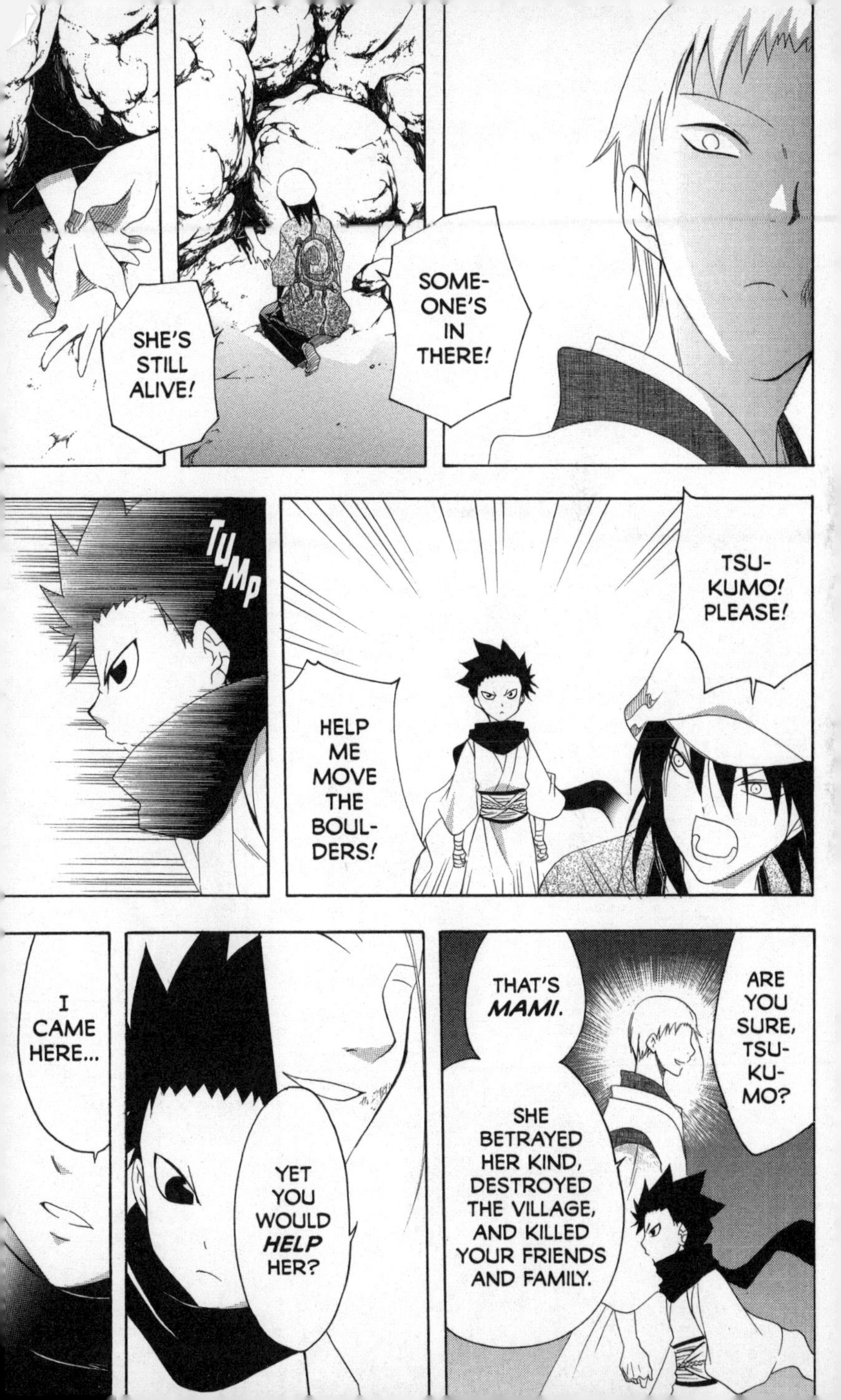
SOME-ONE'S IN THERE!
SHE'S STILL ALIVE!
TSU-KUMO! PLEASE!
HELP ME MOVE THE BOUL-DERS!
TUMP
ARE YOU SURE, TSU-KU-MO?
THAT'S *MAMI*.
SHE BETRAYED HER KIND, DESTROYED THE VILLAGE, AND KILLED YOUR FRIENDS AND FAMILY.
YET YOU WOULD *HELP* HER?
I CAME HERE...

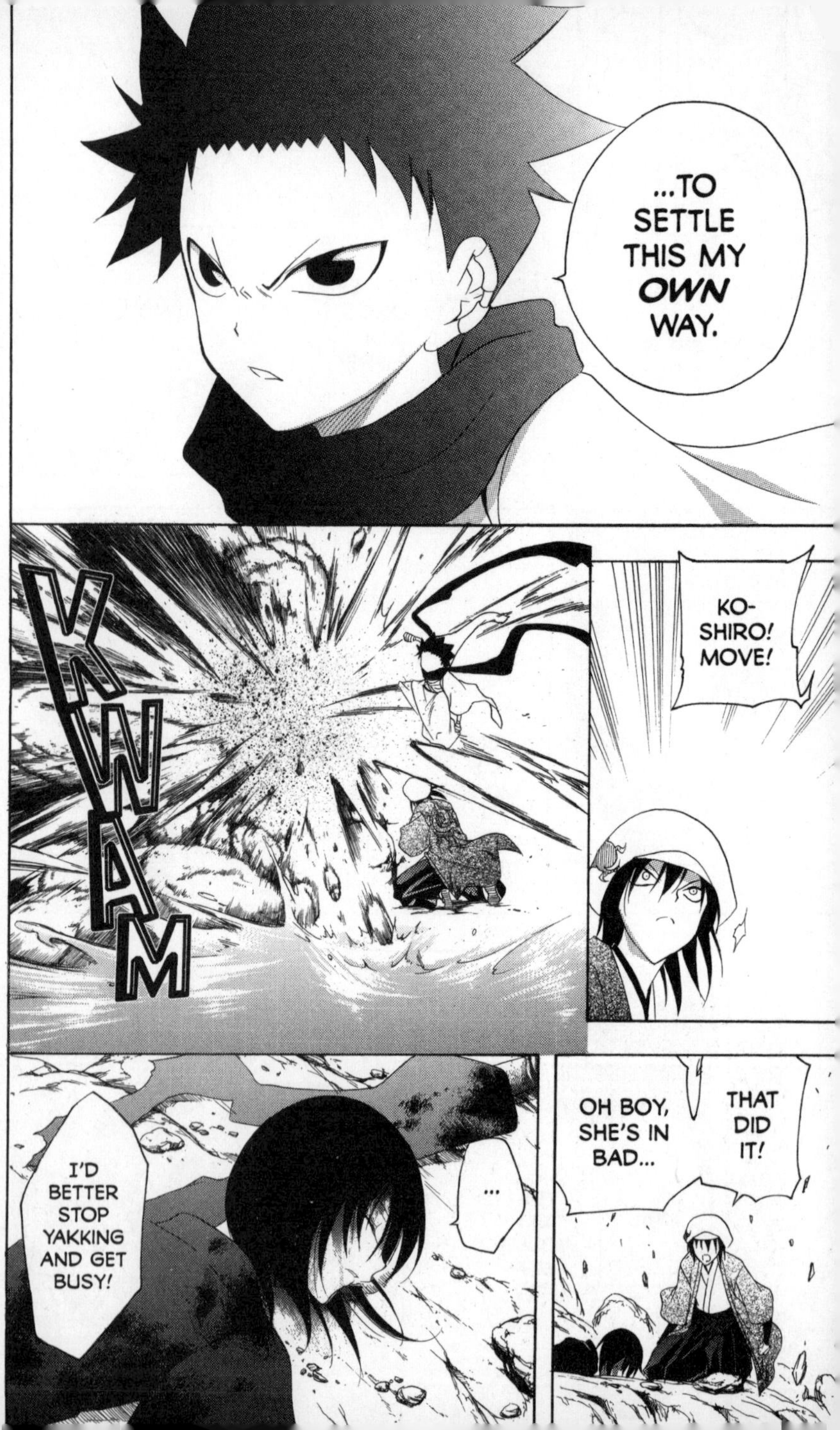
...TO SETTLE THIS MY *OWN* WAY.
KO-SHIRO! MOVE!
KWAM
THAT DID IT!
OH BOY, SHE'S IN BAD...
...
I'D BETTER STOP YAKKING AND GET BUSY!

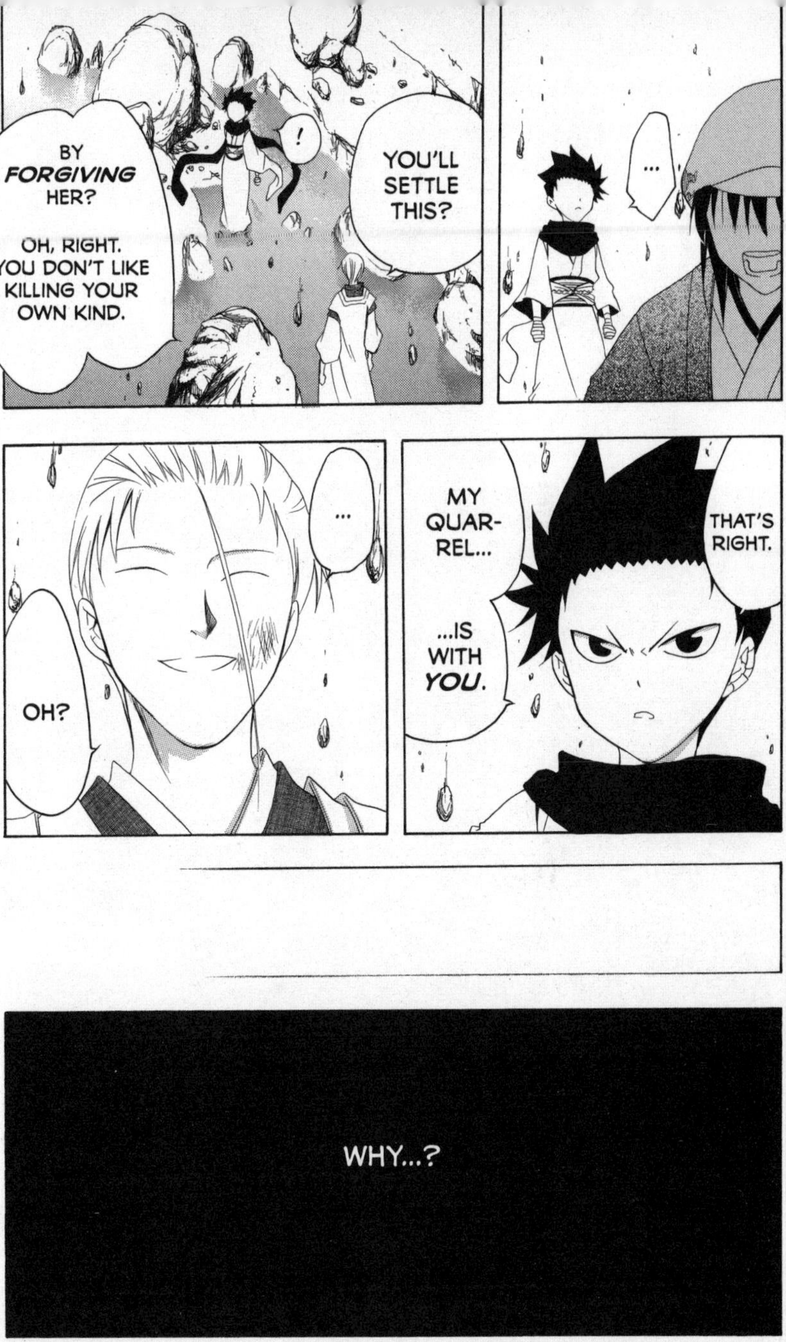
...
YOU'LL SETTLE THIS?
!
BY *FORGIVING* HER?
OH, RIGHT. YOU DON'T LIKE KILLING YOUR OWN KIND.
THAT'S RIGHT.
MY QUAR-REL...
...IS WITH *YOU*.
...
OH?
WHY...?

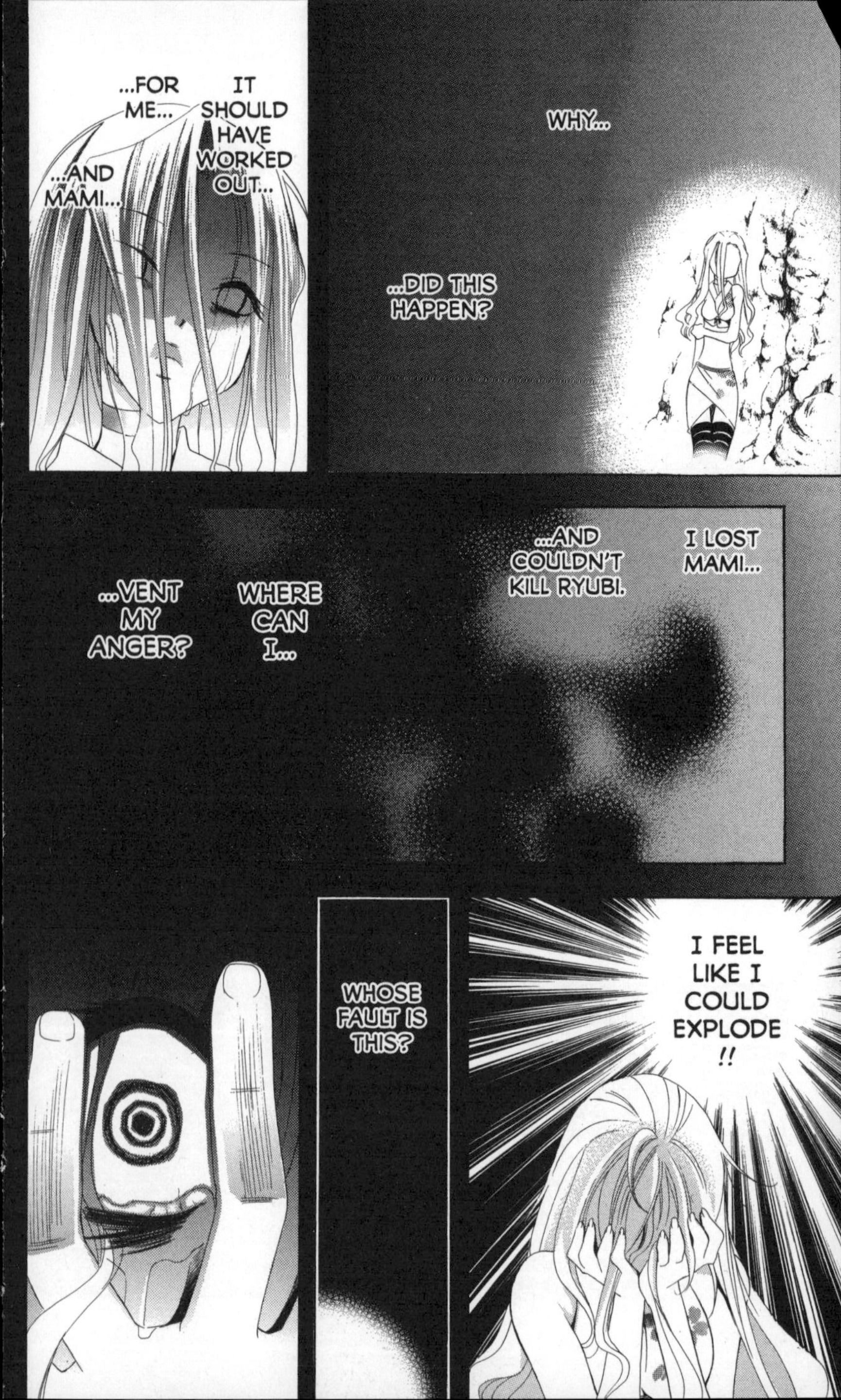
WHY...
...DID THIS HAPPEN?
IT SHOULD HAVE WORKED OUT...
...FOR ME...
...AND MAMI...
I LOST MAMI...
...AND COULDN'T KILL RYUBI.
WHERE CAN I...
...VENT MY ANGER?
I FEEL LIKE I COULD EXPLODE !!
WHOSE FAULT IS THIS?

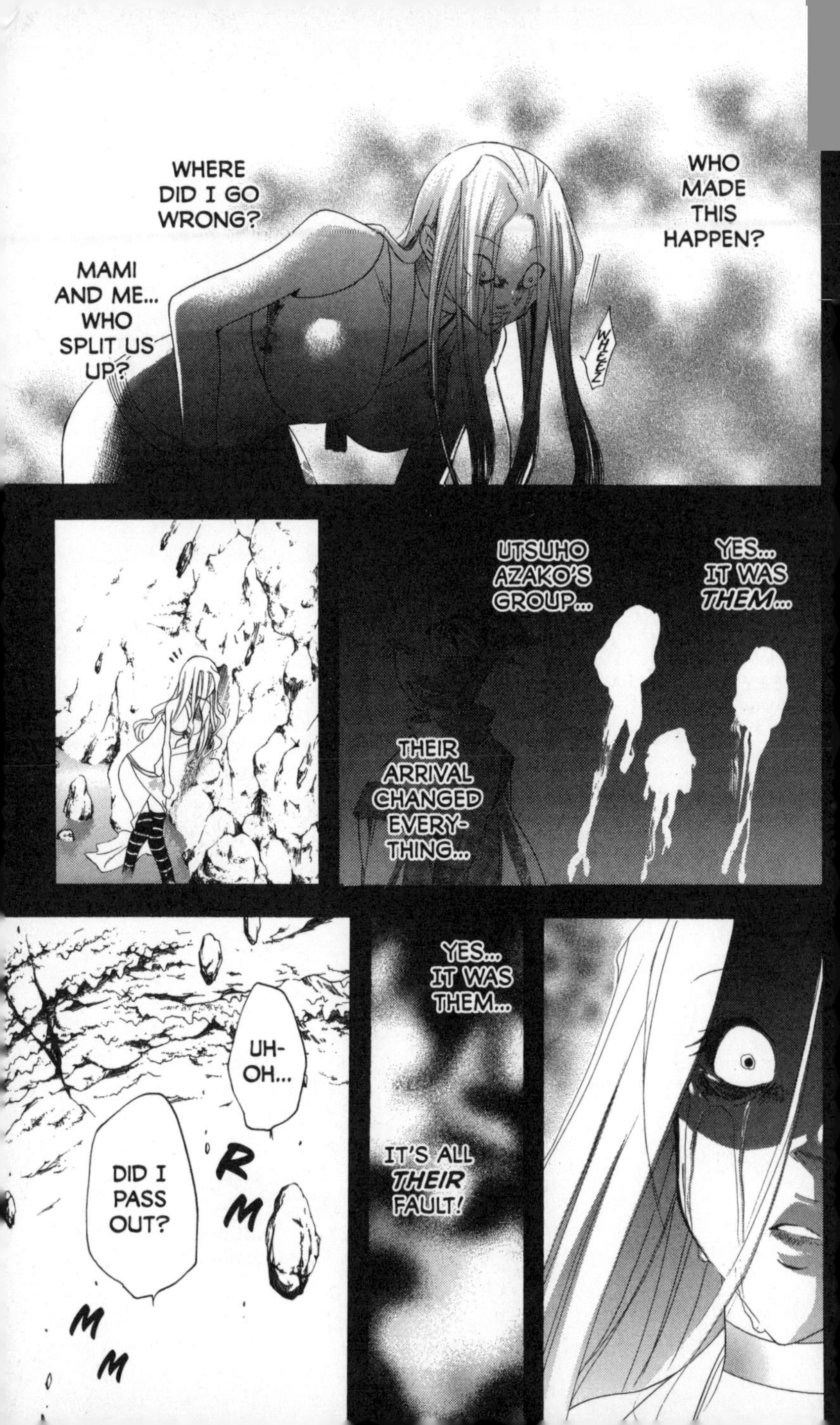

WHO MADE THIS HAPPEN?
WHERE DID I GO WRONG?
WHEEZ
MAMI AND ME... WHO SPLIT US UP?
YES... IT WAS *THEM*...
UTSUHO AZAKO'S GROUP...
THEIR ARRIVAL CHANGED EVERY-THING...
YES... IT WAS THEM...
IT'S ALL *THEIR* FAULT!
UH-OH...
RMM
DID I PASS OUT?
MM

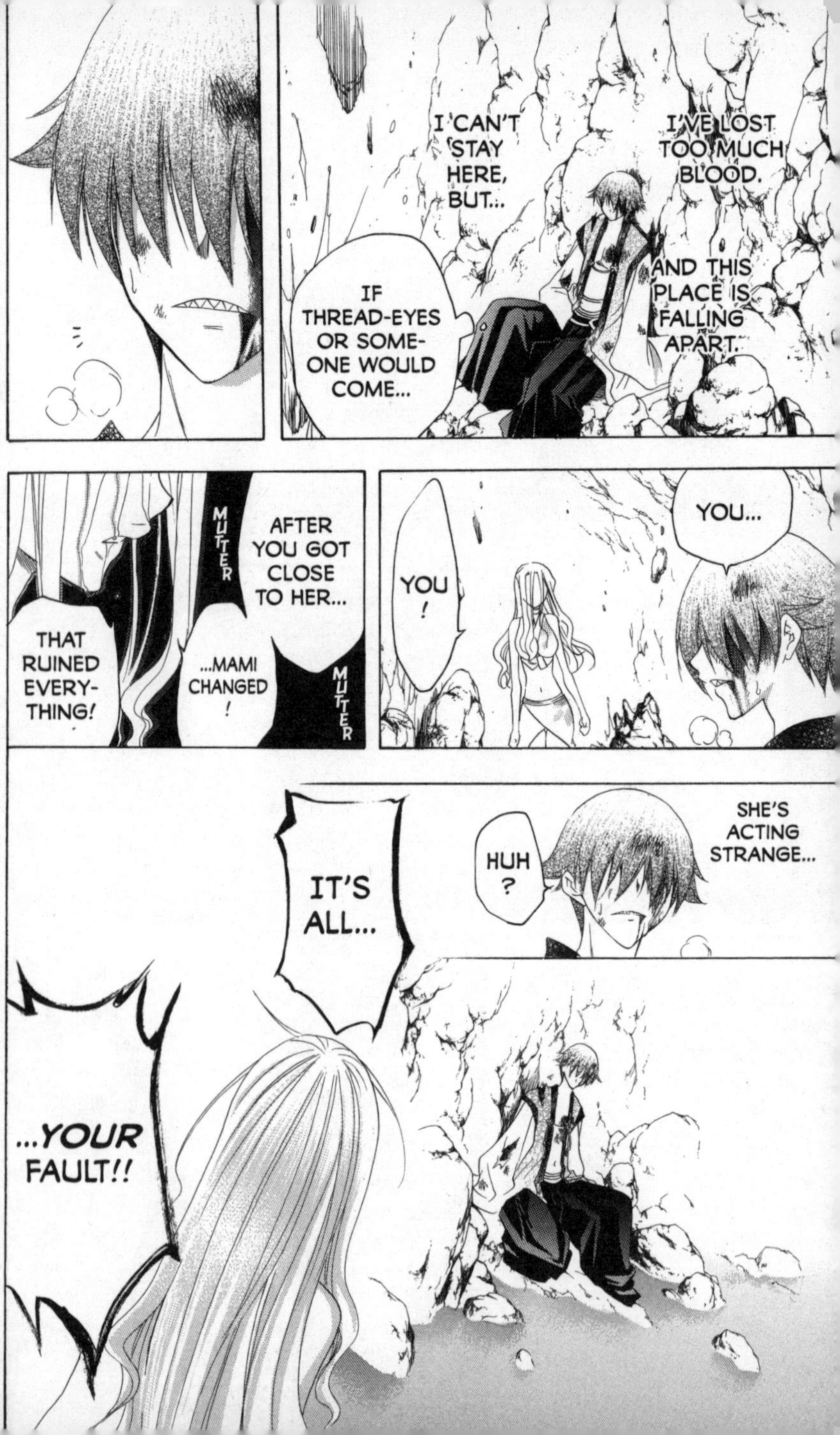
I'VE LOST TOO MUCH BLOOD.
I CAN'T STAY HERE, BUT...
AND THIS PLACE IS FALLING APART.
IF THREAD-EYES OR SOME-ONE WOULD COME...
YOU...
YOU!
MUTTER
AFTER YOU GOT CLOSE TO HER...
MUTTER
...MAMI CHANGED!
THAT RUINED EVERY-THING!
SHE'S ACTING STRANGE...
HUH?
IT'S ALL...
...YOUR FAULT!!

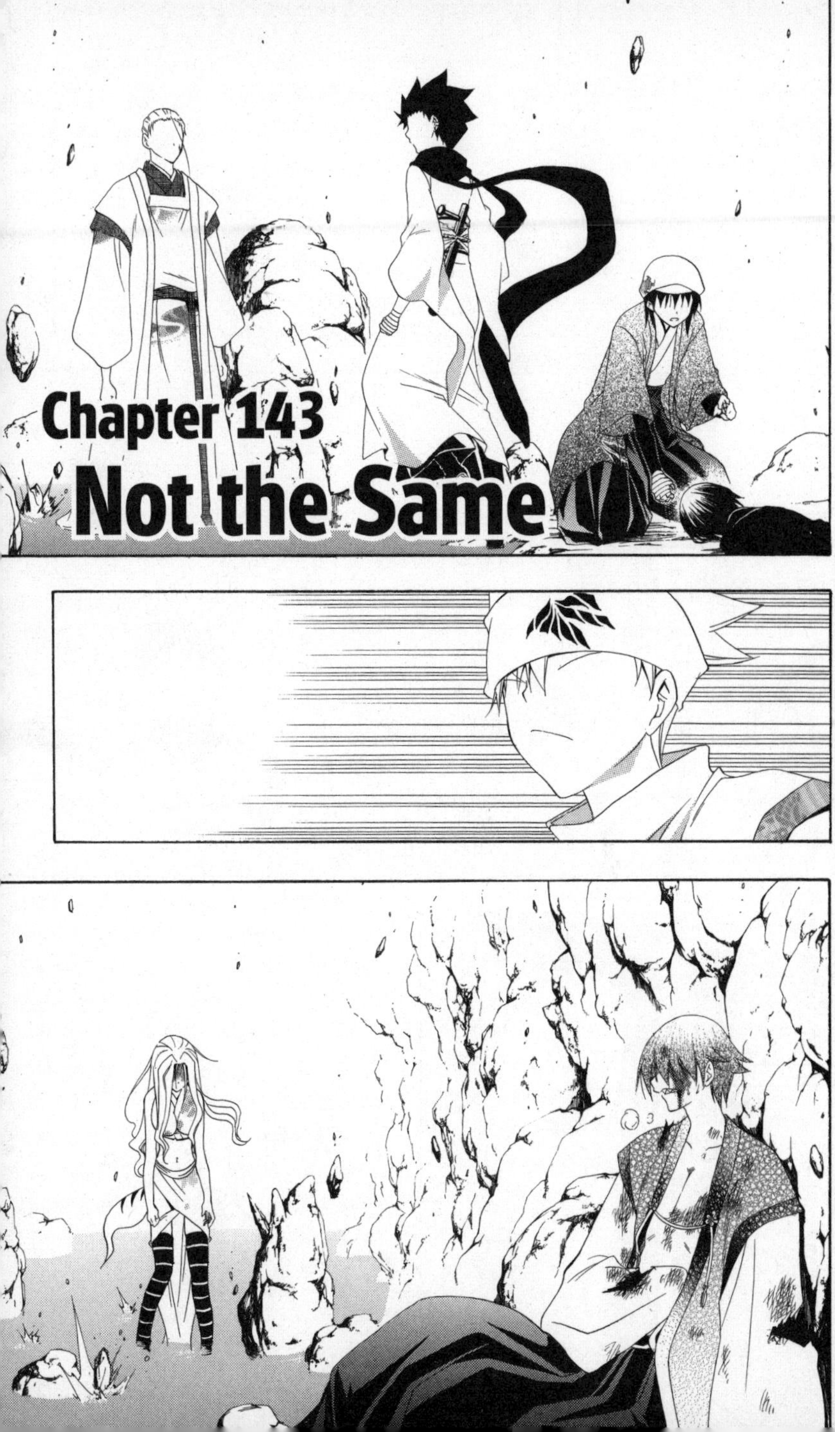
Chapter 143
Not the Same

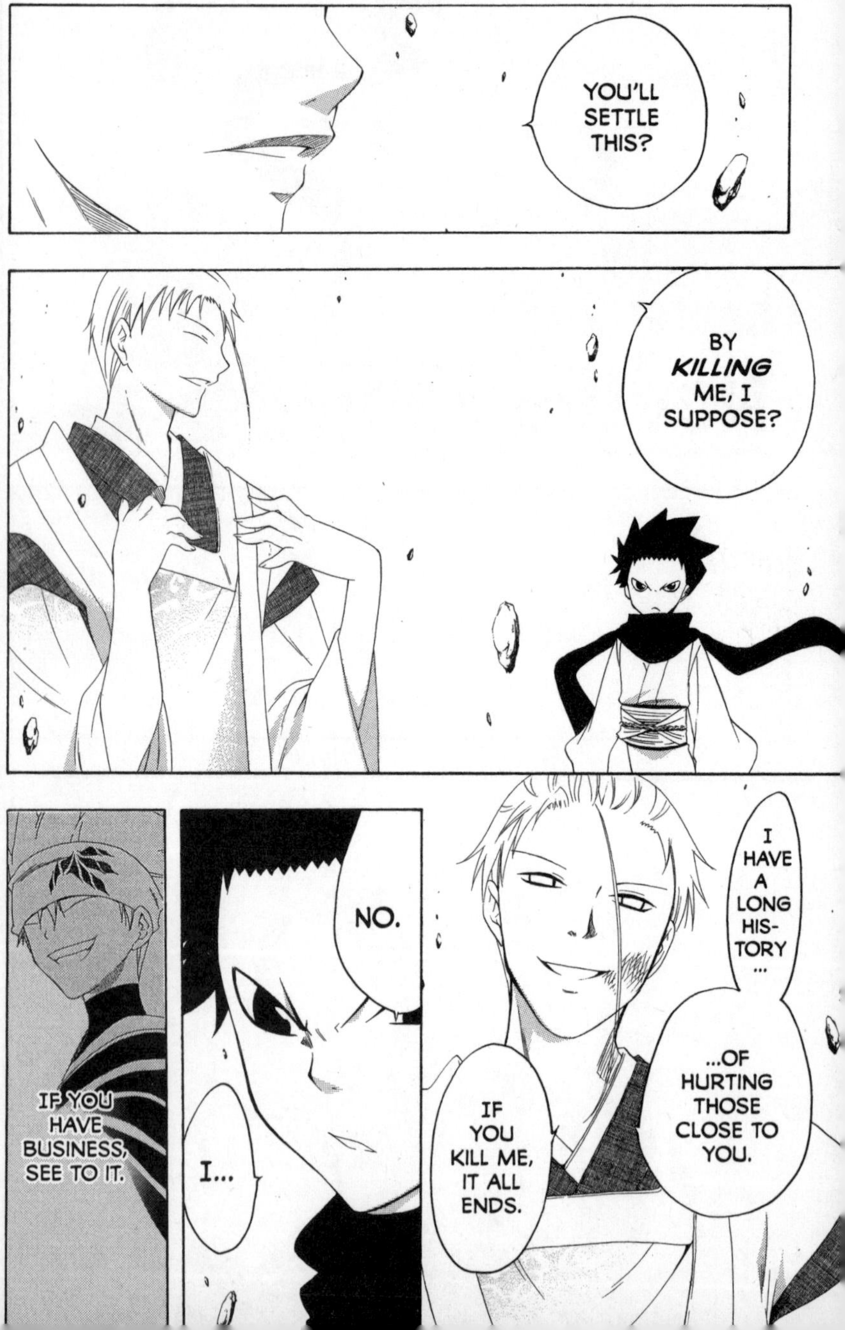
YOU'LL SETTLE THIS?
BY *KILLING* ME, I SUPPOSE?
I HAVE A LONG HIS-TORY...
...OF HURTING THOSE CLOSE TO YOU.
IF YOU KILL ME, IT ALL ENDS.
NO.
I...
IF YOU HAVE BUSINESS, SEE TO IT.

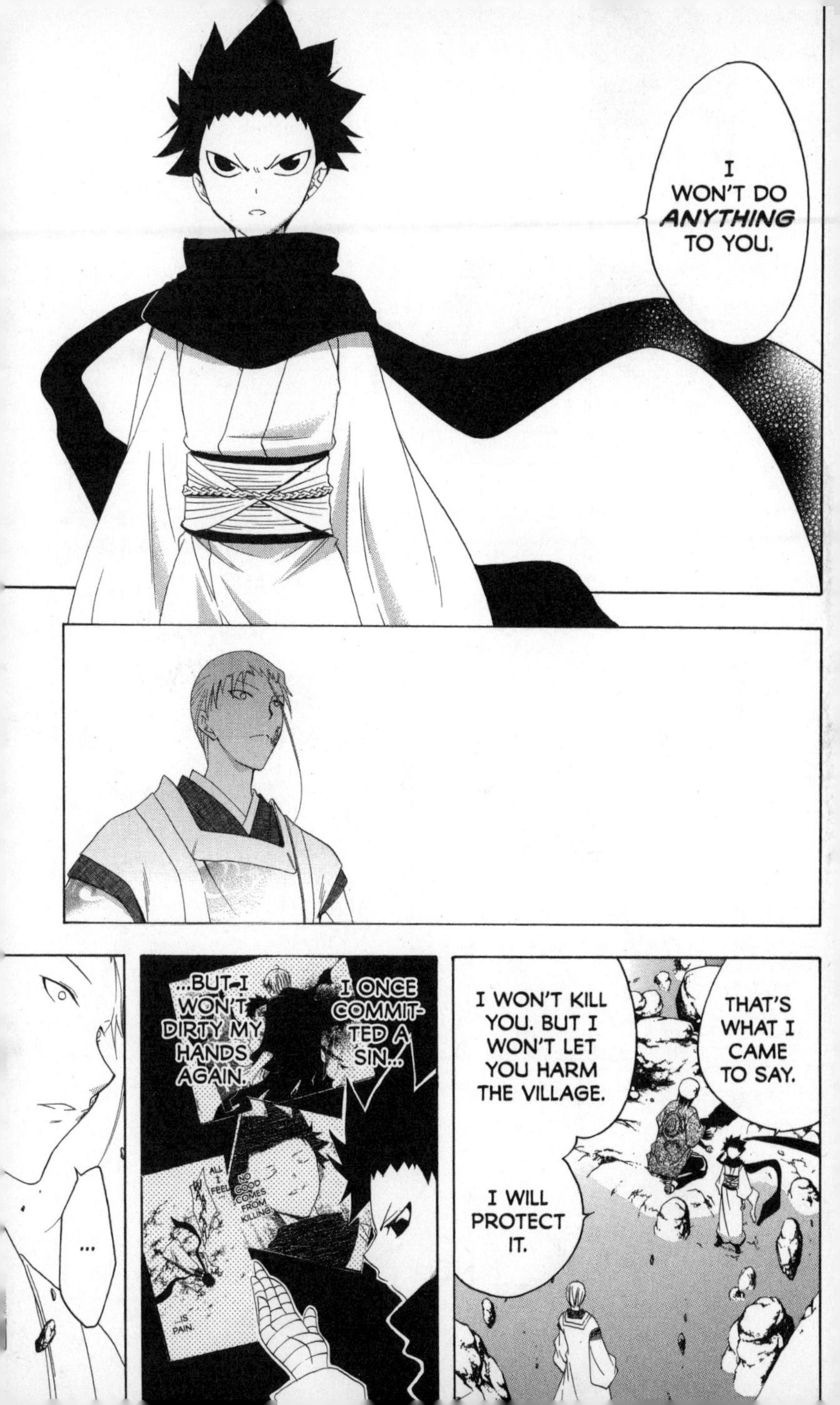
I WON'T DO ANYTHING TO YOU.
I WON'T KILL YOU. BUT I WON'T LET YOU HARM THE VILLAGE.
I WILL PROTECT IT.
THAT'S WHAT I CAME TO SAY.
I ONCE COMMITTED A SIN...
...BUT I WON'T DIRTY MY HANDS AGAIN.
NO GOOD COMES FROM KILLING.
ALL I FEEL
...IS PAIN.
...

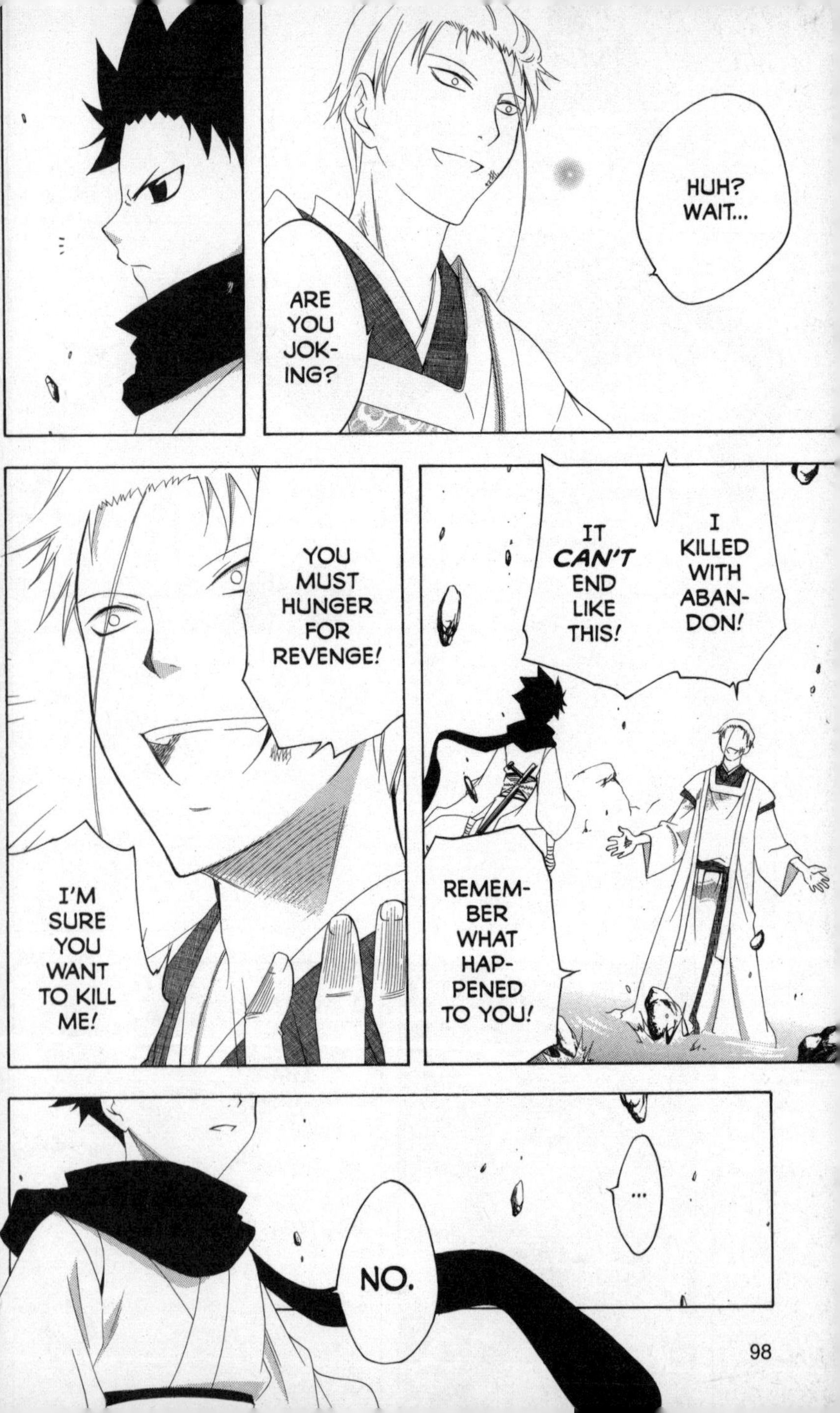
HUH? WAIT...
ARE YOU JOKING?
I KILLED WITH ABANDON!
IT *CAN'T* END LIKE THIS!
REMEMBER WHAT HAPPENED TO YOU!
YOU MUST HUNGER FOR REVENGE!
I'M SURE YOU WANT TO KILL ME!
...
NO.

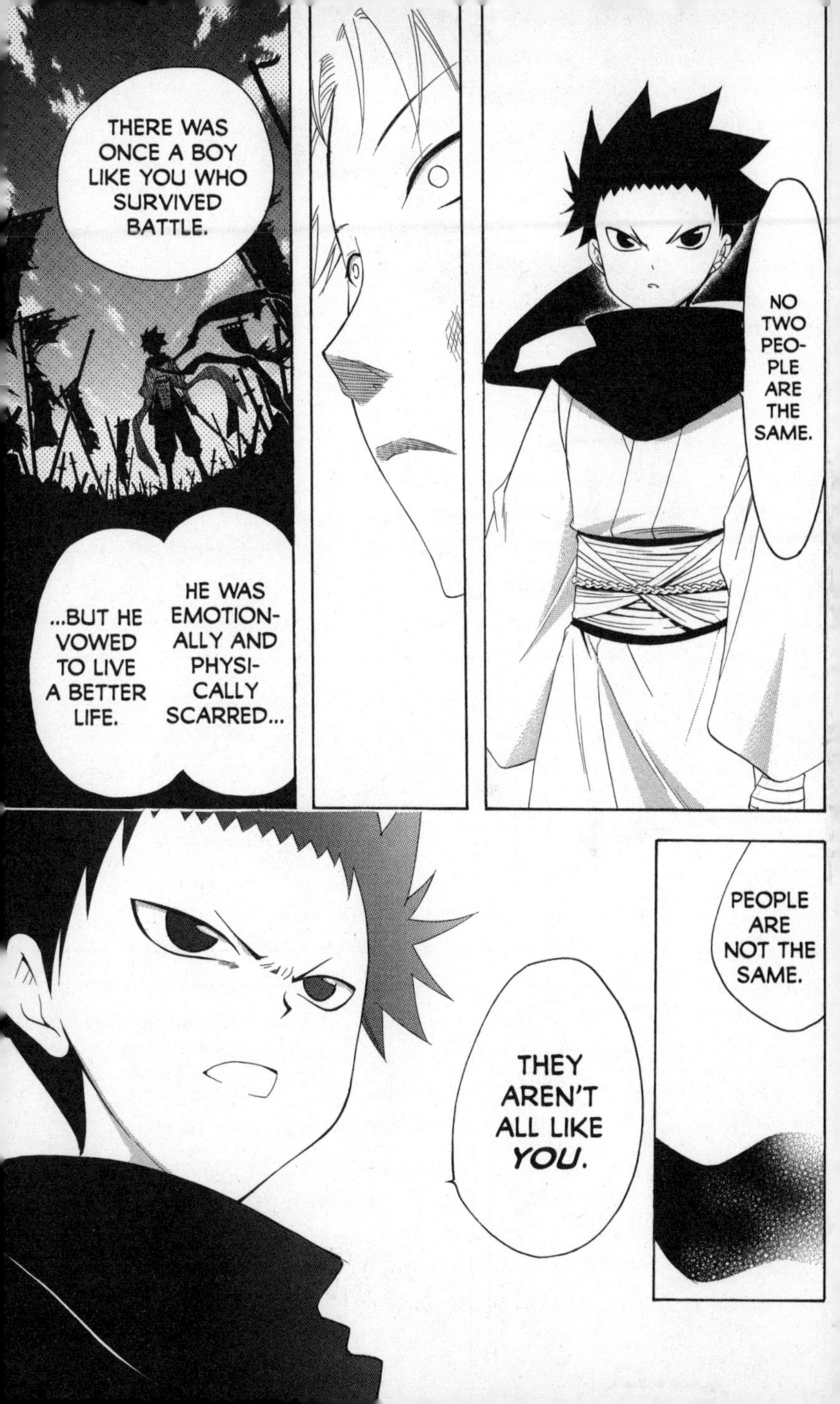
NO TWO PEO-PLE ARE THE SAME.
THERE WAS ONCE A BOY LIKE YOU WHO SURVIVED BATTLE.
HE WAS EMOTION-ALLY AND PHYSI-CALLY SCARRED...
...BUT HE VOWED TO LIVE A BETTER LIFE.
PEOPLE ARE NOT THE SAME.
THEY AREN'T ALL LIKE *YOU*.

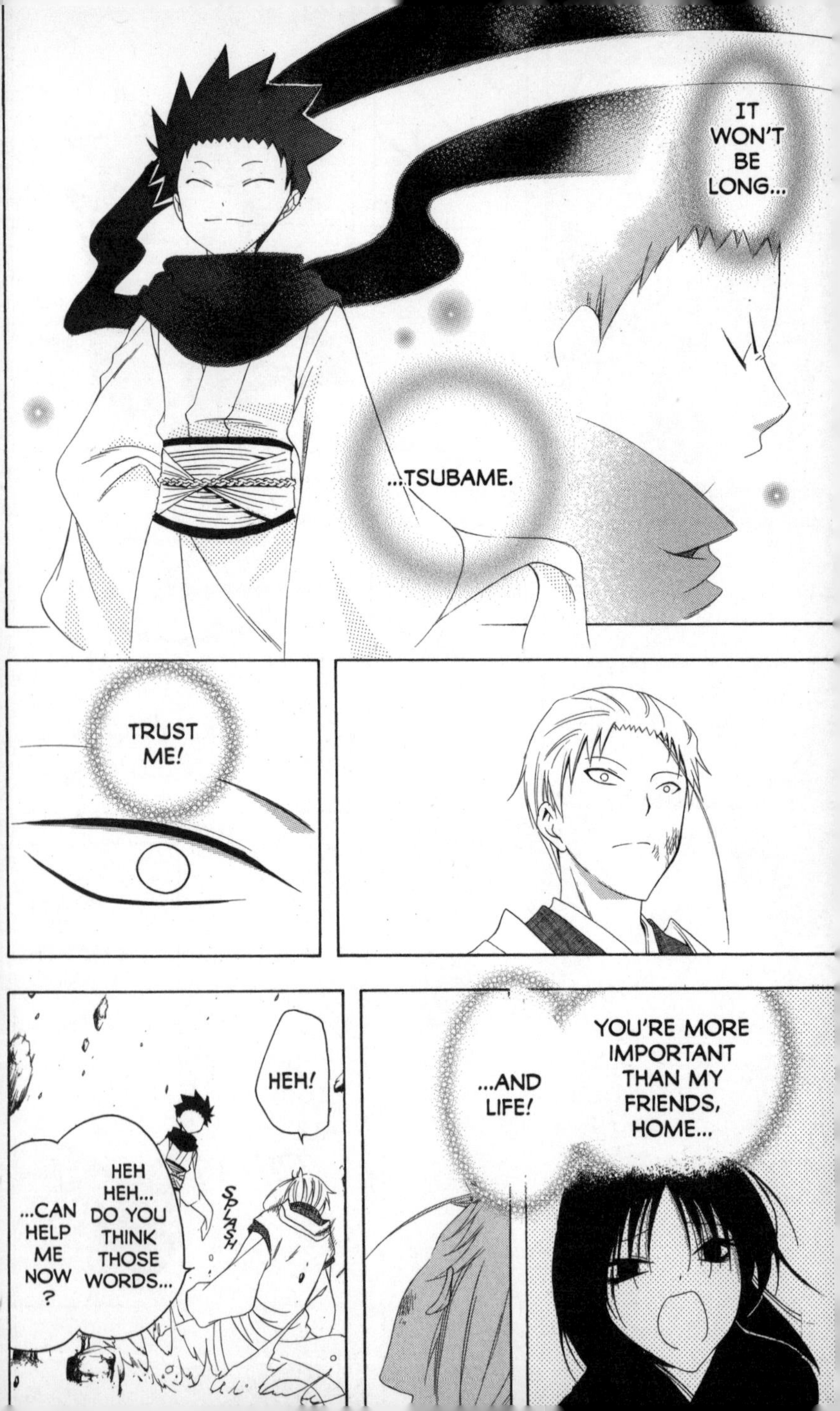
IT WON'T BE LONG...
...TSUBAME.
TRUST ME!
YOU'RE MORE IMPORTANT THAN MY FRIENDS, HOME...
...AND LIFE!
HEH!
SPLASH
HEH HEH... DO YOU THINK THOSE WORDS...
...CAN HELP ME NOW?

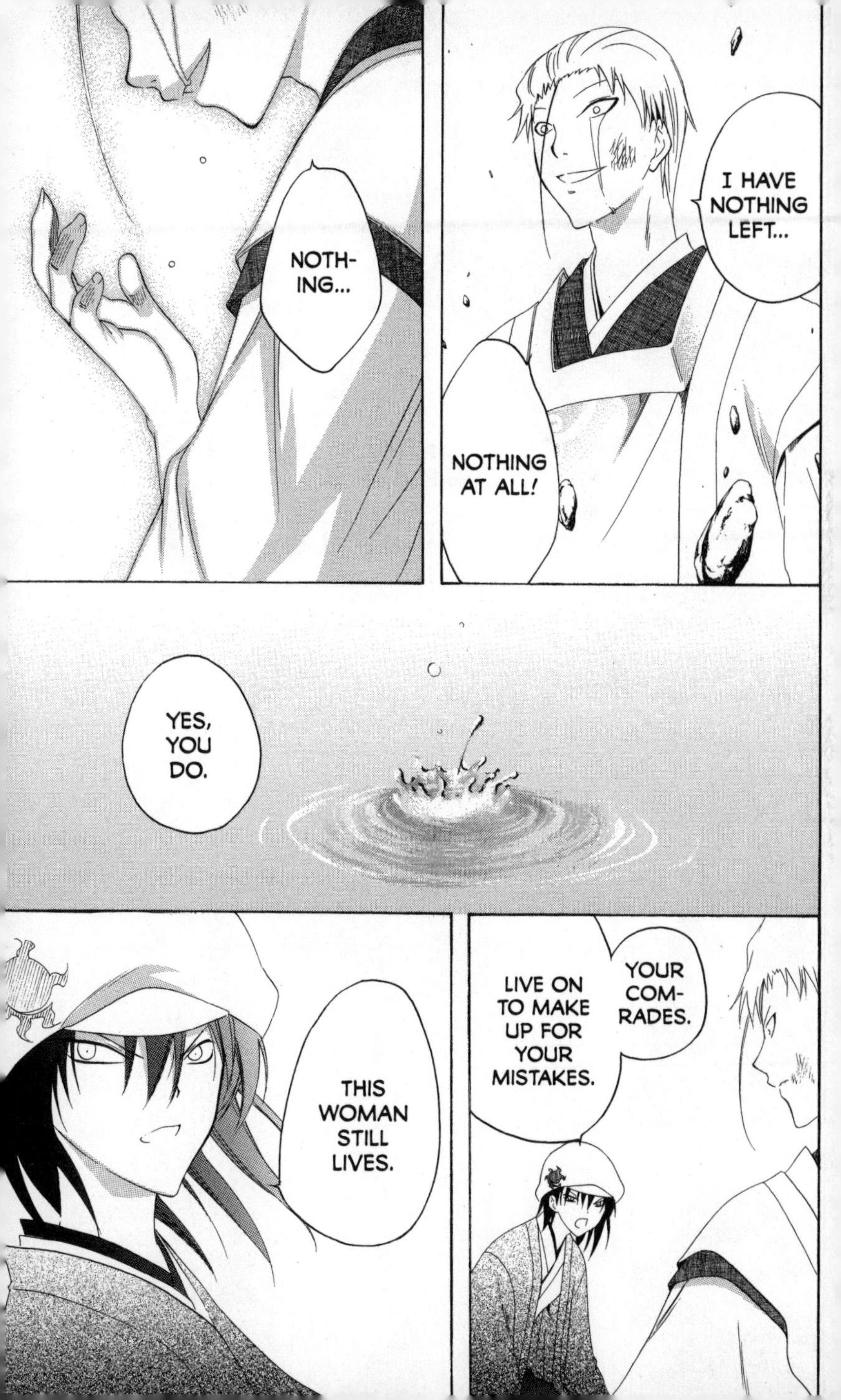
I HAVE NOTHING LEFT...
NOTHING AT ALL!
NOTHING...
YES, YOU DO.
YOUR COMRADES.
LIVE ON TO MAKE UP FOR YOUR MISTAKES.
THIS WOMAN STILL LIVES.

AND SHE'LL RECOVER.

IT'S A KIND OF MIRACLE.

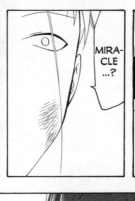

MIRA-CLE...?

...

I SEE...

SLOSH

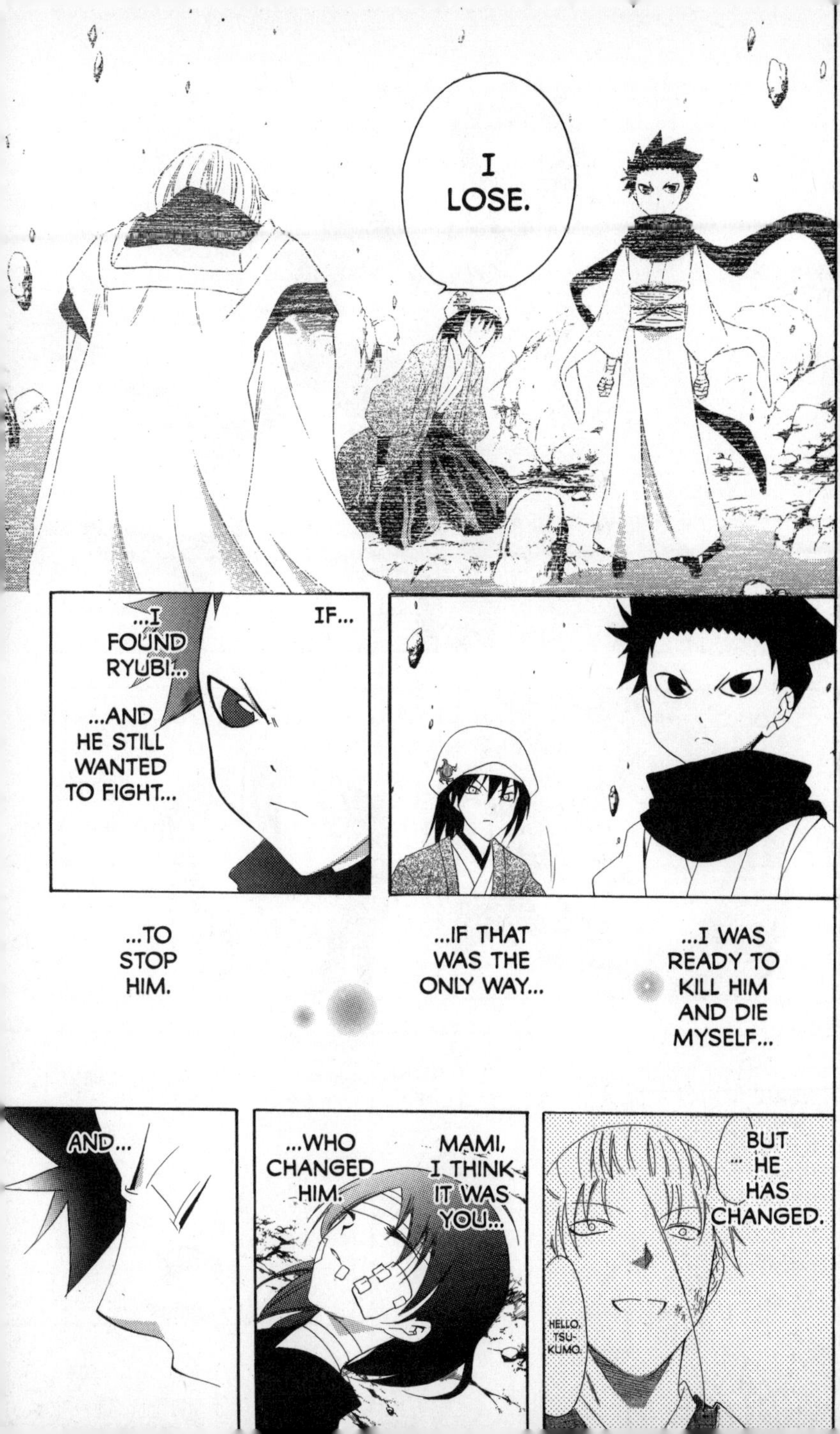
I LOSE.
IF...
...I FOUND RYUBI...
...AND HE STILL WANTED TO FIGHT...
...I WAS READY TO KILL HIM AND DIE MYSELF...
...IF THAT WAS THE ONLY WAY...
...TO STOP HIM.
BUT HE HAS CHANGED.
HELLO, TSU-KUMO.
MAMI, I THINK IT WAS YOU...
...WHO CHANGED HIM.
AND...

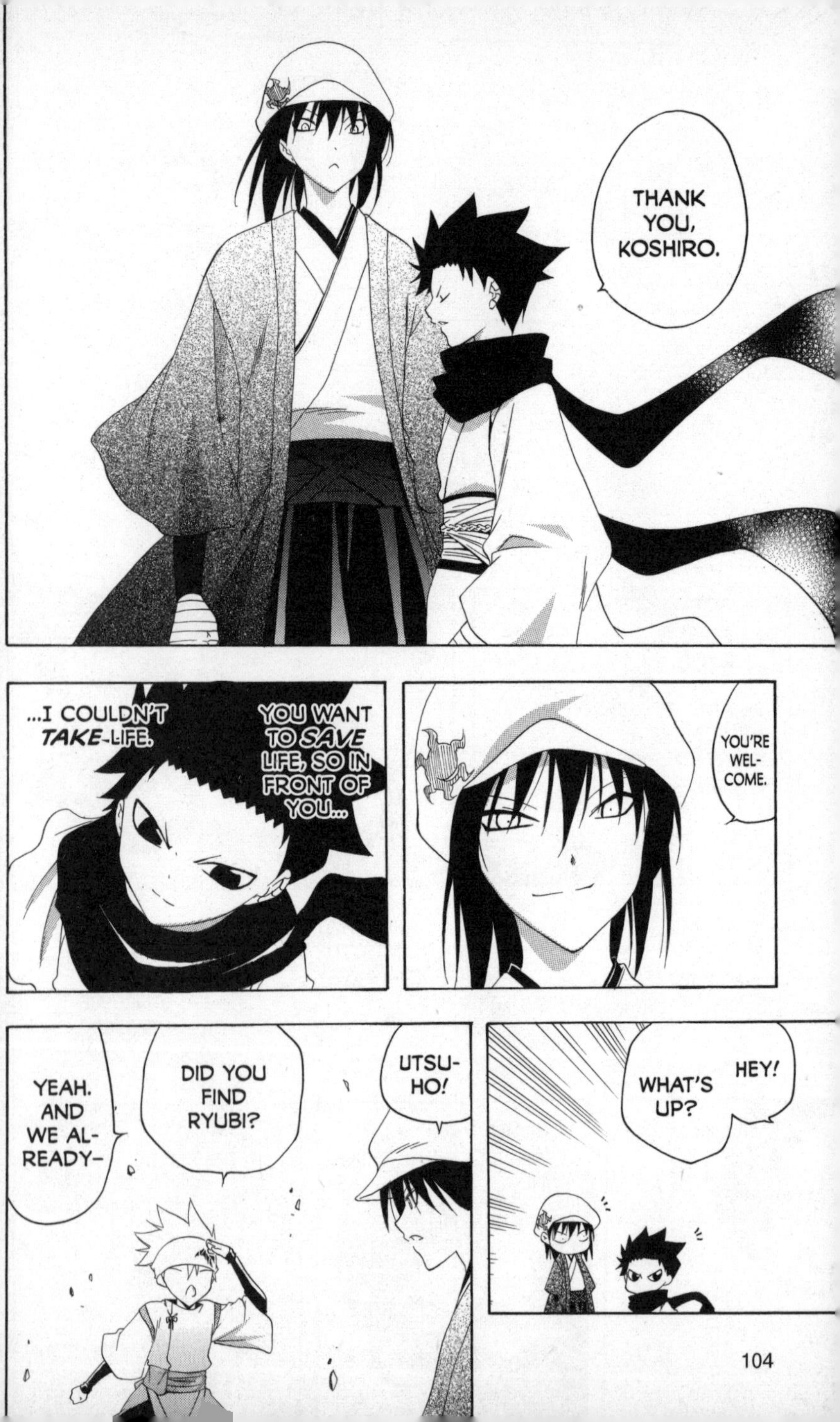
THANK YOU, KOSHIRO.
YOU'RE WEL-COME.
YOU WANT TO SAVE LIFE, SO IN FRONT OF YOU...
...I COULDN'T TAKE-LIFE.
HEY!
WHAT'S UP?
UTSU-HO!
DID YOU FIND RYUBI?
YEAH. AND WE AL-READY-

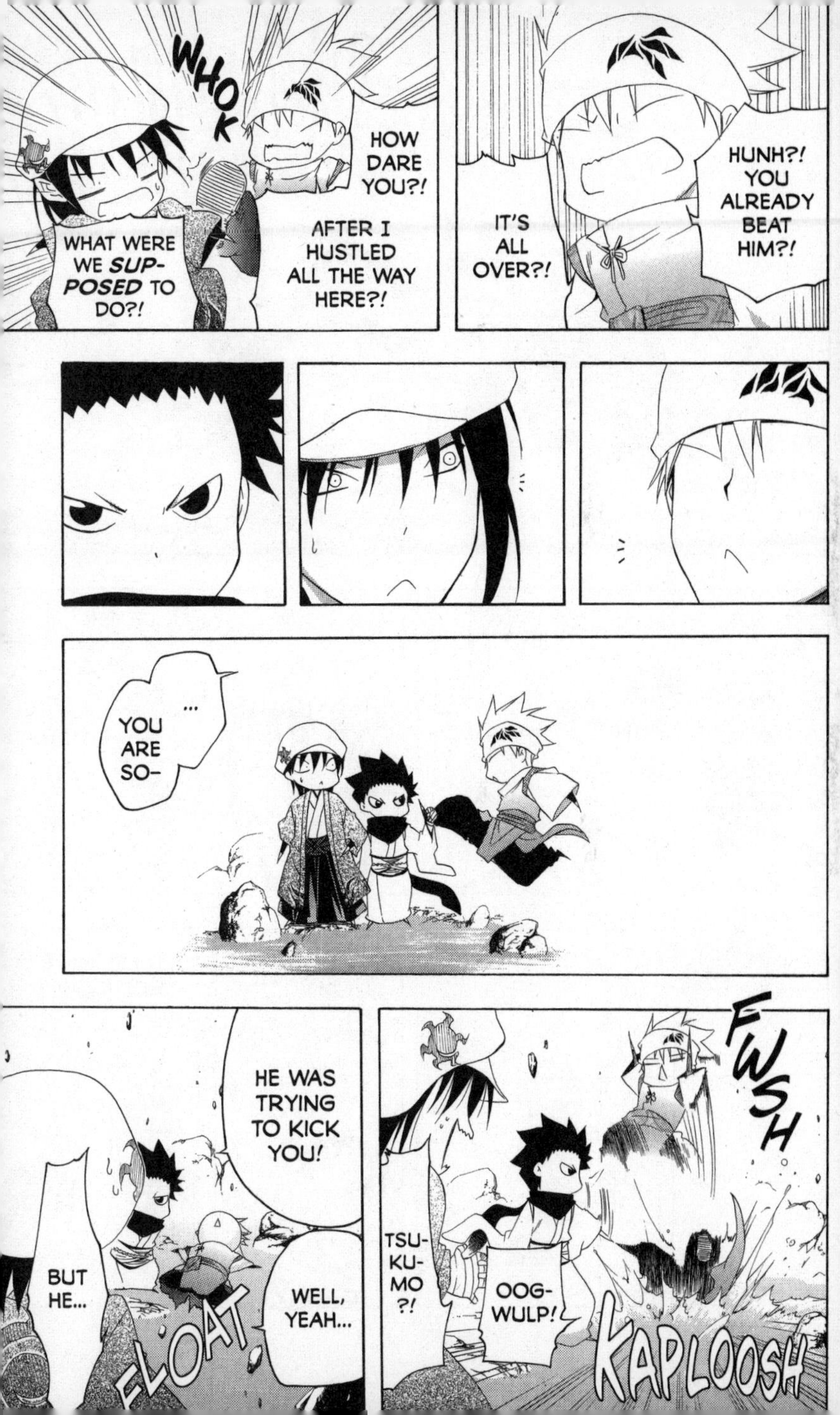
HUNH?! YOU ALREADY BEAT HIM?!
IT'S ALL OVER?!
WHOK
HOW DARE YOU?!
AFTER I HUSTLED ALL THE WAY HERE?!
WHAT WERE WE SUP-POSED TO DO?!
... YOU ARE SO–
FWSH
TSU-KU-MO?!
OOG-WULP!
KAPLOOSH
HE WAS TRYING TO KICK YOU!
WELL, YEAH...
BUT HE...
FLOAT

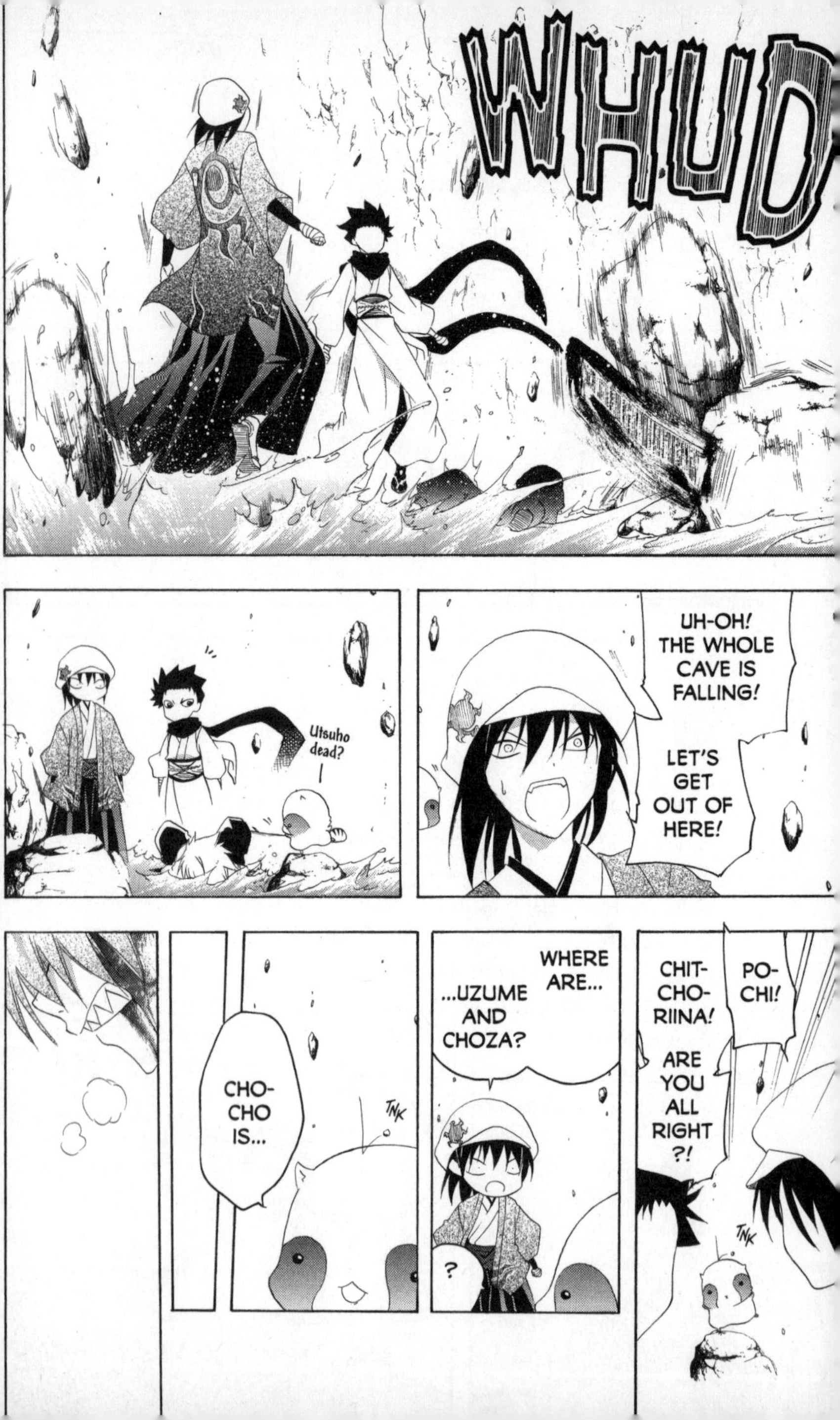
WHUD
UH-OH! THE WHOLE CAVE IS FALLING!
LET'S GET OUT OF HERE!
Utsuho dead?
PO-CHI!
CHIT-CHO-RIINA!
ARE YOU ALL RIGHT?!
TNK
WHERE ARE...
...UZUME AND CHOZA?
?
CHO-CHO IS...
TNK

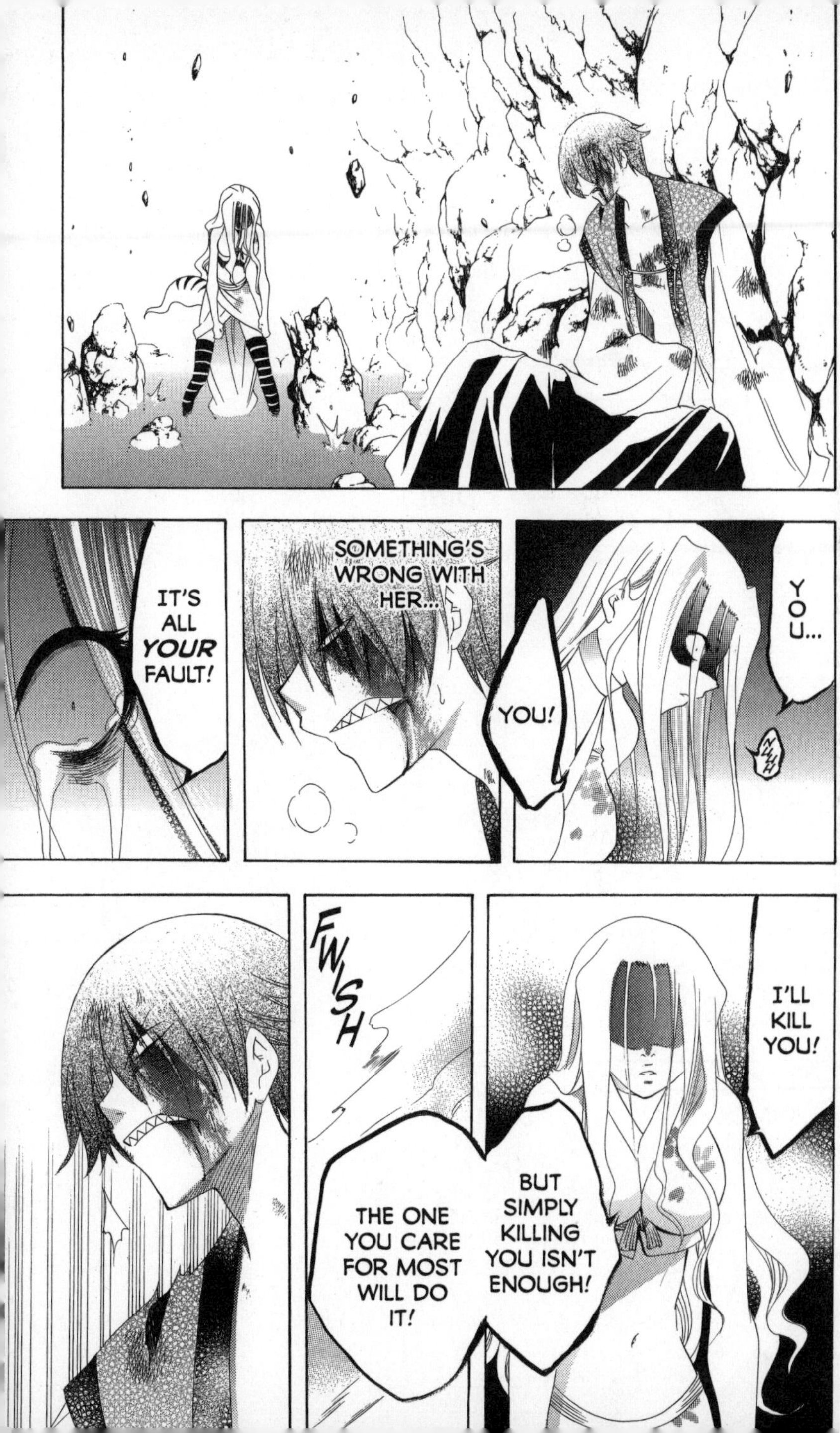

YOU...
YOU!
SOMETHING'S WRONG WITH HER...
IT'S ALL *YOUR* FAULT!
I'LL KILL YOU!
BUT SIMPLY KILLING YOU ISN'T ENOUGH!
THE ONE YOU CARE FOR MOST WILL DO IT!
FWISH

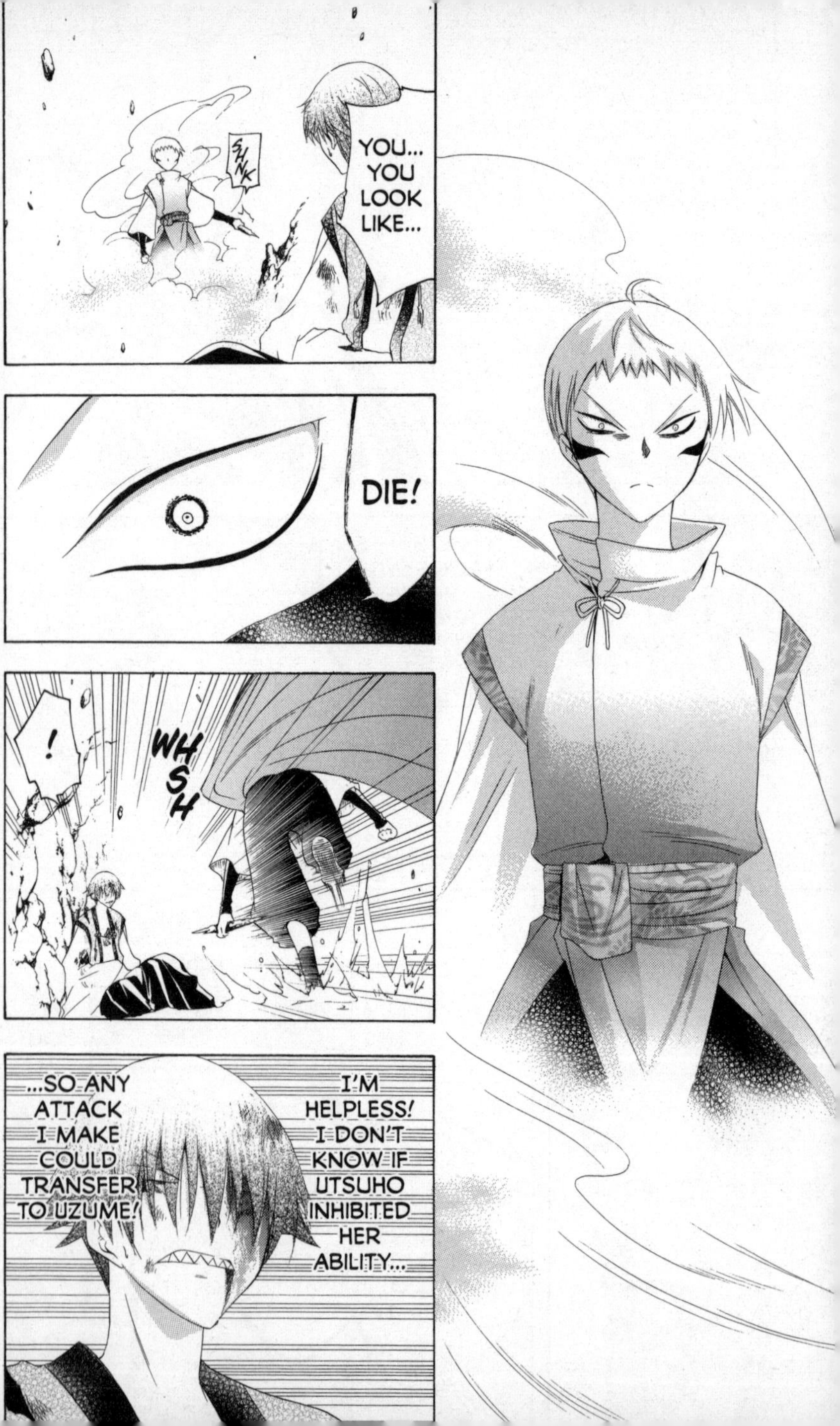
YOU... YOU LOOK LIKE...
SHNK
DIE!
WHSH
!
I'M HELPLESS! I DON'T KNOW IF UTSUHO INHIBITED HER ABILITY...
...SO ANY ATTACK I MAKE COULD TRANSFER TO UZUME!

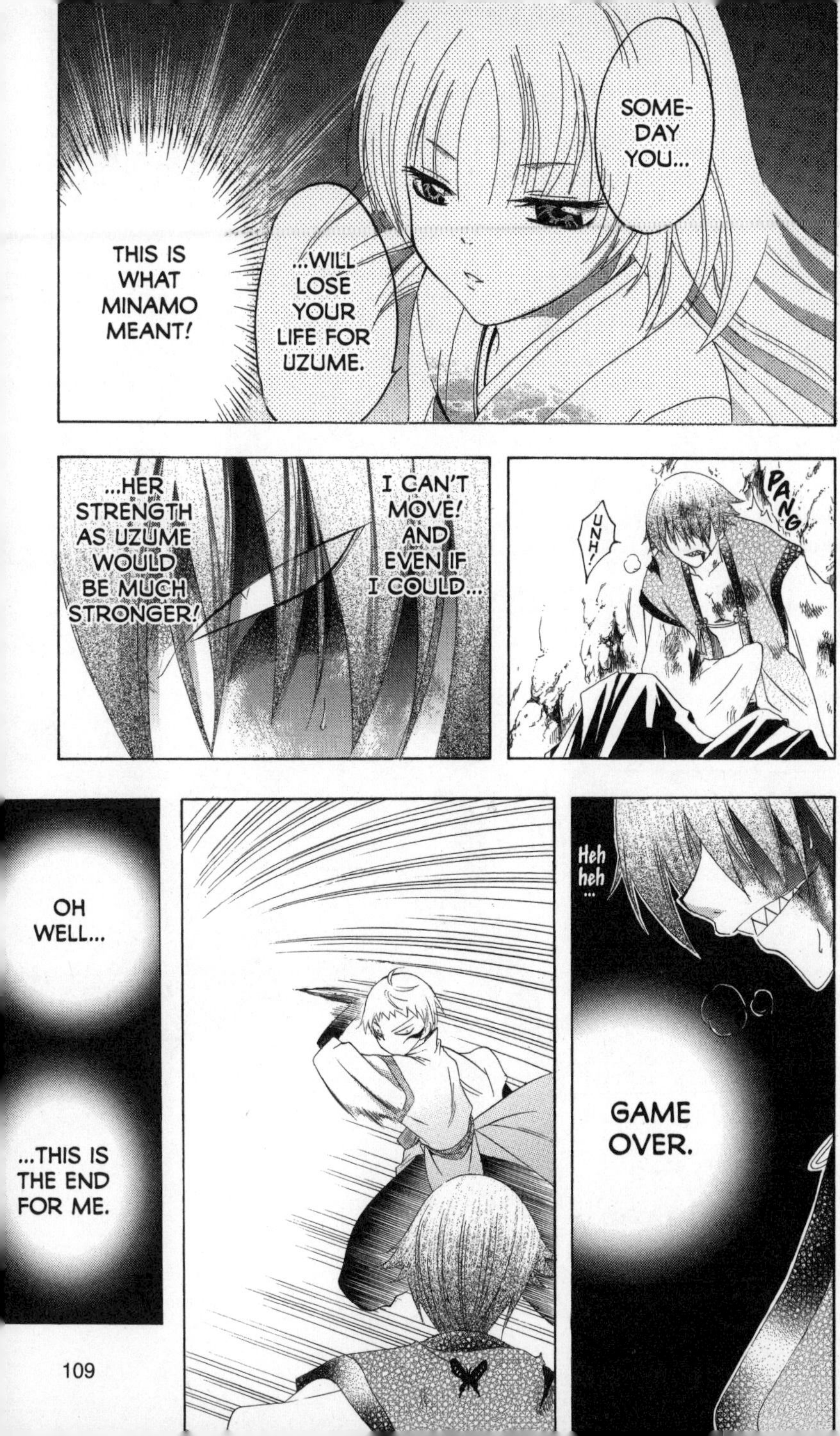

SOME-DAY YOU...
...WILL LOSE YOUR LIFE FOR UZUME.
THIS IS WHAT MINAMO MEANT!
PANG
UNH!
I CAN'T MOVE! AND EVEN IF I COULD...
...HER STRENGTH AS UZUME WOULD BE MUCH STRONGER!
Heh heh...
GAME OVER.
OH WELL...
...THIS IS THE END FOR ME.

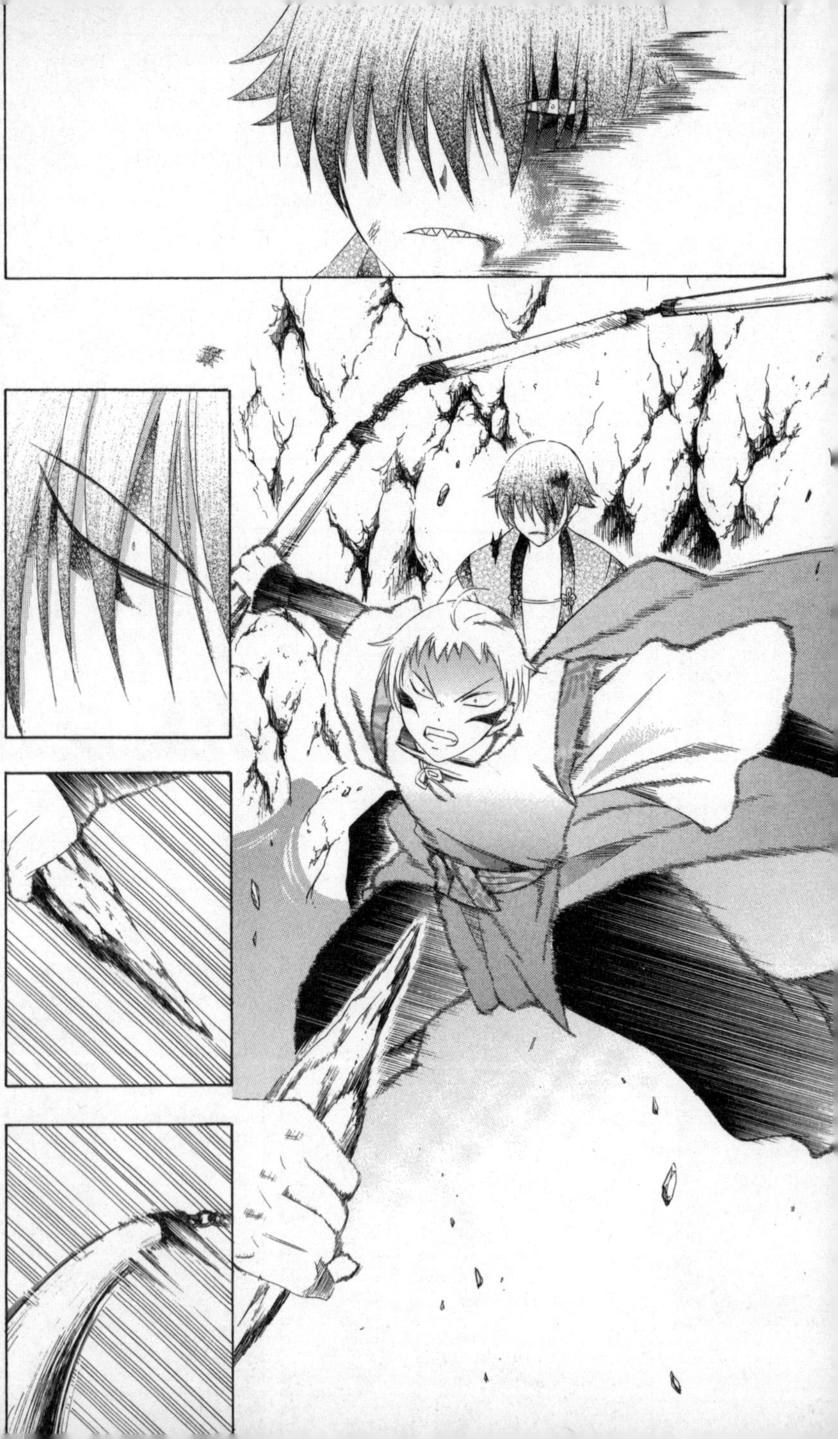

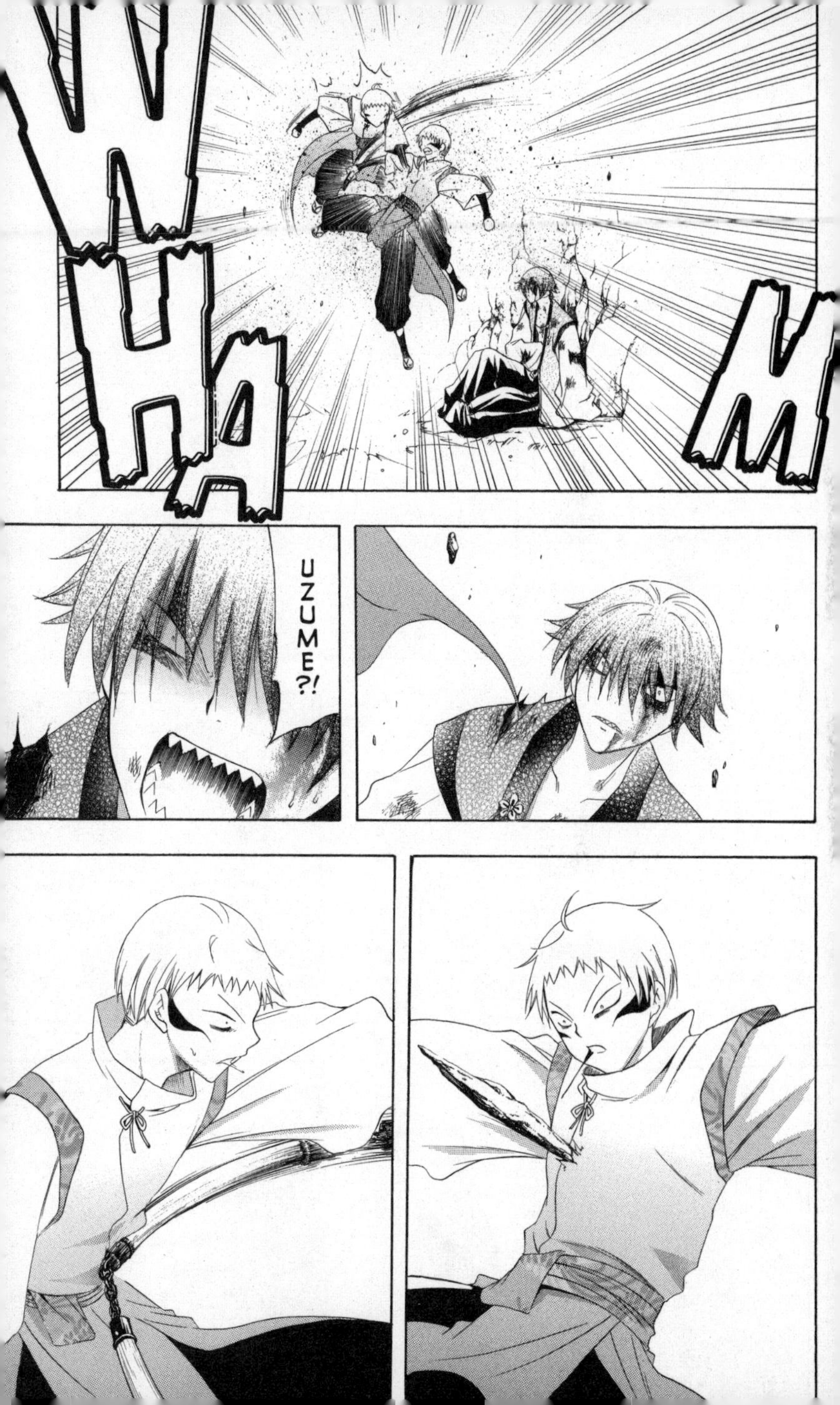
WHAM
UZUME?!

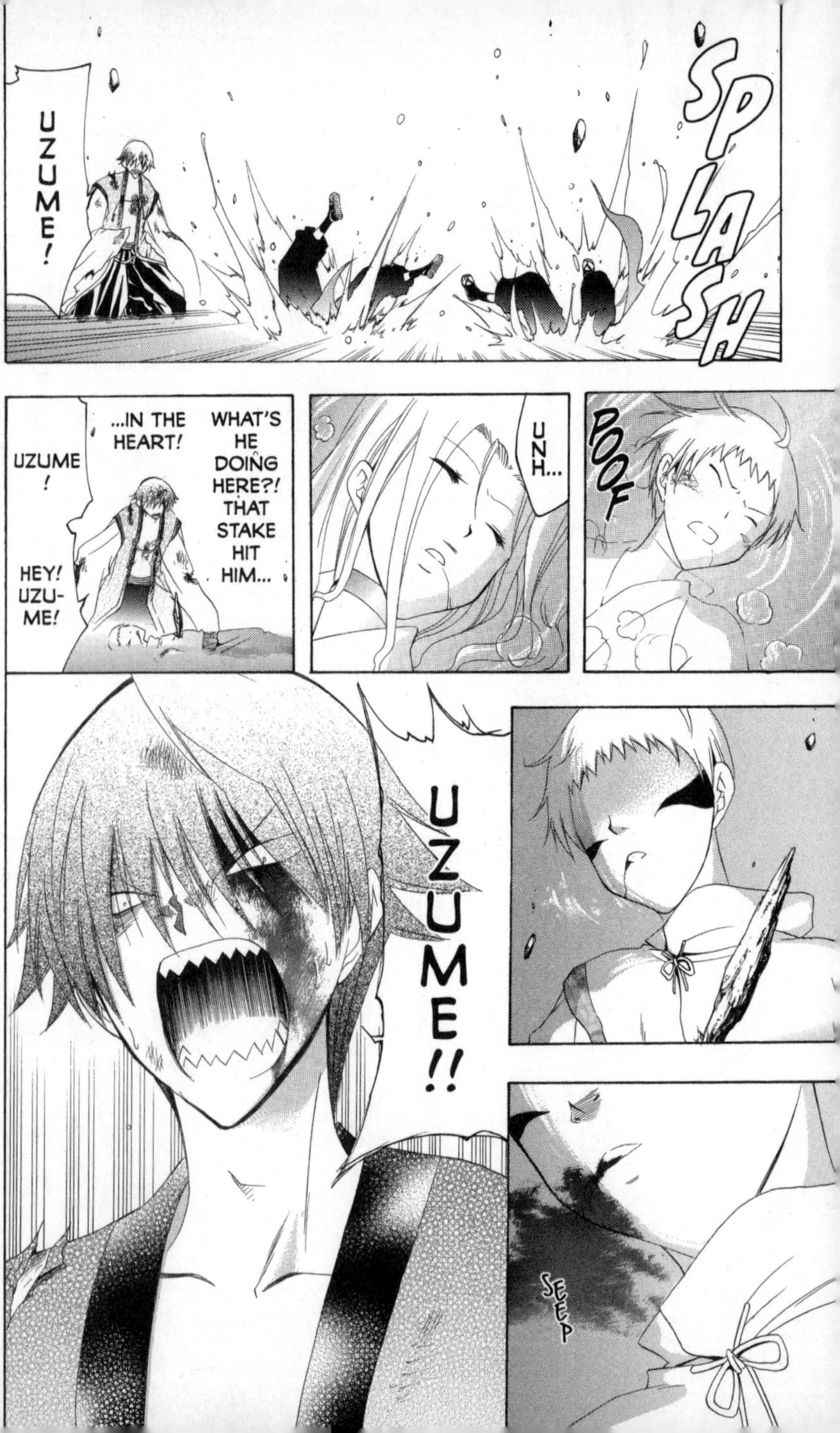
SPLASH
UZUME!
POOF
UNH...
WHAT'S HE DOING HERE?! THAT STAKE HIT HIM...
...IN THE HEART!
UZUME!
HEY! UZUME!
SEEP
UZUME!!

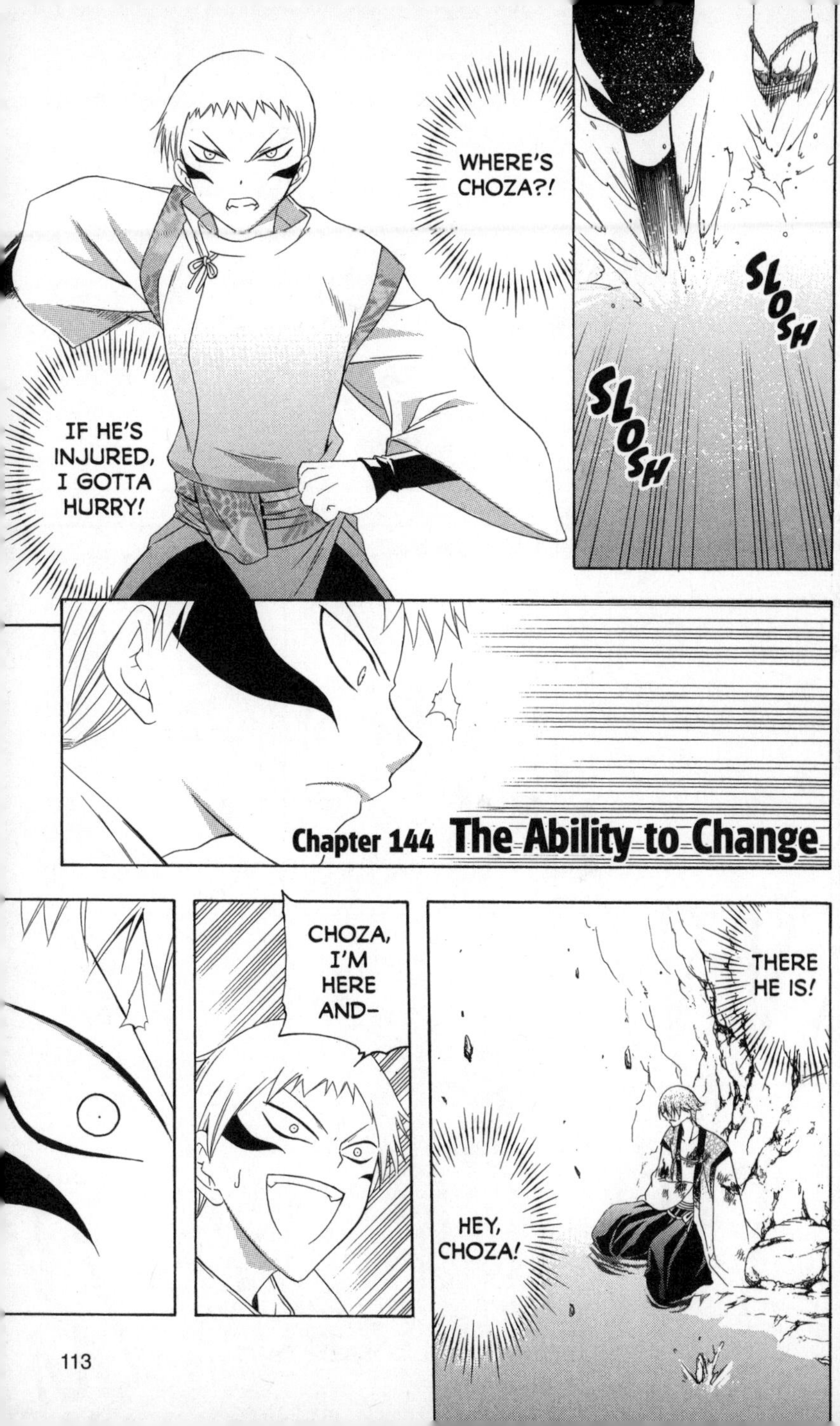
SLOSH
SLOSH
WHERE'S CHOZA?!
IF HE'S INJURED, I GOTTA HURRY!
Chapter 144 The Ability to Change
THERE HE IS!
HEY, CHOZA!
CHOZA, I'M HERE AND-

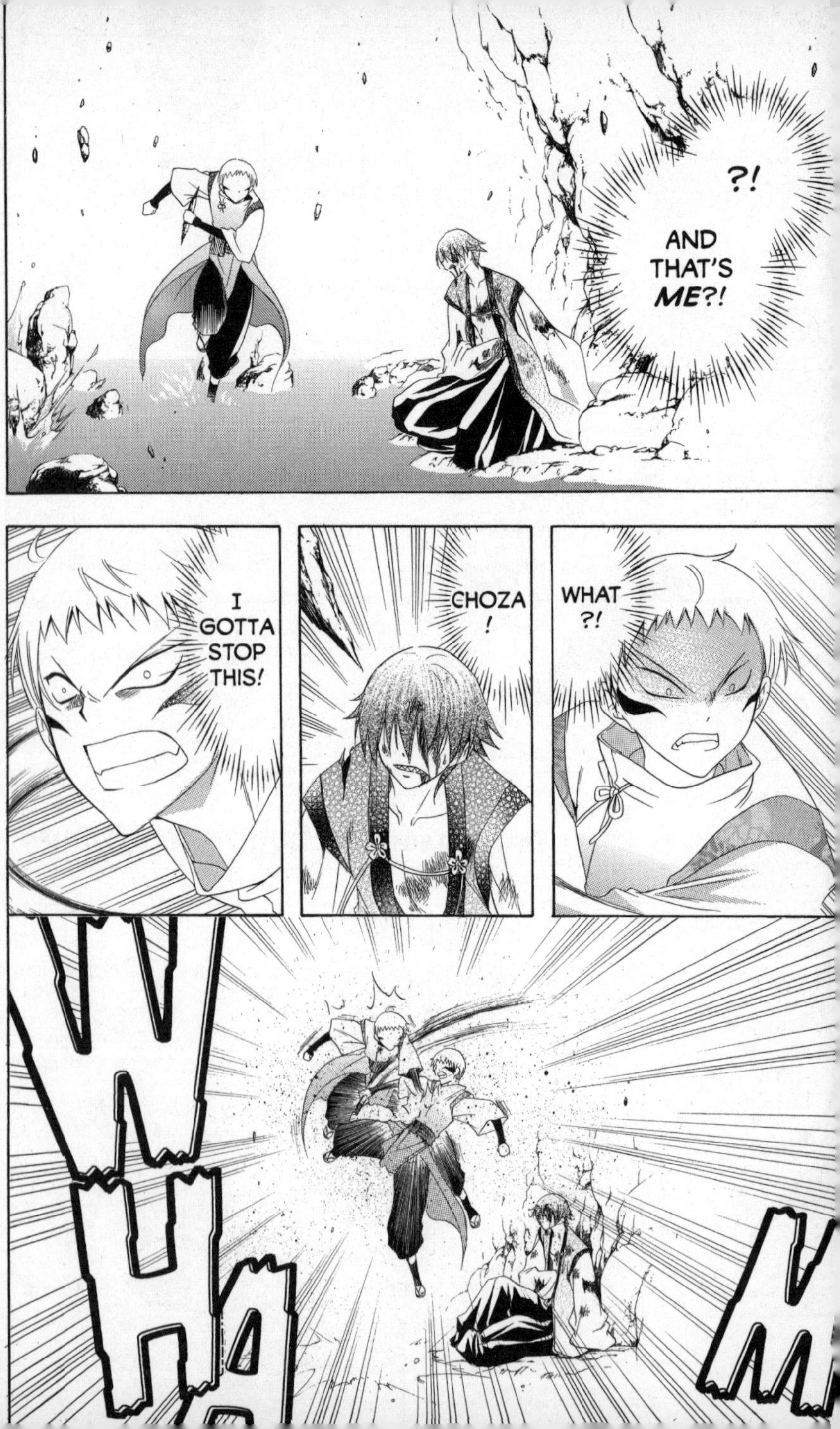
?!
AND THAT'S *ME*?!
WHAT ?!
CHOZA !
I GOTTA STOP THIS!
WHAM

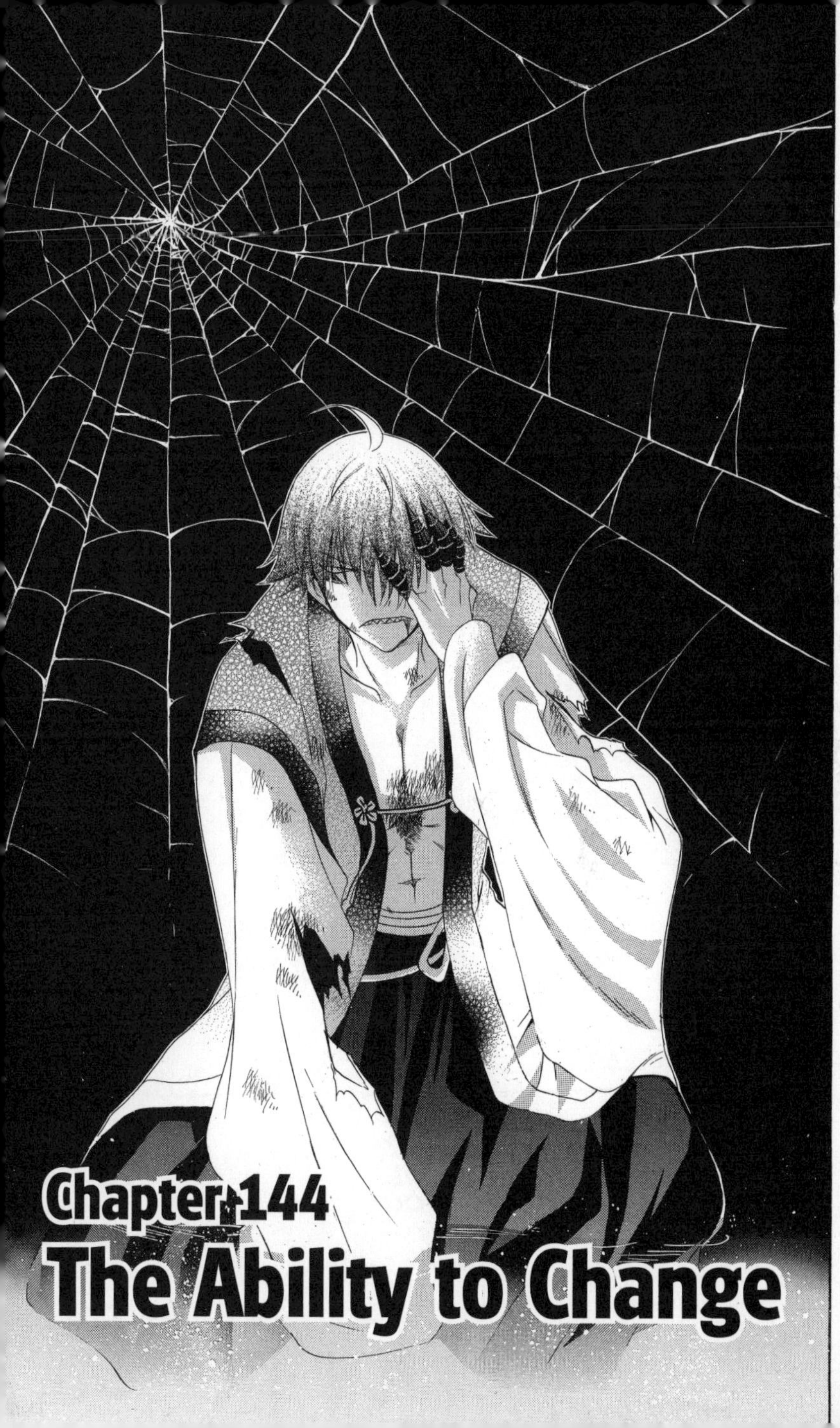
Chapter 144
The Ability to Change

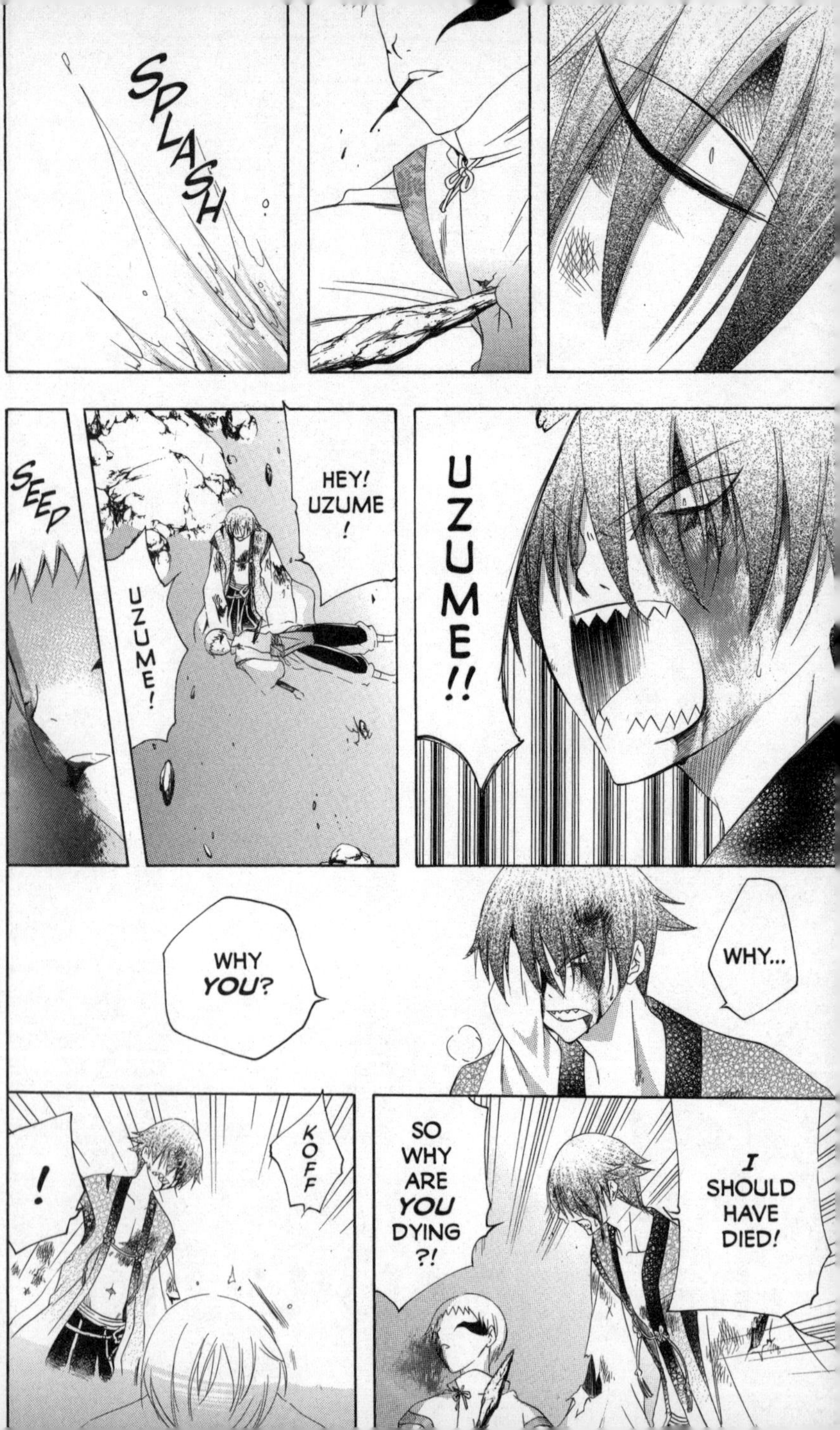

SPLASH
UZUME!!
HEY! UZUME!
UZUME!
SEEP
WHY...
WHY *YOU*?
I SHOULD HAVE DIED!
SO WHY ARE *YOU* DYING?!
KOFF
!

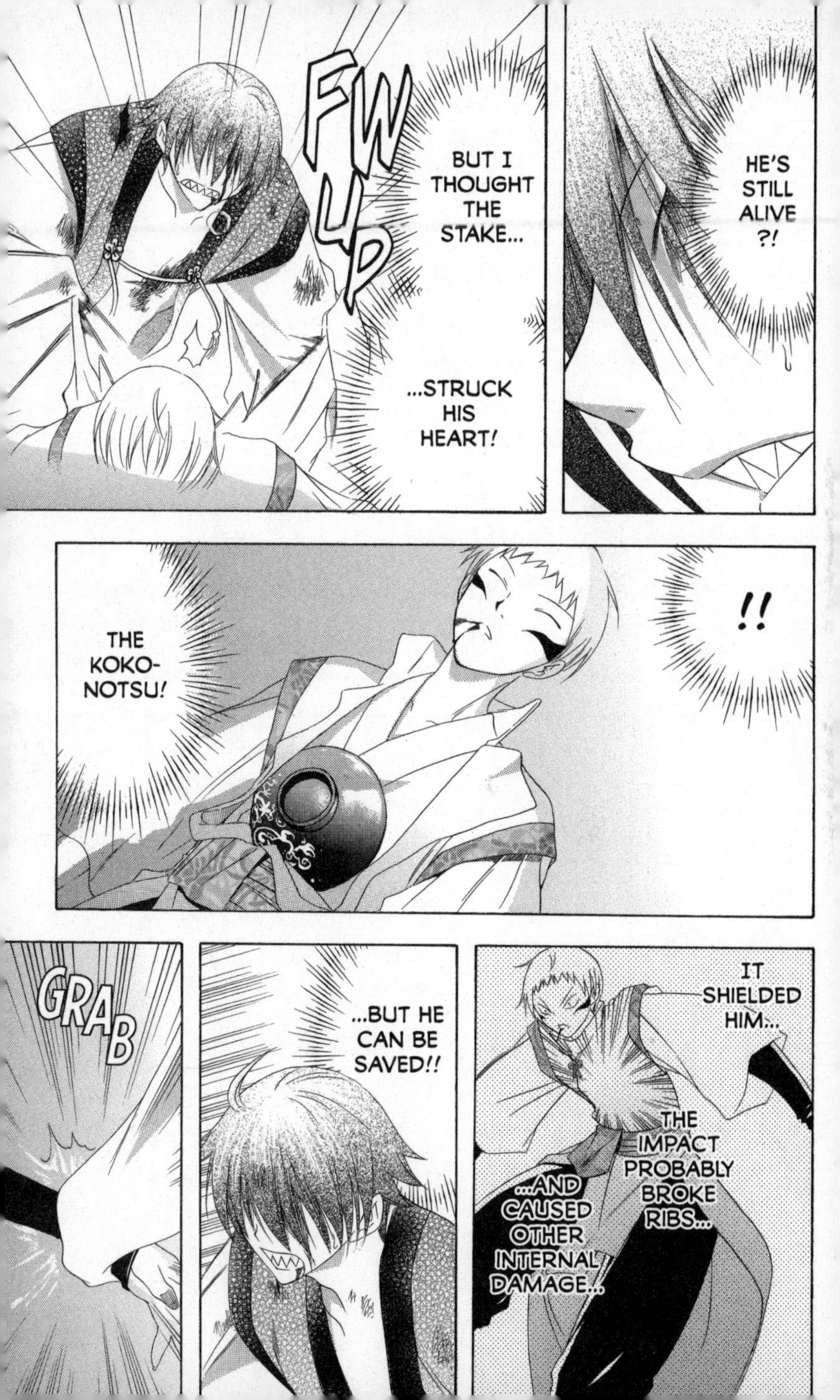
HE'S STILL ALIVE?!
FWUP
BUT I THOUGHT THE STAKE...
...STRUCK HIS HEART!
!!
THE KOKO-NOTSU!
IT SHIELDED HIM...
THE IMPACT PROBABLY BROKE RIBS...
...AND CAUSED OTHER INTERNAL DAMAGE...
...BUT HE CAN BE SAVED!!
GRAB

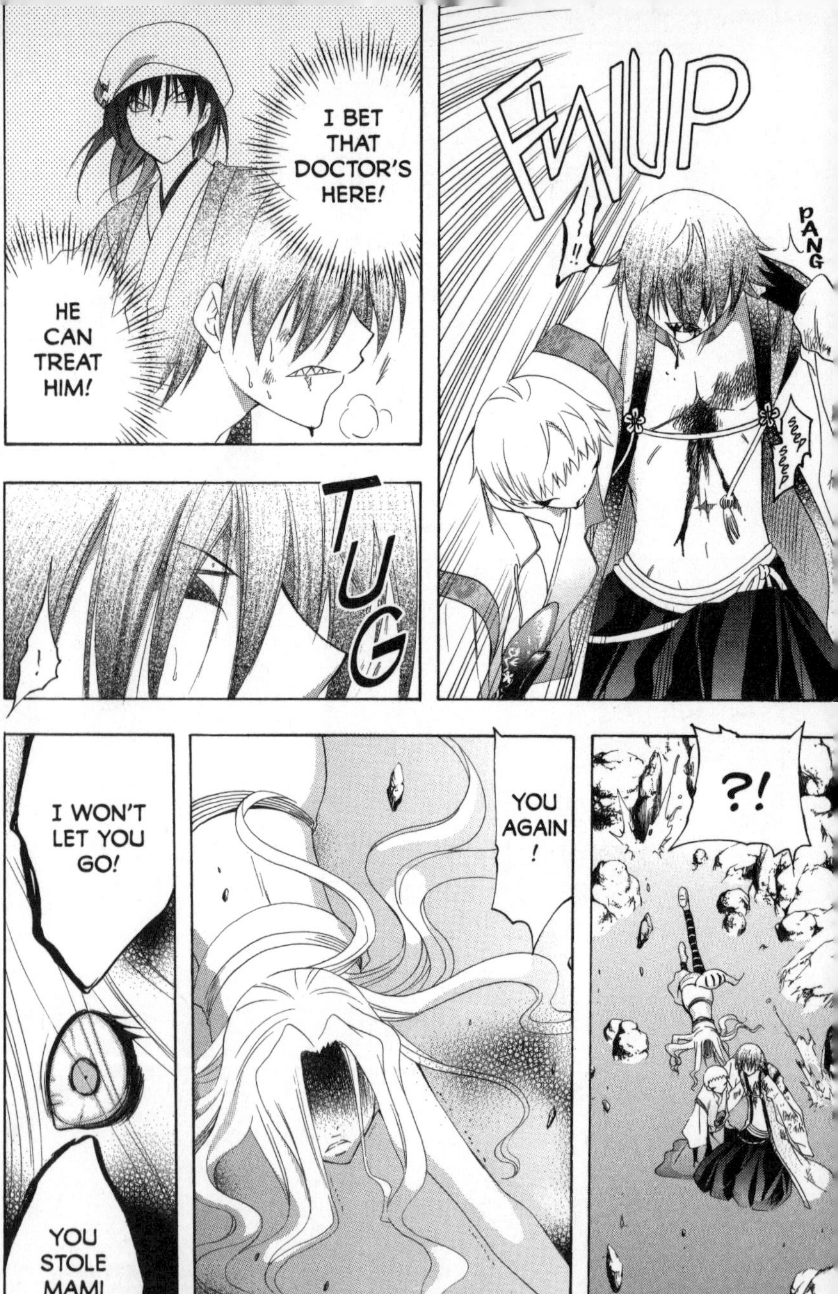

FWUP
!!
PANG
SEEP SEEP
I BET THAT DOCTOR'S HERE!
HE CAN TREAT HIM!
TUG
!
?!
YOU AGAIN!
I WON'T LET YOU GO!
YOU STOLE MAMI FROM ME!

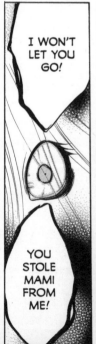

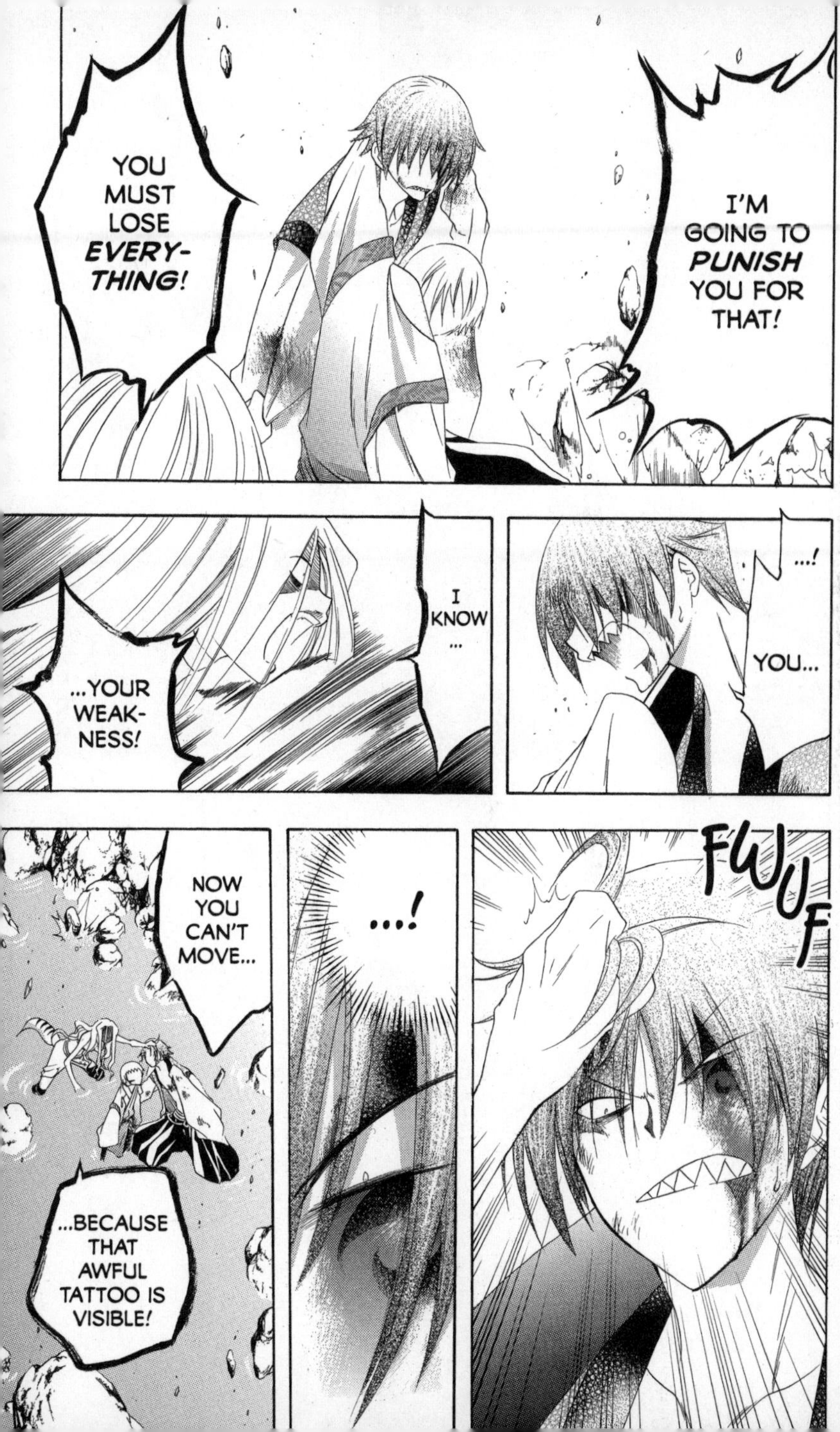
I'M GOING TO *PUNISH* YOU FOR THAT!
YOU MUST LOSE *EVERY-THING!*
...!
YOU...
I KNOW...
...YOUR WEAK-NESS!
FWUF
...!
NOW YOU CAN'T MOVE...
...BECAUSE THAT AWFUL TATTOO IS VISIBLE!

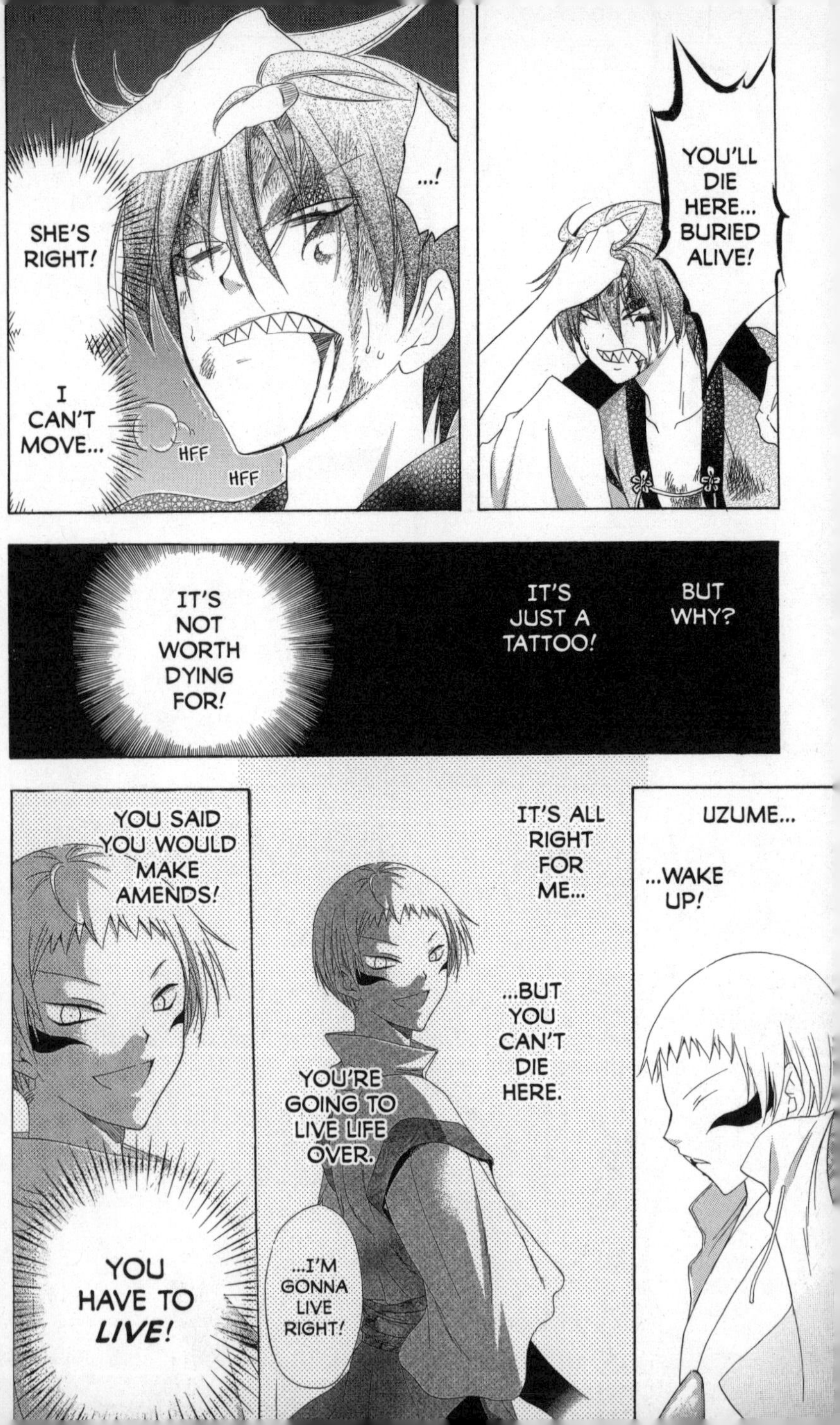
YOU'LL DIE HERE... BURIED ALIVE!
...!
SHE'S RIGHT!
I CAN'T MOVE...
HFF
HFF
BUT WHY?
IT'S JUST A TATTOO!
IT'S NOT WORTH DYING FOR!
UZUME...
...WAKE UP!
IT'S ALL RIGHT FOR ME...
...BUT YOU CAN'T DIE HERE.
YOU'RE GOING TO LIVE LIFE OVER.
...I'M GONNA LIVE RIGHT!
YOU SAID YOU WOULD MAKE AMENDS!
YOU HAVE TO *LIVE*!

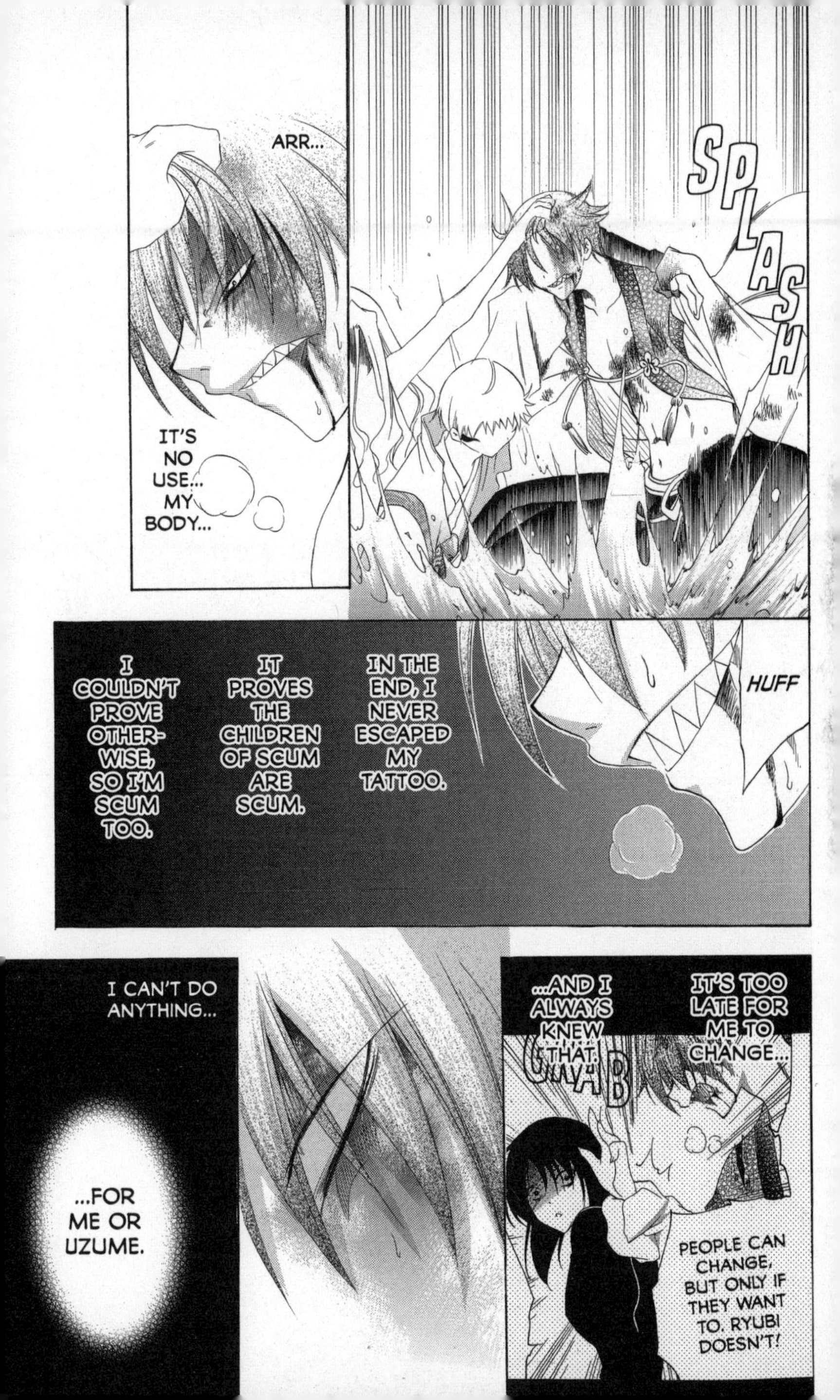
SPLASH
ARR...
IT'S NO USE... MY BODY...
HUFF
IN THE END, I NEVER ESCAPED MY TATTOO.
IT PROVES THE CHILDREN OF SCUM ARE SCUM.
I COULDN'T PROVE OTHER-WISE, SO I'M SCUM TOO.
IT'S TOO LATE FOR ME TO CHANGE...
...AND I ALWAYS KNEW THAT.
GRAB
PEOPLE CAN CHANGE, BUT ONLY IF THEY WANT TO. RYUBI DOESN'T!
I CAN'T DO ANYTHING...
...FOR ME OR UZUME.

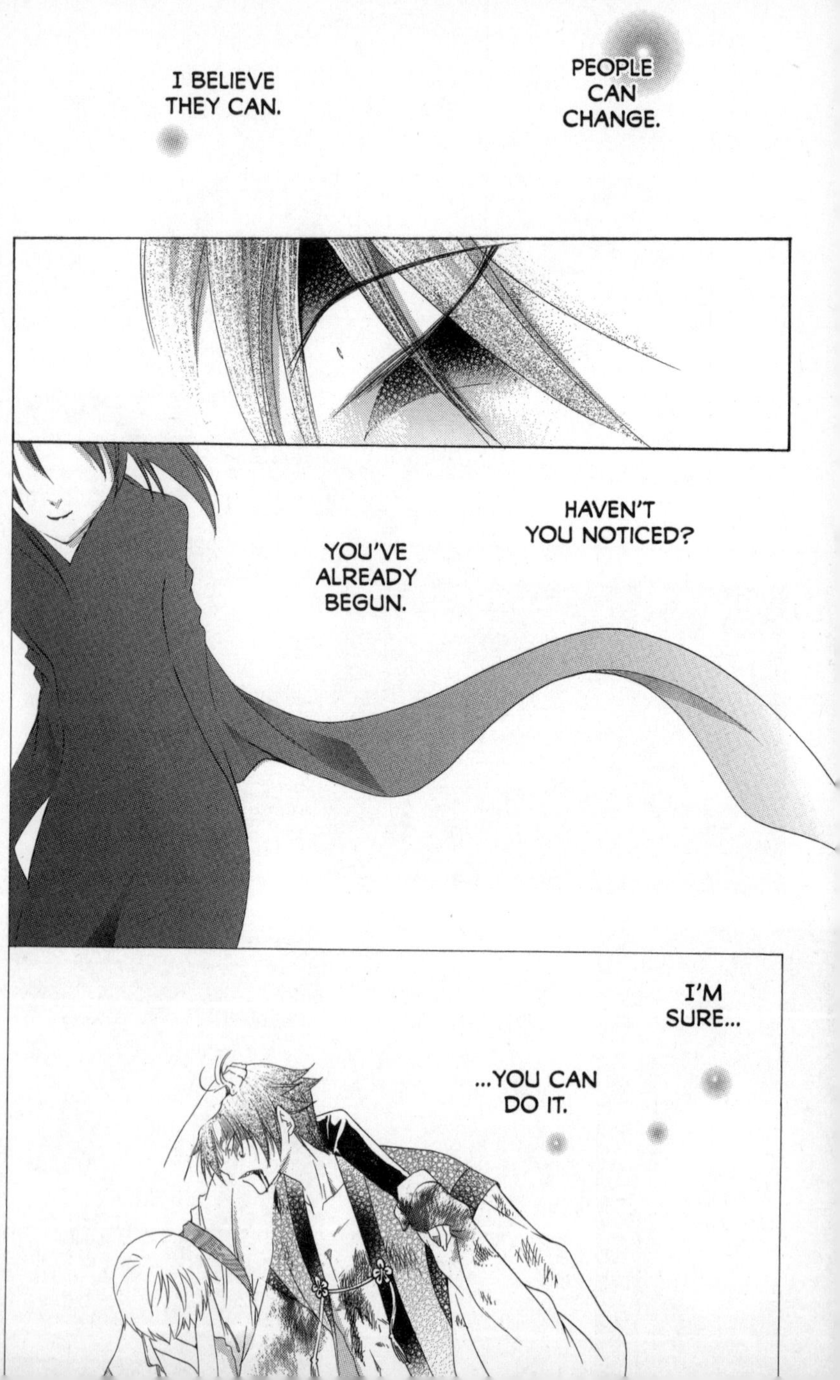
PEOPLE CAN CHANGE.
I BELIEVE THEY CAN.
HAVEN'T YOU NOTICED?
YOU'VE ALREADY BEGUN.
I'M SURE...
...YOU CAN DO IT.

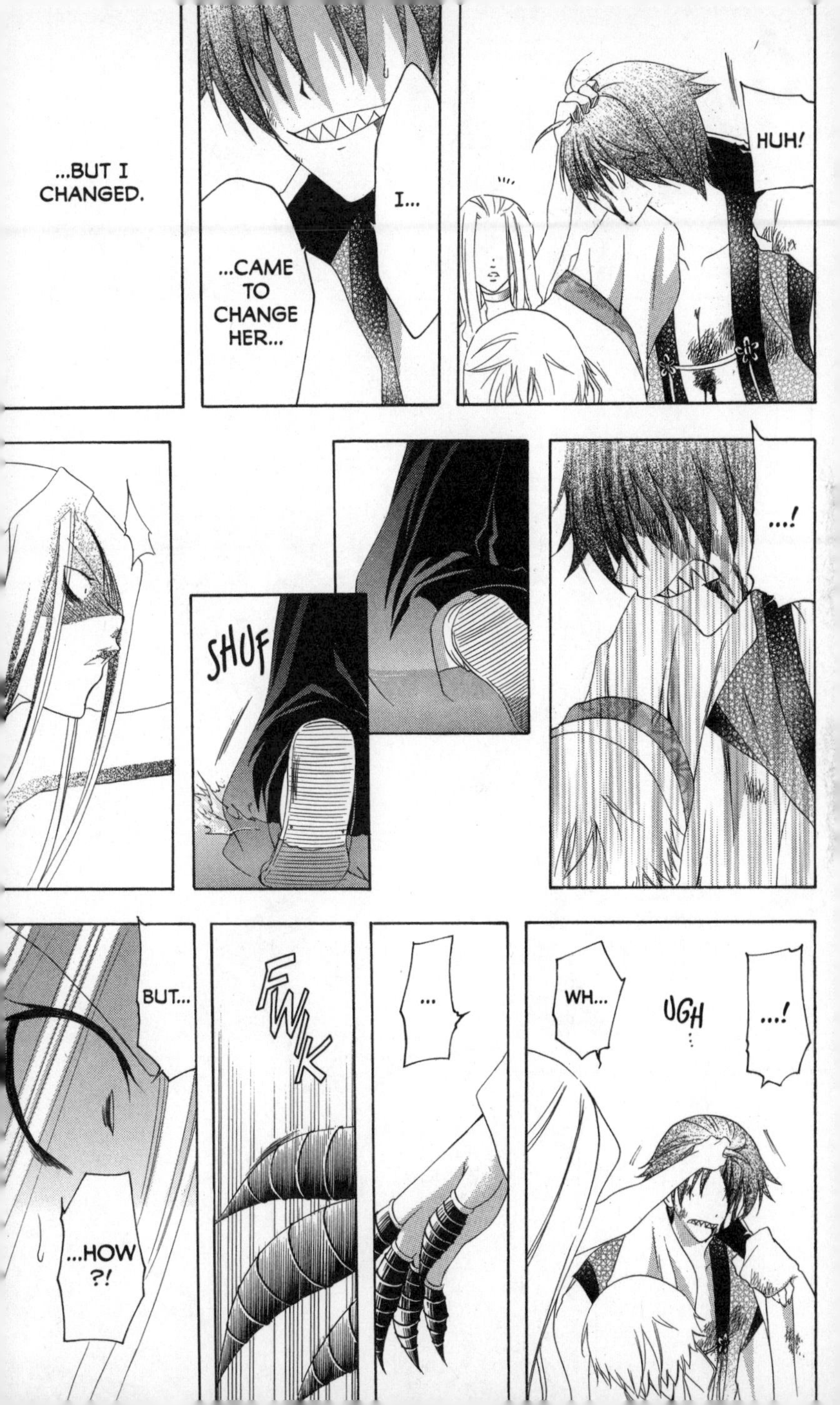
HUH!
I...
...CAME TO CHANGE HER...
...BUT I CHANGED.
...!
SHUF
...!
UGH
WH...
...
FWIK
BUT...
...HOW ?!

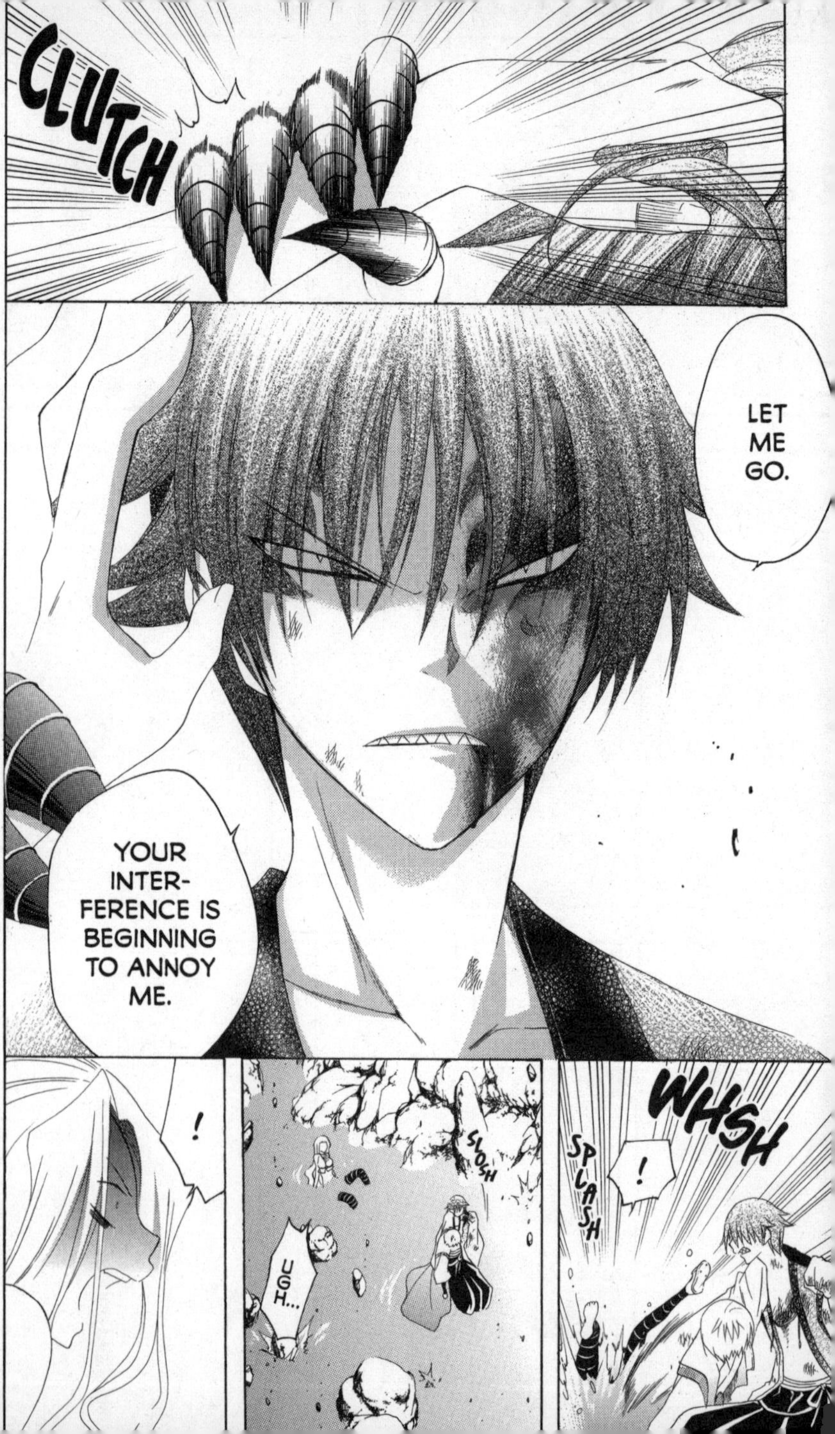
CLUTCH
LET ME GO.
YOUR INTERFERENCE IS BEGINNING TO ANNOY ME.
WHSH
SPLASH
!
SLOSH
UGH...
!

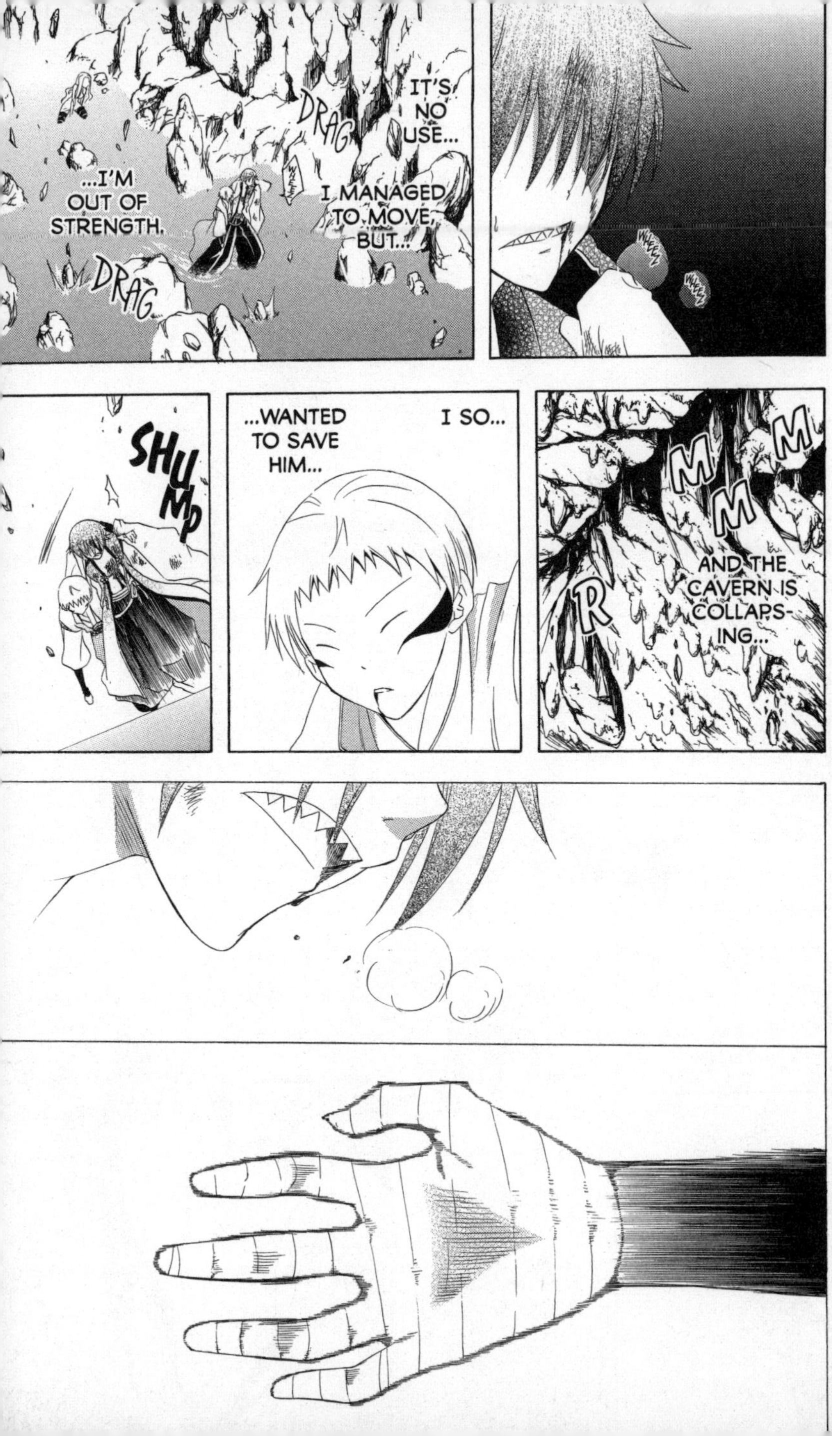
IT'S NO USE...
DRAG
I MANAGED TO MOVE, BUT...
...I'M OUT OF STRENGTH.
DRAG
RMMMM
AND THE CAVERN IS COLLAPS-ING...
I SO...
...WANTED TO SAVE HIM...
SHUMP

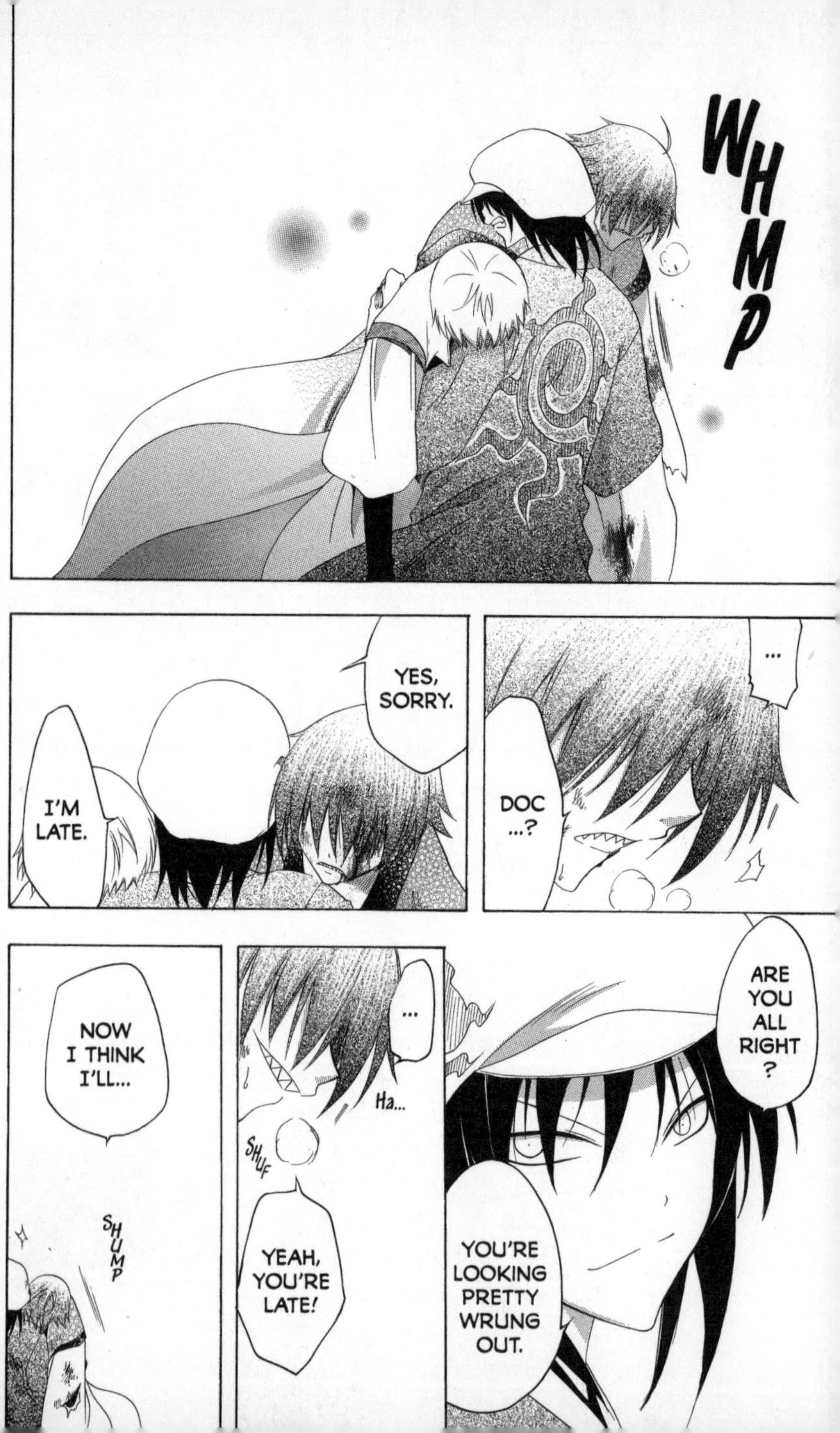
WHMP
...
DOC ...?
YES, SORRY.
I'M LATE.
ARE YOU ALL RIGHT?
YOU'RE LOOKING PRETTY WRUNG OUT.
...
Ha...
SHUF
YEAH, YOU'RE LATE!
NOW I THINK I'LL...
SHUMP

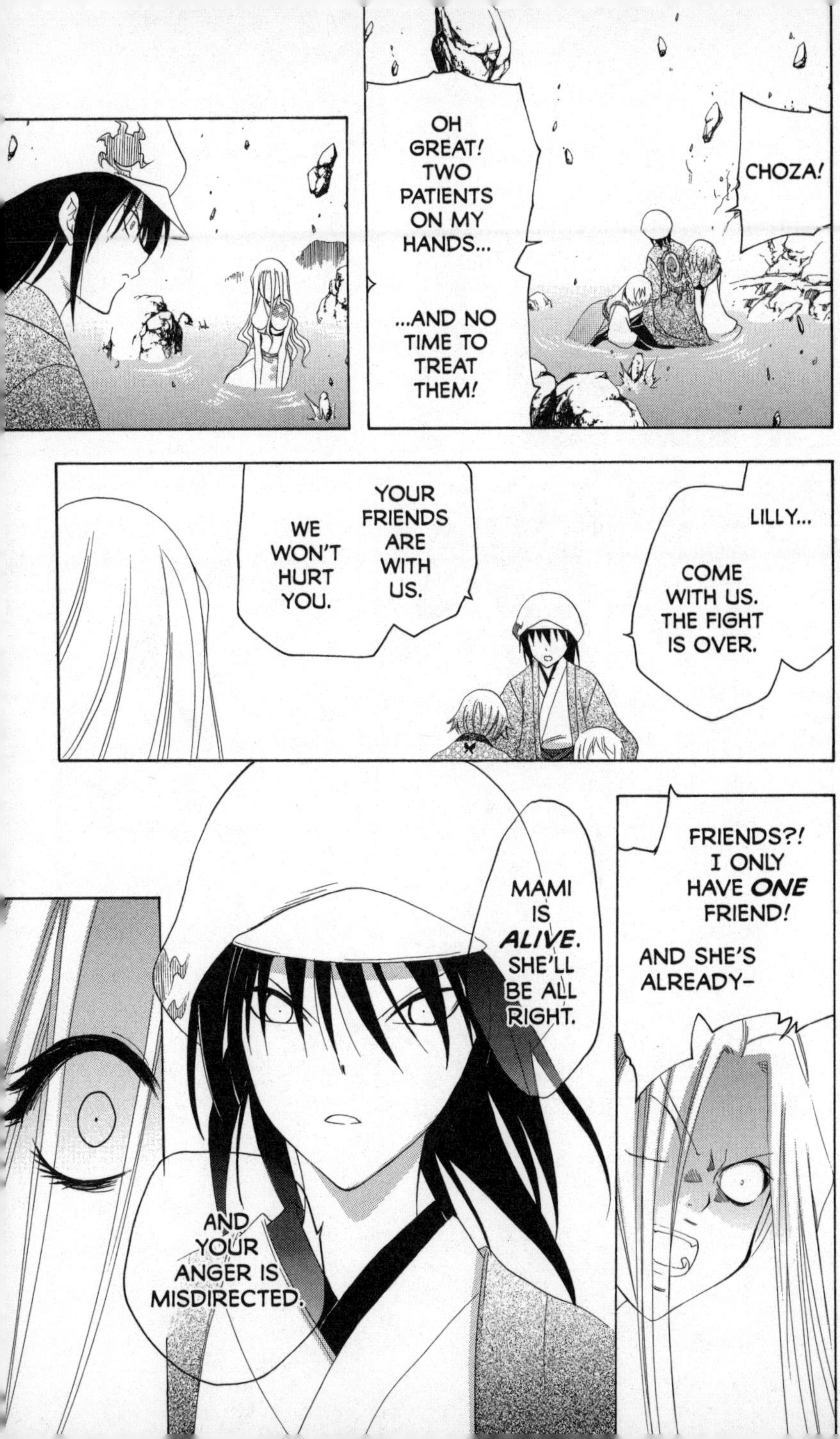
CHOZA!
OH GREAT! TWO PATIENTS ON MY HANDS...
...AND NO TIME TO TREAT THEM!
LILLY...
COME WITH US. THE FIGHT IS OVER.
YOUR FRIENDS ARE WITH US.
WE WON'T HURT YOU.
FRIENDS?! I ONLY HAVE *ONE* FRIEND!
AND SHE'S ALREADY–
MAMI IS *ALIVE*. SHE'LL BE ALL RIGHT.
AND YOUR ANGER IS MISDIRECTED.

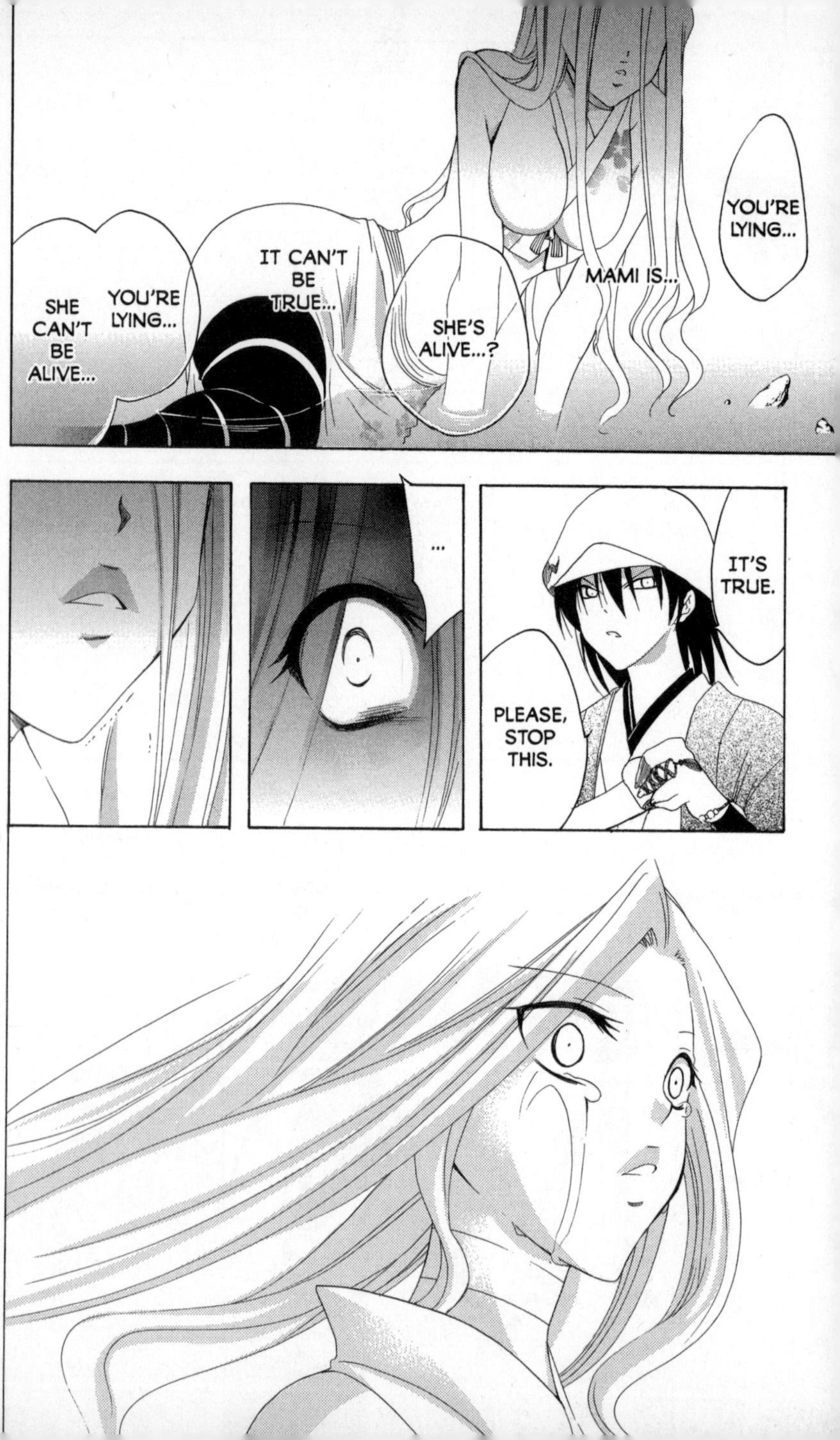
YOU'RE LYING...
MAMI IS...
SHE'S ALIVE...?
IT CAN'T BE TRUE...
YOU'RE LYING...
SHE CAN'T BE ALIVE...
IT'S TRUE.
PLEASE, STOP THIS.
...

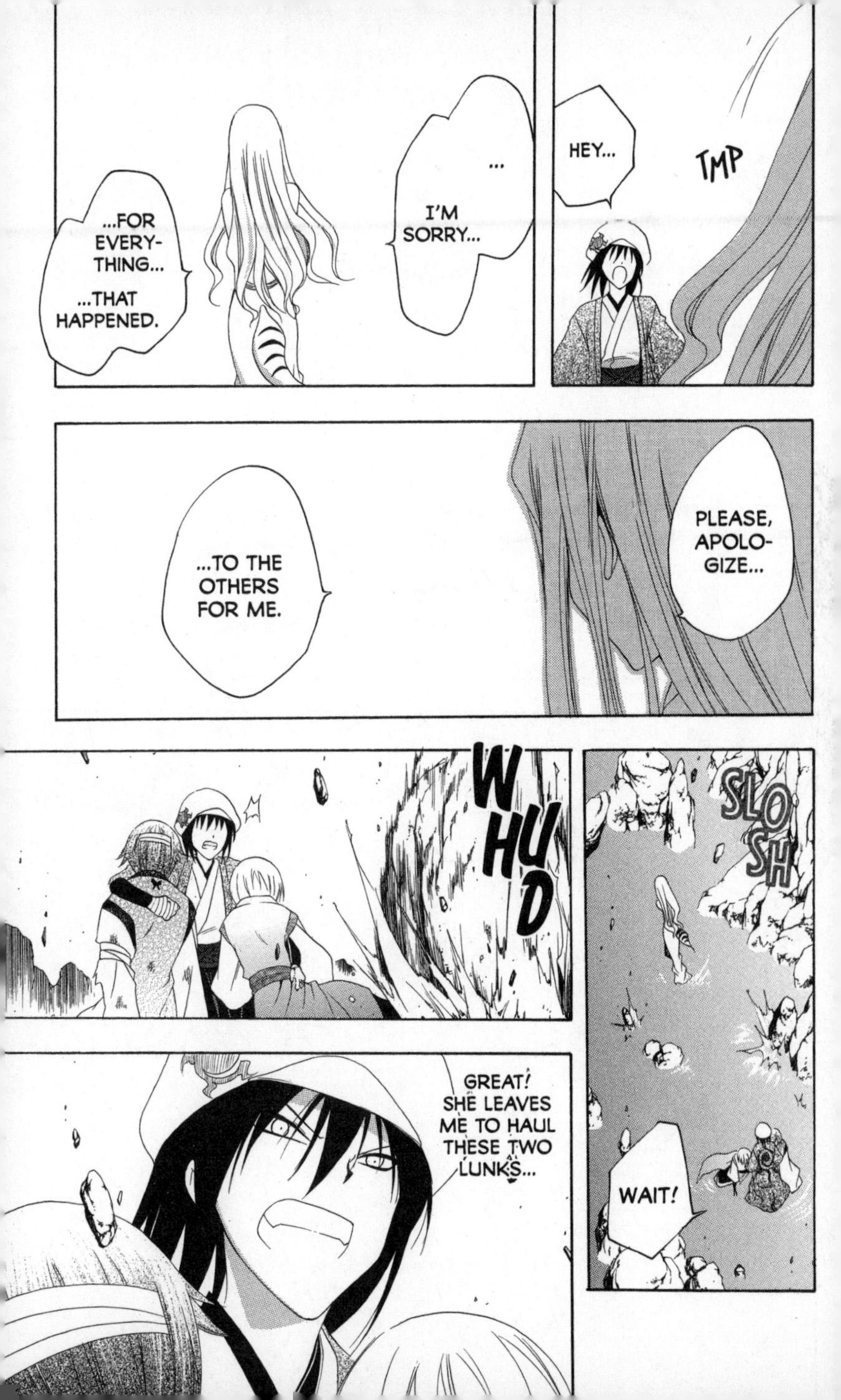
HEY...
TMP
... I'M SORRY...
...FOR EVERY-THING... ...THAT HAPPENED.
PLEASE, APOLO-GIZE...
...TO THE OTHERS FOR ME.
SLOSH
WAIT!
WHUD
GREAT! SHE LEAVES ME TO HAUL THESE TWO LUNKS...

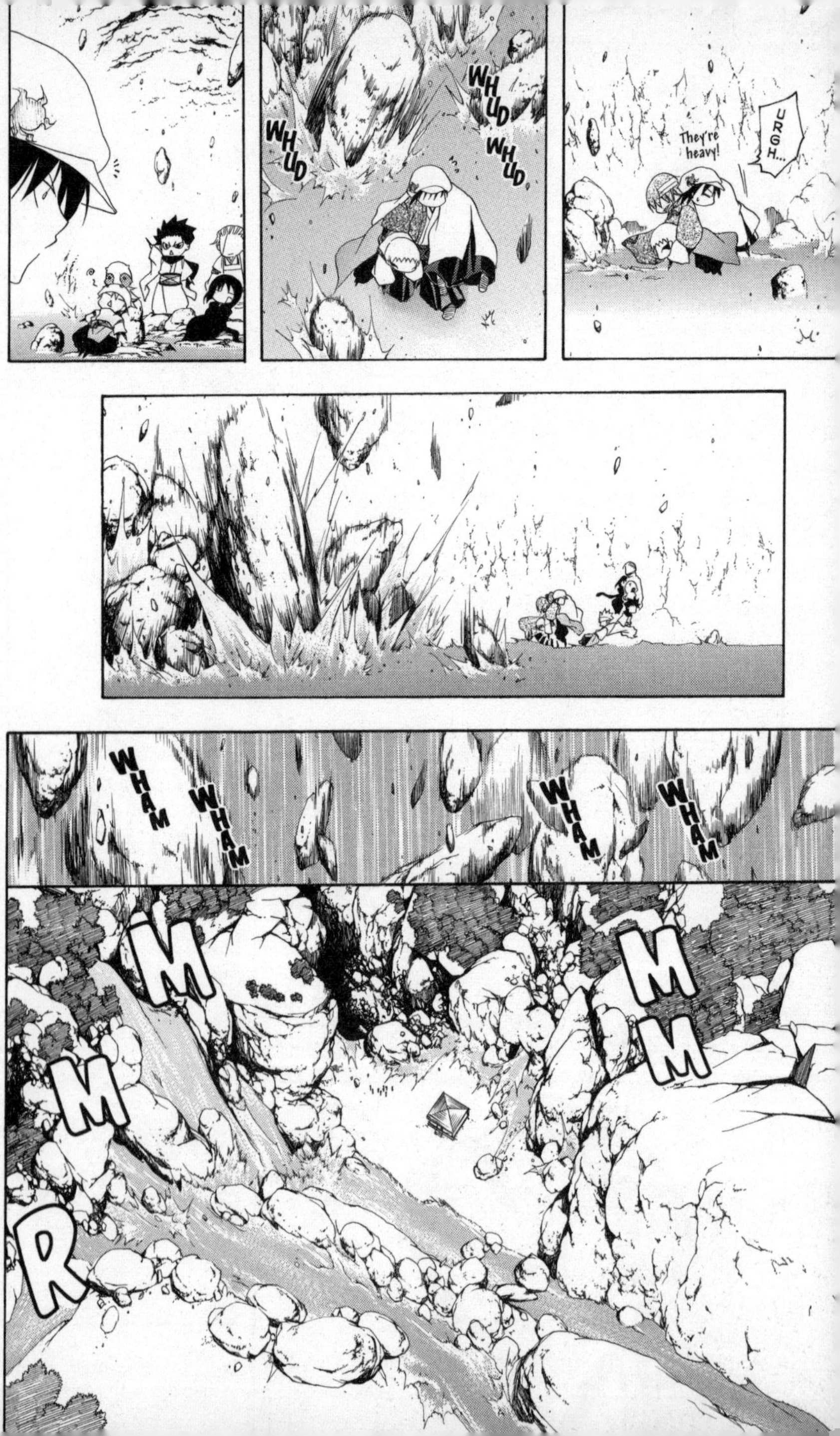
URGH...
They're heavy!
WHUD
WHUD
WHUD
WHAM
WHAM
WHAM
WHAM
M
M
M
M
R

Chapter 145 Hikae's Worries

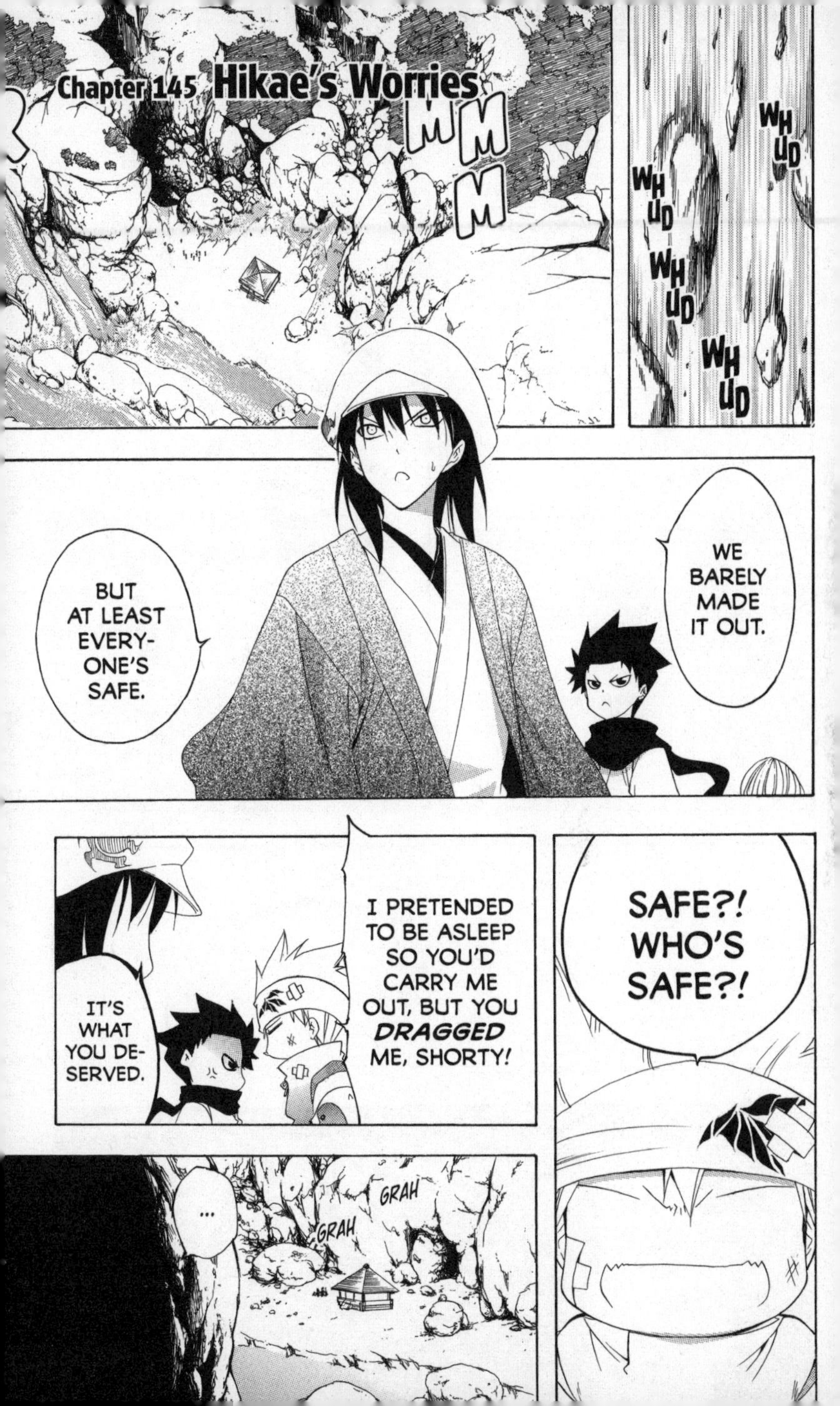
WHUD WHUD WHUD WHUD
MMM
WE BARELY MADE IT OUT.
BUT AT LEAST EVERYONE'S SAFE.
SAFE?! WHO'S SAFE?!
I PRETENDED TO BE ASLEEP SO YOU'D CARRY ME OUT, BUT YOU *DRAGGED* ME, SHORTY!
IT'S WHAT YOU DESERVED.
GRAH
GRAH
...

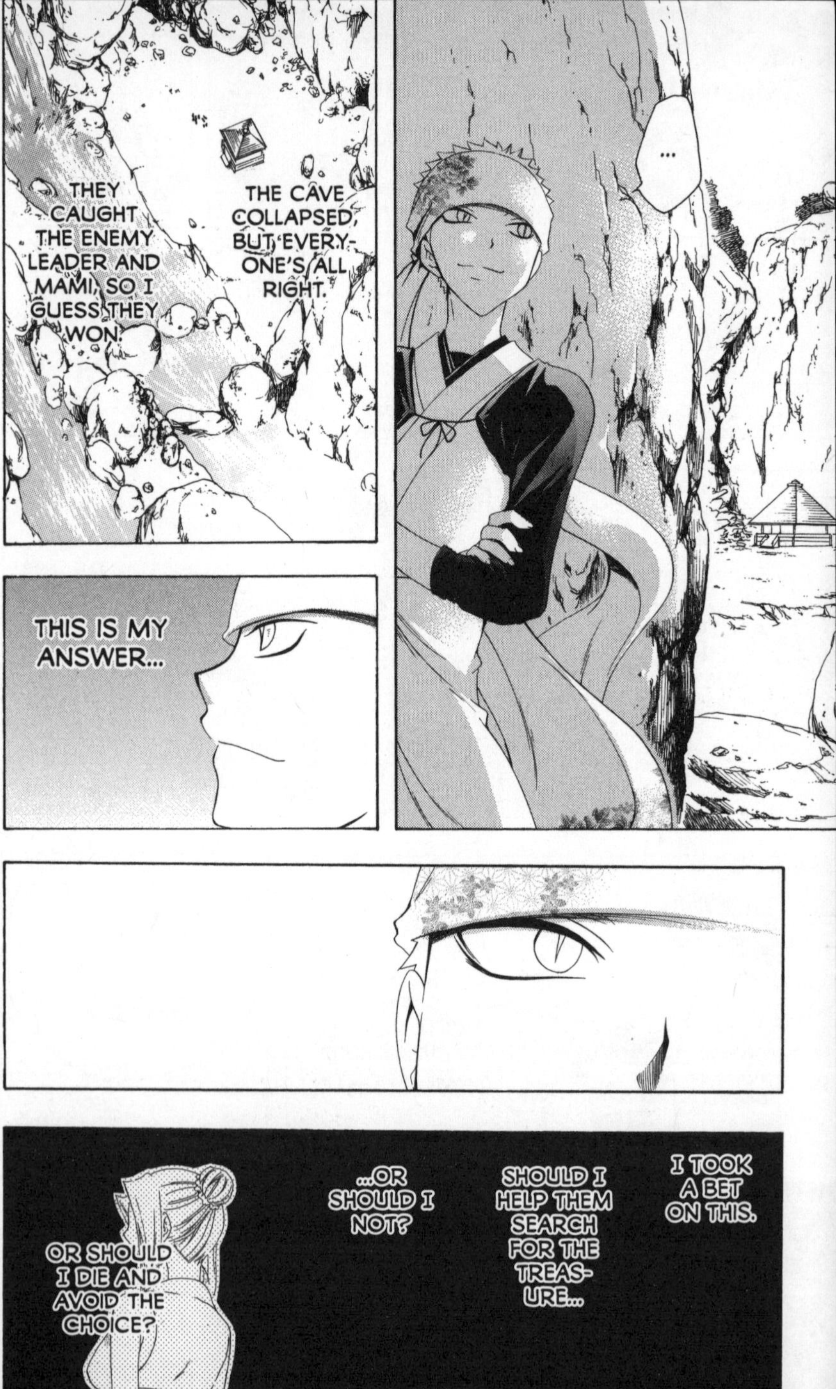
...
THE CAVE COLLAPSED, BUT EVERY-ONE'S ALL RIGHT.
THEY CAUGHT THE ENEMY LEADER AND MAMI, SO I GUESS THEY WON.
THIS IS MY ANSWER...
I TOOK A BET ON THIS.
SHOULD I HELP THEM SEARCH FOR THE TREAS-URE...
...OR SHOULD I NOT?
OR SHOULD I DIE AND AVOID THE CHOICE?

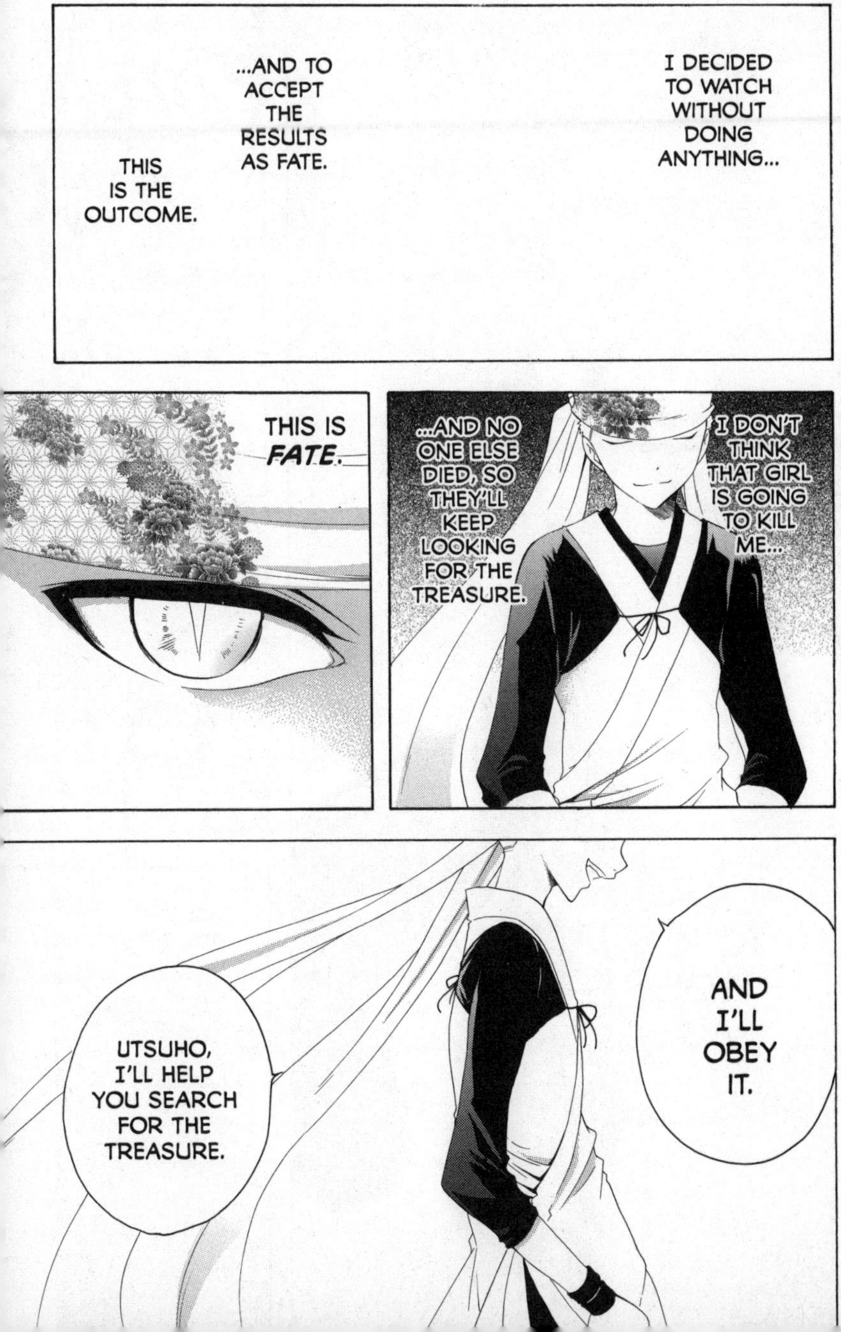
I DECIDED TO WATCH WITHOUT DOING ANYTHING...
...AND TO ACCEPT THE RESULTS AS FATE.
THIS IS THE OUTCOME.
I DON'T THINK THAT GIRL IS GOING TO KILL ME...
...AND NO ONE ELSE DIED, SO THEY'LL KEEP LOOKING FOR THE TREASURE.
THIS IS *FATE*.
AND I'LL OBEY IT.
UTSUHO, I'LL HELP YOU SEARCH FOR THE TREASURE.

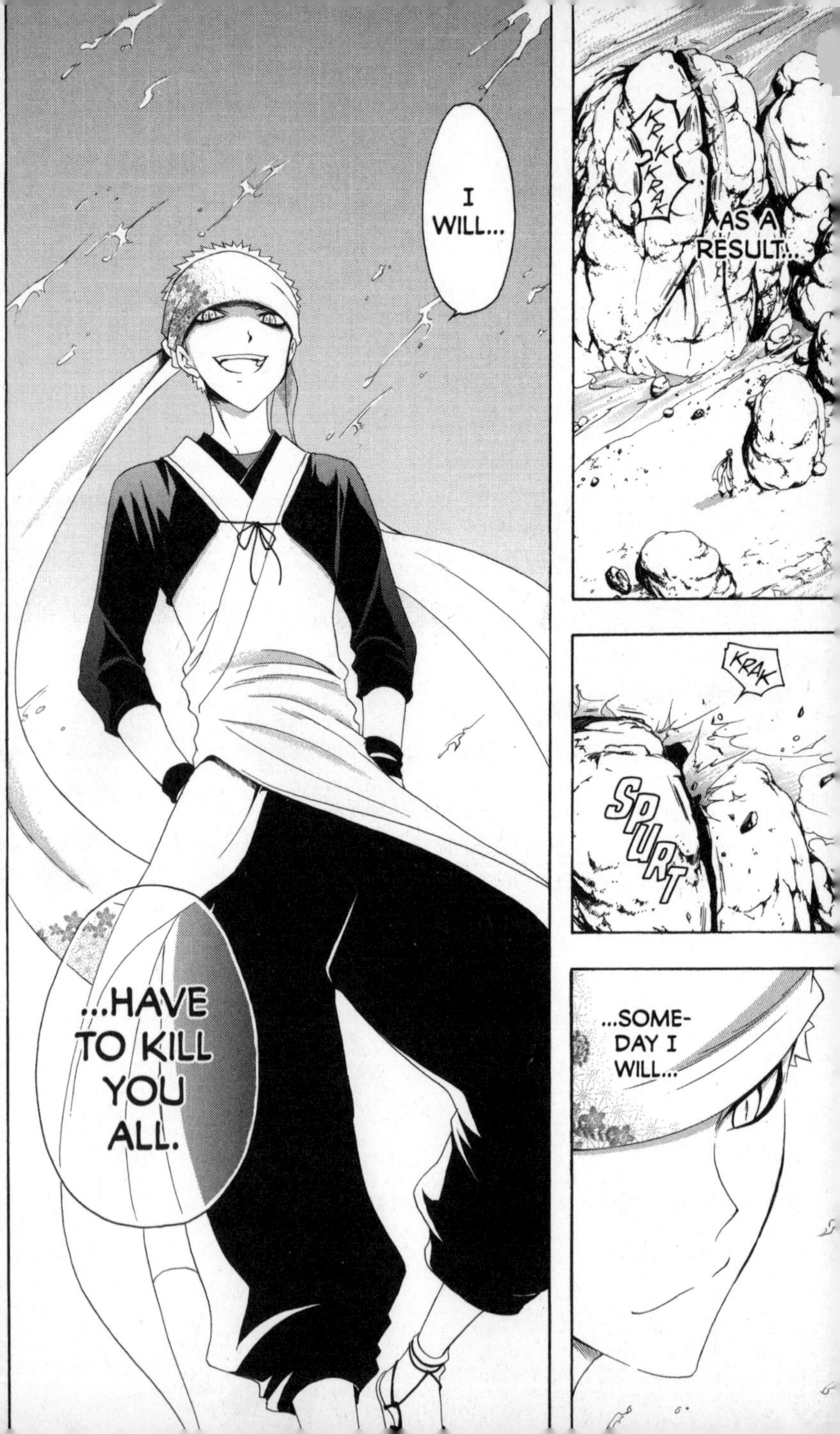
KRIK KRAK
AS A RESULT...
KRAK
SPURT
...SOME-DAY I WILL...
I WILL...
...HAVE TO KILL YOU ALL.

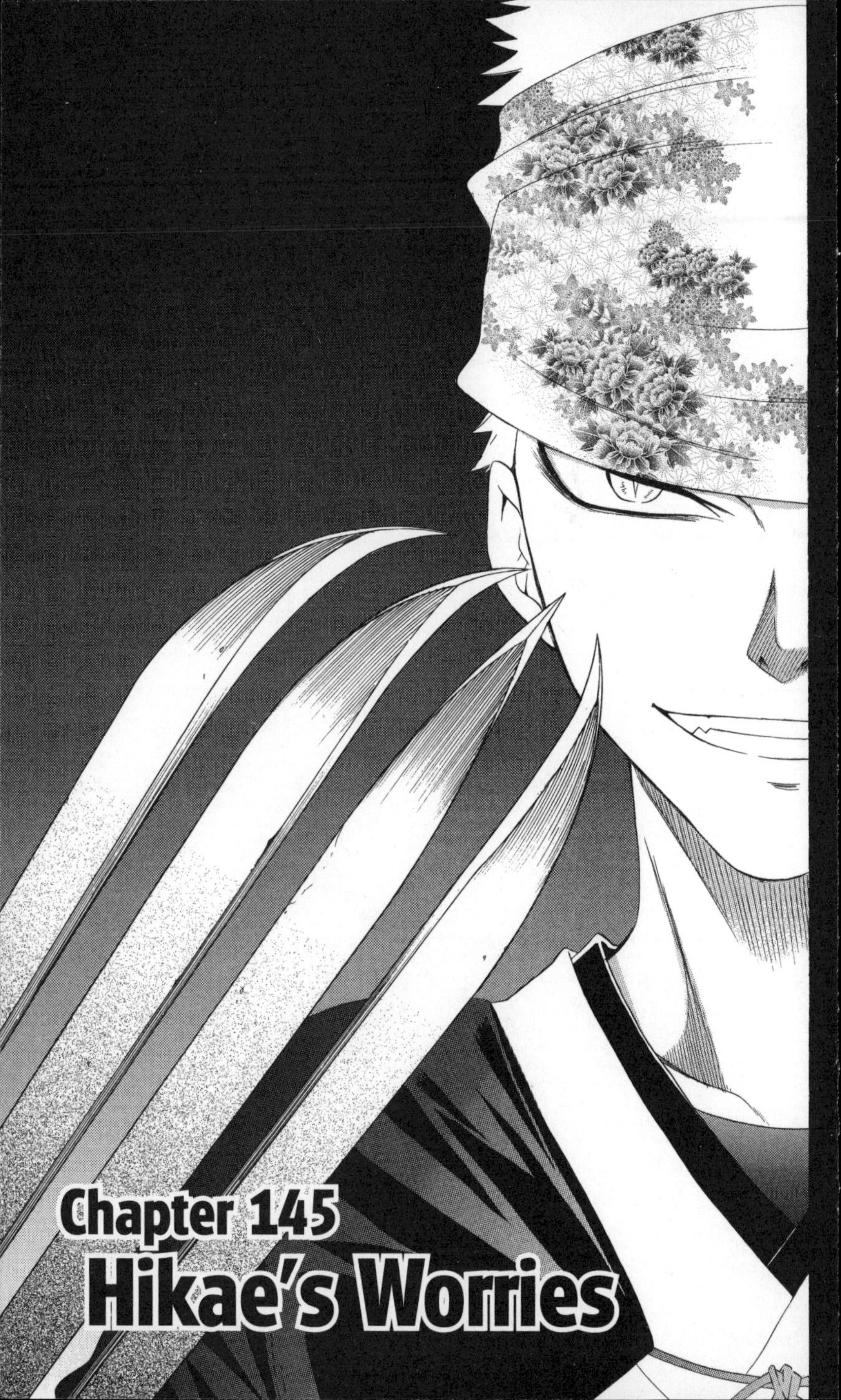
Chapter 145
Hikae's Worries

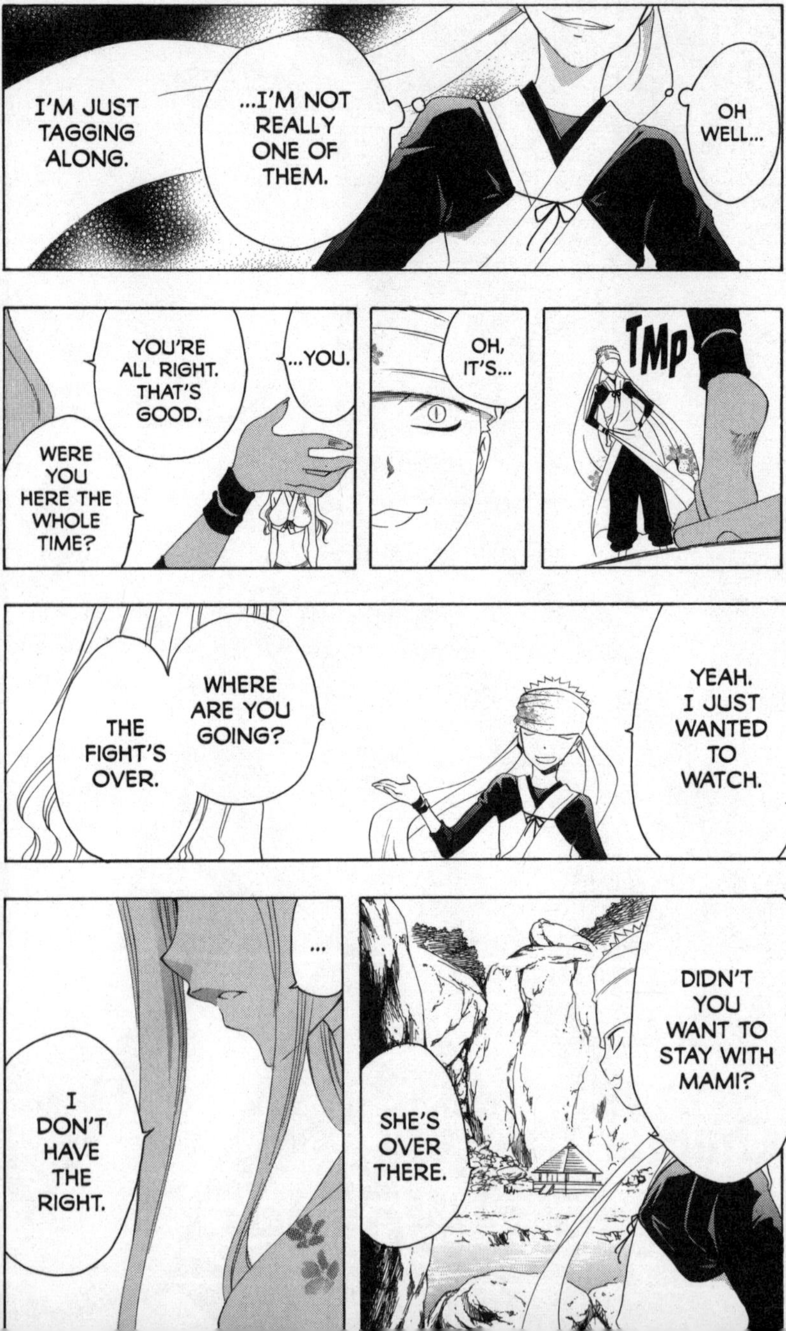
OH WELL...
...I'M NOT REALLY ONE OF THEM.
I'M JUST TAGGING ALONG.
TMP
OH, IT'S...
...YOU.
YOU'RE ALL RIGHT. THAT'S GOOD.
WERE YOU HERE THE WHOLE TIME?
YEAH. I JUST WANTED TO WATCH.
WHERE ARE YOU GOING?
THE FIGHT'S OVER.
DIDN'T YOU WANT TO STAY WITH MAMI?
SHE'S OVER THERE.
...
I DON'T HAVE THE RIGHT.

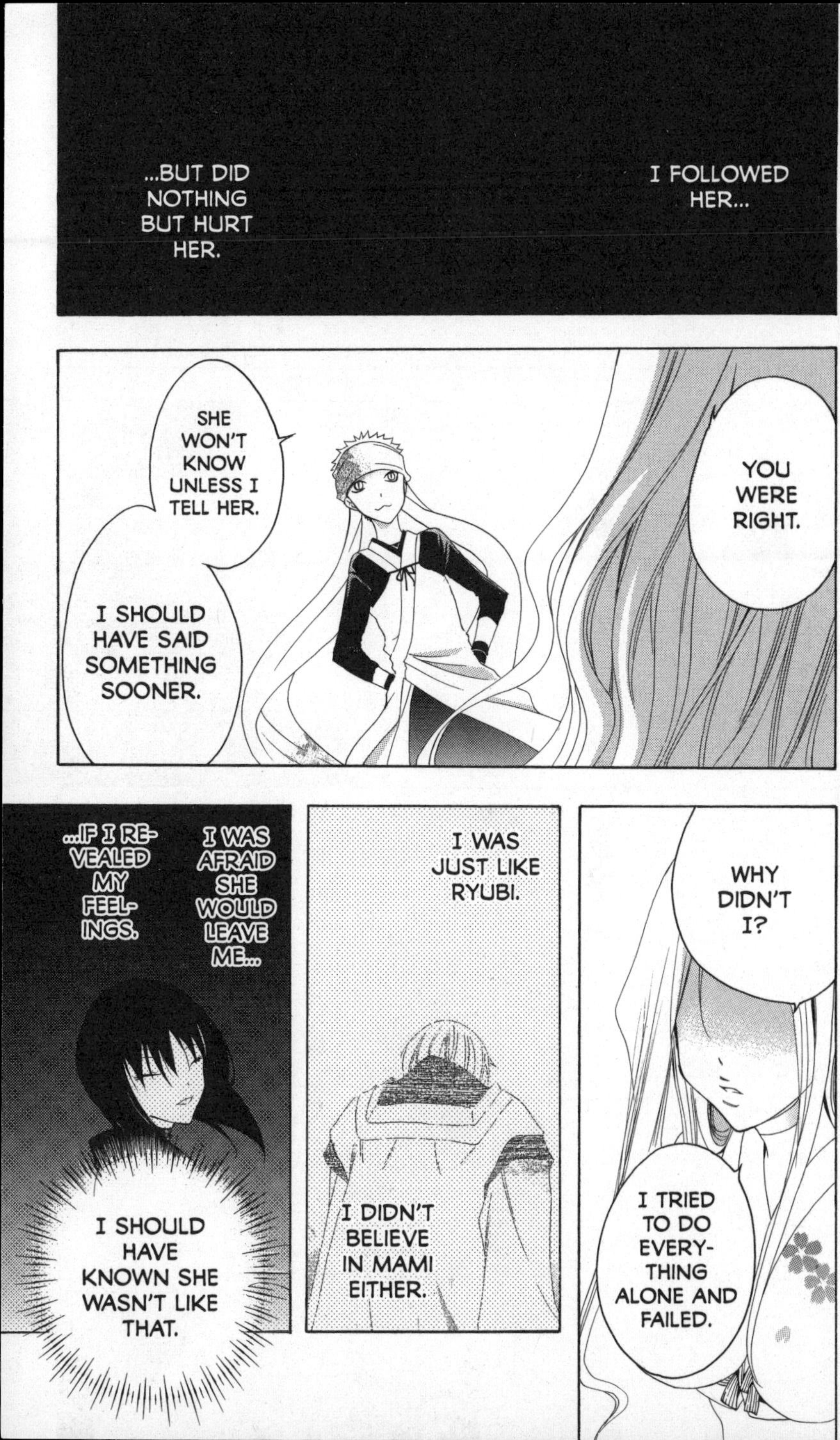
I FOLLOWED HER...
...BUT DID NOTHING BUT HURT HER.
YOU WERE RIGHT.
SHE WON'T KNOW UNLESS I TELL HER.
I SHOULD HAVE SAID SOMETHING SOONER.
WHY DIDN'T I?
I TRIED TO DO EVERY-THING ALONE AND FAILED.
I WAS JUST LIKE RYUBI.
I DIDN'T BELIEVE IN MAMI EITHER.
I WAS AFRAID SHE WOULD LEAVE ME...
...IF I RE-VEALED MY FEEL-INGS.
I SHOULD HAVE KNOWN SHE WASN'T LIKE THAT.

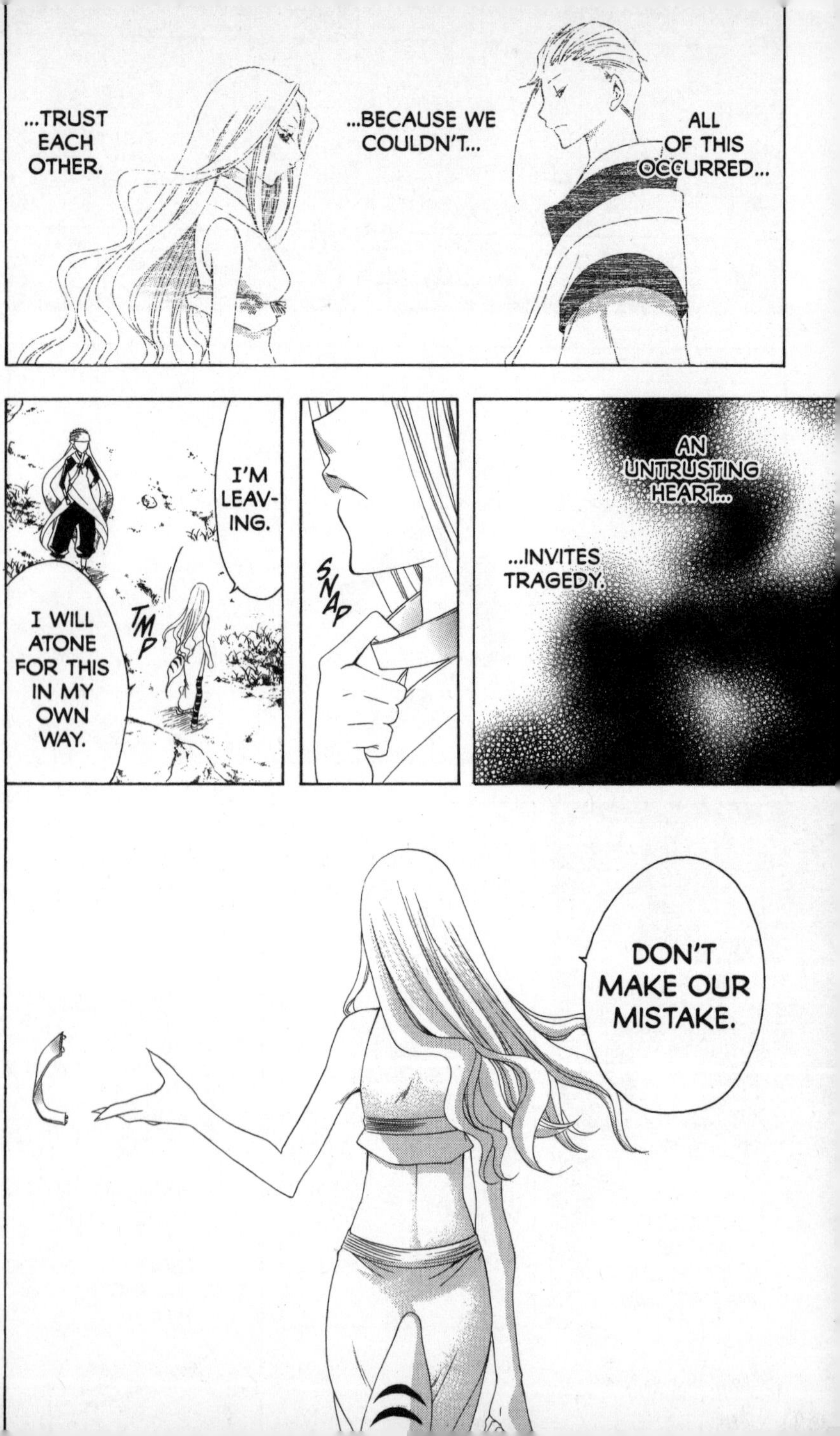
ALL OF THIS OCCURRED...
...BECAUSE WE COULDN'T...
...TRUST EACH OTHER.
AN UNTRUSTING HEART...
...INVITES TRAGEDY.
SNAP
I'M LEAV-ING.
TMP
I WILL ATONE FOR THIS IN MY OWN WAY.
DON'T MAKE OUR MISTAKE.

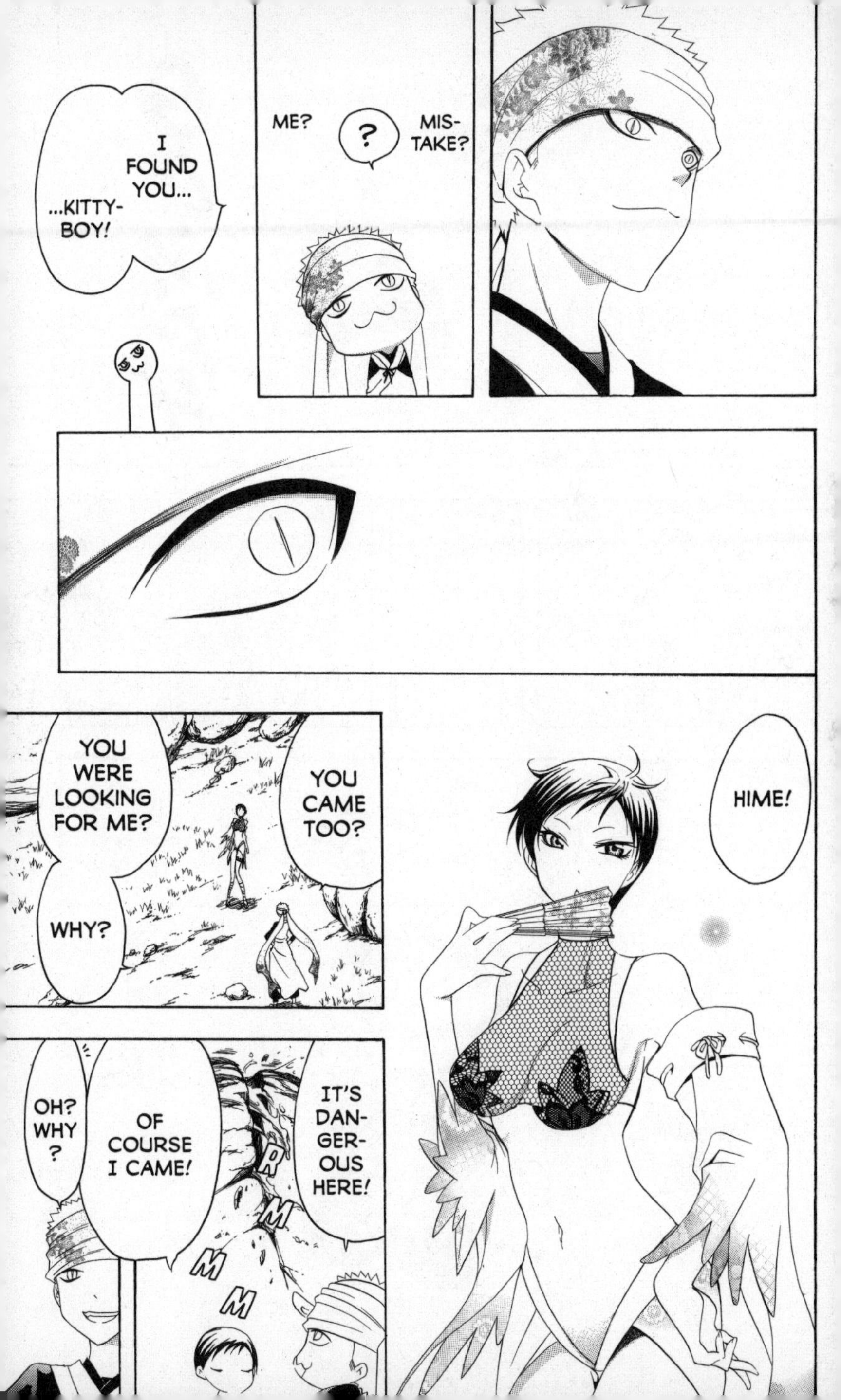
MIS-TAKE?
?
ME?
I FOUND YOU...
...KITTY-BOY!
HIME!
YOU CAME TOO?
YOU WERE LOOKING FOR ME?
WHY?
IT'S DAN-GER-OUS HERE!
RMMMM
OF COURSE I CAME!
OH? WHY?

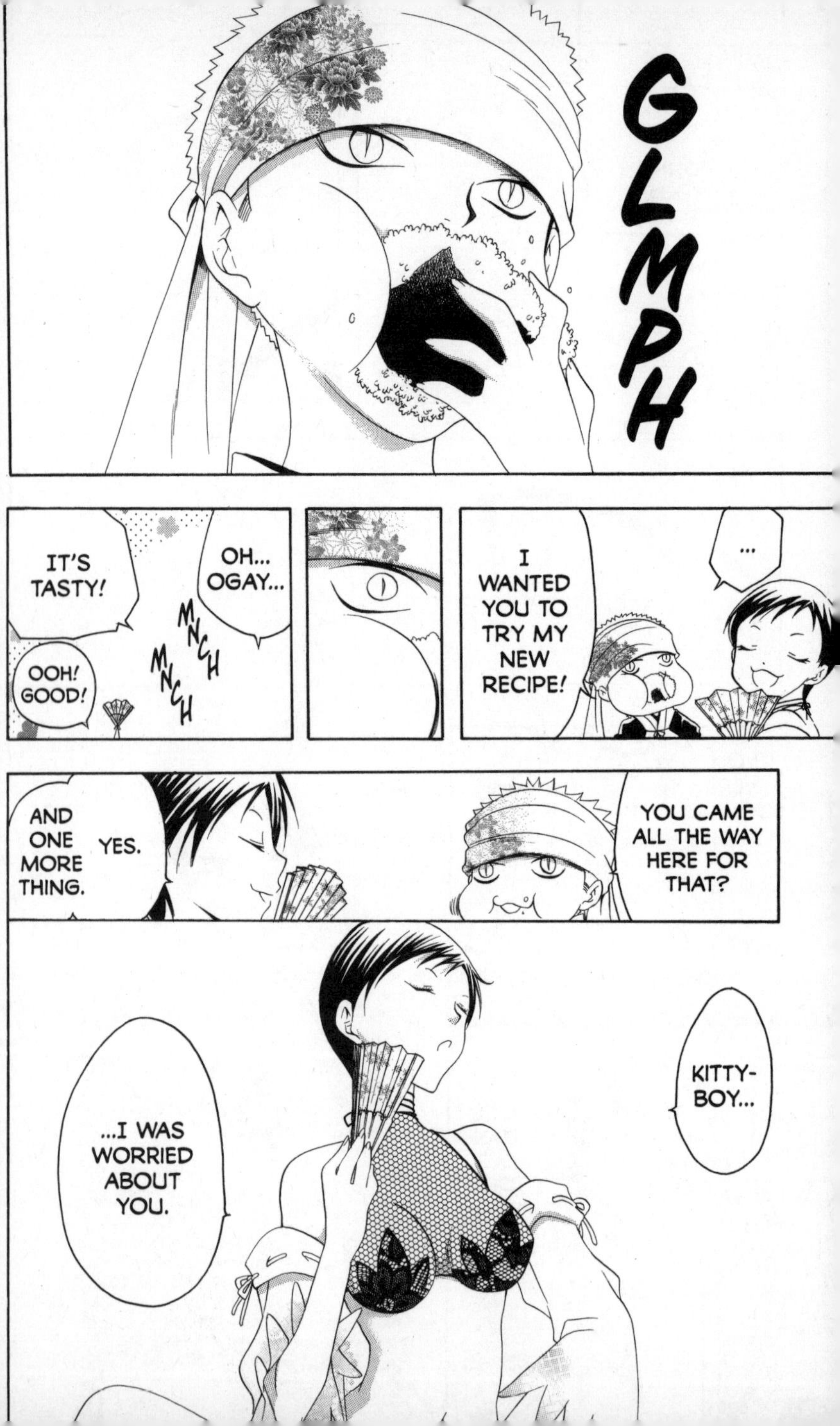
GLMPH
...
I WANTED YOU TO TRY MY NEW RECIPE!
OH... OGAY...
MNCH MNCH
IT'S TASTY!
OOH! GOOD!
YOU CAME ALL THE WAY HERE FOR THAT?
YES.
AND ONE MORE THING.
KITTY-BOY...
...I WAS WORRIED ABOUT YOU.

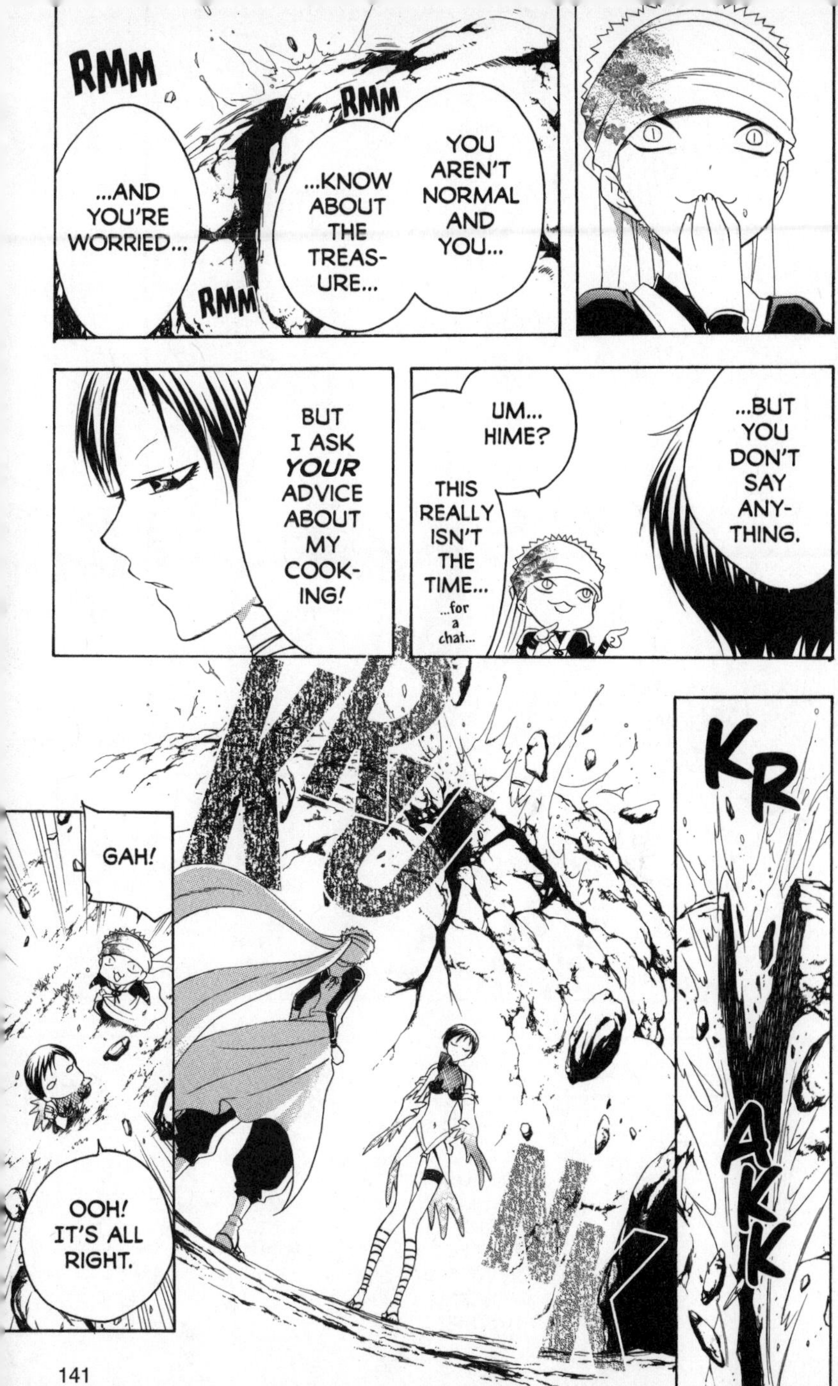
YOU AREN'T NORMAL AND YOU...
...KNOW ABOUT THE TREASURE...
RMM
RMM
RMM
...AND YOU'RE WORRIED...
...BUT YOU DON'T SAY ANYTHING.
UM... HIME?
THIS REALLY ISN'T THE TIME...
...for a chat...
BUT I ASK YOUR ADVICE ABOUT MY COOKING!
KRAKK
KRUMM
GAH!
OOH! IT'S ALL RIGHT.

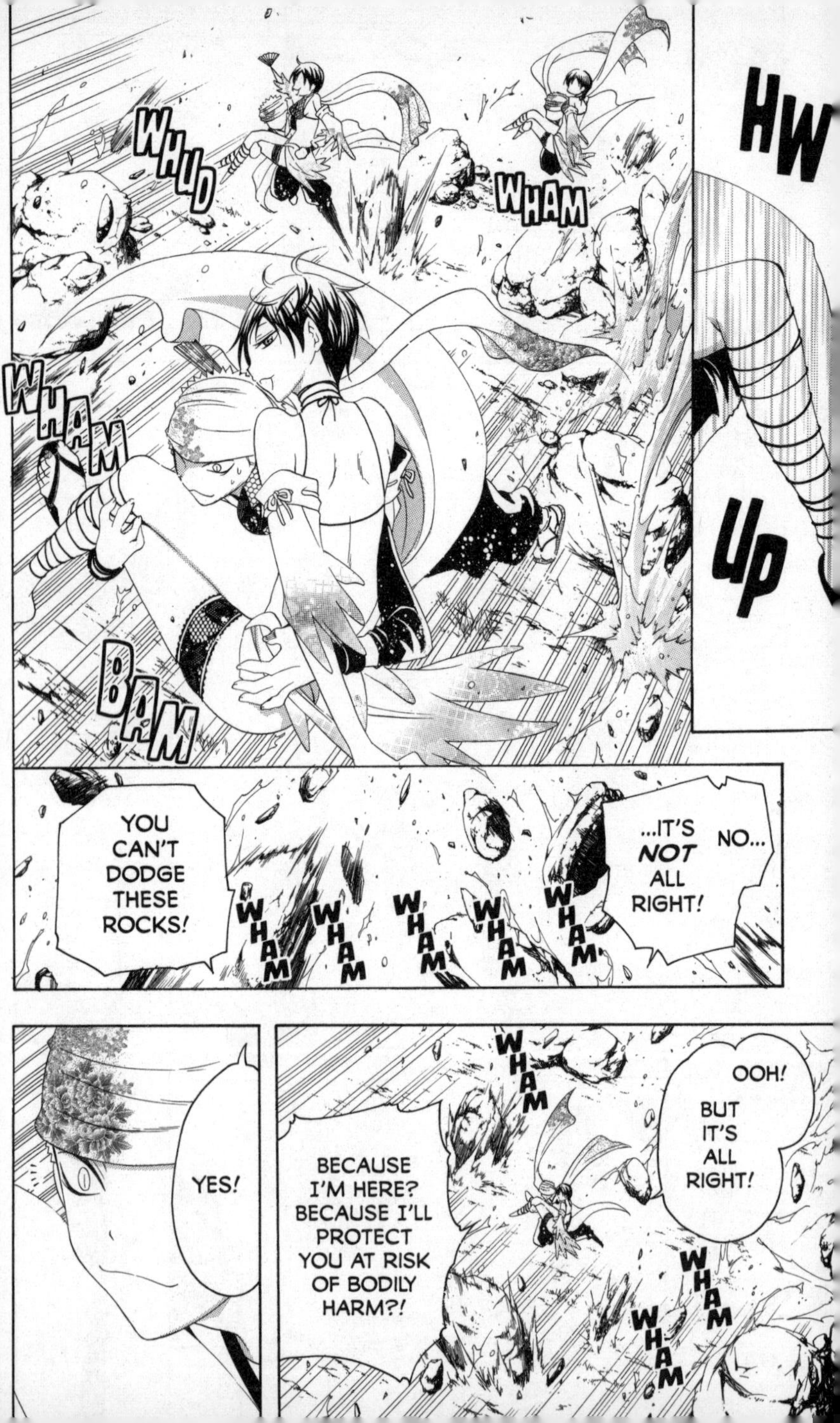
HW
UP
WHAM
WHUD
WHAM
BAM
NO...
...IT'S *NOT* ALL RIGHT!
WHAM WHAM WHAM WHAM WHAM
YOU CAN'T DODGE THESE ROCKS!
OOH! BUT IT'S ALL RIGHT!
WHAM
BECAUSE I'M HERE? BECAUSE I'LL PROTECT YOU AT RISK OF BODILY HARM?!
WHAM
WHAM
YES!

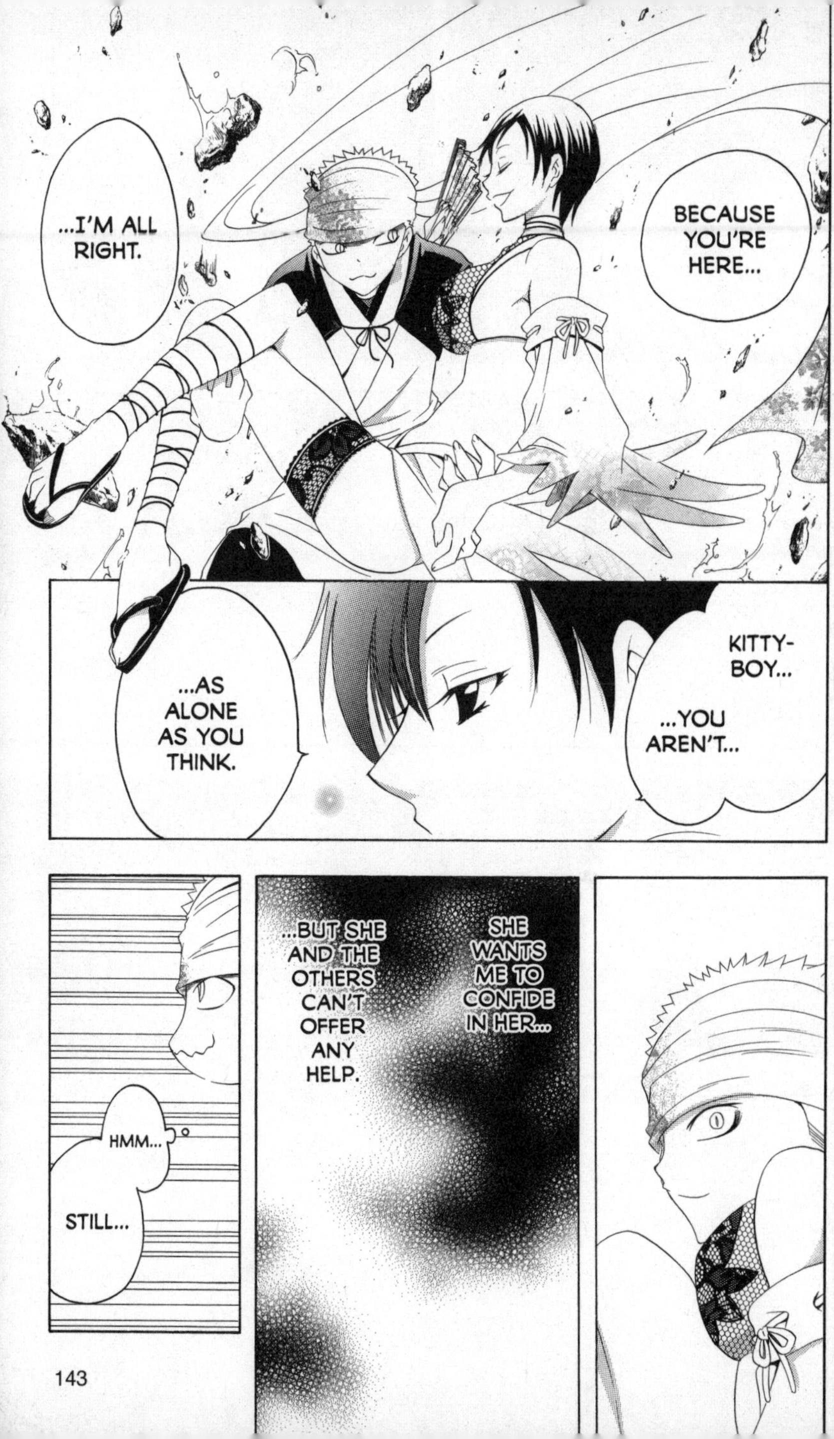
BECAUSE YOU'RE HERE...
...I'M ALL RIGHT.
KITTY-BOY...
...YOU AREN'T...
...AS ALONE AS YOU THINK.
SHE WANTS ME TO CONFIDE IN HER...
...BUT SHE AND THE OTHERS CAN'T OFFER ANY HELP.
HMM...
STILL...

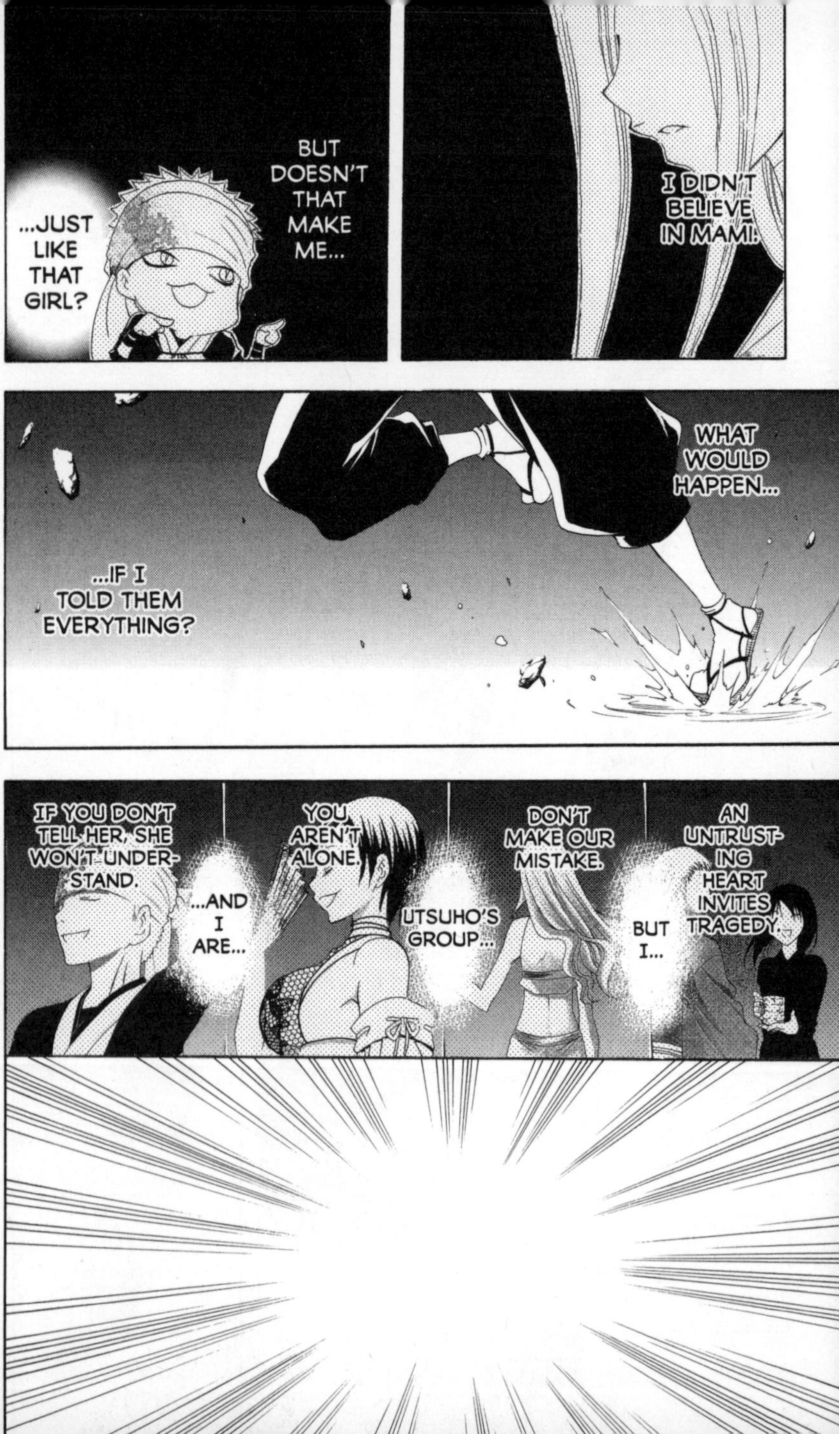
I DIDN'T BELIEVE IN MAMI.
BUT DOESN'T THAT MAKE ME...
...JUST LIKE THAT GIRL?
WHAT WOULD HAPPEN...
...IF I TOLD THEM EVERYTHING?
AN UNTRUSTING HEART INVITES TRAGEDY.
BUT I...
DON'T MAKE OUR MISTAKE.
UTSUHO'S GROUP...
YOU AREN'T ALONE.
...AND I ARE...
IF YOU DON'T TELL HER, SHE WON'T UNDERSTAND.

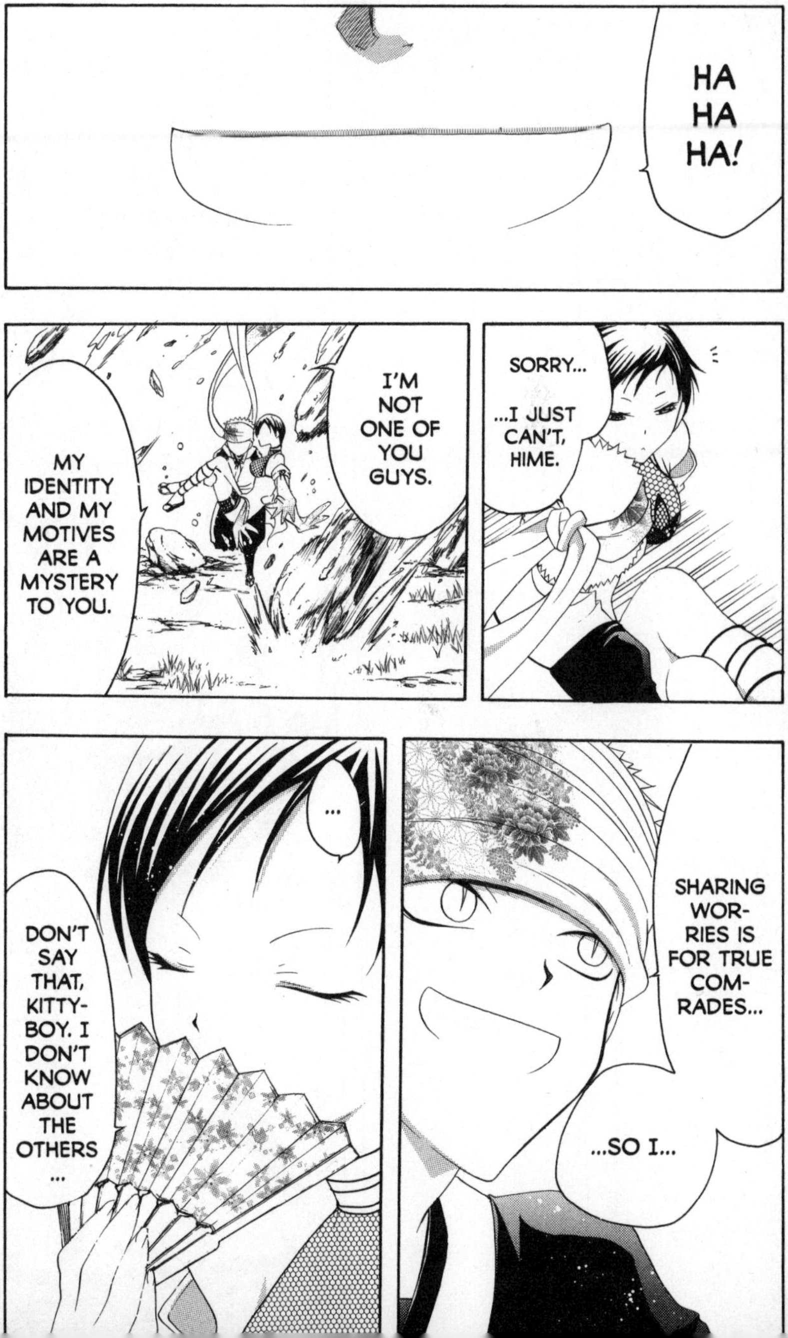
HA HA HA!
SORRY...
...I JUST CAN'T, HIME.
I'M NOT ONE OF YOU GUYS.
MY IDENTITY AND MY MOTIVES ARE A MYSTERY TO YOU.
SHARING WORRIES IS FOR TRUE COMRADES...
...SO I...
...
DON'T SAY THAT, KITTY-BOY. I DON'T KNOW ABOUT THE OTHERS...

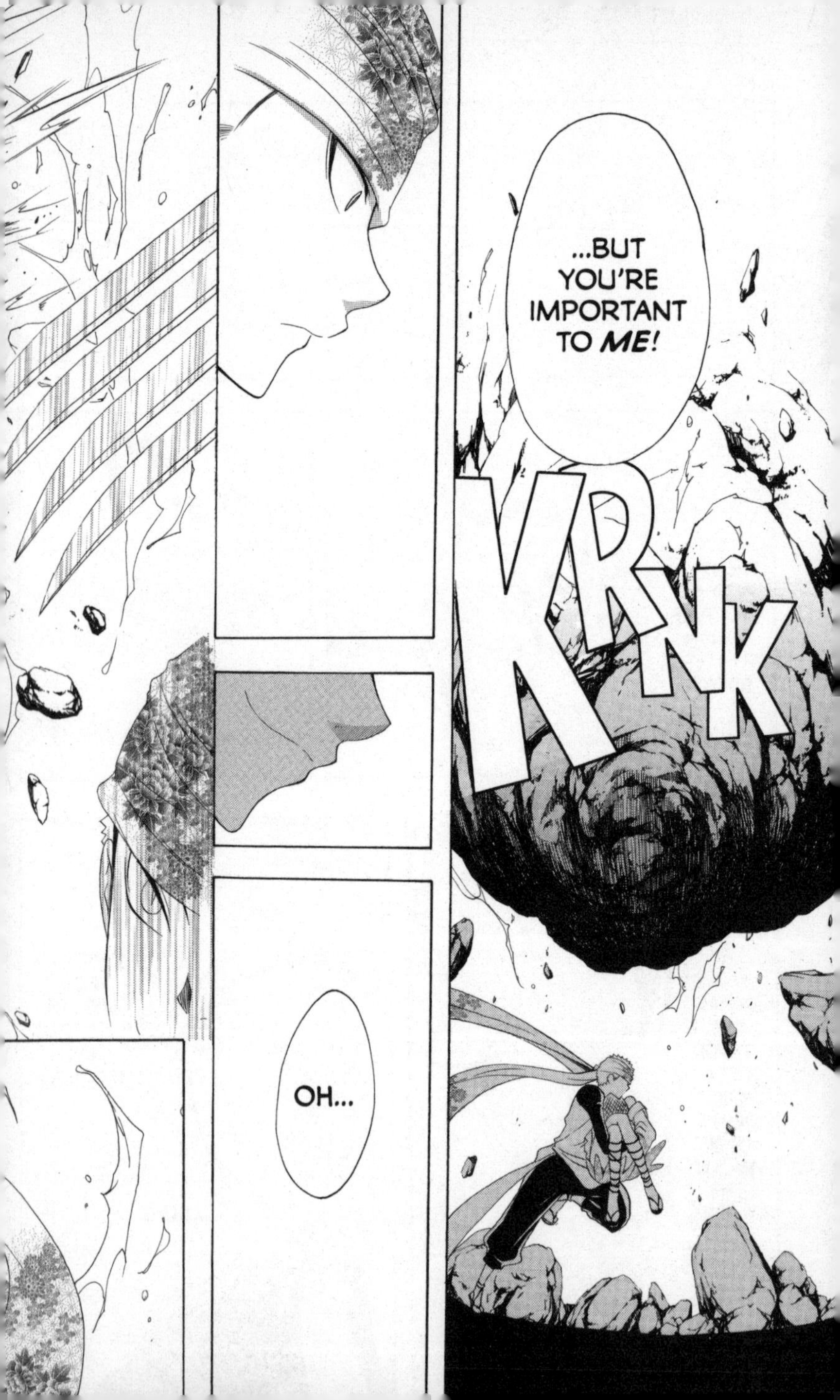
...BUT YOU'RE IMPORTANT TO *ME*!
KRNK
OH...

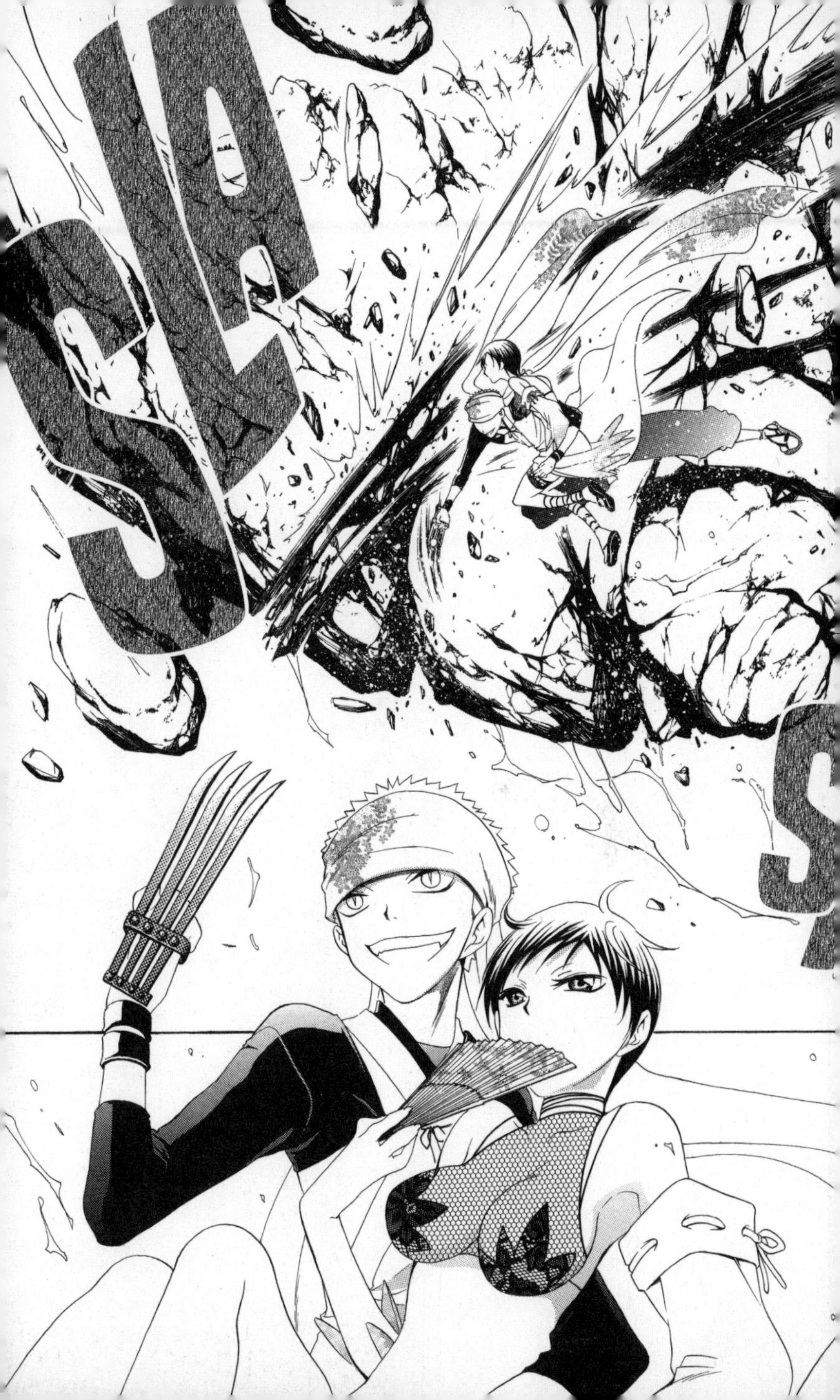

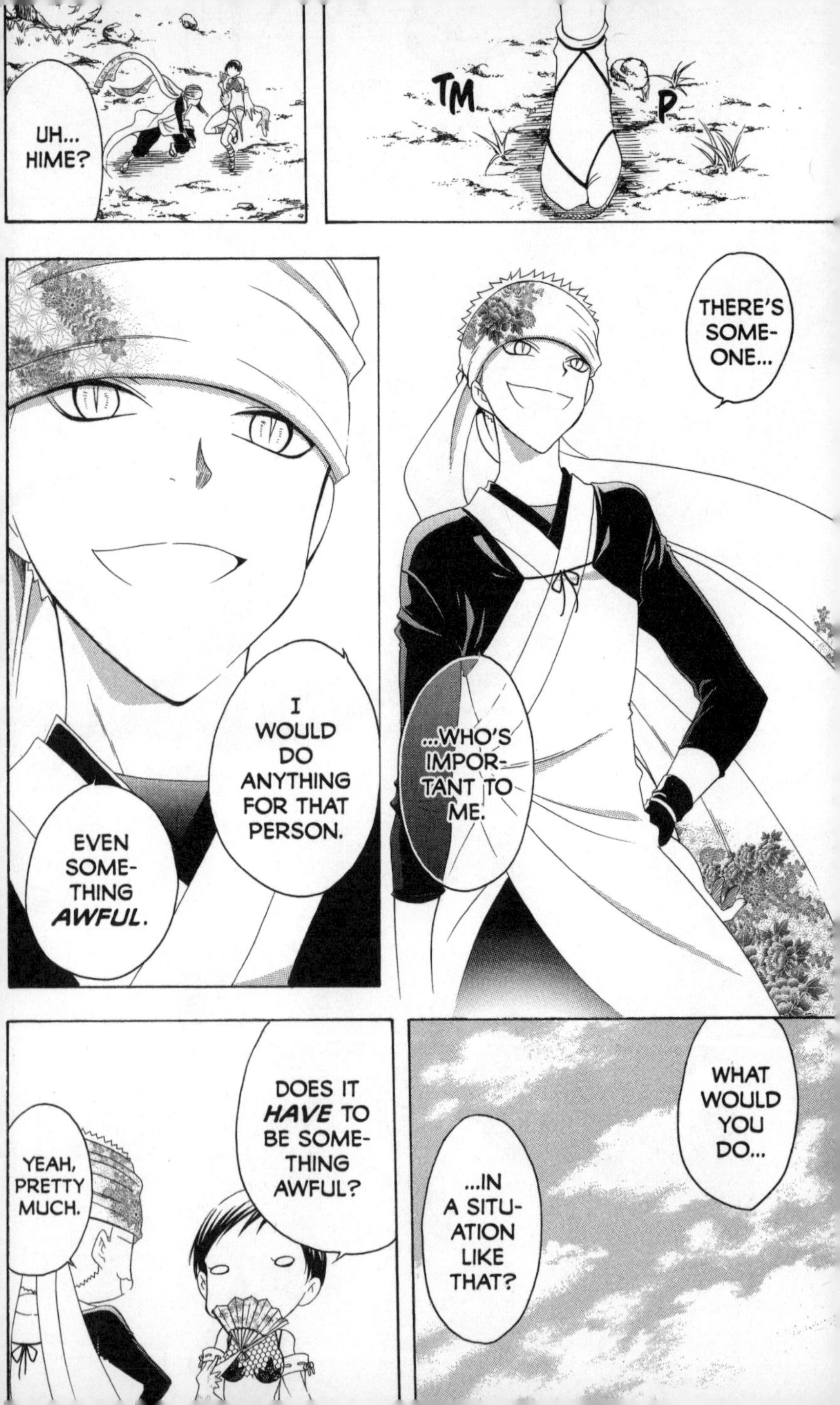
TMP
UH... HIME?
THERE'S SOMEONE...
...WHO'S IMPORTANT TO ME.
I WOULD DO ANYTHING FOR THAT PERSON.
EVEN SOMETHING ***AWFUL***.
WHAT WOULD YOU DO...
...IN A SITUATION LIKE THAT?
DOES IT ***HAVE*** TO BE SOMETHING AWFUL?
YEAH, PRETTY MUCH.

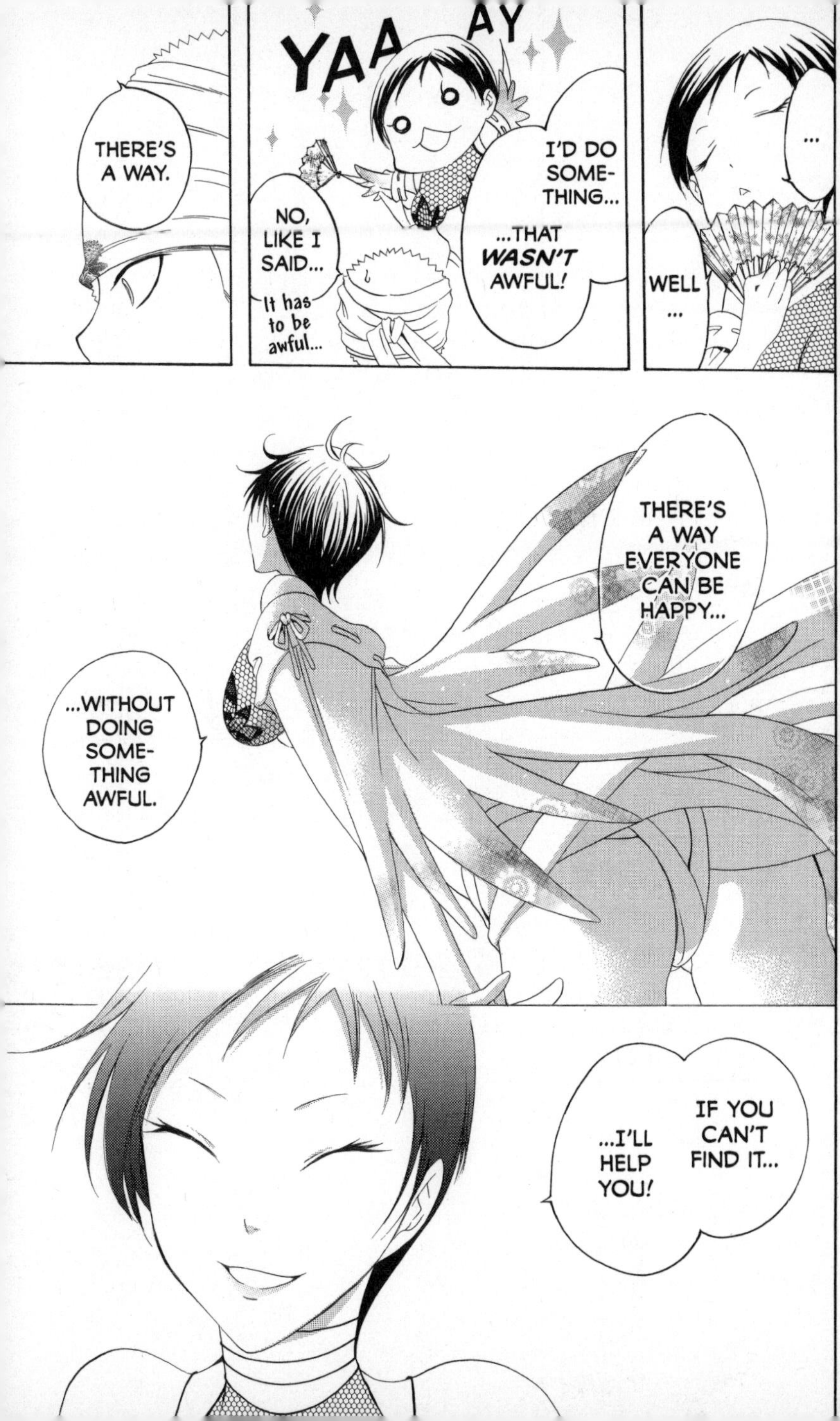
...
WELL ...
YAAAY
I'D DO SOMETHING...
...THAT *WASN'T* AWFUL!
NO, LIKE I SAID...
It has to be awful...
THERE'S A WAY.
THERE'S A WAY EVERYONE CAN BE HAPPY...
...WITHOUT DOING SOMETHING AWFUL.
IF YOU CAN'T FIND IT...
...I'LL HELP YOU!

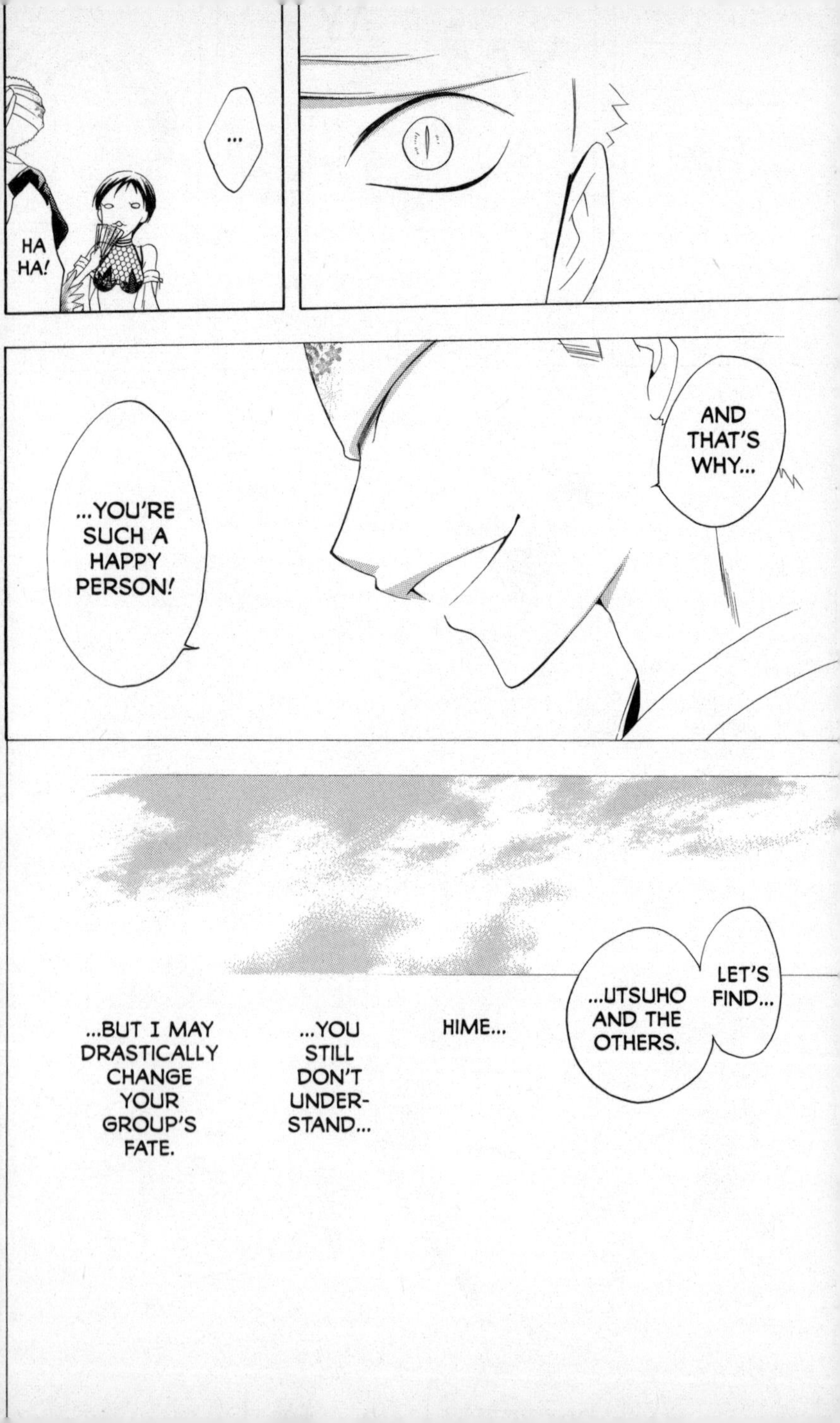
...
HA HA!
AND THAT'S WHY...
...YOU'RE SUCH A HAPPY PERSON!
LET'S FIND...
...UTSUHO AND THE OTHERS.
HIME...
...YOU STILL DON'T UNDER-STAND...
...BUT I MAY DRASTICALLY CHANGE YOUR GROUP'S FATE.

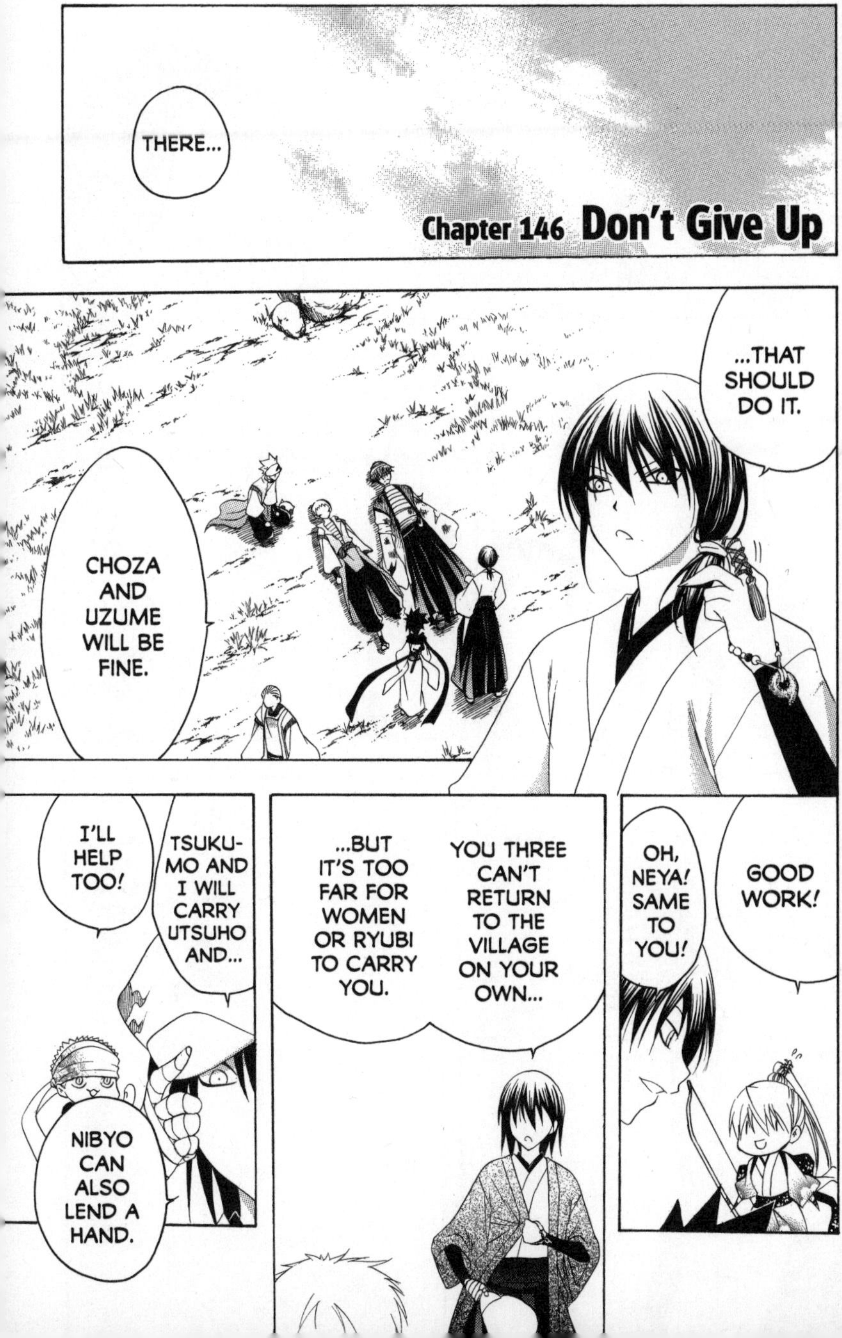
THERE...
Chapter 146 Don't Give Up
...THAT SHOULD DO IT.
CHOZA AND UZUME WILL BE FINE.
GOOD WORK!
OH, NEYA! SAME TO YOU!
YOU THREE CAN'T RETURN TO THE VILLAGE ON YOUR OWN...
...BUT IT'S TOO FAR FOR WOMEN OR RYUBI TO CARRY YOU.
TSUKU-MO AND I WILL CARRY UTSUHO AND...
I'LL HELP TOO!
NIBYO CAN ALSO LEND A HAND.

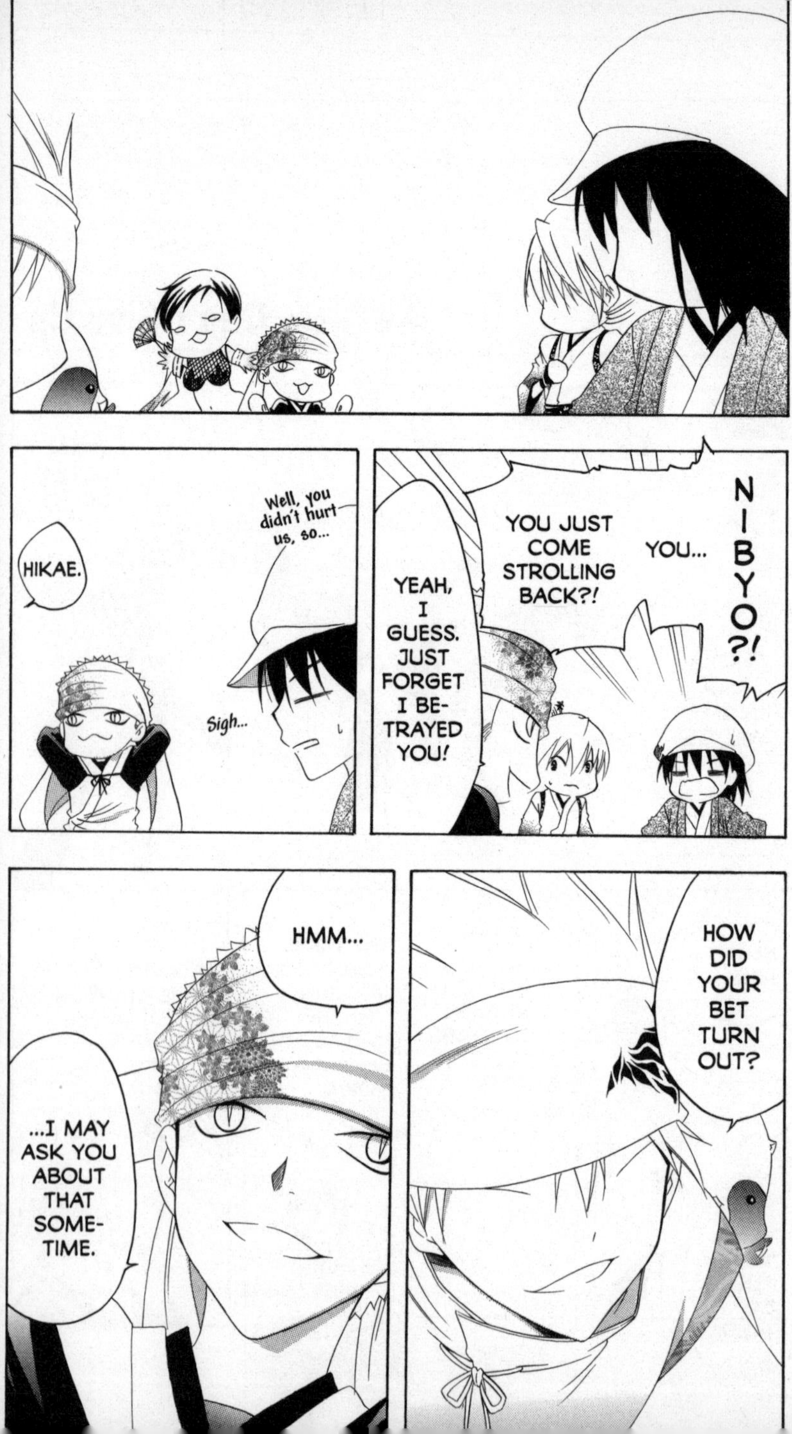
NIBYO?!
YOU...
YOU JUST COME STROLLING BACK?!
YEAH, I GUESS. JUST FORGET I BE-TRAYED YOU!
Well, you didn't hurt us, so...
Sigh...
HIKAE.
HOW DID YOUR BET TURN OUT?
HMM...
...I MAY ASK YOU ABOUT THAT SOME-TIME.

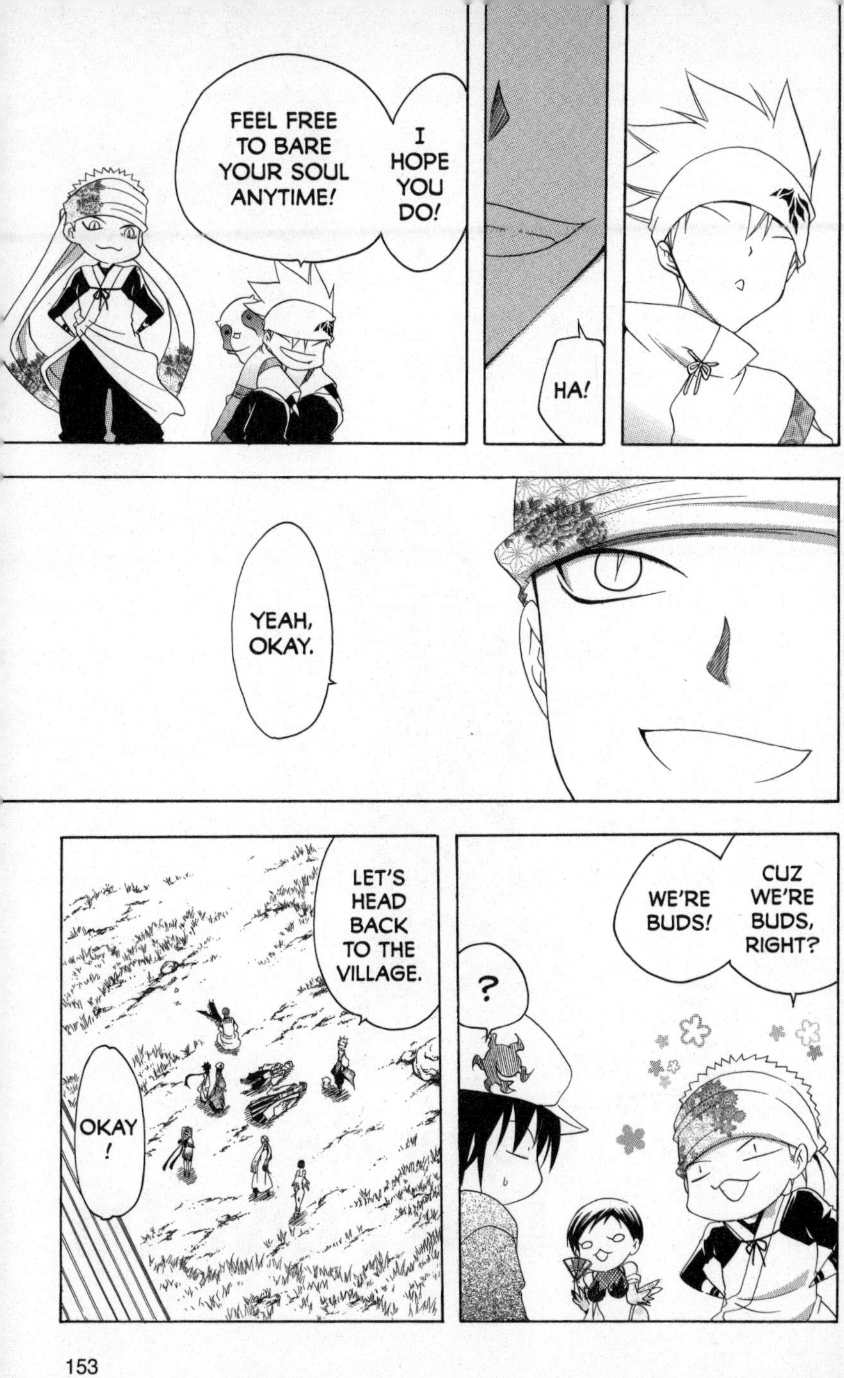
HA!
I HOPE YOU DO!
FEEL FREE TO BARE YOUR SOUL ANYTIME!
YEAH, OKAY.
CUZ WE'RE BUDS, RIGHT?
WE'RE BUDS!
?
LET'S HEAD BACK TO THE VILLAGE.
OKAY!

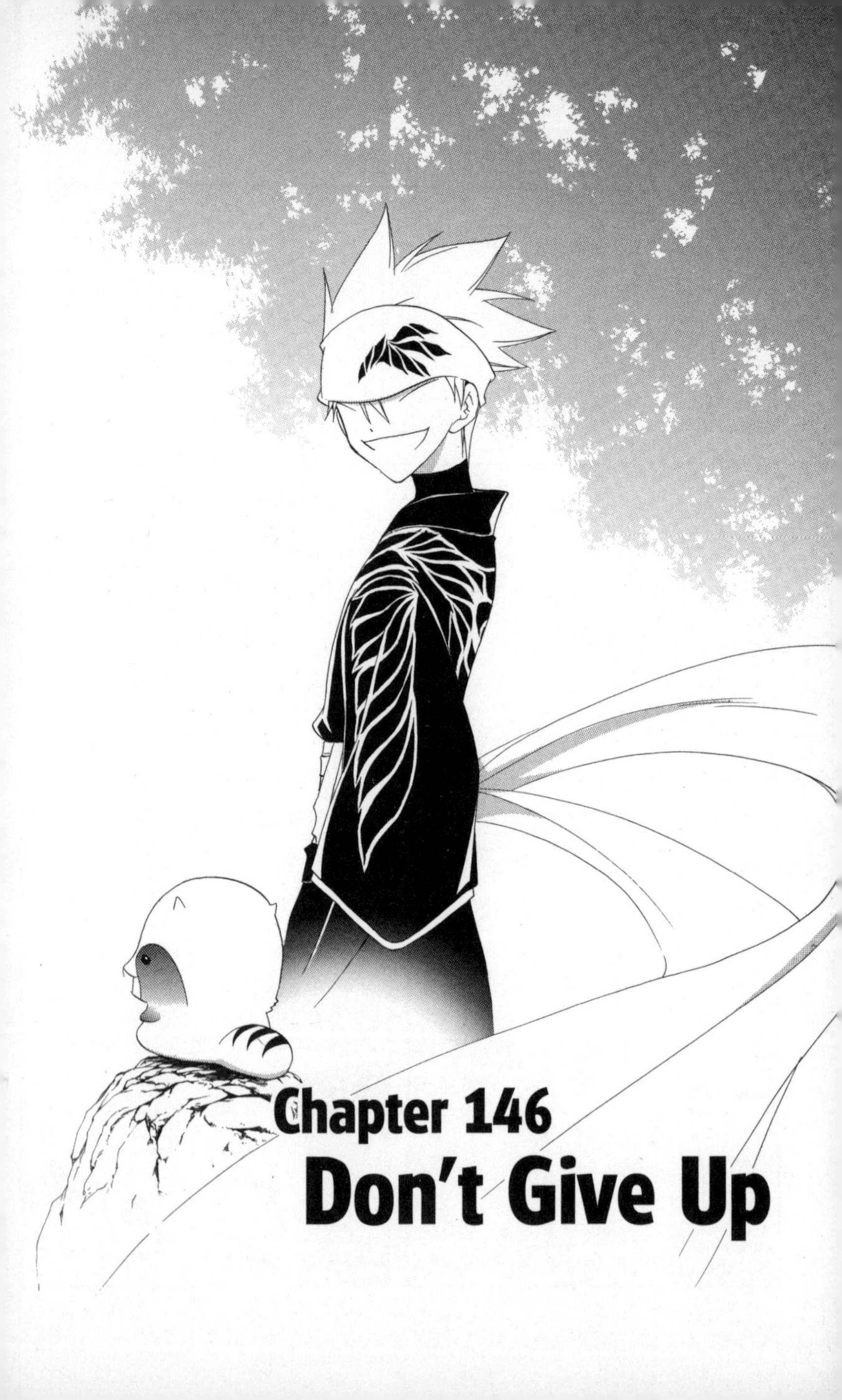

Chapter 146
Don't Give Up

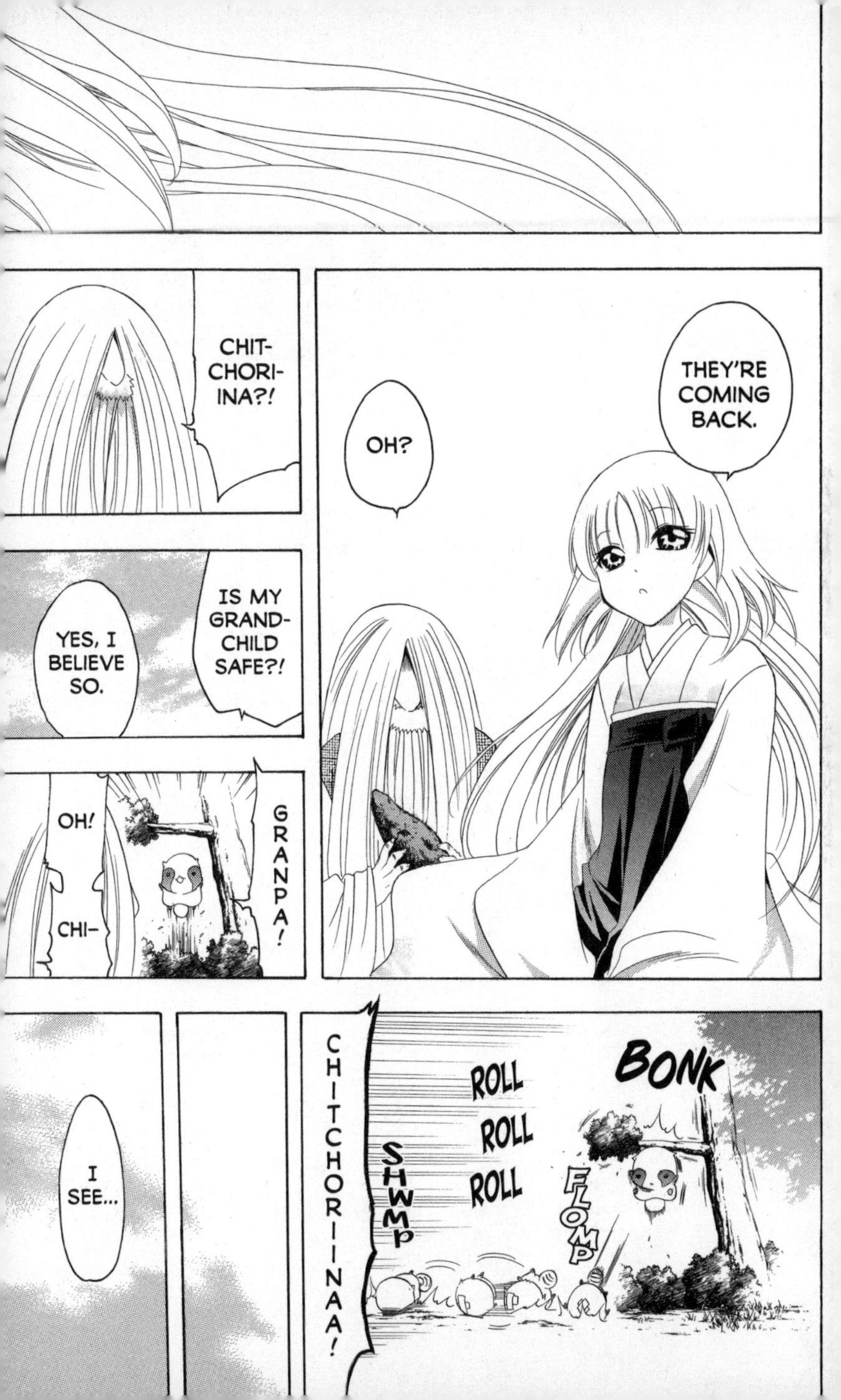
THEY'RE COMING BACK.
OH?
CHIT-CHORI-INA?!
IS MY GRAND-CHILD SAFE?!
YES, I BELIEVE SO.
GRANPA!
OH!
CHI-
BONK
ROLL
ROLL
FLOMP
ROLL
SHWMP
CHITCHORIINAA!
I SEE...

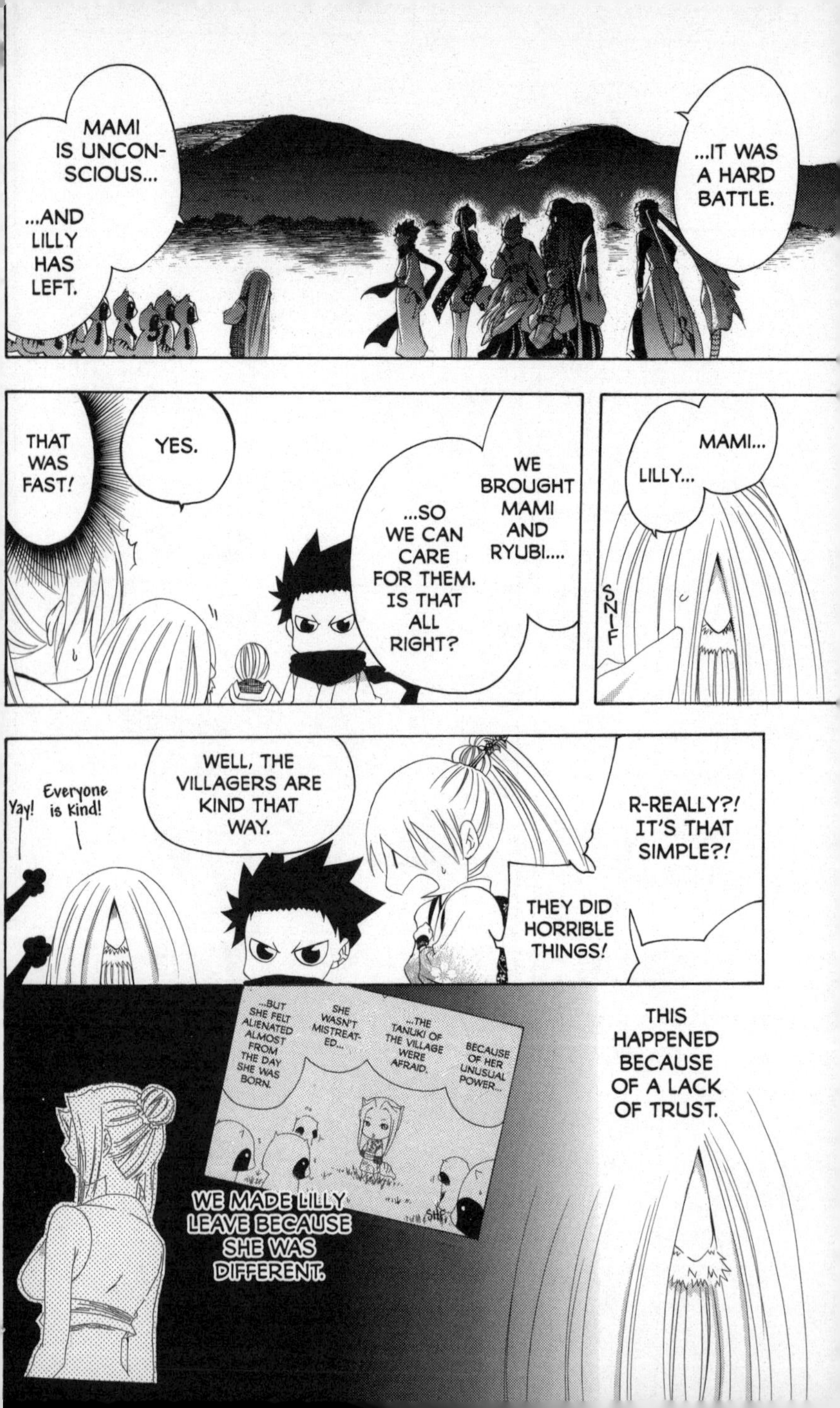
...IT WAS A HARD BATTLE.
MAMI IS UNCONSCIOUS...
...AND LILLY HAS LEFT.
MAMI...
LILLY...
SNIF
WE BROUGHT MAMI AND RYUBI....
...SO WE CAN CARE FOR THEM. IS THAT ALL RIGHT?
YES.
THAT WAS FAST!
R-REALLY?! IT'S THAT SIMPLE?!
THEY DID HORRIBLE THINGS!
WELL, THE VILLAGERS ARE KIND THAT WAY.
Everyone is kind!
Yay!
THIS HAPPENED BECAUSE OF A LACK OF TRUST.
BECAUSE OF HER UNUSUAL POWER...
...THE TANUKI OF THE VILLAGE WERE AFRAID.
SHE WASN'T MISTREATED...
...BUT SHE FELT ALIENATED ALMOST FROM THE DAY SHE WAS BORN.
SHF
WE MADE LILLY LEAVE BECAUSE SHE WAS DIFFERENT.

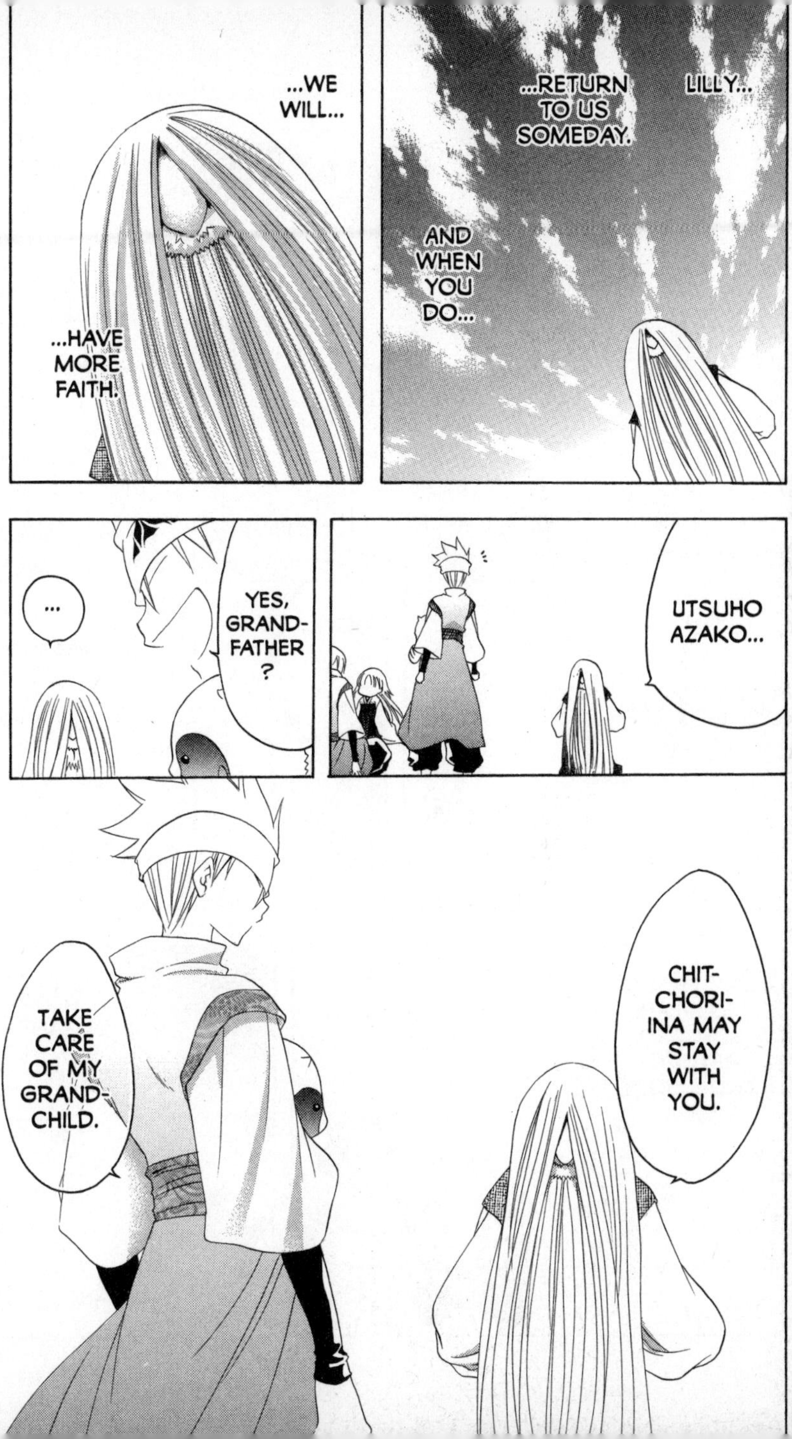
LILLY...
...RETURN TO US SOMEDAY.
AND WHEN YOU DO...
...WE WILL...
...HAVE MORE FAITH.
UTSUHO AZAKO...
YES, GRANDFATHER?
...
CHITCHORIINA MAY STAY WITH YOU.
TAKE CARE OF MY GRANDCHILD.

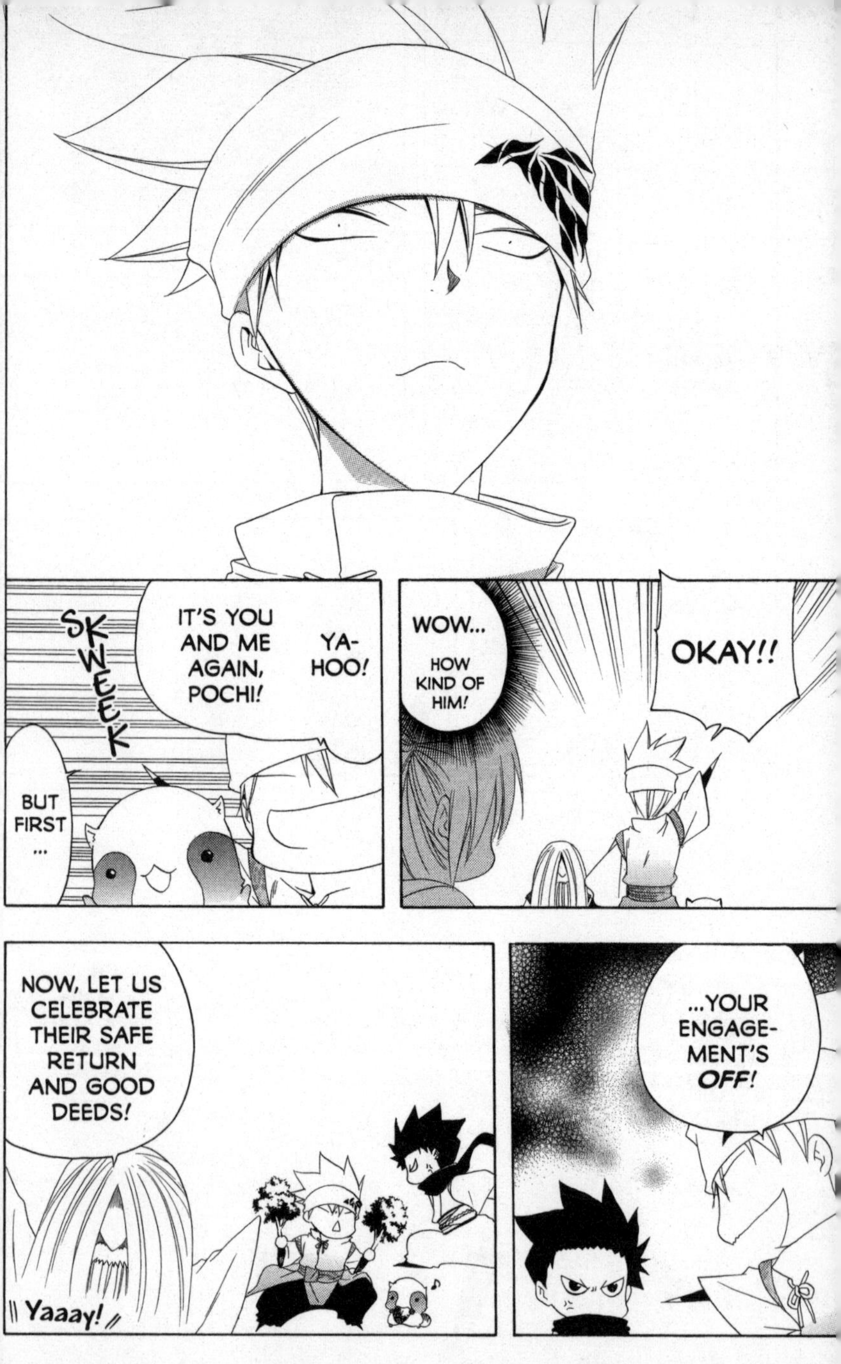
OKAY!!
WOW... HOW KIND OF HIM!
YA-HOO!
IT'S YOU AND ME AGAIN, POCHI!
SKWEEK
BUT FIRST ...
...YOUR ENGAGE-MENT'S *OFF*!
NOW, LET US CELEBRATE THEIR SAFE RETURN AND GOOD DEEDS!
Yaaay!

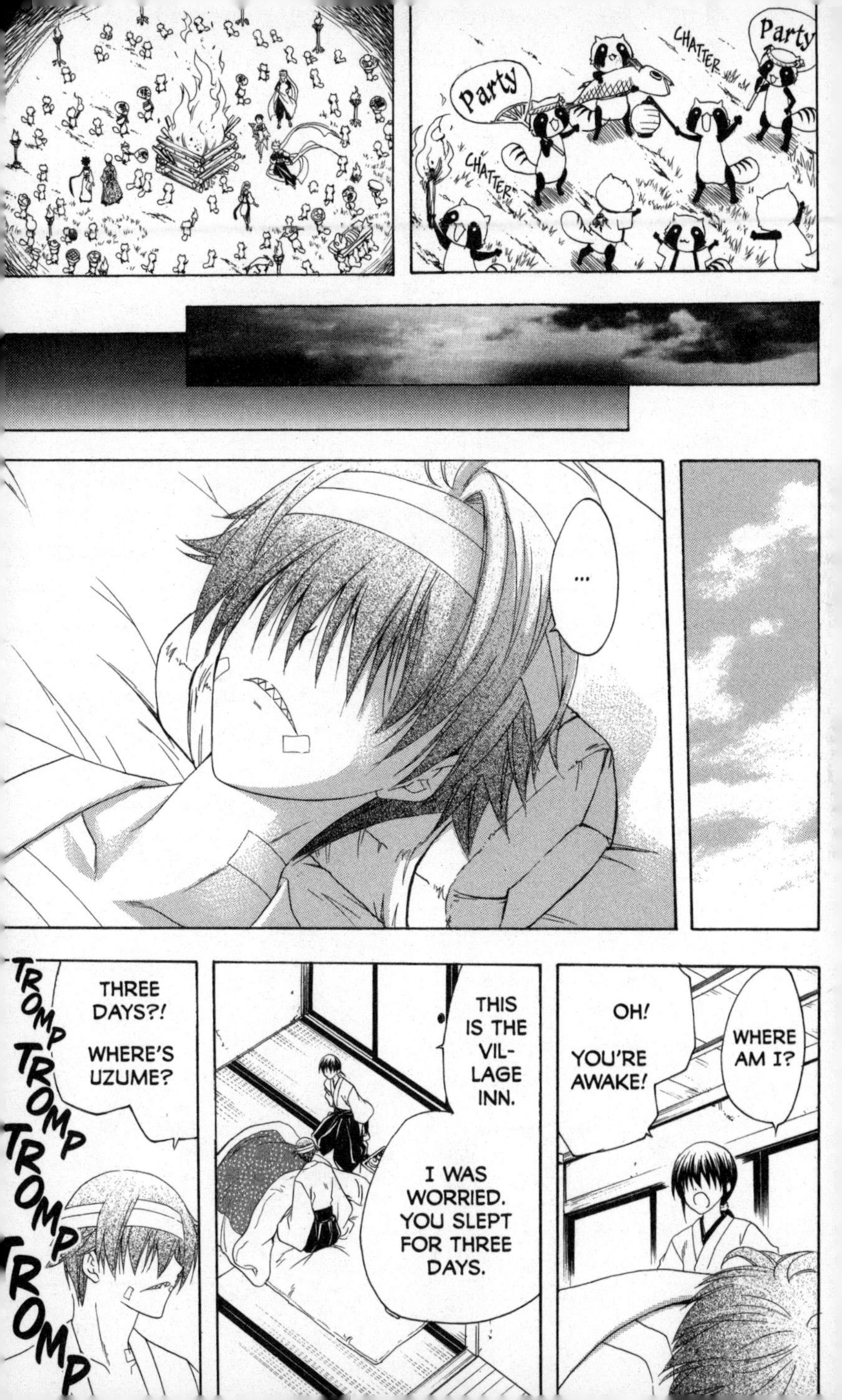

Party
CHATTER
Party
CHATTER
...
WHERE AM I?
OH!
YOU'RE AWAKE!
THIS IS THE VIL-LAGE INN.
I WAS WORRIED. YOU SLEPT FOR THREE DAYS.
THREE DAYS?!
WHERE'S UZUME?
TROMP TROMP TROMP TROMP TROMP TROMP TROMP

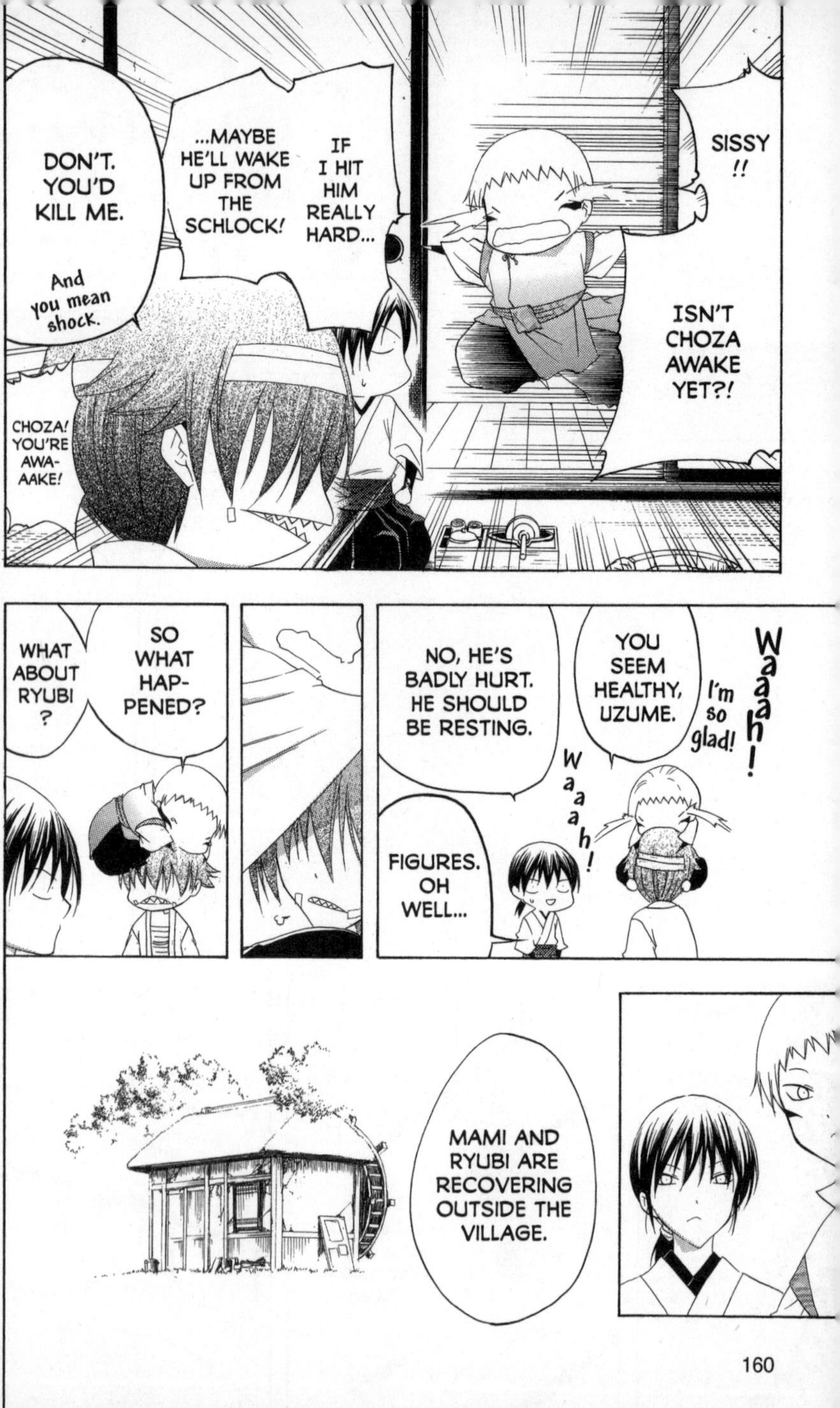
SISSY!!
ISN'T CHOZA AWAKE YET?!
IF I HIT HIM REALLY HARD...
...MAYBE HE'LL WAKE UP FROM THE SCHLOCK!
DON'T. YOU'D KILL ME.
And you mean shock.
CHOZA! YOU'RE AWA-AAKE!
Waaaah!
I'm so glad!
YOU SEEM HEALTHY, UZUME.
Waaah!
NO, HE'S BADLY HURT. HE SHOULD BE RESTING.
FIGURES. OH WELL...
SO WHAT HAP-PENED?
WHAT ABOUT RYUBI?
MAMI AND RYUBI ARE RECOVERING OUTSIDE THE VILLAGE.

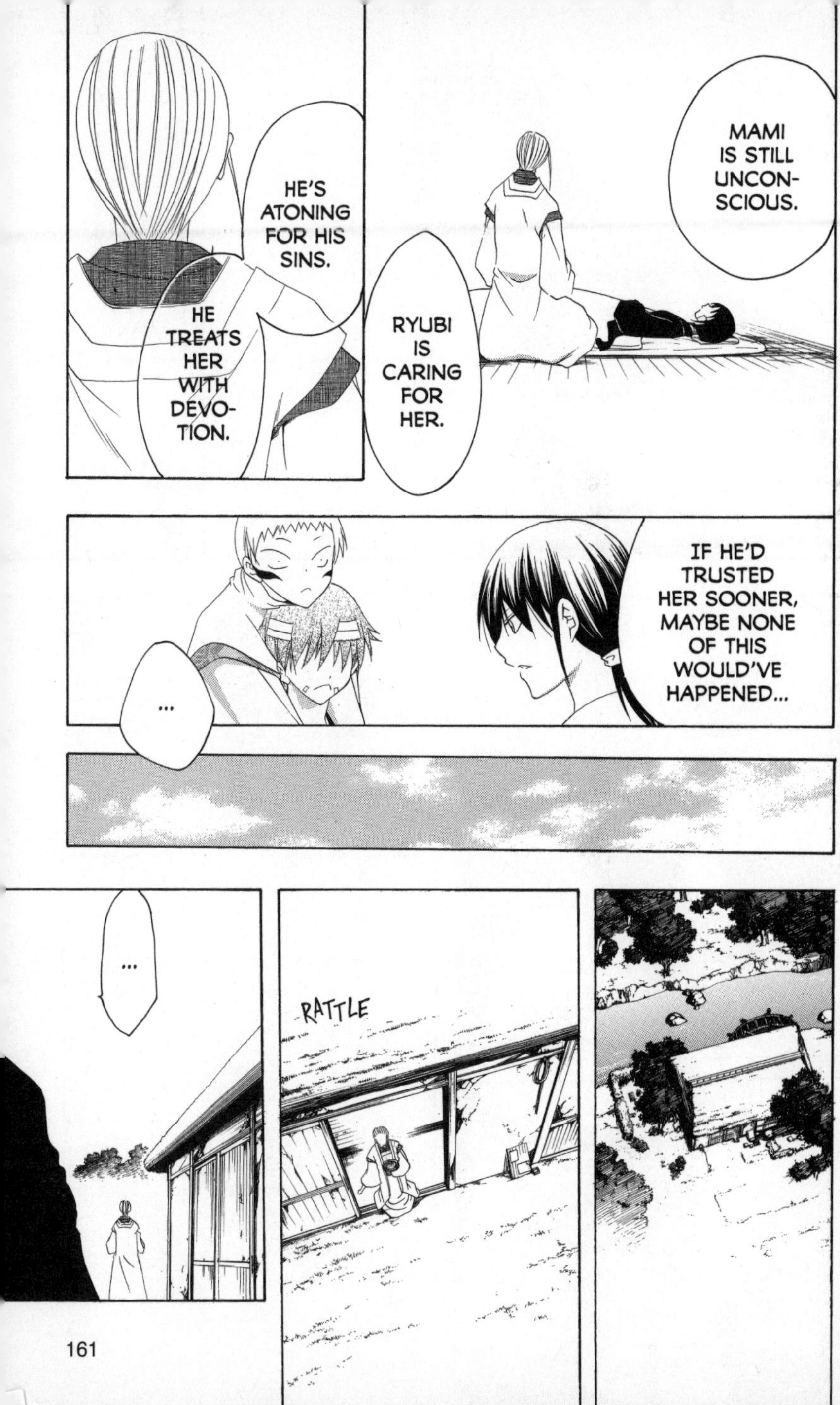
MAMI IS STILL UNCONSCIOUS.
RYUBI IS CARING FOR HER.
HE'S ATONING FOR HIS SINS.
HE TREATS HER WITH DEVOTION.
IF HE'D TRUSTED HER SOONER, MAYBE NONE OF THIS WOULD'VE HAPPENED...
...
RATTLE
...

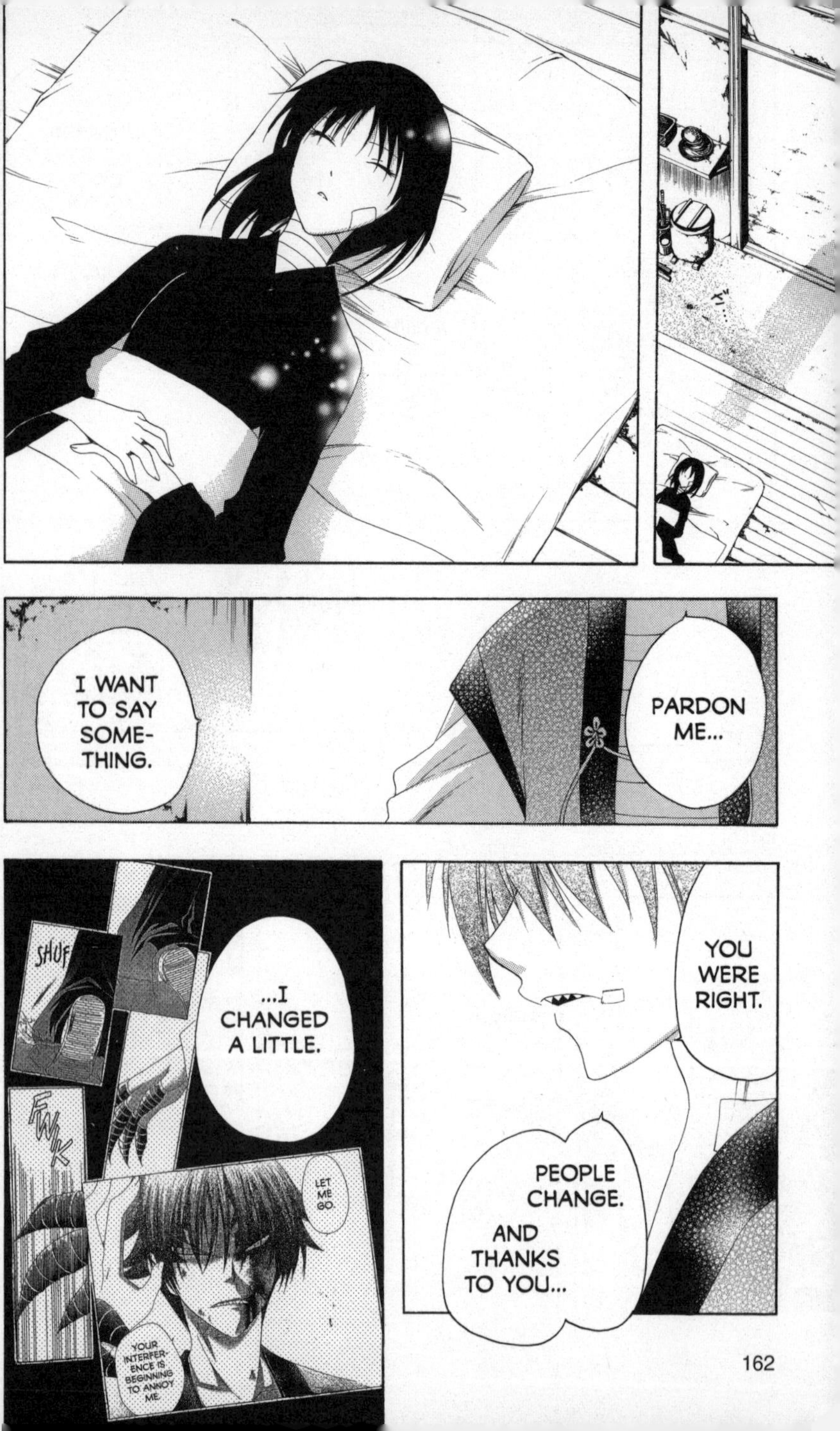
PARDON ME...
I WANT TO SAY SOME-THING.
YOU WERE RIGHT.
PEOPLE CHANGE.
AND THANKS TO YOU...
...I CHANGED A LITTLE.
SHUF
FWIK
LET ME GO.
YOUR INTERFER-ENCE IS BEGINNING TO ANNOY ME.

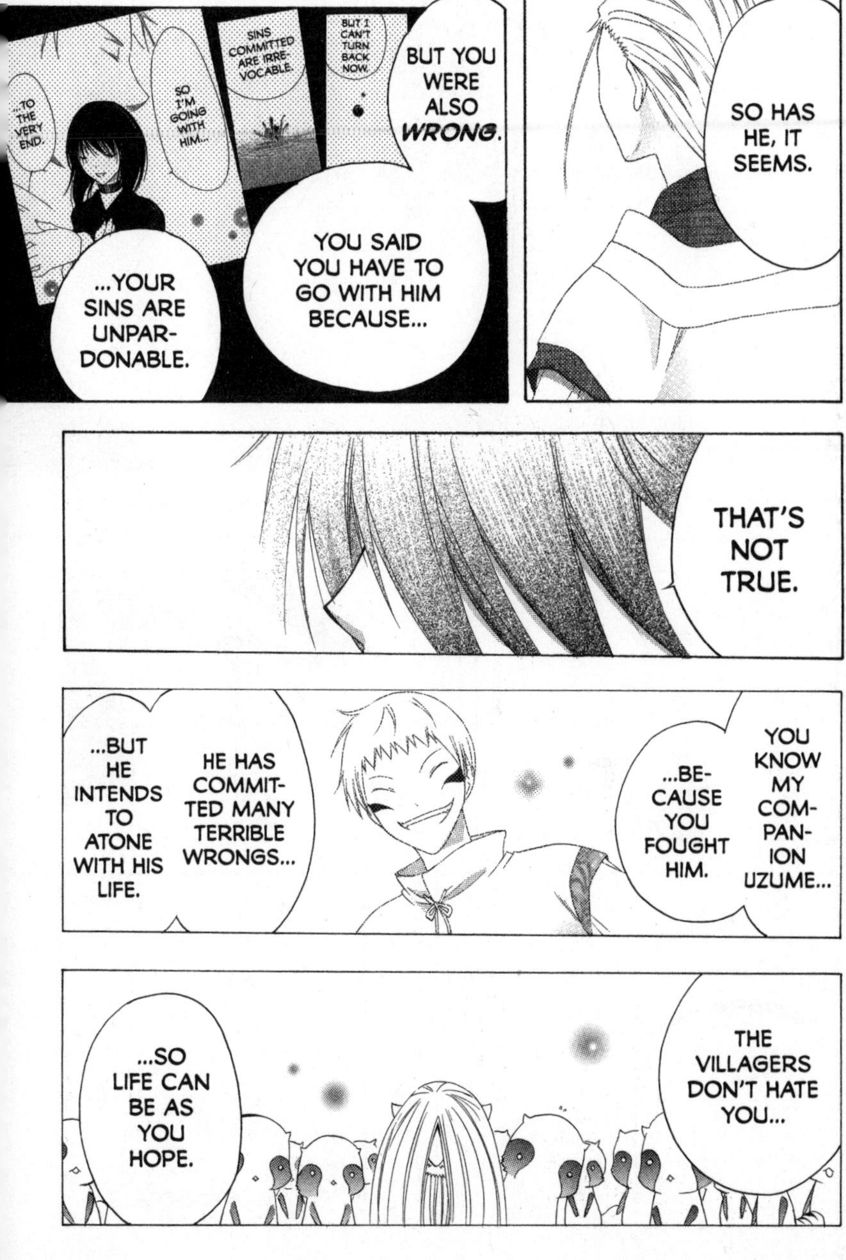
SO HAS HE, IT SEEMS.
BUT YOU WERE ALSO *WRONG*.
BUT I CAN'T TURN BACK NOW.
SINS COMMITTED ARE IRREVOCABLE.
SO I'M GOING WITH HIM...
...TO THE VERY END.
YOU SAID YOU HAVE TO GO WITH HIM BECAUSE...
...YOUR SINS ARE UNPARDONABLE.
THAT'S NOT TRUE.
YOU KNOW MY COMPANION UZUME...
...BECAUSE YOU FOUGHT HIM.
HE HAS COMMITTED MANY TERRIBLE WRONGS...
...BUT HE INTENDS TO ATONE WITH HIS LIFE.
THE VILLAGERS DON'T HATE YOU...
...SO LIFE CAN BE AS YOU HOPE.

LIVE AND BE HAPPY.

DON'T GIVE UP.

TUMP

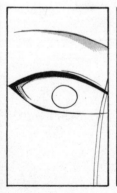

RATTLE

164

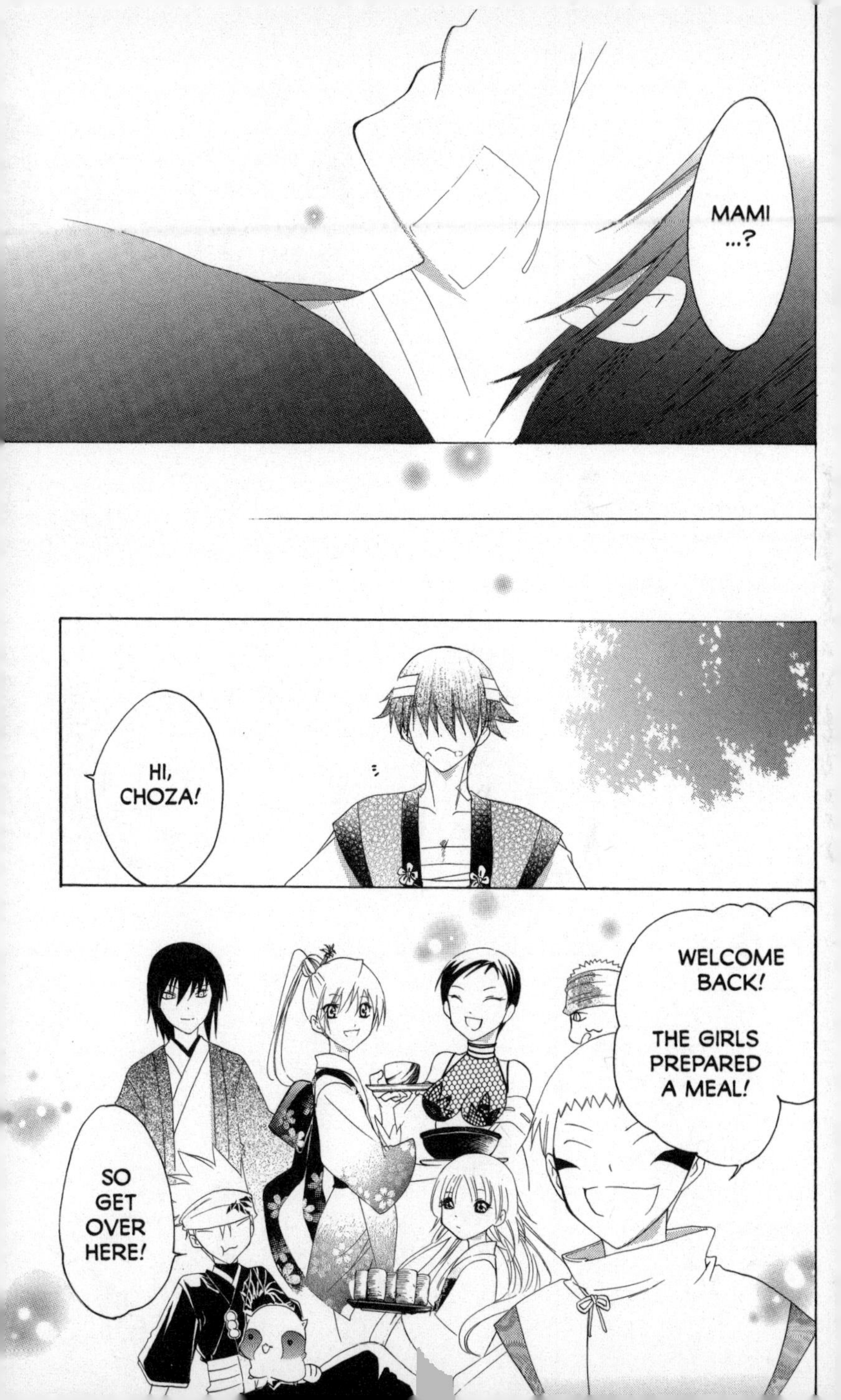
MAMI ...?
HI, CHOZA!
WELCOME BACK!
THE GIRLS PREPARED A MEAL!
SO GET OVER HERE!

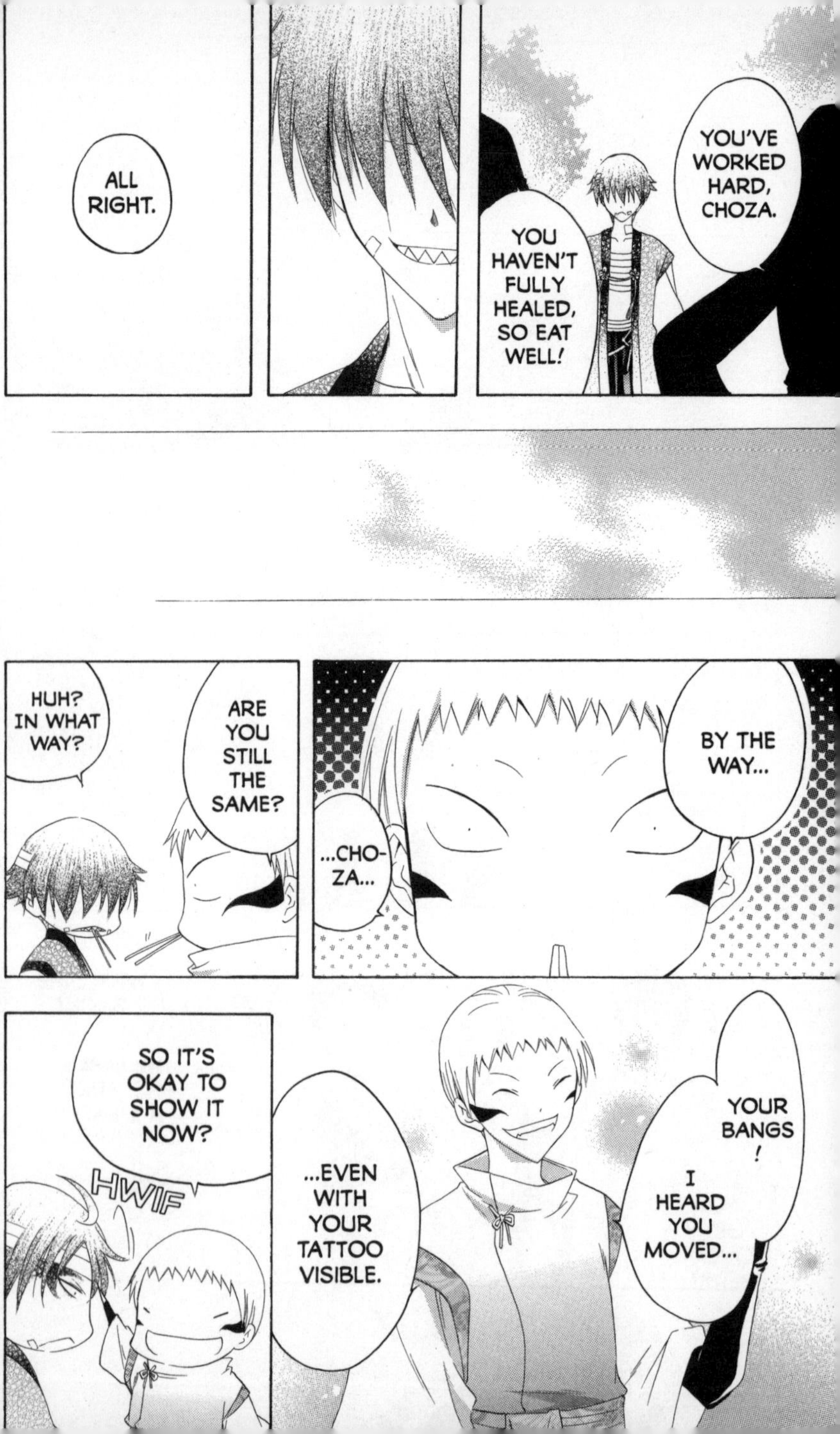
YOU'VE WORKED HARD, CHOZA.
YOU HAVEN'T FULLY HEALED, SO EAT WELL!
ALL RIGHT.
BY THE WAY...
...CHO-ZA...
ARE YOU STILL THE SAME?
HUH? IN WHAT WAY?
YOUR BANGS!
I HEARD YOU MOVED...
...EVEN WITH YOUR TATTOO VISIBLE.
SO IT'S OKAY TO SHOW IT NOW?
HWIF

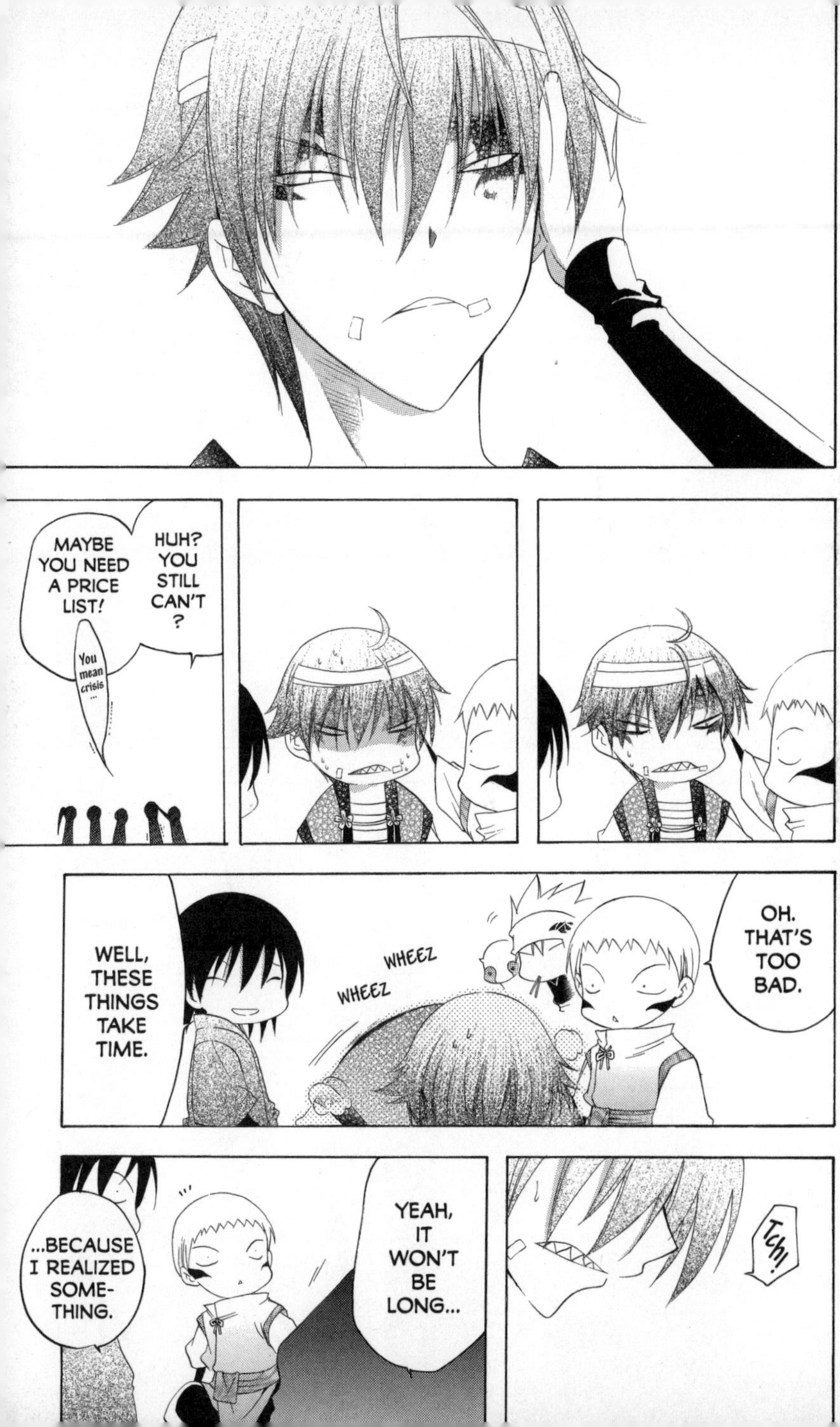
HUH? YOU STILL CAN'T ?
MAYBE YOU NEED A PRICE LIST!
You mean crisis...
OH. THAT'S TOO BAD.
WHEEZ
WHEEZ
WELL, THESE THINGS TAKE TIME.
Tch!
YEAH, IT WON'T BE LONG...
...BECAUSE I REALIZED SOME-THING.

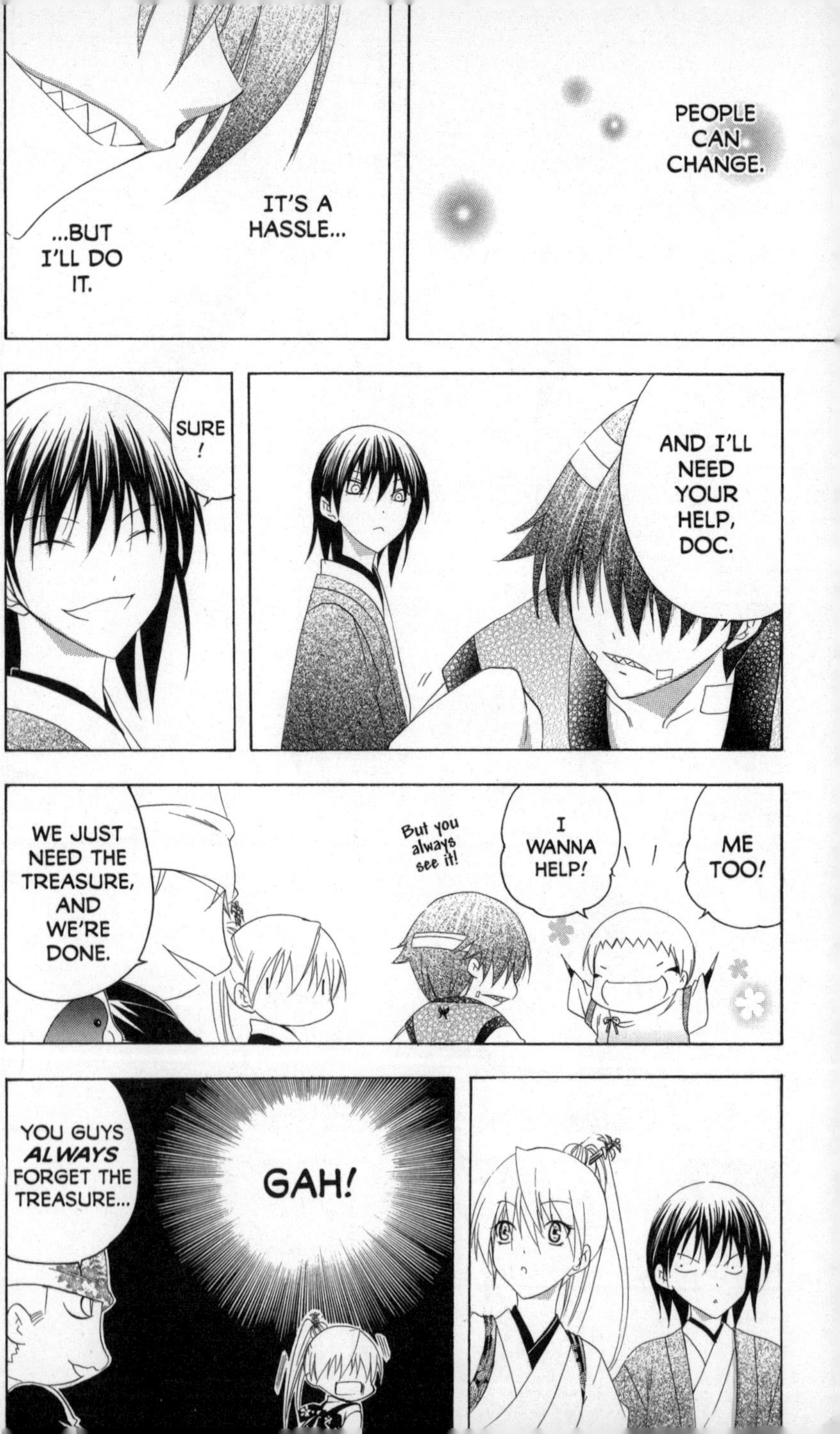
PEOPLE CAN CHANGE.
IT'S A HASSLE...
...BUT I'LL DO IT.
AND I'LL NEED YOUR HELP, DOC.
SURE!
ME TOO!
I WANNA HELP!
But you always see it!
WE JUST NEED THE TREASURE, AND WE'RE DONE.
YOU GUYS *ALWAYS* FORGET THE TREASURE...
GAH!

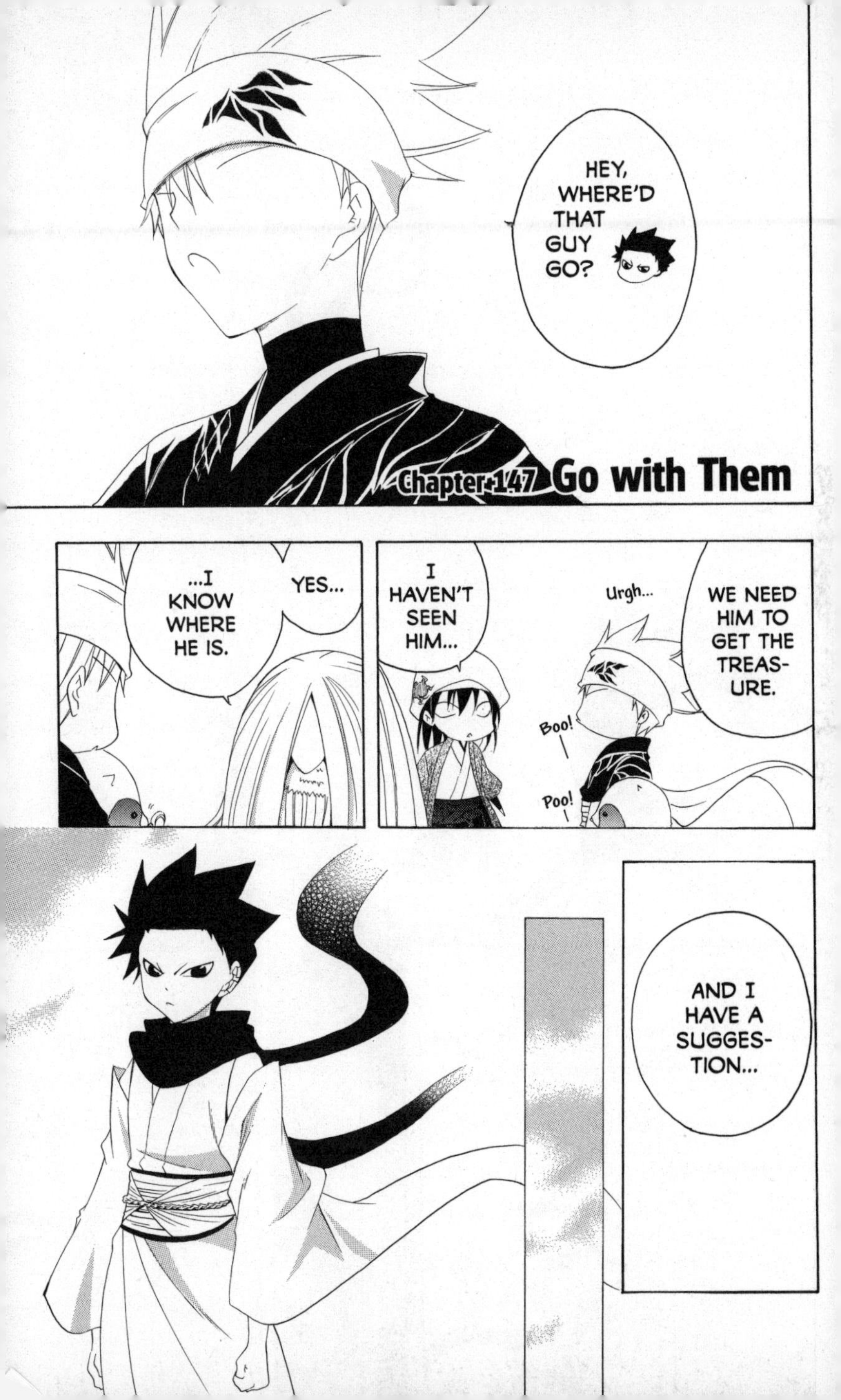
HEY, WHERE'D THAT GUY GO?
Chapter 147 Go with Them
WE NEED HIM TO GET THE TREASURE.
Urgh...
Boo!
Poo!
I HAVEN'T SEEN HIM...
YES...
...I KNOW WHERE HE IS.
AND I HAVE A SUGGESTION...

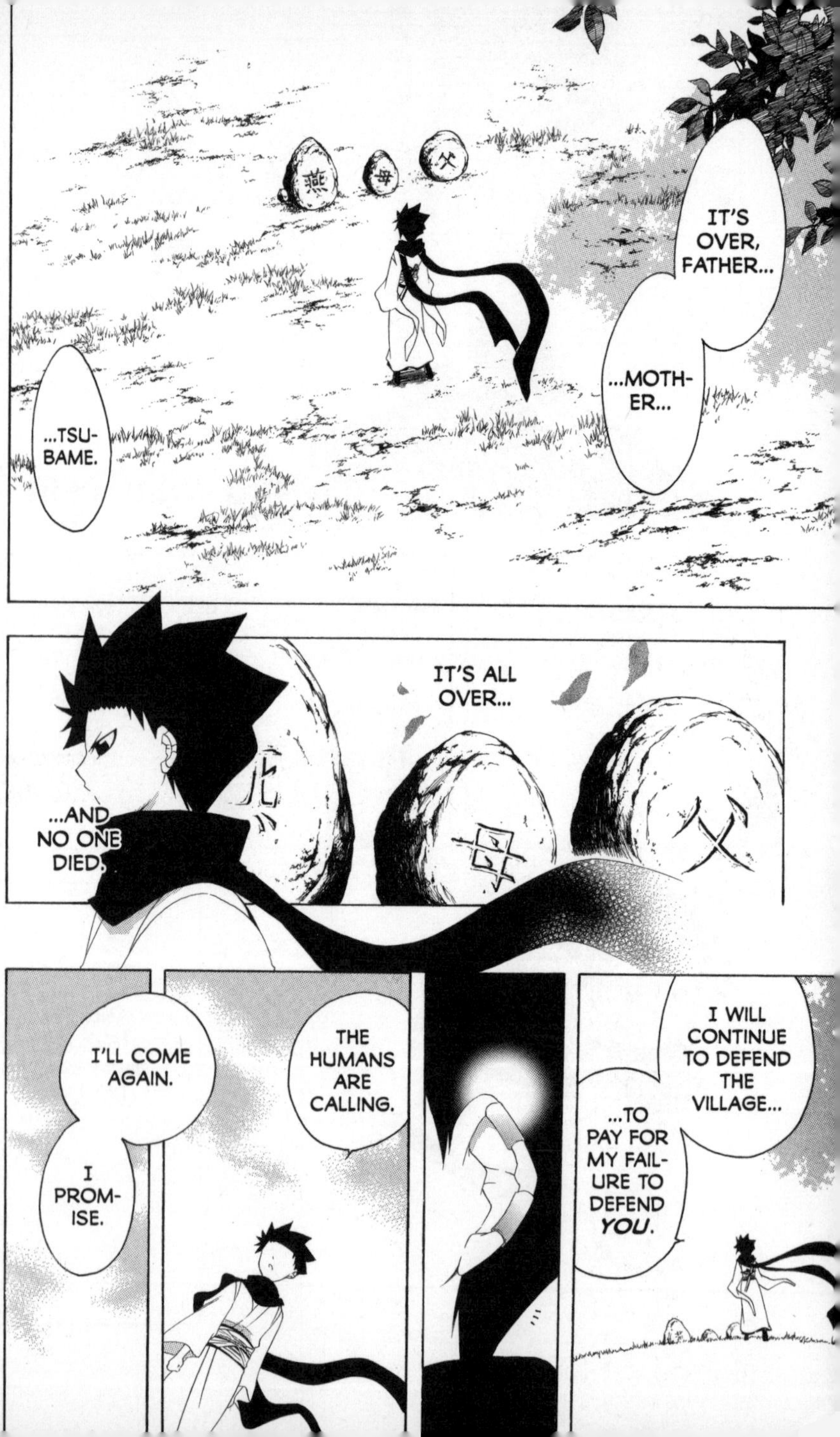
IT'S OVER, FATHER...
...MOTH-ER...
...TSU-BAME.
IT'S ALL OVER...
...AND NO ONE DIED.
I WILL CONTINUE TO DEFEND THE VILLAGE...
...TO PAY FOR MY FAIL-URE TO DEFEND *YOU*.
THE HUMANS ARE CALLING.
I'LL COME AGAIN.
I PROM-ISE.

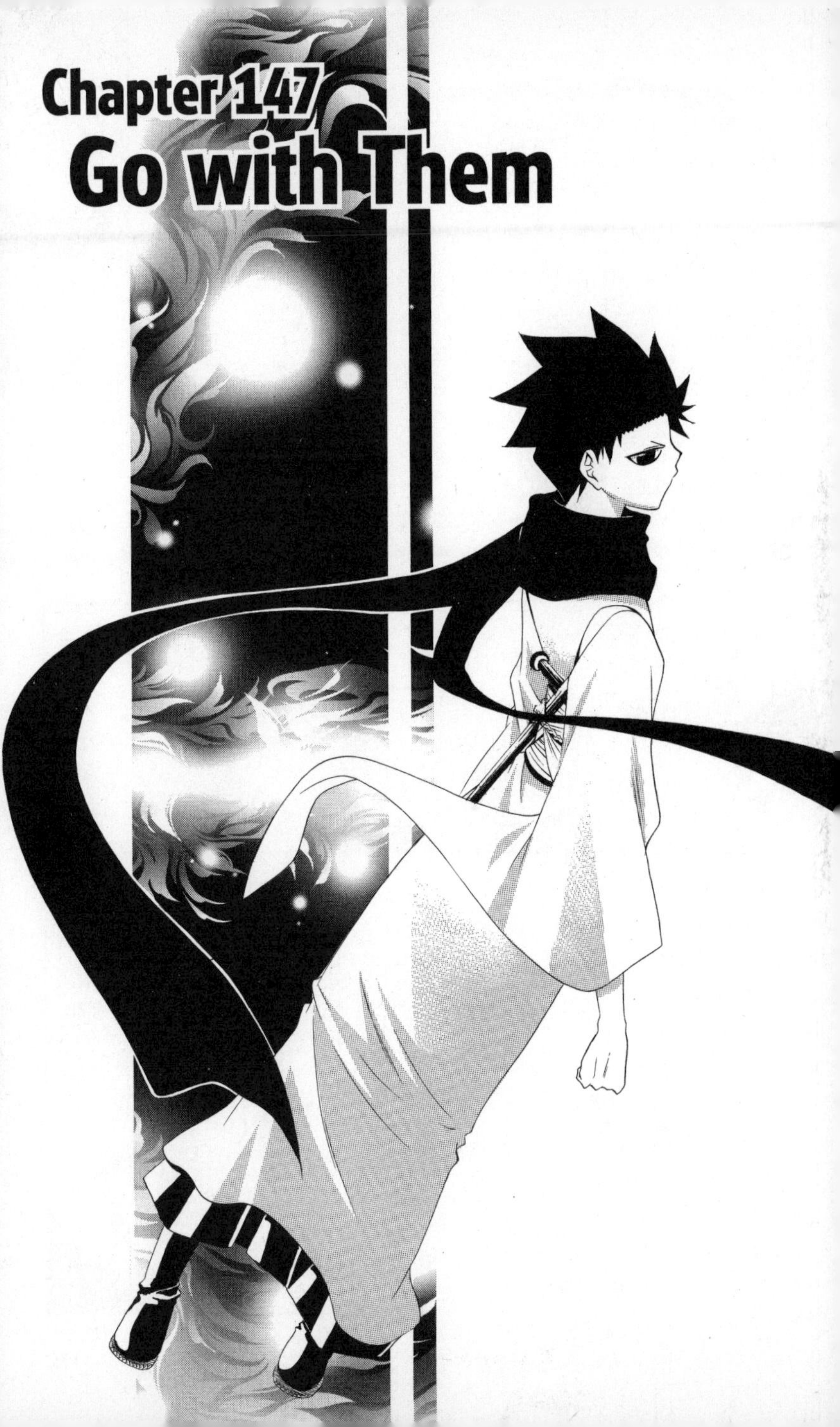
Chapter 147
Go with Them

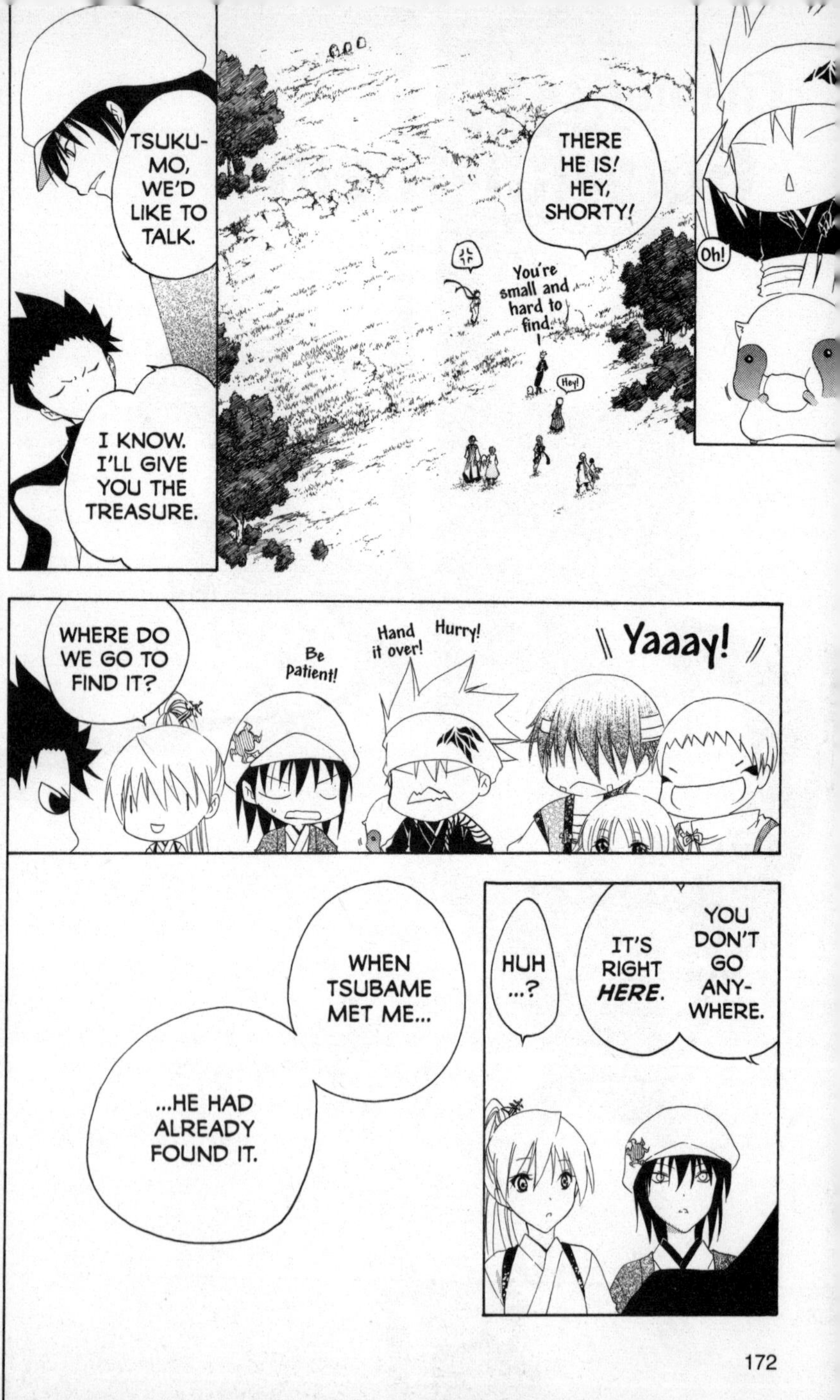
Oh!
THERE HE IS! HEY, SHORTY!
You're small and hard to find!
Hey!
TSUKU-MO, WE'D LIKE TO TALK.
I KNOW. I'LL GIVE YOU THE TREASURE.
Yaaay!
Hurry!
Hand it over!
Be patient!
WHERE DO WE GO TO FIND IT?
YOU DON'T GO ANY-WHERE.
IT'S RIGHT *HERE*.
HUH ...?
WHEN TSUBAME MET ME...
...HE HAD ALREADY FOUND IT.

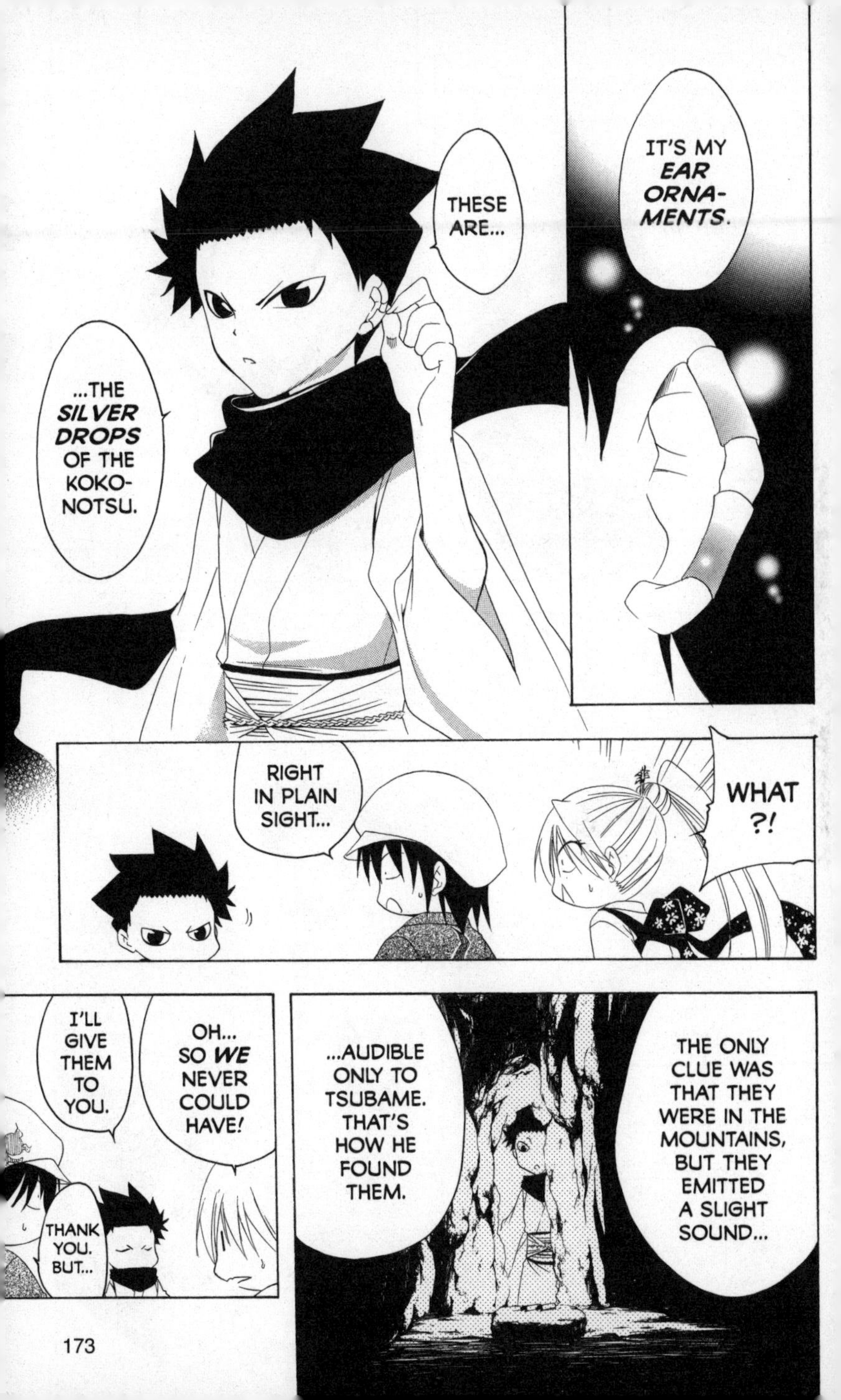
IT'S MY EAR ORNAMENTS.
THESE ARE...
...THE SILVER DROPS OF THE KOKONOTSU.
WHAT?!
RIGHT IN PLAIN SIGHT...
THE ONLY CLUE WAS THAT THEY WERE IN THE MOUNTAINS, BUT THEY EMITTED A SLIGHT SOUND...
...AUDIBLE ONLY TO TSUBAME. THAT'S HOW HE FOUND THEM.
OH... SO WE NEVER COULD HAVE!
I'LL GIVE THEM TO YOU.
THANK YOU. BUT...

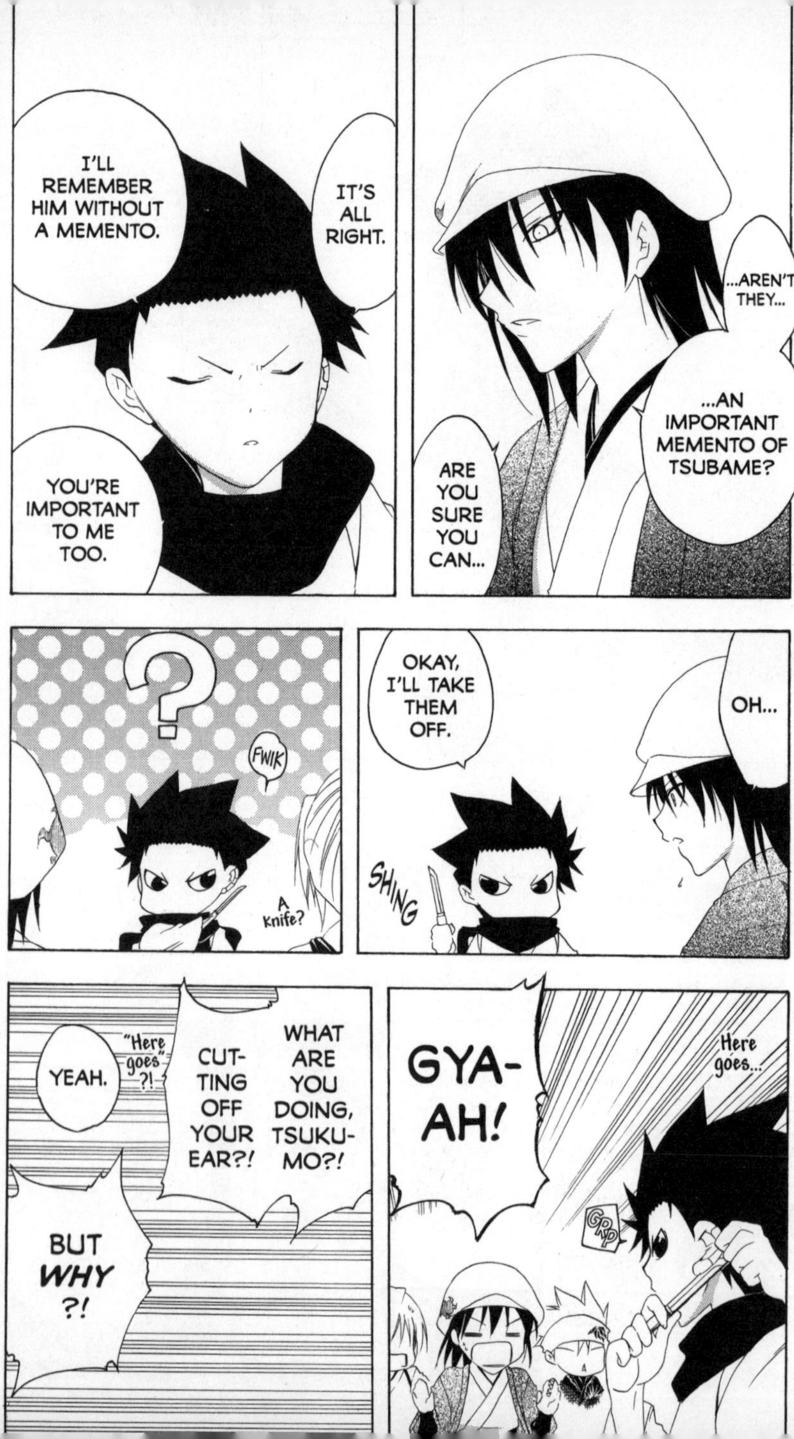
...AREN'T THEY...
...AN IMPORTANT MEMENTO OF TSUBAME?
ARE YOU SURE YOU CAN...
IT'S ALL RIGHT.
I'LL REMEMBER HIM WITHOUT A MEMENTO.
YOU'RE IMPORTANT TO ME TOO.
OH...
OKAY, I'LL TAKE THEM OFF.
SHING
?
FWIK
A knife?
Here goes...
GYA-AH!
GRP
WHAT ARE YOU DOING, TSUKUMO?!
CUT-TING OFF YOUR EAR?!
"Here goes"?!
YEAH.
BUT *WHY* ?!

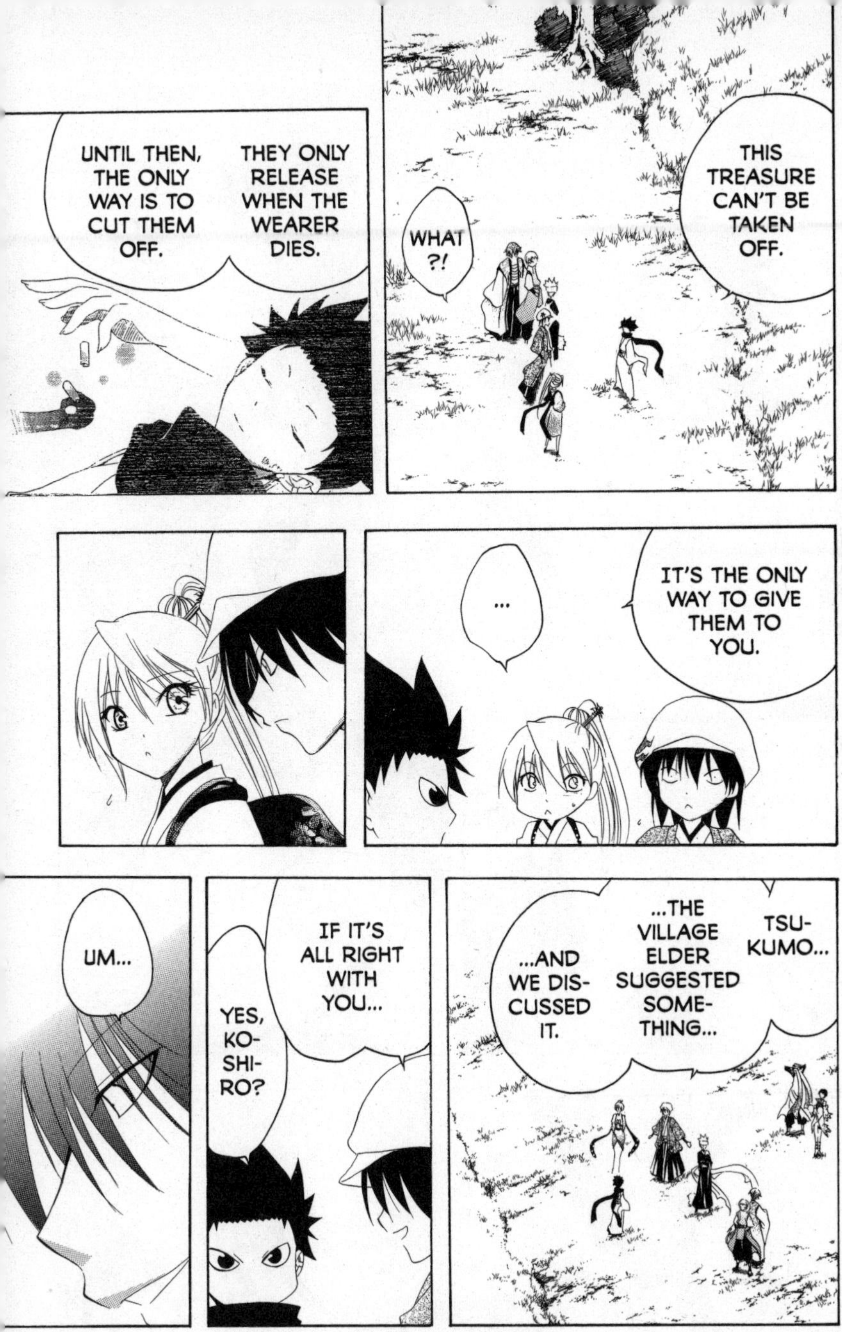
THIS TREASURE CAN'T BE TAKEN OFF.
WHAT ?!
THEY ONLY RELEASE WHEN THE WEARER DIES.
UNTIL THEN, THE ONLY WAY IS TO CUT THEM OFF.
IT'S THE ONLY WAY TO GIVE THEM TO YOU.
...
TSU-KUMO...
...THE VILLAGE ELDER SUGGESTED SOME-THING...
...AND WE DIS-CUSSED IT.
IF IT'S ALL RIGHT WITH YOU...
YES, KO-SHI-RO?
UM...

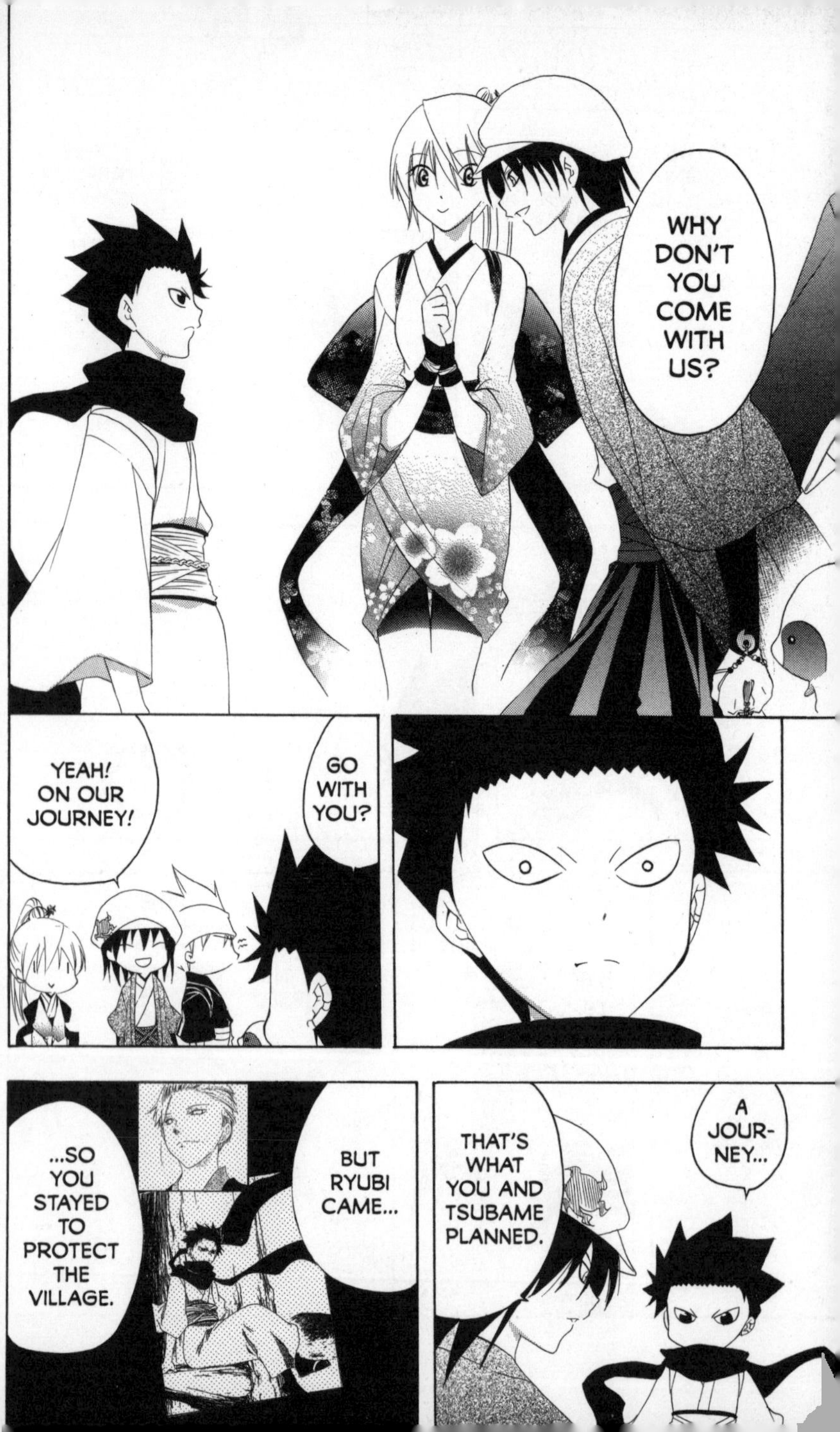
WHY DON'T YOU COME WITH US?
GO WITH YOU?
YEAH! ON OUR JOURNEY!
A JOUR-NEY...
THAT'S WHAT YOU AND TSUBAME PLANNED.
BUT RYUBI CAME...
...SO YOU STAYED TO PROTECT THE VILLAGE.

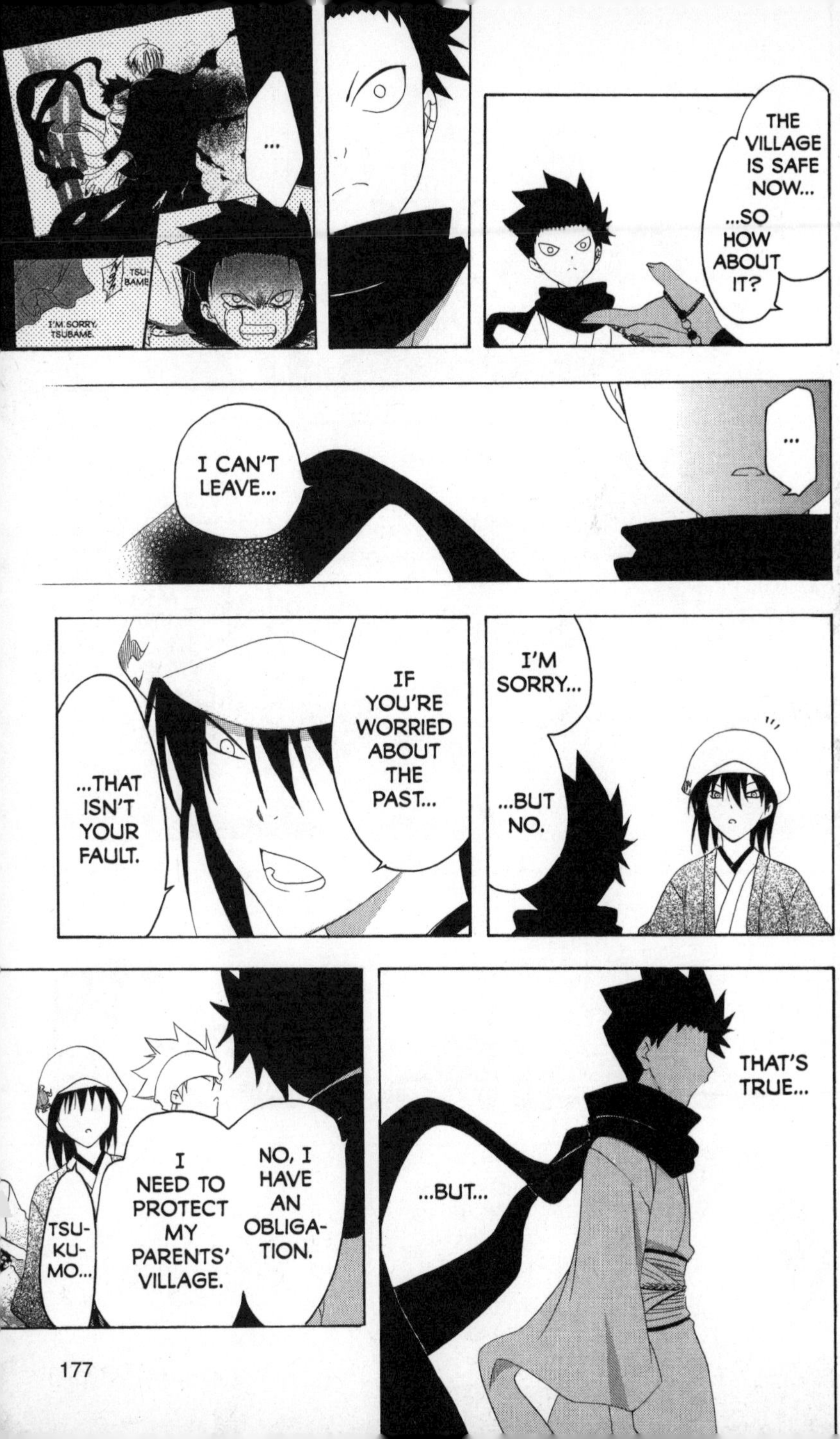
THE VILLAGE IS SAFE NOW...
...SO HOW ABOUT IT?
...
TSU-BAME
I'M SORRY, TSUBAME.
...
I CAN'T LEAVE...
I'M SORRY...
...BUT NO.
IF YOU'RE WORRIED ABOUT THE PAST...
...THAT ISN'T YOUR FAULT.
THAT'S TRUE...
...BUT...
NO, I HAVE AN OBLIGA-TION.
I NEED TO PROTECT MY PARENTS' VILLAGE.
TSU-KU-MO...

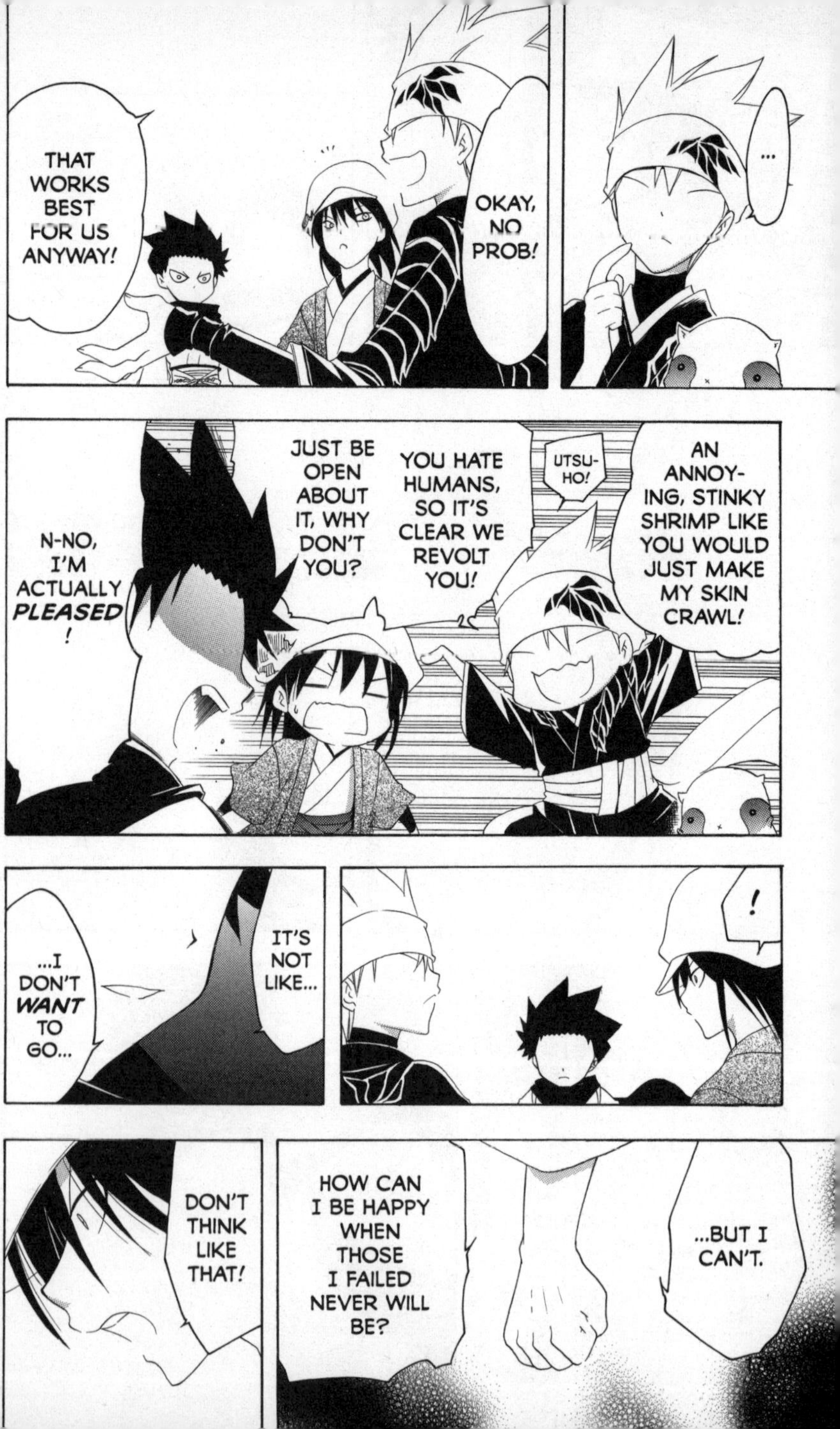
...
OKAY, NO PROB!
THAT WORKS BEST FOR US ANYWAY!
AN ANNOY-ING, STINKY SHRIMP LIKE YOU WOULD JUST MAKE MY SKIN CRAWL!
UTSU-HO!
YOU HATE HUMANS, SO IT'S CLEAR WE REVOLT YOU!
JUST BE OPEN ABOUT IT, WHY DON'T YOU?
N-NO, I'M ACTUALLY *PLEASED*!
!
IT'S NOT LIKE...
...I DON'T *WANT* TO GO...
...BUT I CAN'T.
HOW CAN I BE HAPPY WHEN THOSE I FAILED NEVER WILL BE?
DON'T THINK LIKE THAT!

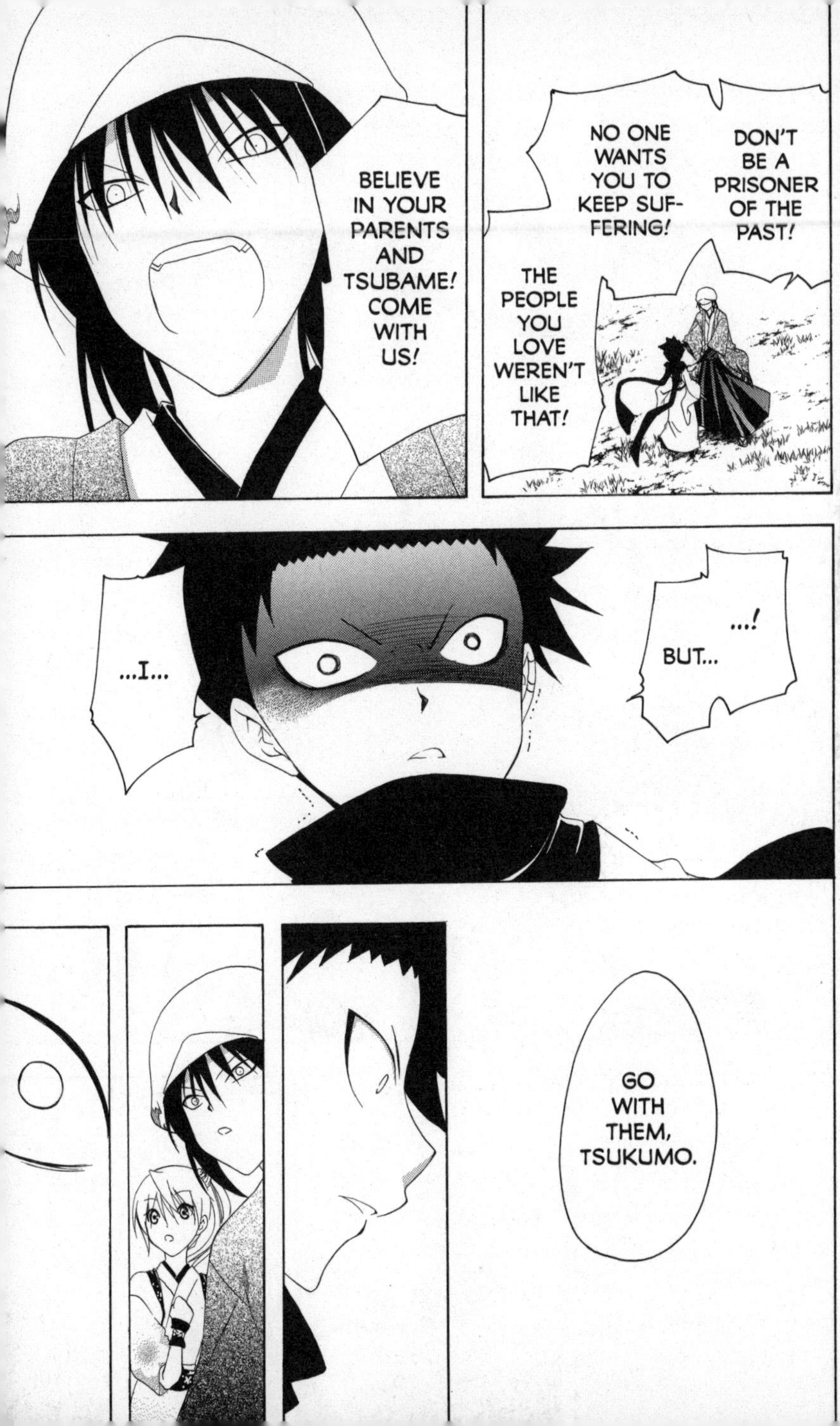
DON'T BE A PRISONER OF THE PAST!
NO ONE WANTS YOU TO KEEP SUF-FERING!
THE PEOPLE YOU LOVE WEREN'T LIKE THAT!
BELIEVE IN YOUR PARENTS AND TSUBAME! COME WITH US!
...!
BUT...
...I...
GO WITH THEM, TSUKUMO.

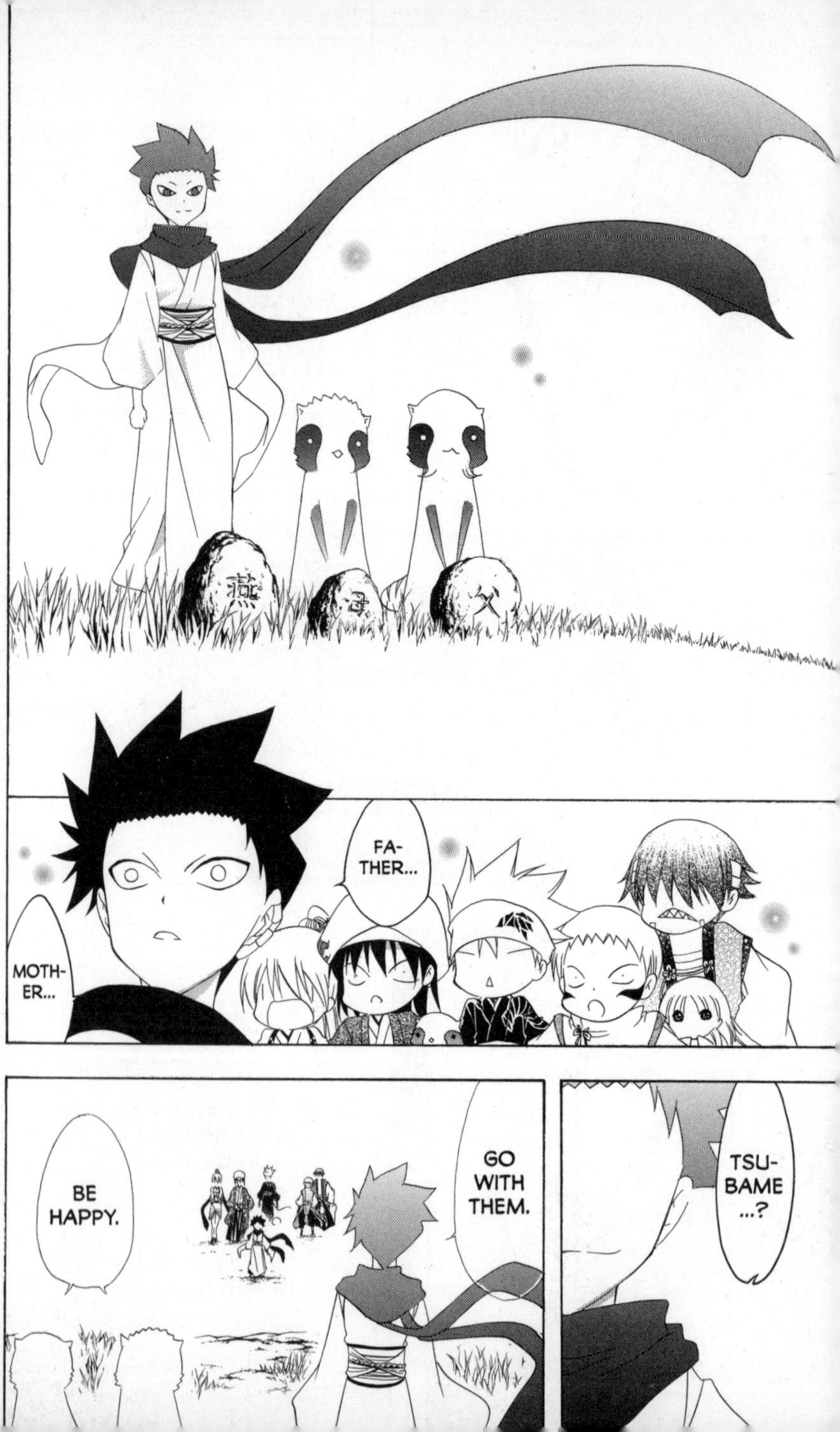
父
母
燕
FA-THER...
MOTH-ER...
TSU-BAME ...?
GO WITH THEM.
BE HAPPY.

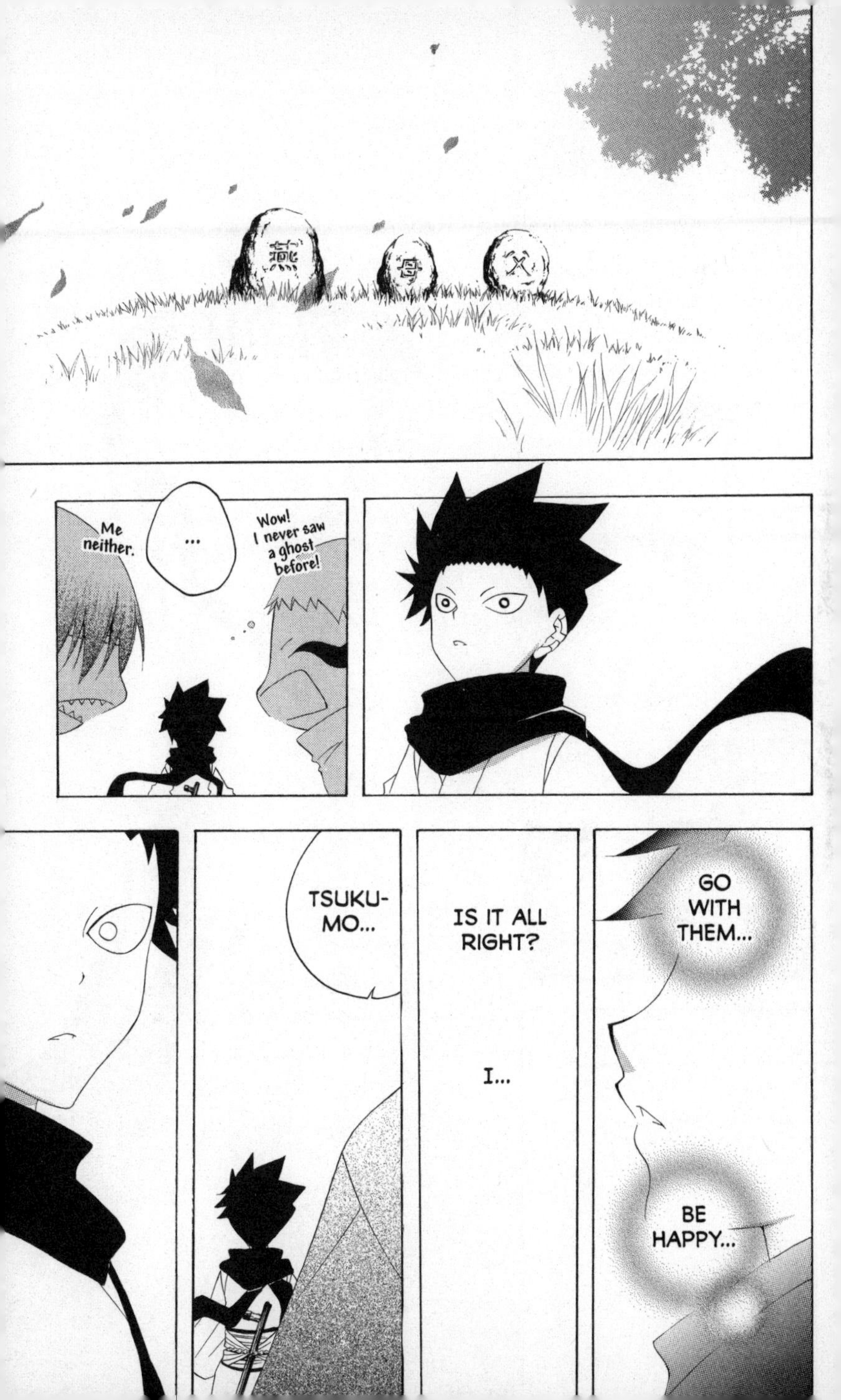
Wow! I never saw a ghost before!
...
Me neither.
GO WITH THEM...
BE HAPPY...
IS IT ALL RIGHT?
I...
TSUKU-MO...

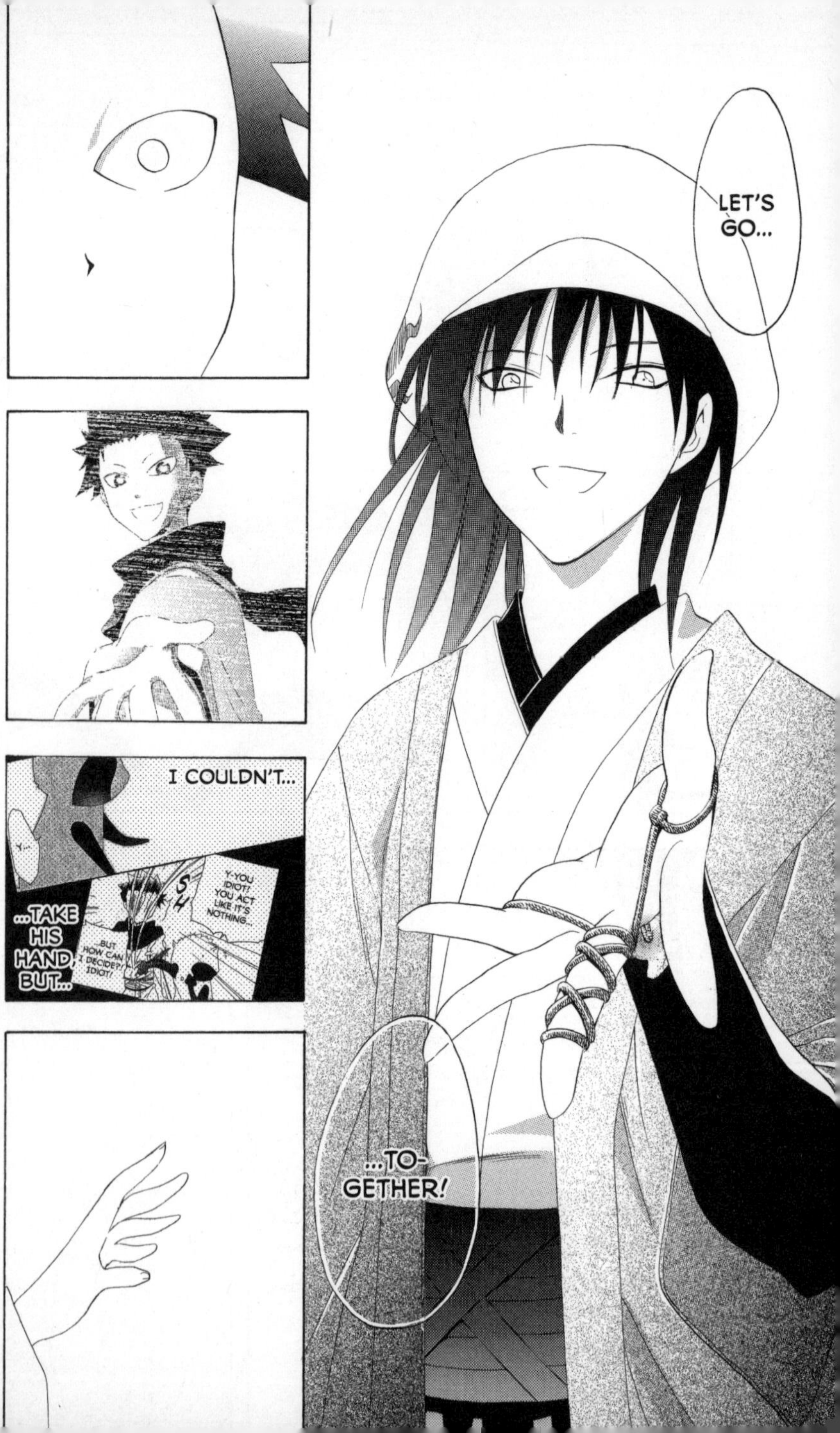
LET'S GO...
...TO-GETHER!
I COULDN'T...
Y...
Y-YOU IDIOT! YOU ACT LIKE IT'S NOTHING...
SH
...BUT HOW CAN I DECIDE?! IDIOT!
...TAKE HIS HAND, BUT...

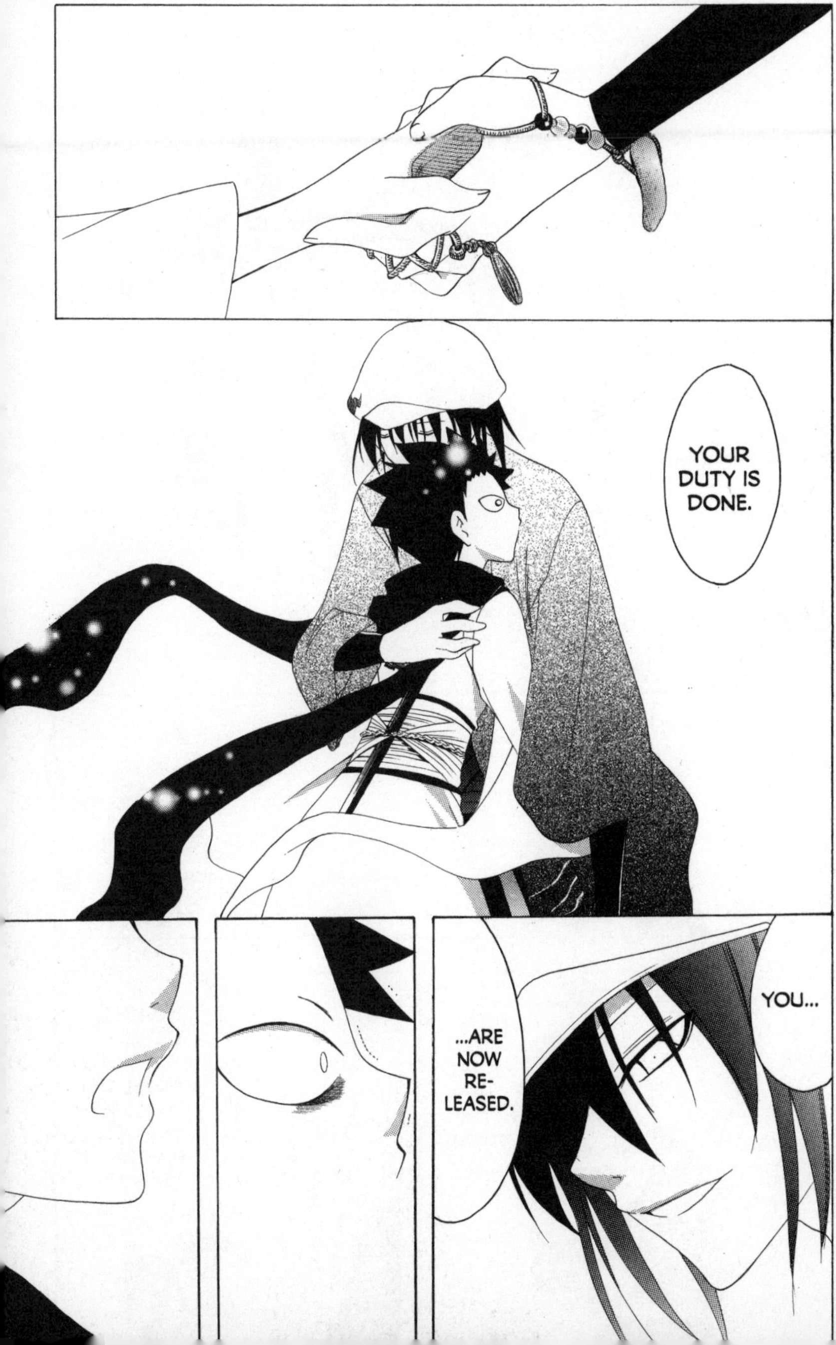
YOUR DUTY IS DONE.
YOU...
...ARE NOW RE-LEASED.

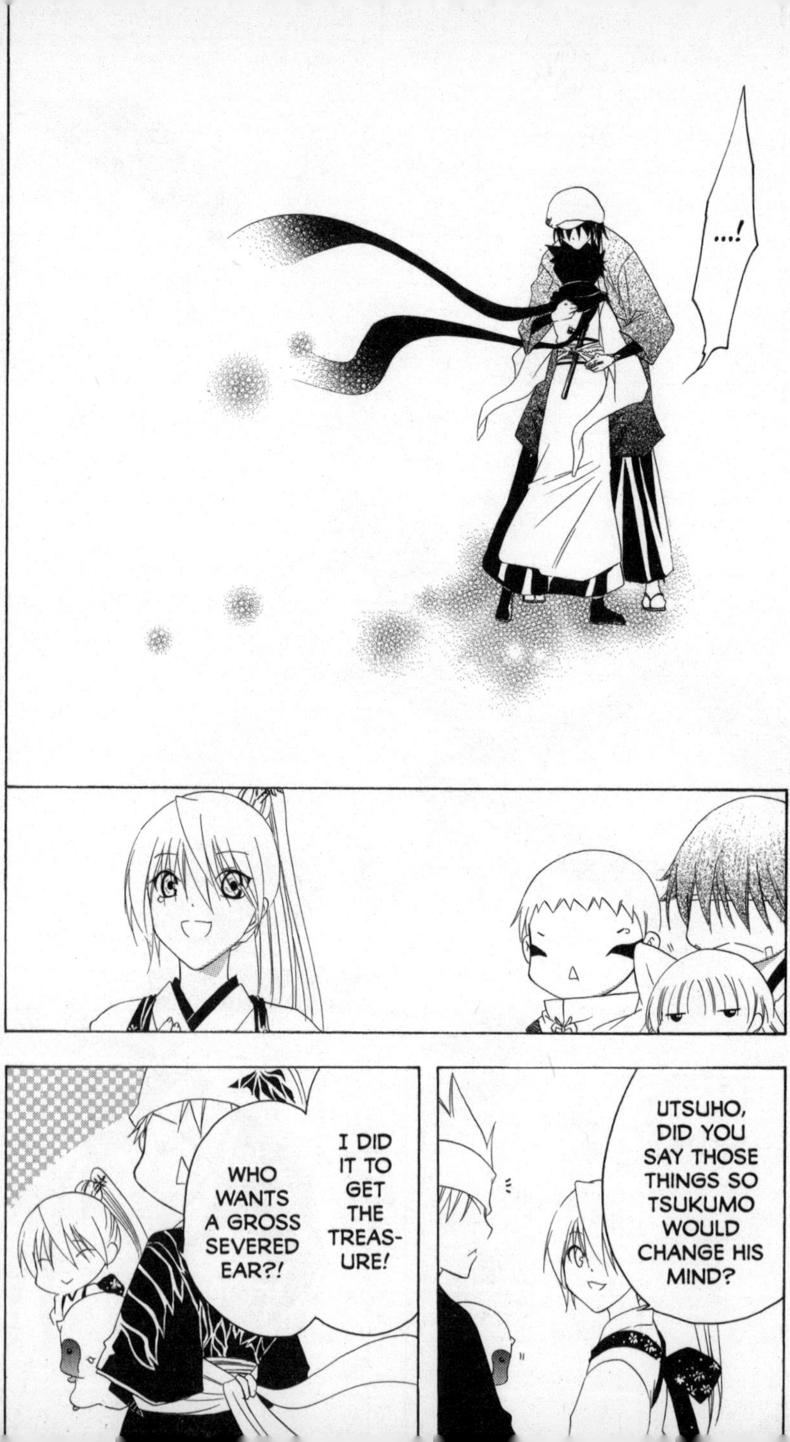
...!
UTSUHO, DID YOU SAY THOSE THINGS SO TSUKUMO WOULD CHANGE HIS MIND?
I DID IT TO GET THE TREASURE!
WHO WANTS A GROSS SEVERED EAR?!

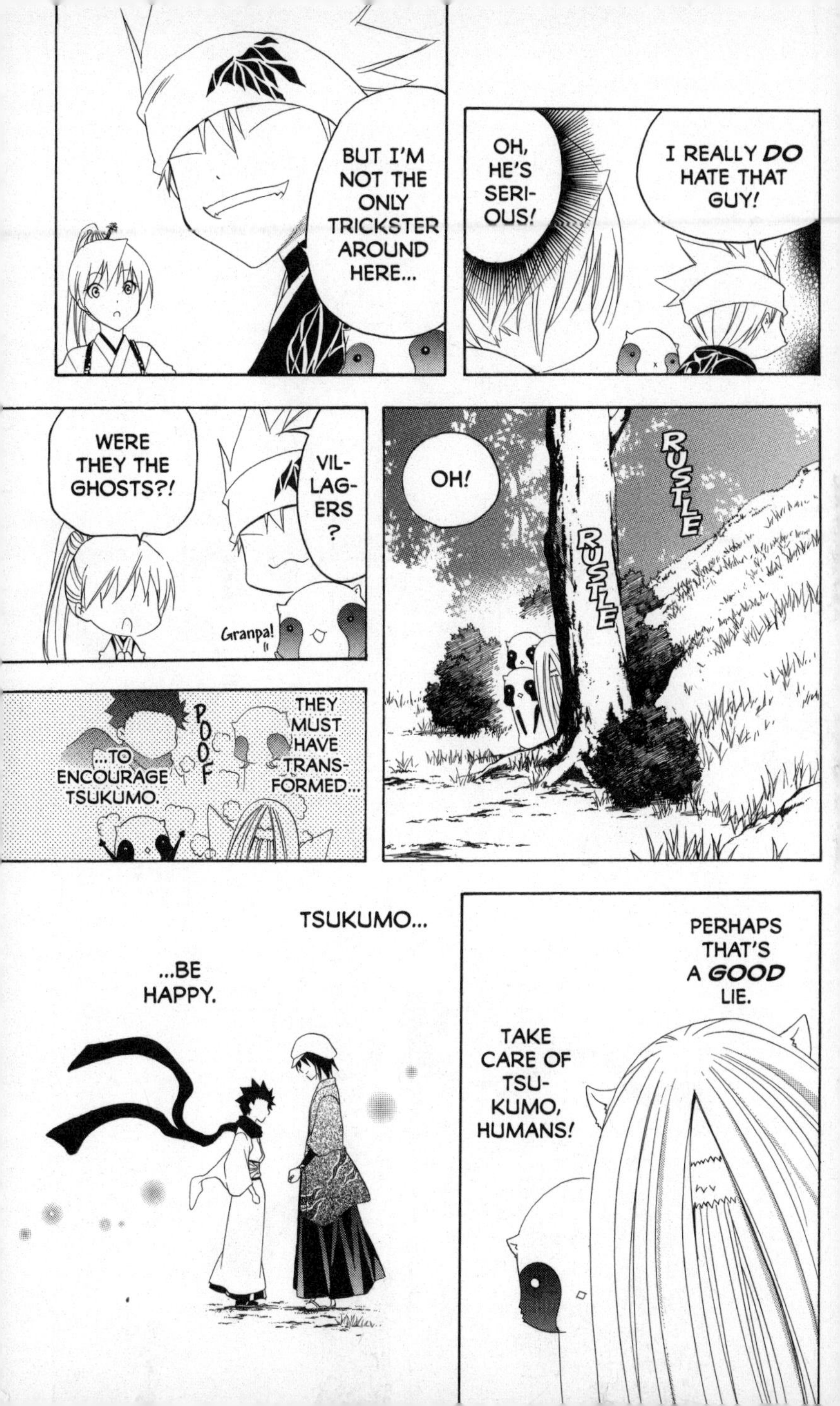
I REALLY DO HATE THAT GUY!
OH, HE'S SERIOUS!
BUT I'M NOT THE ONLY TRICKSTER AROUND HERE...
OH!
RUSTLE
RUSTLE
VILLAGERS?
WERE THEY THE GHOSTS?!
Granpa!
THEY MUST HAVE TRANSFORMED...
POOF
...TO ENCOURAGE TSUKUMO.
PERHAPS THAT'S A GOOD LIE.
TAKE CARE OF TSUKUMO, HUMANS!
TSUKUMO...
...BE HAPPY.

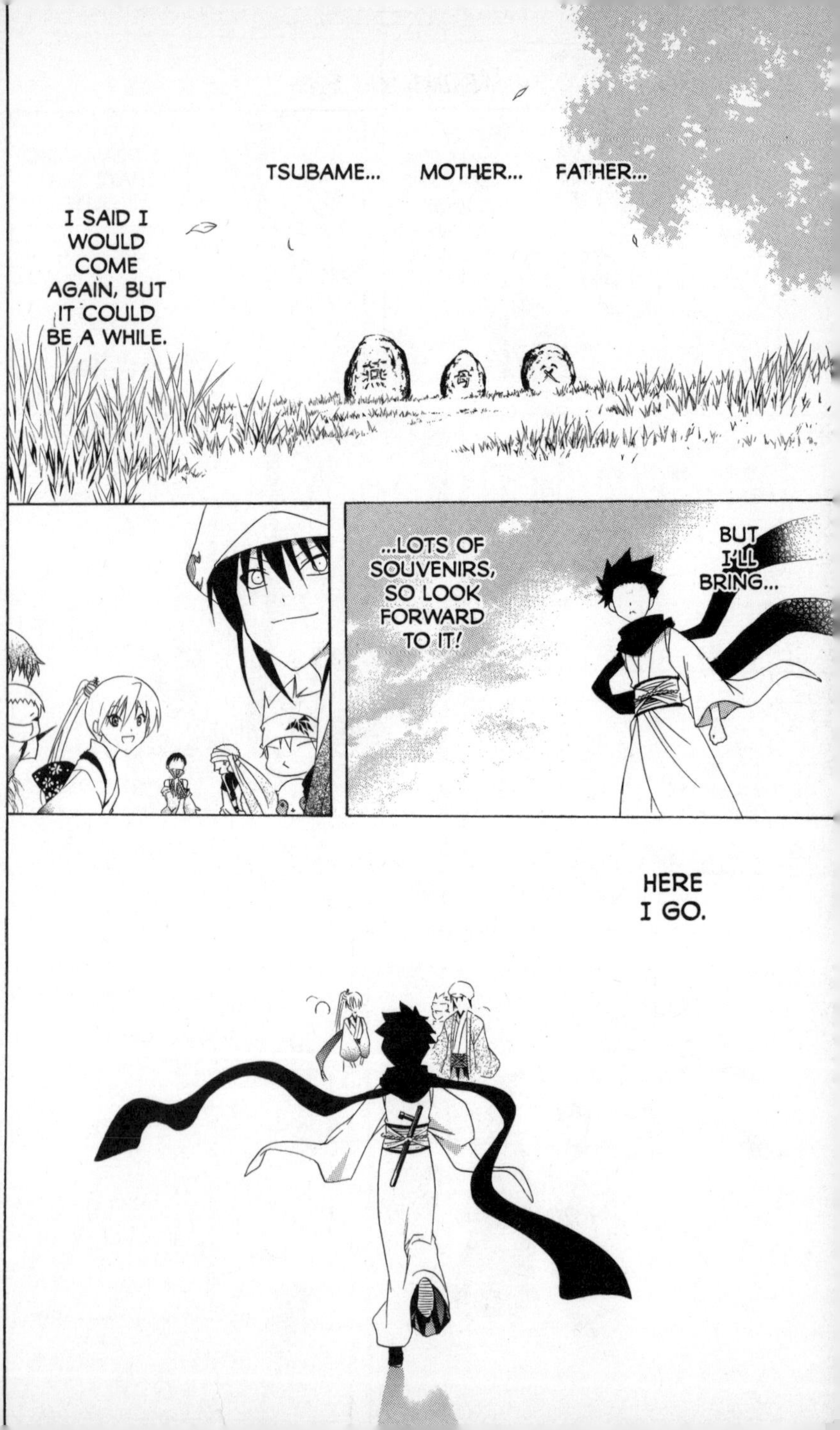
TSUBAME... MOTHER... FATHER...
I SAID I WOULD COME AGAIN, BUT IT COULD BE A WHILE.
BUT I'LL BRING...
...LOTS OF SOUVENIRS, SO LOOK FORWARD TO IT!
HERE I GO.

Bonus Manga

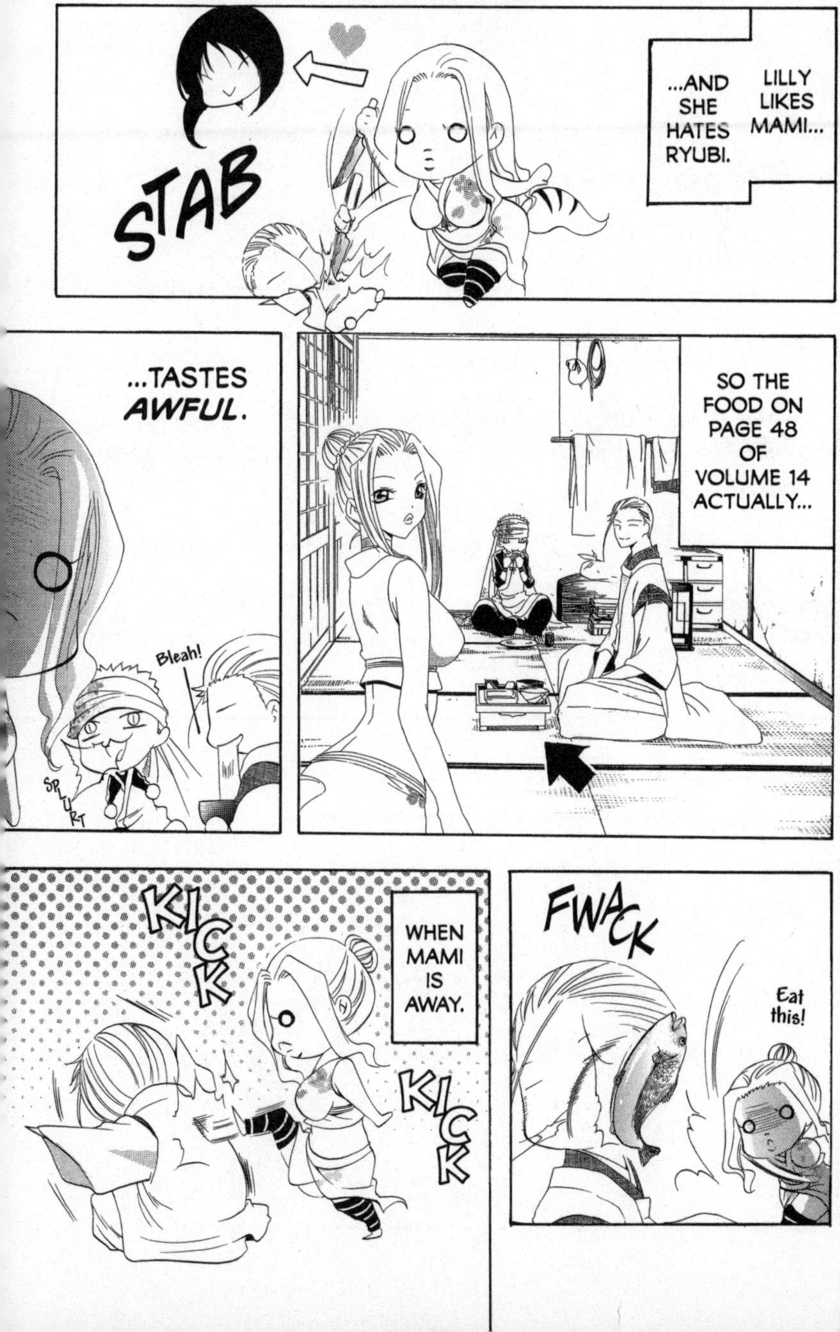
LILLY LIKES MAMI...
...AND SHE HATES RYUBI.
STAB
SO THE FOOD ON PAGE 48 OF VOLUME 14 ACTUALLY...
...TASTES AWFUL.
Bleah!
SPLURT
FWACK
Eat this!
WHEN MAMI IS AWAY.
KICK
KICK

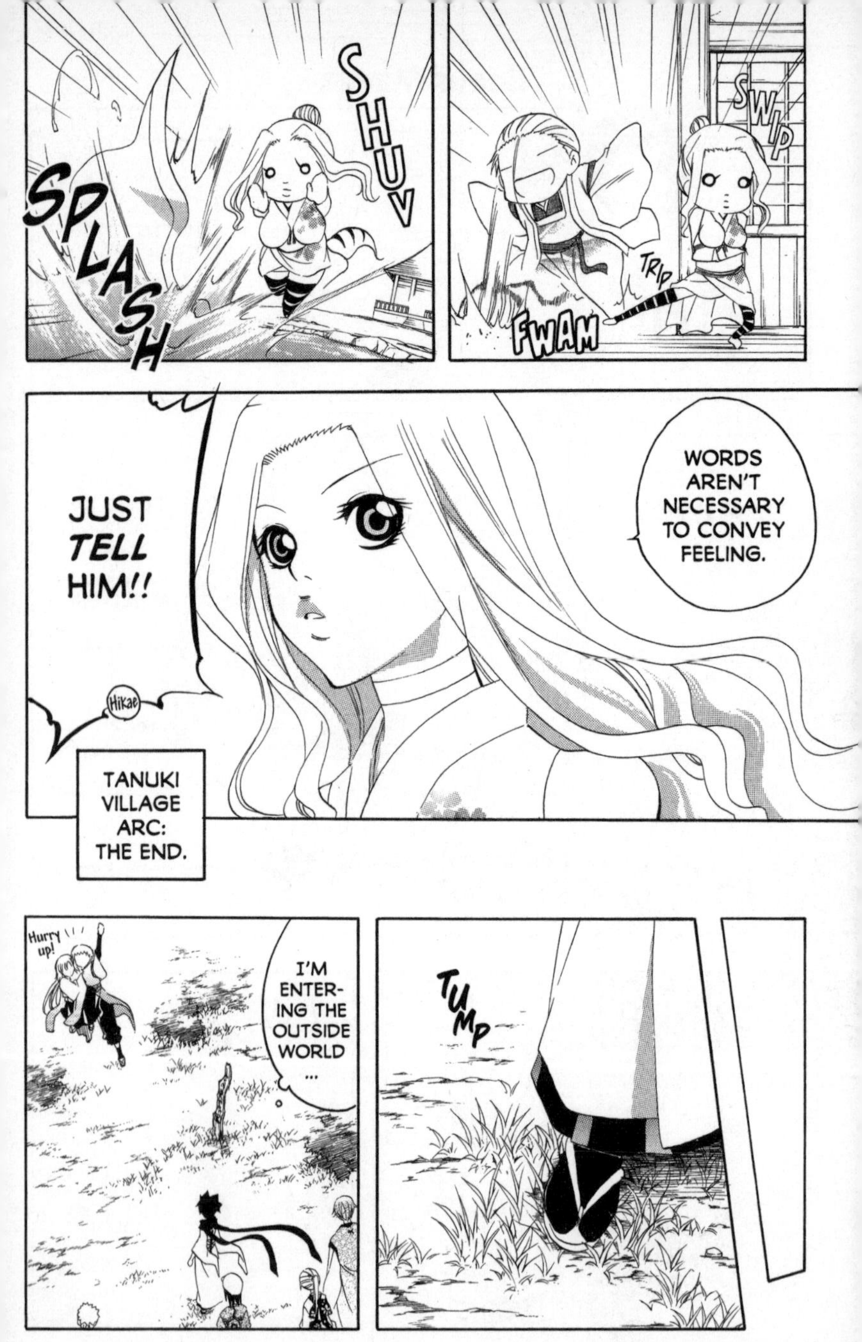
SWIP
TRIP
FWAM
SHUV
SPLASH
WORDS AREN'T NECESSARY TO CONVEY FEELING.
JUST *TELL* HIM!!
Hikae
TANUKI VILLAGE ARC: THE END.
TUMP
I'M ENTERING THE OUTSIDE WORLD ...
Hurry up!

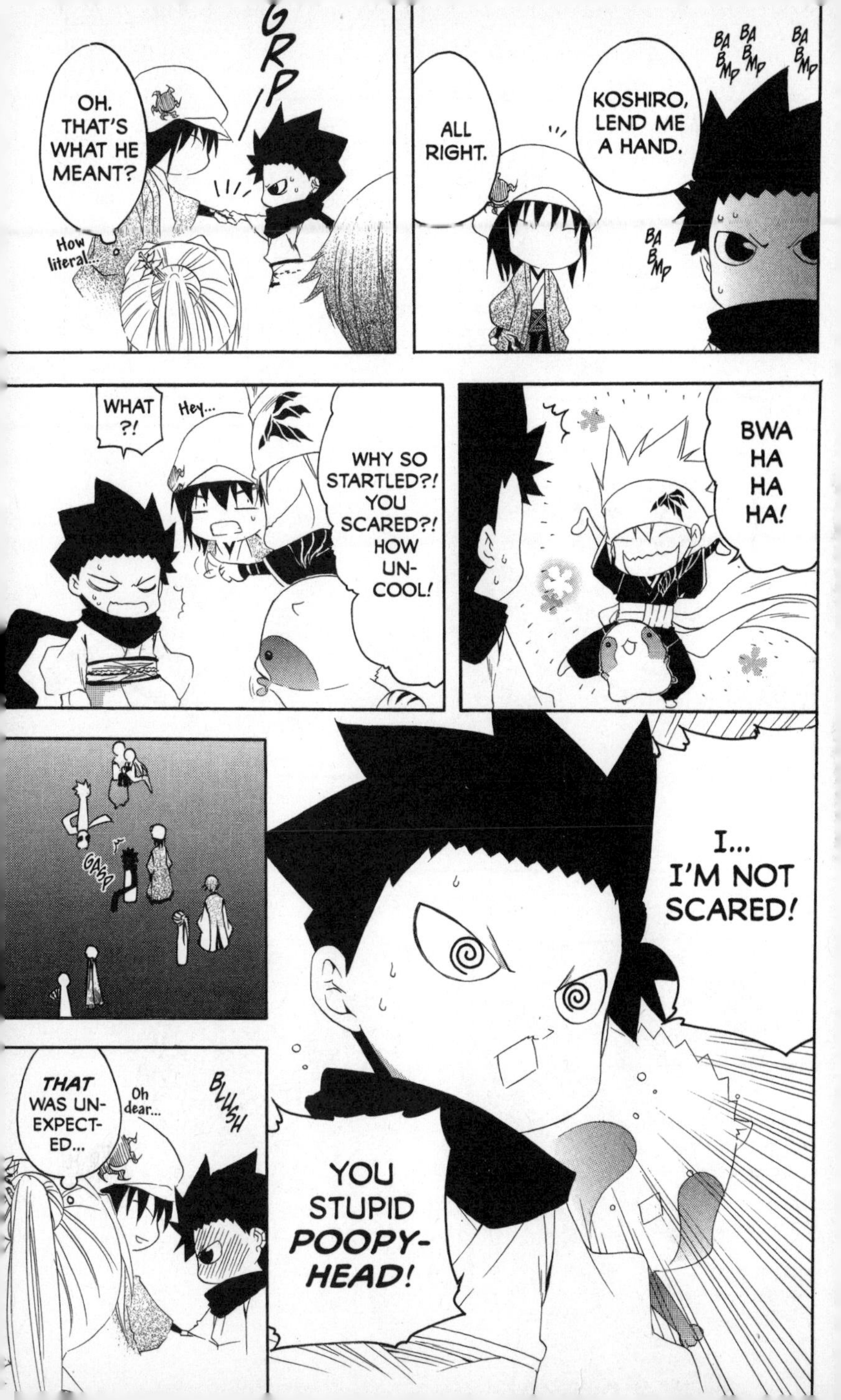
BA BMP BA BMP BA BMP
KOSHIRO, LEND ME A HAND.
ALL RIGHT.
BA BMP
GRP
OH. THAT'S WHAT HE MEANT?
How literal...
BWA HA HA HA!
WHY SO STARTLED?! YOU SCARED?! HOW UN-COOL!
Hey...
WHAT ?!
I... I'M NOT SCARED!
YOU STUPID *POOPY-HEAD!*
GASP
THAT WAS UN-EXPECT-ED...
Oh dear...
BLUSH

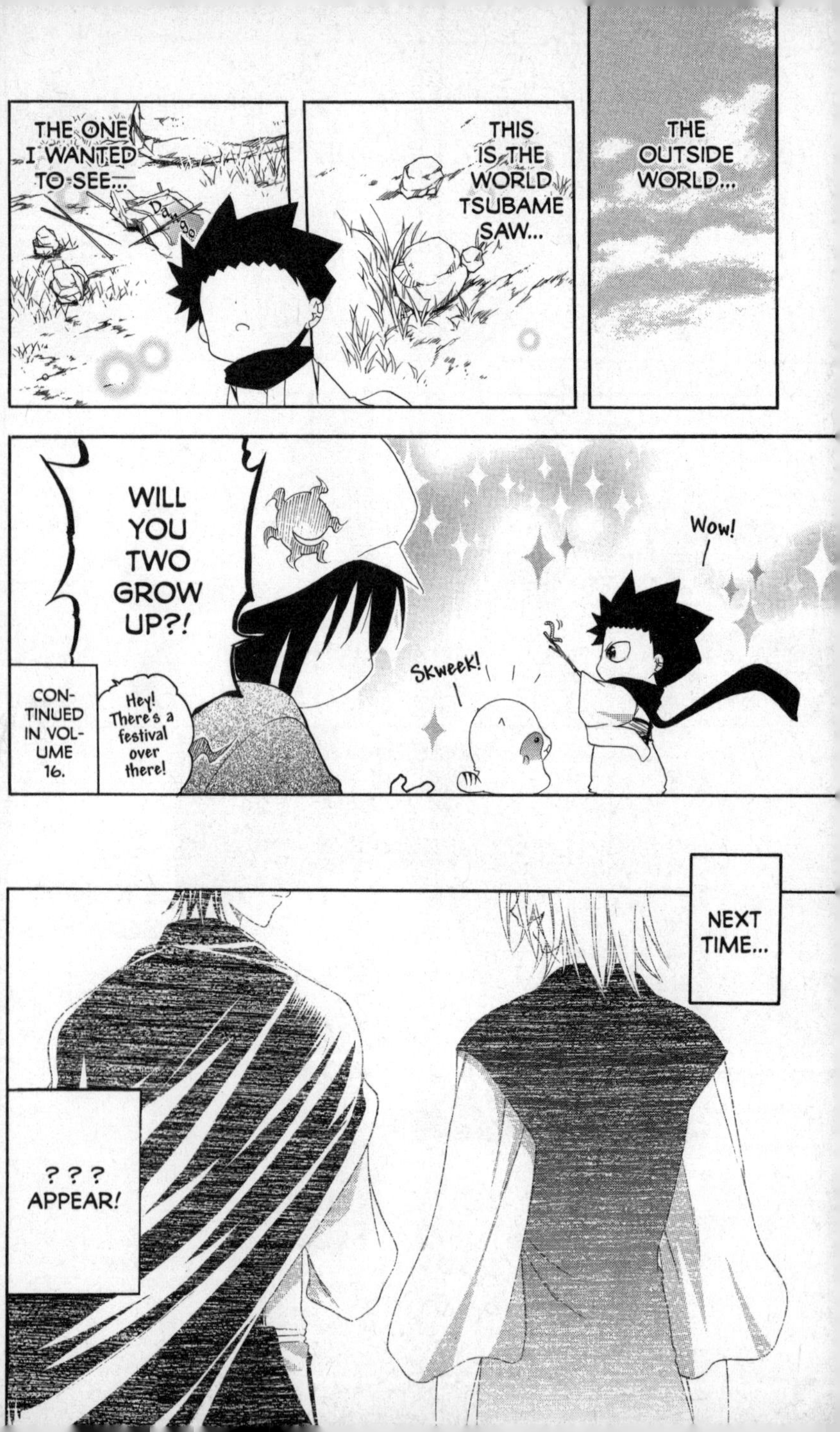
THE OUTSIDE WORLD...
THIS IS THE WORLD TSUBAME SAW...
THE ONE I WANTED TO SEE...
Dango
Wow!
Skweek!
WILL YOU TWO GROW UP?!
Hey! There's a festival over there!
CONTINUED IN VOLUME 16.
NEXT TIME...
? ? ? APPEAR!

ITSUWARIBITO
Volume 15
Shonen Sunday Edition

Story and Art by
YUUKI IINUMA

ITSUWARIBITO ◆ UTSUHO ◆ Vol. 15
by Yuuki IINUMA
© 2009 Yuuki IINUMA
All rights reserved.
Original Japanese edition published by SHOGAKUKAN.
English translation rights in the United States of America and Canada
arranged with SHOGAKUKAN.

Translation/John Werry
Touch-up Art & Lettering/Susan Daigle-Leach
Design/Matt Hinrichs
Editor/Gary Leach

The stories, characters and incidents mentioned
in this publication are entirely fictional.

Printed in the U.S.A.

Published by VIZ Media, LLC
P.O. Box 77010
San Francisco, CA 94107

10 9 8 7 6 5 4 3 2 1
First printing, August 2015

www.viz.com   WWW.SHONENSUNDAY.COM

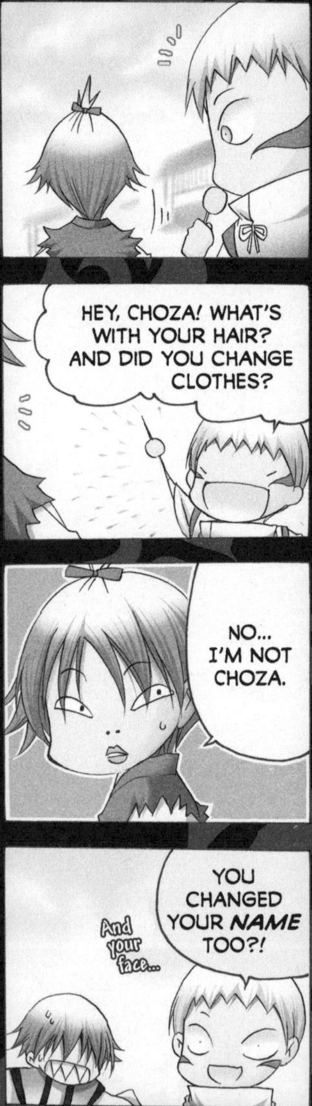
HEY, CHOZA! WHAT'S WITH YOUR HAIR? AND DID YOU CHANGE CLOTHES?
NO... I'M NOT CHOZA.
YOU CHANGED YOUR *NAME* TOO?!
And your face...

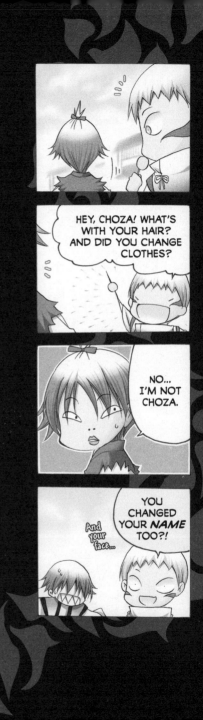